# The Rule Against Perpetuities

## Volume 1

A LAW CLASSIC

# The Rule Against Perpetuities

## Volume 1

### John Chipman Gray
*Late Royall Professor of Law
in Harvard University*

Fourth Edition

*Edited by* **Roland Gray**

**BeardBooks**

Washington, D.C.

Boston: Little, Brown and Company

ISBN 1-58798-115-7

Reprinted 2002 by Beard Books, Washington, D.C.
Printed in the United States of America.

# PREFACE TO THE FOURTH EDITION

The third edition of this work was sent to the press by the author shortly before his death in 1915. Since then over thirteen hundred new cases have been reported and much discussion has taken place on the topics here treated. The third edition is out of print; and the demand for a new edition has become urgent in many quarters.

In preparing a new edition of a legal textbook after the author's death, two courses are open. The author's language may be kept intact, and the additions and qualifications necessary to bring the work up to date inserted in separate sentences or clauses. On the other hand, the editor may proceed as if he were writing a new book, following the general plan of the earlier work, but adopting only so much of its language as seems to him to state accurately the present law or to indicate the historical development of the law where he thinks it necessary to show such development. I have endeavored to steer between these two courses.

In those portions of the book where no radical changes have seemed necessary, I have followed the course of preserving the author's work. In such instances, the language of the third edition has been reprinted with only slight modifications, and the new authorities inserted in the notes with further remarks of an explanatory or illustrative nature. This method is the more appropriate since the author, in preparing the second and third editions, followed a similar course. In the preface to the third edition, he said: "If this had been the first edition of this work, I should undoubtedly have adopted a more consecutive and compact arrangement in several respects than it now exhibits. It has seemed to me, however, to be advantageous to the reader to retain in the present edition a form which shows the development not only of the law but of the author's views during a period of twenty-eight years." I have therefore refrained from omitting, without careful consideration, any of the discussion of the older cases. Even after a case has ceased to be of present interest, the author's remarks in the course of his discussion may retain some value.

But in those places where the weight of authority, or a reconsideration of the subject in the light of recent discussions, has brought me to the conclusion that the author's statements do not represent the existing law, I have expressed the views which I have myself reached after careful study of all the cases. This has involved the insertion of new material of considerable length, in the text as well as in the notes, and sometimes even a complete rewriting of several sections. The portions of the work where this has been done are often concerned with important subjects.*

After some hesitation, it was decided not to attempt to distinguish the new matter from the old by any system of marks. Such marks impair the good appearance and even the readability of the printed page. Moreover, it would have been very difficult, in the present revision, to apply any consistent scheme for making such distinctions. To indicate every alteration or omission of a word would have been almost intolerable; and to draw the line between those changes which were important and those which were not would have been very difficult. Where I have made no change of substance, I have not thought it necessary to indicate changes of form or additions of illustrative or corroborative material. But where I have departed, on any important point, from the author's conclusions, I have tried to indicate, in one way or another, that there has been a departure, unless it seemed evident from the context. In some places in the notes, or in appendices which were originally published as articles in magazines, the author has spoken in the first person, and this fact

---

\* E. g. §§ 39–41, on possibilities of reverter in the United States; §§ 259–267, on Conflict of Laws; §§ 487–509.18, on powers of sale; §§ 541–561.7, on election with respect to appointments under powers; and Appendix H, §§ 894–909, on gifts for non-charitable purposes. Appendix N, §§ 975–977, on the Statute *Quia Emptores*, is entirely new. §§ 753–772, on Foreign Law, have also been rewritten.

makes my mention of him elsewhere in the third person inconsistent. I have taken no great pains, however, to iron out these and similar irregularities of form where they brought no danger of confusion of thought.

Throughout the revision of the entire work I have been assisted by my learned friend, Charles Young Wadsworth, Esquire, of the Boston Bar, who is also responsible for the Index. Without the suggestions received from him, and his unremitting attention to detail, I should have had difficulty in completing the revision. My learned friend and associate, Cecil Heber Smith, Esquire, of the Boston Bar, has likewise made valuable suggestions. My learned friend, Ralph Vincent Rogers, Esquire, at present a research fellow in the Harvard Law School, has not only been of great assistance in preparing Appendix N, on the Statute of *Quia Emptores,* but has seen the book through the press and prepared the Table of Cases. And finally, it would have been impossible for me to carry the work through without the assiduity and accuracy of my secretary, Miss A. E. Steutermann.

To Professor William Barton Leach, of the Harvard Law School, I have to acknowledge my indebtedness, not only for his published writings, but also for an instructive correspondence on several points. My obligations to other learned writers are acknowledged in various places throughout the work. But I have especially to thank Professor James Bradley Thayer (*clarum et venerabile nomen*), of the Harvard Law School, for rewriting the sections in Appendix D on the Roman Law, Modern Civil Law, and the law of Louisiana.

ROLAND GRAY.

*Boston, February, 1942.*

# PREFACE TO THE FIRST EDITION

I have long thought that in the present state of legal learning a chief need is for books on special topics, chosen with a view, not to their utility as the subjects of convenient manuals, but to their place and importance in the general system of the law. When such books have been written, it will then, for the first time, become possible to treat fully the great departments of the law, or even to construct a *corpus juris*.

Such a book should deal with the whole of its subject, its history, its relation to other parts of the law, its present condition, the general principles which have been evolved and the errors which have been eliminated in its development, and the defects which still mar its logical symmetry, or, what is of vastly greater moment, lessen its value as a guide to conduct.

A treatise of this nature I have tried to write on the legal doctrine governing the creation of future interests in property, commonly known as the Rule against Perpetuities.

The doctrines derived from the feudal law, which so closely limited the creation and transfer of future estates, have passed or are fast passing away. Any reasons for their existence have gone, and under the joint action of the Legislatures and Courts they have themselves almost disappeared. Of all that forest of learning there remains here and there only a stump over which an unlucky testator may stumble. But the Rule against Perpetuities is in full vigor; where the Legislature has interfered, it has been to increase its stringency. Indeed, the Rule is substantially, at the present day, *the* law of future interests.

Though I have been desirous to keep as closely to the subject as possible, it seemed almost indispensable to show how the law of future interests has been thus simplified and reduced to the Rule against Perpetuities. Chapter II., which treats of this, cost more labor than any other in the book.

On the other hand, questions of construction have been rigorously excluded, unless where, as in Chapter XIX., the Rule against Perpetuities is concerned in their solution. There is an enormous number of cases reported where an interest did or did not violate the Rule, according as one or another construction was adopted. But the adoption of one construction rather than another was not affected by the existence of the Rule, and when a construction had been adopted there was no doubt whether or not the Rule applied to it. The consideration of such cases belongs to a treatise on Interpretation. It has always seemed to me a blemish in Mr. Lewis's admirable work that so large a part of it is devoted to these questions.

The learned reader will observe that some parts of the subject are treated at much greater length than others. The guide in determining the room to be allotted to each question has been its comparative difficulty. On points which have raised serious doubts in the minds of others, or in my own mind, the authorities and arguments have been fully given; but although I hope the book may be of service not only in practice but to students, it is not written *in usum tironum*, and undisputed doctrines have been stated with as much brevity as is consistent with accuracy.

The ambiguity in the meaning of terms, which is perhaps the chief reproach of our law, has worked great harm with the matters here considered. The Rule against Perpetuities should have been called the Rule against Remoteness. It is aimed at the control of future interests; it has nothing to do, save incidentally, with present interests. But its name is a constant temptation to treat it as aimed against restraints on the alienation of present interests.[1] Hence frequent lapses into error, from which the courts have recovered themselves slowly and painfully; and hence also statutes, like those of New York, whose interpretation has cost, and will cost, a subsidy.[2] If this book has any merit, it is in the more or less

[1] See § 119, and the other sections there cited.
[2] See §§ 747–750.

successful attempt to free the subject from this source of confusion and mistake.[3]

In many legal discussions there is, in the last resort, nothing to say but that one judge or writer thinks one way, and another writer or judge thinks another way. There is no exact standard to which appeal can be made. In questions of remoteness this is not so; there is for them a definite recognized rule: if a decision agrees with it, it is right; if it does not agree with it, it is wrong. In no part of the law is the reasoning so mathematical in its character; none has so small a human element.

A degree of dogmatism, therefore, may be permitted here which would be unbecoming in other branches of the law. If the answer to a problem does not square with the multiplication table one may call it wrong, although it be the work of Sir Isaac Newton; and so if a decision conflicts with the Rule against Perpetuities, one may call it wrong, however learned and able the court that has pronounced it.

That I have done all my own sums correctly, I do not venture to hope. There is something in the subject which seems to facilitate error. Perhaps it is because the mode of reasoning is unlike that with which lawyers are most familiar. The study and practice of the Rule against Perpetuities is indeed a constant school of modesty. A long list might be formed of the demonstrable blunders with regard to its questions made by eminent men, blunders which they themselves have been sometimes the first to acknowledge; and there are few lawyers of any practice in drawing wills and settlements who have not at some time either fallen into the net which the Rule spreads for the unwary, or at least shuddered to think how narrowly they have escaped it.

Finally, I must acknowledge my great obligations to Mr.

---

[3] When I began to collect the authorities, I did not clearly apprehend that the Rule against Perpetuities had no direct connection with restraints on alienation, and I intended to devote a chapter to these restraints; but as I went on I saw that such a chapter would be out of place, and therefore concluded to treat the subject in a separate essay,—Restraints on the Alienation of Property, Boston, 1883, (2d ed.) 1895.

Lewis's classical treatise. He is prolix, and his prolixity makes him occasionally obscure; but no writer on the Common Law excels him in acuteness and candor. I have never consulted him but with renewed respect. On a few points I have ventured to disagree with him, but always with diffidence. To Mr. Marsden's excellent treatise I also take pleasure in recognizing my indebtedness. From him, too, I have at times differed; but much oftener I have been fortified in my conclusions on doubtful questions by finding that they agreed with his.

With two such books on our shelves I feel I owe an apology for adding another to the overgrown literature of the law. My excuse must be that it is thirty-six years since Mr. Lewis published the Supplement to his book, and that Mr. Marsden's plan excludes consideration of the history of the Rule; but chiefly that neither of them deals with the American cases.

I have to thank Professor E. W. Gurney for kindly revising the sections in the Appendix on the Roman Law.[4]

J. C. G.

*Boston, January, 1886.*

---

[4] In the preface to the second edition the author acknowledged the assistance of Messrs. Charles Lowell Barlow and John Gorham Palfrey in the preparation of that edition, and in the preface to the third edition, that of William Rodman Fay, Esquire, and the present editor.

# TABLE OF CONTENTS

Volume 1

## CHAPTER I

## CHAPTER II

xiii

## CHAPTER III

## CHAPTER IV

# CHAPTER V

# CHAPTER VI

# xvi

TABLE OF CONTENTS

SECTION

5. Lives in Being ........................ 216–219.2
6. Period of Gestation ...................... 220–222
7. Term of Twenty-one Years ............... 223, 224
8. Limitations of an Estate for Life or not exceeding Twenty-one Years .................. 225–229
9. Covenants to renew Leases ............. 230–230.3
10. Time runs from Testator's Death .............. 231
11. Enough if Interest begins within the Required Limits ................................ 232–246
12. Effect of Remote Interests on Prior Limitations ................................ 247–250
13. Effect of Remote Interests on Subsequent Limitations ............................. 251–258.1
14. Conflict of Laws ........................ 259–267

## CHAPTER VII

Interests, though Alienable, may be too Remote
268–278.4

## CHAPTER VIII

Interests Subject to the Rule against Perpetuities ...................................... 279–330.3
Present Rights in Lands of Others not Subject 279–282
I. Legal Interests ........................ 283–321.2
    A. Real Estate ........................ 283–318
        (1) Reversions and Vested Remainders .. 283
        (2) Contingent Remainders ....... 284–298.9
        (3) Rights of Entry .............. 299–311.1
        (4) Possibilities of Reverter ........ 312, 313
        (5) Curtesy and Dower .............. 313.1
        (6) Rights in Land of Others ....... 314–316
        (7) Escheat ......................... 316.1
        (8) Conditional Limitations ............ 317
            Copyholds ..................... 318
    B. Personal Property ................. 319–321.2

Volume 2

## CHAPTER IX

## CHAPTER X

## CHAPTER XI

## CHAPTER XII

## CHAPTER XIII

## CHAPTER XIV

## CHAPTER XV

## CHAPTER XVI

## CHAPTER XVII

## CHAPTER XVIII

## CHAPTER XIX

# CHAPTER XX

# APPENDIX

# TABLE OF CASES CITED

## A

## B

Bould v. Wynston—§ 146.
Boulton's Case—§ 138 n. 3.
Bourne, Re—§ 924.
Bourne v. Buckton—§ 704 n. 1; § 711 nn. 4, 6, 12.
Bourne v. Keane—§ 896 n. 1.
Bowditch v. Andrew—§ 117.2 n. 3.
Bowen, Re—§ 593 n. 1; § 594 n. 1; § 603.9 & n. 3; § 631 n. 1.
Bowen v. Hackney—§ 108 n. 2.
Bowerman v. Taylor—§ 245.2; § 392 n. 3.
Bowles, Re—§ 258 n. 3; § 295; § 298.9 n. 3; § 321 n. 2; § 480 n. 2; § 509.11 n. 4.
Bowlin v. R. I. Hosp. Trust Co.— § 215.1 n. 4.
Bowling v. Dobyns—§ 88 n. 2.
Bowling v. Grace—§ 737 n. 1.
Bowman, Re—§ 626 n. 3.
Bowyer v. West—§ 374 n. 1.
Boyce v. Hanning—§ 489 n. 2; § 499 n. 1.
Boyd's Estate—§ 522 n. 1; § 523.2 n. 3; § 523.3; § 526.2 n. 2; § 963.
Boyd, Re—§ 428 n. 1; § 437.
Boyd v. Allen—§ 490 n. 3.
Boyd v. U. S.—§ 739 n. 6.
Boydell v. Golightly—§ 362 n. 3.
Bracebridge's Case—§ 137 n. 3; § 144 & n. 2.
Bracebridge v. Cook—§ 144 n. 2.
Brackenbury v. Gibbons—§ 922; § 923.
Bradford v. Andrew—§ 540.1 n. 1.
Bradford v. Griffin—§ 62 n. 1; § 232 n. 11; § 398.1.
Bradley v. Mosby—§ 91 n. 1.
Bradshaw v. Bradshaw—§ 561.1 n. 1; § 561.5; § 561.6.
Bradshaw v. Jackman—§ 896 n. 1; § 896.1 n. 3.
Bradshaw v. Lawson—§ 977.

Braithwaite v. A. G.—§ 681 n. 3; § 896.2 n. 5.
Brandenburgh v. Thorndike— § 214.1; § 214.3.
Brandon v. Woodthorpe—§ 215.1 n. 4.
Brandt, Charles T., Inc. v. Y. W. C. A.—§ 245.2 n. 19.
Brannigan v. Murphy—§ 898 n. 1.
Brasher v. Marsh—§ 740 n. 2.
Braswell v. Morehead—§ 88 n. 3; § 848 n. 1.
Brattan v. Graham—§ 746 n. 1.
Brattleboro v. Mead—§ 594 n. 1.
Brattle Square Church v. Grant— § 40.3 n. 2; 247 n. 1; § 269 nn. 2, 7; § 305.2; § 305.6; § 305.7; § 308 n. 1; § 312 n. 6; § 593 n. 1.
Braund v. Devon—§ 685.1 n. 3.
Bray v. Bree—§ 477 n. 3; § 524 n. 1; § 957.
Bray v. Hammersley—§ 477 n. 3.
Breckenbury v. Gifford—§ 110.1 n. 1.
Breheny, Re—§ 374 n. 3.
Brent's Case—§ 137 nn. 2, 3; § 142.
Brent v. Gilbert—§ 131 n. 2; § 137 n. 3; § 142.
Brett v. Sawbridge—§ 362.
Brewer v. Brewer—§ 259.1 n. 1.
Brewer v. Hardy—§ 57 n. 1.
Brewer v. Penniman—§ 259.1 n. 1.
Brewster v. McCall—§ 88 n. 2.
Brice v. All Saints Mem. Chapel —§ 282 n. 1; § 590 n. 4; § 593 n. 1.
Bridgeport City Trust Co. v. All-ing—§ 633 n. 1.
Bridgeport Public Library v. Bur-roughs Home—§ 590 n. 4.
Bridgeport Trust Co. v. Parker— § 739 n. 5.

# D

# E

# F

# G

## H

James v. Allen—§ 894 n. 1.
James v. Masters—§ 852 n. 7.
James v. Wynford—§ 380 n. 2.
Janey v. Latane—§ 616 n. 1.
Jansen v. Godair—§ 607 n. 1.
Jarman's Estate, Re—§ 894 n. 1.
Jay v. Jay—§ 159 n. 4.
Jee v. Audley—§ 182; § 215;
    § 215.1; § 339; § 373; § 537
    & n. 1.
Jeefers v. Lampson—§ 108 n. 1.
Jefferies, Re—§ 692 n. 1.
Jeffersonville, etc., R. Co. v. Bar-
    bour—§ 309 n. 1.
Jefferys, Re—§ 701 n. 2.
Jeffries v. Jeffries—§ 282 n. 1.
Jenkins v. Guarantee Trust Co.—
    § 267 n. 1.
Jenkins v. Jenkins University—
    § 40.15 n. 2; § 51.1 n. 2;
    § 603.9 nn. 1, 3.
Jennings v. Jennings—§ 110 n. 2.
Jensen v. Jensen—§ 19 n. 4.
Jermyn v. Orchard—§ 808 n. 2.
Jesson v. Wright—§ 881 & n. 2.
Jocelyn v. Nott—§ 605 n. 1; § 622.
John's Will, Re—§ 597 n. 5; § 607
    n. 1.
John Osborn v. The Prior of Es-
    ton—§ 33.2 n. 2.
Johns Hopkins Univ. v. Uhrig—
    § 263.3 n. 1.
Johnson, Re—§ 349.5 n. 2; § 385
    n. 2.
Johnson's Trusts—§ 269 nn. 6, 9;
    § 365 n. 1; § 366 n. 1; § 594
    n. 1.
Johnson v. Battelle—§ 112 n. 1.
Johnson v. De Pauw Univ.—§ 683
    n. 2.
Johnson v. Edmond—§ 101 n. 1;
    § 113.1 n. 8; § 118 n. 1; § 739
    n. 5.
Johnson v. Holifield—§ 898 n. 1.
Johnson v. Jacob—§ 108 n. 2.

Johnson v. Johnson—§ 97 n. 2;
    § 613 n. 1; § 737 n. 1; § 852
    n. 7.
Johnson v. Lane—§ 39 n. 2.
Johnson v. Lish—§ 228 nn. 1, 5.
Johnson v. Mitchell—§ 91 n. 4.
Johnson v. Norway—§ 50.
Johnson v. Preston—§ 214.4 n. 2;
    § 237.3 n. 2; § 249.4 n. 1.
Johnson v. Webber—§ 739 n. 5.
Johnston's Estate—§ 232 nn. 2,
    13; § 242 n. 2; § 245.2 n. 6;
    § 249.2 & n. 3; § 249.3; § 475
    n. 1.
Johnston, Re—§ 120 n. 2; § 365 n.
    1; § 407 n. 3.
Johnston v. Cosby—§ 239 n. 2;
    § 249.3 n. 3; § 370 n. 1.
Johnston v. Spicer—§ 205.1 nn. 2,
    13.
Johnston v. Stubbs—§ 476.1 n. 3.
Johnstone     v.     Commissioner—
    § 540.2 n. 11.
Jones, Re—§ 205.1 & n. 9; § 323
    n. 1; § 365 n. 1; § 367 n. 1;
    § 626 n. 3; § 896 n. 6; § 898
    n. 1; § 909.2 n. 1.
Jones' Trusts—§ 249.2.
Jones v. Davies—§ 15 n. 1.
Jones v. Habersham—§ 311 n. 3;
    § 590 n. 4; § 597; § 607 n. 1.
Jones v. Hoskins—§ 91 n. 1.
Jones v. Langhorn—§ 88 n. 2;
    § 849 n. 1.
Jones v. Maggs—§ 704 n. 1; § 711
    n. 7.
Jones v. Postell—§ 14 n. 3; § 313
    n. 2; § 455 n. 6.
Jones v. Roe—§ 12 n. 1.
Jones v. Sothoron—§ 848 n. 1.
Jones v. Webster—§ 683 n. 2.
Jones v. Zollicoffer—§ 88 n. 3.
Jordan v. Jordan—§ 110 n. 2;
    § 215.1 n. 4.

## L

# M

## O

Rector of Chedington's Case—
§ 125 n. 2; § 133 n. 1; § 151
n. 7; § 169; § 288 & n. 1.
Rector v. Dalby—§ 120 n. 2;
§ 121.2 n. 2.
Redington v. Browne—§ 209 n. 3;
§ 230 n. 7; § 275.1 n. 4;
§ 320; § 330 n. 2.
Redmond v. Redmond—§ 746 n. 1.
Reece v. Steel—§ 656 n. 1.
Reed's Estate—§ 509.16 n. 2.
Reed v. McIlvain—§ 245.2;
§ 249.9 n. 2; § 394.1 n. 2;
§ 522 n. 1; § 526.2 n. 2; § 537
n. 3; § 963.
Reed v. Stouffer—§ 39 n. 2; § 40.8
n. 2.
Reeder v. Antrim—§ 744 n. 4.
Reeve v. Long—§ 173 n. 2.
Reeves v. Comfort—§ 735 n. 2.
Reffon Realty Co. v. Adams Land
Co.—§ 896 n. 1.
Regular Predestinarian Baptist
Church v. Parker—§ 13 n. 3;
§ 40.17 n. 1.
Reichenbach v. Quin—§ 898 n. 1.
Reid v. Earle—§ 374 n. 1.
Reid v. Reid—§ 255 n. 6; § 431
n. 3.
Reid v. Shergold—§ 526.3 n. 1.
Reid v. Voorhees—§ 249.3; § 249.4
n. 1.
Reid's Trustees v. Cattanach—
§ 894 n. 1.
Reid's Trustees v. Dashwood—
§ 220 n. 2; § 758 n. 1.
Reimer v. Smith—§ 236 n. 1.
Reinhart v. Lantz—§ 19 n. 4.
Renaker v. Tanner—§ 737 n. 1.
Retherick v. Chappel—§ 153 & n.
7; § 157.
Rex v. Croyden—§ 124 n. 3.
Rex v. Skingle—§ 43 n. 1.
Rhoads v. Rhoads—§ 121.2 n. 2.
Rhode Island Hospital Trust Co.
v. Dunnell—§ 540.2 n. 11.

Rhode Island Hospital Trust Co.
v. Granger—§ 370 n. 3.
Rhode Island Hospital Trust Co.
v. Harris—§ 108 n. 2.
Rhode Island Hospital Trust Co.
v. Peck—§ 246 n. 2.
Rhode Island Hospital Trust Co.
v. Proprietors of Swan Point
Cemetery—§ 898 n. 1.
Rhodes's Estate—§ 209 n. 3; § 232
n. 13; § 242 n. 2; § 322 n. 1.
Rhodes v. Rhodes—§ 613 n. 1.
Riccards's Trusts, Re—§ 215.1 n.
4.
Rice v. Boston & Worcester R. R.
Co.—§ 12 n. 1.
Rice v. Key—§ 769 n. 3.
Rice v. Lincoln and N. W. Ry.—
§ 330 n. 2.
Richards v. Coal Co.—§ 51 n. 2.
Richards v. Hartshorne—§ 107 n.
4.
Richardson, Re—§ 282 n. 1; § 648
n. 2; § 652 n. 5; § 656 n. 2.
Richardson v. Richardson—§ 103
n. 1.
Richardson v. Warfield—§ 110 n.
2.
Richardson v. Wilson—§ 614 n. 3.
Richman v. Hopkins—§ 68.1 n. 5.
Richmond v. Davis—§ 744 n. 4.
Rickard v. Robson—§ 898 n. 1.
Ricketts, Re—§ 374 n. 1.
Rider, Estate of—§ 415 n. 3.
Rider v. Ford—§ 230.2; § 230.3
n. 1.
Ridgway, Re—§ 77 n. 1.
Ridley, Re—§ 121.5; § 121.8 n. 2;
§ 436; § 441 n. 1.
Riggs v. New Castle—§ 38 n. 7.
Riley v. Jaeger—§ 249.1.
Ring v. Hardwick—§ 374 n. 1;
§ 427.
Ripley v. Brown—§ 679.1 n. 2.
Risher's Will, Re—§ 263.3 nn. 1,
7.

# S

# W

Webb v. Sadler—§ 440; § 477 n.
4; § 527 n. 1; § 534 n. 1.
Webb v. Webb—§ 678 n. 2; § 697
n. 2; § 726.1 n. 1.
Webber v. Webber—§ 751.3 n. 3.
Weber v. Texas Co.—§ 330 n. 2.
Webster v. Boddington—§ 380;
§ 382; § 391.
Webster v. Morris—§ 23.2 n. 5;
§ 607 n. 1; § 683 n. 2; § 751.3
n. 3; § 916 n. 3.
Webster v. Parr—§ 385 n. 2.
Webster v. Wiggin—§ 597 n. 6.
Weed v. Woods—§ 40.7 n. 2.
Weekly v. Wildman—§ 576 n. 4;
§ 579 n. 1.
Weeks v. Hobson—§ 590 n. 4.
Weinmann's Estate—§ 718 n. 2.
Weir v. Simmons—§ 282 n. 1.
Welcden v. Elkington—§ 80 n. 3;
§ 83; § 151; § 152 n. 4; § 808;
§ 809 nn. 1, 2; § 813; § 815
n. 1; § 826 n. 1; § 827.
Welch v. Kinard—§ 91 n. 2.
Weld v. Traip—§ 71 n. 1.
Welkden & Elkington's Case—See
Welcden v. Elkington.
Wellbeloved v. Jones—§ 685.1 n.
8.
Welles v. Olcott—§ 19 n. 4.
Wellington v. Wellington—§ 33.11.
Wellock v. Hammond—§ 138 n. 5.
Wells, Re—§ 51 & nn. 4, 9; § 205.1
& n. 12.
Wells v. Heath—§ 590 n. 4; § 593
n. 1.
Wells v. Olcott—§ 663 n. 1.
Wells v. Wells—§ 367 n. 1.
Welsch v. Belleville Bank—§ 88
n. 2; § 95 n. 2.
Welsh v. Foster—§ 57 n. 1; § 413
n. 2.
Welsh v. Woodbury—§ 112 n. 1.
Wenmoth's Estate, Re—§ 641 n. 2.
Wentworth v. Fernald—§ 607 n. 1.

Wentworth v. Wentworth—§ 214
n. 1; § 398.2 n. 2.
West v. Ashby—§ 737 n. 1.
West v. Knight—§ 685.1 n. 8.
Westby, Jack d., v. Fetherstone—
§ 447 n. 1.
Westcott v. Cady—§ 88 n. 2.
Weston v. Trustees of Boston
College—§ 607 n. 1.
Westport Co. v. Staples—§ 631
n. 1.
Westropp v. Congested Districts
Board—§ 316 n. 6; § 579 n. 1.
West Texas Bank v. Matlock—
§ 413 n. 2.
Wetherell v. Wetherell—§ 641
n. 2.
Wharton v. Masterman—§ 679.1
n. 1.
Wheaton v. Peters—§ 674.1 n. 7.
Wheeler v. Chase—§ 394.1 n. 2.
Wheeler v. Fellowes—§ 259.1 n. 1;
§ 269 n. 3; § 739 n. 5.
Wheeler v. St. Johnsbury—§ 107
n. 2.
Wheeler v. Smith—§ 616 n. 1.
Whipple v. Fairchild—§ 118 n. 2.
Whistler v. Webster—§ 541 n. 3;
§ 558; § 559; § 561.5 n. 2.
Whitaker v. Burhans—§ 577 n. 2.
Whitby v. Mitchell—§ 125 n. 2;
§ 133 n. 1; § 199 n. 7; § 285
n. 4; § 290 n. 1; § 298.1;
§ 298.2; § 298.3; § 298.4;
§ 298.8 & n. 10; § 298.9 &
n. 3; § 318 n. 2; § 325.1;
§ 437 n. 8; § 521 n. 2; § 522
n. 1; § 530.4 n. 1; § 931;
§ 932; § 945; § 946; § 947
& n. 1.
Whitby v. Von Luedecke—§ 108
n. 2; § 298.9; § 522 n. 1.
White's Estate—§ 717 n. 1; § 718
n. 1.
White, Re—§ 215.1 n. 4; § 690 n.
4; § 700 n. 2; § 714 n. 5.

## Z

†

# THE RULE AGAINST PERPETUITIES

# NOTE

ON CORRESPONDENCE OF SECTIONS BETWEEN THE FOURTH
AND EARLIER EDITIONS

The numbering of the sections is the same as in earlier
editions, with two exceptions noted below. All new matter
has been inserted under the old numbers, except Appendix N
at the end of the book. But the sections formerly designated
by a number and a letter have been designated by a decimal
number; e. g. 121 *a* has become 121.1. The arrangement of
sections with decimal headings does not always correspond
with that of the lettered sections; e. g., a case which was
treated in 40 *a* may now be found under 40.17. A few whole
sections have been omitted. But matter in earlier editions,
which has not been omitted, will be found under the same
section number, or some decimal number following it. Omission of sections, or important passages, which appeared in
the third edition, has generally been noted. The instances
where the numbers have been changed are: 118 *a* has become 119; and 258 *a* is now 259.

# CHAPTER I

## INTRODUCTION

**§ 1. Nature of Rule.** Certain transfers of rights in their nature alienable the law forbids. Sometimes the reason of this inhibition is the character of the person who is to make the transfer; thus an infant cannot convey his land. Sometimes it is the character of the person who is to receive the transfer; thus Mortmain Acts forbid devises to charitable corporations. Sometimes it is the nature of the right; thus the right to recover damages for a libel is not assignable. And sometimes the transfer is to take effect at too remote a period; thus a bequest to those descendants of the testator who shall be living fifty years after his death is bad. The rule of the Common Law, which determines this last class by fixing the limit beyond which future interests cannot be created, is called the Rule against Perpetuities.

**§ 2. A Rule against Remoteness.** The Rule against Perpetuities is often spoken of as aimed at restraints upon alienation. Now it is true that future interests, to confine the creation of which within precise limits is the object of the Rule, make the interest of the present owner of an estate less marketable, and therefore may be loosely said to restrain alienation; but, speaking accurately, a future interest does not render a present interest inalienable. The present owner has less to convey than he would have if the future interest did not exist; but all that he has he can convey freely. Suppose land is devised to A. and his heirs, with an executory devise over should he die unmarried, A. can sell his interest, and in the hands of the purchaser the land is subject to precisely the same devise over as it was in the hands of A., no more no less.[1] The misconception has been

---

§ 2. [1] Of course, if the contingency on which the future interest is to arise is an alienation by
the present owner, then the fu-

aided by the name given to the Rule. It would have been better had it been called the Rule against Remoteness.[2] But usage has settled the name as the Rule against Perpetuities.[3]

§ 2.1. The system of rules disallowing restraints on alienation and the Rule against Perpetuities are the two modes adopted by the Common Law for forwarding the circulation of property which it is its policy to promote. The rules disallowing restraints against alienation and the Rule against Perpetuities have, therefore, it is true, the same ultimate end, but they serve that end by different means.[1]

§ 3. The practice of confounding the rule against remoteness with the rules disallowing restraints on alienation[1] has led to grave errors,[2] as, for example, (1) that future interests, if alienable, cannot be obnoxious to the Rule against Perpetuities;[3] (2) that a trust to pay the income of property to A. and his heirs violates the Rule.[4]

§ 4. As the Rule against Perpetuities is the law limiting the time within which future interests can be created, we must first see what future interests can be created, apart from any question of remoteness. We shall find that originally the common law subjected their creation to many restrictions, but that these restrictions have been gradually so far removed that the Rule against Perpetuities is now almost the only legal check upon the granting of future interests.

ture interest may be truly called a restraint on alienation. Such a case is the gift of a life estate to A., until he attempts to part with it, and then to B.

[2] This suggestion is due to the late Mr. Justice Gray of the United States Supreme Court.

[3] See 1 Jarm. Wills (7th ed.) 267, note; 1 Tiffany, Real Prop. (3d ed.), §§ 391, 398; 1 Perry, Trusts (7th ed.) 377; 42 Am. Law Rev. 112; Mass. Gen. Laws (1932),

c. 184, § 3; Report of Amer. Bar Asso. (1916) 531. Cf. Re Gump's Estate, 97 Pac. 2d 301 (Cal. Ap.).

§ 2.1. [1] See §§ 119 et seq., post.

§ 3. [1] As to these latter rules see the author's essay, "Restraints on Alienation" (2d ed.) Boston, 1895.

[2] See § 119.

[3] See Chap. VII., §§ 268 et seq., post.

[4] See §§ 235 et seq., post.

## CHAPTER II

## FUTURE INTERESTS

§ 5. In this chapter it is proposed to treat of future estates and interests in property, and of the restrictions on their creation other than the Rule against Perpetuities.

### I. REAL ESTATE

#### A. LANDS OF FREEHOLD TENURE

##### 1. COMMON LAW

§ 6. **No Ownership could begin in Future.** No seisin or ownership of a freehold estate in corporeal hereditaments of freehold tenure can begin *in futuro.* This is owing to the fundamental doctrine of the feudal law, that such seisin can be given only by a present livery, actual or constructive.

§ 7. The future freehold interests in real estate allowed by the common law are: (1) Remainders and Reversions; (2) Interests Arising on Entry for Condition Broken; (3) Possibilities of Reverter; (4) Curtesy and Dower; (5) Interests less than Ownership in Land of Others; and (6) Interests by Escheat.

§ 8. **Remainders and Reversions.** Though seisin of a freehold estate can be given only by livery, yet the ownership may be cut up into several successive life estates, either with or without an ultimate estate in fee. The first life estate is called a particular estate; the succeeding life estates, and the ultimate estate in fee, if any, are remainders.[1] The essential qualities and the restrictions on the creation of a remainder are that it must be created by the same conveyance as the previous freehold estate or estates, and that it must become a present freehold estate on the expiration of the previous freehold estate or estates as originally

---

§ 8. [1] Each remainder for life is, in its relation to the follow-ing remainders, also a particular estate. See § 100, post.

limited.  A remainder cannot cut short or overlap the preceding estate, and no interval of time must separate it
from such estate.  The particular estate and the remainders
form an unbroken series.  Each remainder is said to be
supported by the preceding estates.  There can be no remainder after a fee simple.  A freehold estate subject to
a term for years is not a future estate of freehold at all,
but  a present estate of freehold; the holder of such estate
has the present seisin.[2]

§ 9. **Remainders Vested or Contingent.**  Remainders are
either vested or contingent.  A remainder is vested if, at
every moment during its continuance, it becomes a present
estate, whenever and however the preceding freehold estates
determine.  A remainder is contingent if, in order for it to
become a present estate, the fulfilment of some condition
precedent, other than the determination of the preceding
freehold estates, is necessary.  If an estate is given to A.
for life, remainder to his eldest born son in fee, the remainder is contingent until the birth of A.'s first-born son, and
then vests.  The distinction between vested and contingent
remainders is developed in the following chapter.

§ 10. **Contingent Remainders.**  Unless a contingent remainder becomes vested on or before the determination of
the preceding vested freehold estates, it can never become
a present estate: it has perished.  It makes no difference
whether the preceding estates have ended by reaching the
limit originally imposed on them, or whether they have been
cut short by merger, forfeiture, or otherwise.  It has been
doubted whether the common law originally allowed of
contingent remainders; they were, however, recognized as
valid as early as the fifteenth century.[1]

§ 11. **Reversions.**  A future estate may be indirectly created by giving livery of seisin for one or more life estates,
without an ultimate remainder in fee.  The estate remaining in the former owner ready to come into possession on the

[2] Wakefield Bank v. Yates,
[1916] 1 Ch. 452.  Challis, Real

Prop. (3d ed.) 80, 99.  § 970, note
3, post.

§ 10. [1] See §§ 100, 134, post.

termination of the life estate or estates is a reversion. The same result is reached when an ultimate remainder in fee is contingent. Until it vests, there is a reversion in the feoffor and his heirs.[1]

§ 12. **Interests arising on Entry for Condition Broken.** Future interests sometimes arose from conveyances being on condition, implied or express. All estates were conveyed on the implied condition that the tenants should not deny tenure. Express conditions might also be attached to a conveyance. On breach of a condition the feoffor had a right to enter; but, until entry, the estate remained with the feoffee. The right of entry was inalienable, and therefore advantage of a condition could be taken only by the feoffor and his heirs.[1]

§ 11. [1] When a conveyance is by way of use or devise, there is, unquestionably, during the contingency of a remainder in fee, a reversion in the grantor or devisor and his heirs; and the prevailing opinion seems to be the same way upon a feoffment at common law. Plunket v. Holmes, 1 Lev. 11, 1 Sid. 47, T. Raym. 28. Purefoy v. Rogers, 2 Wms. Saund. 380, 382, and note. Carter v. Barnardiston, 1 P. Wms. 505, 511–518. Egerton v. Massey, 3 C. B., N. S. 338, 358. Co. Lit. 191 a, Butler's note. Fearne, C. R. 360–364. Wms. Settlements 207–210. Wms. Real Prop. (23d ed.) 388. See Pinkney v. Weaver, 216 Ill. 185, 74 N. E. 714; Belding v. Parsons, 258 Ill. 422, 101 N. E. 570; Collins v. Sanitary District, 270 Ill. 108, 110 N. E. 318; Bigley v. Watson, 98 Tenn. 353, 39 S. W. 525. Contra, see Y. B. Hil. 40 Edw. III. fol. 9 b; Co. Lit. 342 b; 2 Prest. Abs. 101–107; Cornish, Rem. 175–178; 4 Kent, Com. 257–

260; Bohon v. Bohon, 78 Ky. 408. Cf. 1 Simes, Fut. Int., § 45; Amer. Law Inst. Restatement, Property, § 25 (2), Comment g.

The transfer in futuro of remainders and reversions already existing is considered in § 17, post.

§ 12. [1] See Ashuelot Nat. Bank v. Keene, 74 N. H. 148, 65 N. E. 826; Whitmore v. Cong. Parish, 121 Me. 391, 117 Atl. 469; Perry v. Smith, 231 S. W. 340 (Tex.); 3 Simes, Fut. Int., §§ 716, 717, 732; 24 Cal. Law Rev. 512, 518. But this rule has been largely abrogated by statute or decision in the United States. See 54 Harv. Law Rev. 248, 252; 14 Univ. Cinn. Law Rev. 524; Amer. Law Inst. Restatement, Property, §§ 160, 161. In England rights of entry are now alienable. See 8 & 9 Vict., c. 106, § 6, and the Wills Act (1837). In Massachusetts it has been held that the right of entry cannot pass by deed, Rice v. Boston & Worcester R. R.

**§ 13. Possibilities of Reverter.** Some estates were terminable by special or collateral limitations; for instance, an estate to A. till B. returned from Rome; or an estate to A. and his heirs until they ceased to be tenants of the Manor of Dale.[1] On the happening of the contingency, the feoffor was in of his old estate without entry. The estate was not cut short, as it would have been by entry for breach of condition, but expired by the terms of its original limitation. After a life estate of this kind a remainder could be limited. After such a fee it has commonly been supposed that there could be no remainder;[2] but there was a so-called possibility of reverter to the feoffor and his heirs which was not alienable.[3]

**§ 14. Fee Simple Conditional.** An estate in "fee simple conditional" was by far the most common of these estates

Co., 12 Allen 141; but it has also been held, apparently on a misunderstanding of Doe v. Scott, 3 M. & S. 300, and Jones v. Roe, 3 T. R. 88, that it can be devised. Hayden v. Stoughton, 5 Pick. 528. Austin v. Cambridgeport Parish, 21 Pick. 215. See Dyer v. Siano, 298 Mass. 537, 11 N. E. 2d 451. On breach of a condition attached to an estate for years, the lessor may put an end to the estate without entry. Leake, Law of Property in Land (1st ed.) 226.

**§ 13.** [1] See Co. Lit. 27 a, Harg. note 157; Challis, Real Prop., c. 17. A conditional or determinable fee was regarded as a variety of fee simple, and was usually called a "fee simple conditional" or "determinable." Co. Lit. 18 a. Edw. Seymor's Case, 10 Rep. 97 b. Walsingham's Case, 2 Plowd. 547, 557. § 32, post.

[2] See Buckhurst Peerage, 2 Ap. Cas. 1, 23, 24. But cf. § 14, post, note 8.

[3] See the following section. In Pennsylvania, where possibilities of reverter have been assumed to still exist (see § 38, post), the Court seems also, in Scheetz v. Fitzwater, 5 Pa. 126, to have thought them assignable, and has so held in Slegel v. Lauer, 148 Pa. 236, 23 Atl. 996. See also Battistone v. Banusky, 110 Conn. 267, 147 N. E. 820; Regular Predestinarian Baptist Church v. Parker, 373 Ill. 607, 27 N. E. 2d 522; Dyer v. Siano, 298 Mass. 537, 11 N. E. 2d 451; 3 Simes, Fut. Int., §§ 715, 732; 39 Yale L. J. 910. The rule stated in the text has been largely abrogated in the United States by statute or decision. See Amer. Law Inst. Restatement, Property, §§ 44, 159. In England, such interests (so far as they exist) are now alienable. See 8 & 9 Vict., c. 106, § 6, and the Wills Act (1837).

with special limitations.[1]  This was an estate to the donee
and the heirs of his body (either all the heirs of his body
or some special class of them), with a provision that on the
failure of such heirs the land should revert to the donor
and his heirs.  Sometimes this provision was expressed; but,
even though not expressed, yet on a gift in frankmarriage,
or simply to A. and the heirs of his body, it was tacitly implied.[2]  If the donee of such an estate had issue born, then
he could alienate the land[3] so as to pass a fee simple.  If
he never had issue born, or if he alienated before issue born,[4]
or if his issue, though born, had all died before there had
been any alienation of the estate, then, on his death, or the
subsequent failure of his issue, the land reverted to the

§ 14. [1] See Challis, Real Prop.,
c. 18; 2 P. & M. Hist. Eng. Law
(2d ed.) 14–19; 3 Holdsworth,
Hist. Eng. Law (3d ed.) 111–113;
2 Law Quart. Rev. 276.  Notwithstanding its name, this estate was
one with special limitation rather
than on condition.  The writ of
formedon in reverter alleges no
entry by the donor, F. N. B. 219;
Rast. Ent. 375; and this writ was
the one in use at the common law.
See St. De Donis, 13 Edw. I., c. 1,
§ 4.  Cf. Willion v. Berkley, 1
Plowd. 223, 242; 2 P. & M. Hist.
Eng. Law (2d ed.) 23, note 2, 28;
19 Am. & Eng. Enc. of Law (1st
ed.) Real Property, 1054.  But
see Butler's note to Co. Lit. 241 a.
(In previous editions of this
work, there is a discussion of Mr.
Butler's note, and of the question
of dower in conditional and determinable fees, as bearing on the
point that a conditional fee was
an estate with a special limitation.  As the question of dower
in such estates, which is not otherwise within the scope of this
work, is obscure and disputed, this

discussion has been omitted.)
Conditional fees still exist in
South Carolina, Iowa, Oregon,
and perhaps Nebraska.     § 19,
note 4, post.

[2] St. De Donis, 13 Edw. I., c. 1,
§ 1.  Bract. 17 b.  See Glenn v.
Glenn, 21 So. Car. 308.

[3] It is held in South Carolina,
where estates in fee simple conditional still exist, that they are
never devisable.  Jones v. Postell,
Harp. 92.

[4] Co. Lit. 19 a.  See Anon., Fitz.
Ab. Formedon, 65; Willion v.
Berkley, 1 Plowd. 223, 235, 245;
Barksdale v. Gamage, 3 Rich. Eq.
271, 279.  But in Powers v. Bullwinkle, 33 So. Car. 293, 302, 303,
11 S. E. 971, 975, on a mistaken
statement of what had been decided in Barksdale v. Gamage, it
was held that though the alienation was before issue born, yet if
issue were born afterward, the
possibility of reverter was barred;
and Powers v. Bullwinkle was followed in Dillard v. Yarboro, 77
So. Car. 227, 57 S. E. 841.

donor and his heirs.[5] This possibility of reverter was inalienable;[6] but it could be released to the tenant of the fee simple conditional.[7] There could be no remainder after a fee simple conditional.[8]

[5] Anon., Fitz. Ab. Formedon, 65. Co. Lit. 19 a. See Willion v. Berkley, 1 Plowd. 223, 235; Barksdale v. Gamage, 3 Rich. Eq. 271, 279, 280; Powers v. Bullwinkle, 33 So. Car. 293, 302, 303, 11 S. E. 971, 975.

[6] It cannot be devised. See Bedon v. Bedon, 2 Bail. 231, 248; Adams v. Chaplin, 1 Hill Ch. 265, 280; Deas v. Horry, 2 Hill Ch. 244; but cf. Cruger v. Heyward, 2 Des. 94; note to Mazyck v. Vanderhorst, Bail. Eq. 48, 56; Powers v. Bullwinkle, 33 So. Car. 293, 302, 11 S. E. 971, 975. But see Copenhaver v. Pendleton, 155 Va. 463, 155 S. E. 802; 6 Notre Dame Lawyer 442; 17 Va. Law Rev. 402; 24 Cal. Law Rev. 512, 518–523; 14 Univ. Cinn. Law Rev. 524; 3 Simes, Fut. Int., § 732. The possibility of reverter after a fee simple conditional in copyhold lands (see § 70, post) is devisable under the Wills Act (1 Vict., c. 26), § 3, which also makes a right of entry for condition broken devisable. Pemberton v. Barnes, [1899] 1 Ch. 544. The fee simple conditional does not merge in the possibility of reverter. Adams v. Chaplin, 1 Hill Ch. 265. The contrary has been held in the case of copyholds. Doe d. Simpson v. Simpson, 4 Bing. N. C. 333, 5 Scott 770. Doe d. Blesard v. Simpson (in Cam. Scacc.) 3 Man. & G. 929. See Bishop of Sodor and Man v. Derby, 2 Ves. Sr. 337, 355.

[7] Pearse v. Killian, McMull. Eq. 231. See Adams v. Chaplin, 1 Hill Ch. 265, 278; Vaughan v. Langford, 81 So. Car. 282, 62 S. E. 316.

[8] Willion v. Berkley, 1 Plowd. 223, 235, 242. Co. Lit. 18 a. 2 Inst. 336. Mazyck v. Vanderhorst, Bail. Eq. 48. Bedon v. Bedon, 2 Bail. 231, 248. Bailey v. Seabrook, Rich. Ch. Cas. 419, 426 et seq. Adams v. Chaplin, 1 Hill Ch. 265. Edwards v. Barksdale, 2 Hill Ch. 184, 197. Deas v. Horry, Id. 244. Williams v. Caston, 1 Strob. 130, 133. Buist v. Dawes, 4 Strob. Eq. 37, 48. The case of Cruger v. Heyward, 2 Des. 94, if it decides the contrary, must be considered overruled; see note to Mazyck v. Vanderhorst, Bail. Eq. 48, 58.

In modern times the belief and practice have been in accordance with the text. But Sir Frederick Pollock and Professor Maitland have shown good reason to doubt whether this was so originally. 2 P. & M. Hist. Eng. Law (2d ed.) 23–25, 28; and see an article by Professor Maitland, 6 Law Quart. Rev. 22; criticised, Challis, Real Prop. (3d ed.) 85, 428. Cf. also 2 Bract. Note Book 77, 347; Bract. 18 b; Fleta, Lib. 3, c. 9, § 9; Rowden v. Maltster, Cro. Car. 42, 43; Doe d. Simpson v. Simpson, 4 Bing. N. C. 333, 345, 5 Scott 770, 788; Gardner v. Sheldon, Vaugh. 259, 269; 2 Prest. Est. 318, 319, 323–354; note to Mazyck v. Van-

## § 15. Curtesy and Dower. Curtesy is the estate for life which a man has in an estate of inheritance of his wife after

derhorst, Bail. Eq. 48, 53, 55, 56.

At the present day, apart from the objection of remoteness, there seems no reason why a limitation in a will after a fee simple conditional should not be good as an executory devise. Gardner v. Sheldon, Vaugh. 259, 270. Cruger v. Heyward, 2 Des. 94 (see note to Mazyck v. Vanderhorst, Bail. Eq. 48, 58). Rowland v. Warren, 10 Ore. 129. See Amer. Law Inst. Restatement, Property, §§ 25, 47, 76. (But cf. Doe d. Simpson v. Simpson, ubi sup.) And several cases in which an executory devise after a fee simple conditional has been held to be too remote seem to imply, by raising and deciding the question of remoteness, that such a devise, if not too remote, would be good. Mazyck v. Vanderhorst, Bail. Eq. 48. Bedon v. Bedon, 2 Bail. 231, 248. Adams v. Chaplin, 1 Hill Ch. 265, 280. See Barksdale v. Gamage, 3 Rich. Eq. 271, 276. The South Carolina cases in which it had been decided or said that there could be no executory devise after a fee simple conditional, Bailey v. Seabrook, Rich. Ch. Cas. 419, Williams v. Caston, 1 Strob. 130, 133, Buist v. Dawes, 4 Strob. Eq. 37, 48 et seq., Barksdale v. Gamage, 3 Rich. Eq. 271, 274, seemed to rest on no valid reason, as was strongly intimated in the carefully considered opinion of Dorgan, C., in Buist v. Dawes, 4 Strob. Eq. 37, 48. The only reason given was in Bailey v. Seabrook, Rich. Ch. Cas. 419, viz., the rule that a

limitation must always be construed, if it can be, as a remainder instead of as an executory devise; but as this limitation confessedly cannot be construed as a remainder, the rule seems rather a reason for construing it as an executory devise. In Edwards v. Barksdale, 2 Hill Ch. 184, 197, 198, it was said by O'Neall, J., that if an estate which would otherwise be deemed a fee simple conditional is followed by an executory devise not too remote, the first estate must be construed to be an estate in fee simple. But it has now been held in South Carolina that there may be an executory devise limited on a fee simple conditional. Powers v. Bullwinkle, 33 So. Car. 293, 11 S. E. 971. Selman v. Robertson, 46 So. Car. 262, 24 S. E. 187. See Buist v. Dawes, before the Court of Errors, 4 Rich. Eq. 421, 426; McCorkle v. Black, 7 Rich. Eq. 407, 410, 419; Bethea v. Bethea, 48 So. Car. 440, 26 S. E. 716; Barber v. Crawford, 85 So. Car. 54, 67 S. E. 7; Davis v. Hodge, 102 So. Car. 178, 86 S. E. 478; § 455, post. Cf. also Whitworth v. Stuckey, 1 Rich. Eq. 404; M'Lure v. Young, 3 Rich. Eq. 559; Graham v. Moore, 13 So. Car. 115; Mangum v. Piester, 16 So. Car. 316. And see two later cases, in which the doctrine of O'Neall, J., stated above, is approved; Bomar v. Corn, 150 So. Car. 111, 147 S. E. 659; Prudential Ins. Co. v. Monk, 165 So. Car. 111, 162 S. E. 911. And so after any fee simple determinable,

issue born between them who could inherit the estate. It
has been questioned whether the estate vests in possession
on the birth of the issue, or on the death of the wife.[1] Dower
is the estate for life which a widow has in such land of which
her husband was seised during the coverture as her issue,
should there be any, could inherit. Anciently the more common form of dower seems to have been dower *ad ostium
ecclesiæ* (of which dower *ex permissu patris* was a variety).
By this a woman was endowed at the time of marriage with
certain lands into which she could enter immediately upon
her husband's death. This kind of dower has become entirely obsolete. The right of dower at common law is the right
of a woman to have assigned to her by the heir one-third
of the land in which she is dowable.

§ **16. Interests in Land of Others.** Interests in land owned
by others, such as commons and other profits, ways and other easements, rents, etc., cannot, from their nature, be created by livery of seisin. They, therefore, lie in grant, that
is, are created by deed, and consequently can begin *in futuro*.[1]

where such an estate is allowed, an executory devise may be good, if not too remote. See First Universalist Society v. Boland, 155 Mass. 171, 29 N. E. 524; Institution for Savings v. Home for Aged Women, 244 Mass. 583, 139 N. E. 301; Yarbrough v. Yarbrough, 151 Tenn. 221, 269 S. W. 236; Challis, Real Prop. (3d ed.) 257; Amer. Law Inst. Restatement, Property, § 47.

In Fletcher v. Fletcher, 88 Ind. 418, a deed of land to A. for life, and after his death to his children in fee simple, was held to give A. an estate in fee simple conditional, which on the birth of children became absolute. It is unnecessary to point out to the learned reader the errors in this opinion.

§ **15.** [1] The former view was adopted in Foster v. Marshall, 22 N. H. 491; the latter in Jones v. Davies, 5 H. & N. 766, aff'd 7 H. & N. 507. See 1 Tiffany, Real Prop. (2d ed.), § 244, 2 Tiffany, Real Prop. (3d ed.), § 552. Cf. Doyle v. Amer. Fire Ins. Co., 181 Mass. 139, 63 N. E. 394.

§ **16.** [1] By the common law, all interests in real estate that can be created by livery have to be so created, and are called corporeal hereditaments; interests that from their nature do not admit of livery can be created or conveyed by deed, and are called incorporeal hereditaments. This genus of incorporeal hereditaments contains two species: (1) Existing future estates, i. e. remainders and reversions; (2) jura in alieno solo, i. e. profits, ease-

§ 17. Though interests in others'. lands could at common law be created to begin *in futuro*, yet such interests *when once existing* could not be granted *in futuro;* and the same was true of existing reversions and remainders. Thus a rent might be granted to A. and his heirs, to begin ten years from date, and A. could transfer by grant the rent to B.; but A. could not grant the rent to B. to have it from and after A.'s death. So, again, if land had been conveyed to G. for life, remainder to H. and his heirs, H. could grant his remainder to I., but he could not grant to I. the remainder from and after H.'s death.[1] The reason given is that "if a reversion might be granted at a day to come, from thence it would follow that the grantor would have a particular estate in it, in the meantime, of his own creation, which cannot be by the rule of law that a man should be lessor to himself."[2]

§ 17.1. **Escheat.** When tenant in fee simple dies without heirs (which may happen either *per defectum sanguinis* or *per delictum tenentis*) the land falls by escheat to the lord of whom it is held.[1]

ments, rents, etc. The tie uniting these two very unlike classes is that neither of them lies in livery. Cf. Mr. Sweet's note on Corporeal and Incorporeal Hereditaments in Challis, Real Prop. (3d ed.) 48.

§ 17. [1] Buckler v. Harvy, Cro. El. 450, 585, Moore 423, 2 Co. 55 a. See Swift v. Heirs, March 31, sub nom. Vicars Choral de Litchfield v. Ayres, W. Jones 435, sub nom. Swyft v. Eyres, Cro. Car. 546, 1 Roll. Ab. 828, pl. 3; Prisot, C. J., Y. B. Trin. 38 Hen. VI. 38; Vavasour, J., Y. B. Trin. 8 Hen. VII. fol. 3 b; Throckmerton v. Tracy, 1 Plowd. 145, 152, 155, 156; Wrotesley v. Adams, Id. 187, 197;

Plowd. Qu., § 302; 1 Roll. Ab. 829, pl. 7. Cf. § 279, post.

[2] 1 Plowd. 155. This seems the real reason why the Rule was established, and not that given in 1 Preston, Est. 216–220. Challis, Real Prop. (3d ed.) 104, 112.

Under the Statutes of Uses and Wills existing incorporeal hereditaments can now be transferred in futuro; for a shifting use or executory devise does not create a particular estate in the settlor or in the testator's heirs, but the settlor or heirs retain the fee until the future event happens, upon which the fee shifts. § 54, post.

§ 17.1. [1] See §§ 115, 204, 205.1, post.

## 2. Statute De Donis

§ **18. Statutory Origin.** In 1285, by St. Westm. II., 13 Edw. I., c. 1, *De Donis Conditionalibus,* estates in fee simple conditional were turned into estates tail, the donor's possibility of reverter became a reversion,[1] and a remainder could be created after a fee tail as after a life estate. Interests were thus secured to future generations of a family, and, failing these, to the remainderman or donor, which could not be destroyed by the tenant for the time being of the estate.

§ **19.** By the gradual operation of (1) the doctrine of Collateral Warranty; (2) the allowance, by the courts, of Common Recoveries as a means of barring estates tail;[1] and (3) the Statutes of Fines, 4 Hen. VII., c. 24, and 32 Hen. VIII., c. 36, estates tail became alienable, and the reversions and remainders after them destructible.[2] By St. 3 & 4 Wm. IV., c. 74, fines and recoveries were abolished and simpler modes of assurance substituted.[3] Wherever in any of the United States estates tail have been preserved, simpler forms of conveyance have also generally taken the place of fines and recoveries.[4]

§ 18. [1] See §§ 29.1, 452, post.

§ 19. [1] Taltarum's Case (1472), Y. B. Mich. 12 Edw. IV. 19, pl. 25.

[2] Digby, Hist. Law Real Prop., c. 5, § 2. 2 Bl. Com. 348–364. Wms. Real Prop. (24th ed.), Part II., c. 2.

[3] See now Law of Prop. Act (1925), c. 20; Wms. Real Prop. (24th ed.) 148–149.

[4] See, for example, Me. Rev. Sts. (1916), c. 78, § 10; 2 Mass. Gen. Laws, c. 183, §§ 45–48; R. I. Gen. Laws (1923), c. 296, §§ 5, 14–17; Del. Rev. Sts. (1915), c. 92, § 39; 1 Md. Pub. Gen. Laws (1924), Art. 21, § 25. See also Ewing v. Nesbitt, 88 Kans. 708, 129 Pac. 1131.

The Statute De Donis was brought by the colonists to America. Cf. 78 Univ. Pa. Law Rev. 195. On Dec. 12, 1712, South Carolina passed an Act declaring that certain British Statutes particularly mentioned should be in force; and, § 10, that all others should be declared impracticable. This Act does not mention the Statute De Donis; and the Statute is therefore not in force in that State. Mr. Dane, 6 Dane, Ab. 606, says that this Act applied also to North Carolina, Tennessee, Georgia, Alabama, and Mississippi; but either it did not apply to them, or the enumeration of Statutes in the Act did not include all those in

### 3. Statute Quia Emptores

**§ 20. Tenure at Common Law.** At common law a tenant in fee could either, (1) with the consent of the lord, sub-

force, for in all the above States the Statute De Donis seems to have been in force until repealed by later legislation. No. Car. St. 1749, c. 46; St. 1784, c. 204, § 5. Patterson v. Patterson, 1 Hayw. 163. Den d. Lane v. Davis, Id. 277. Minge v. Gilmour, Id. 279. Moore v. Bradley, 2 Hayw. 142. Polk v. Faris, 9 Yerg. 209, 234. Ga. Const. (1777), Art. 51. Ga. Const. (1789), Art. 4, § 6. Ga. St. Feb. 16, 1799, § 5; St. Dec. 21, 1821. Gray v. Gray, 20 Ga. 804. Hertz v. Abrahams, 110 Ga. 707, 36 S. E. 409. Davis v. Hollingsworth, 113 Ga. 210, 38 S. E. 827. Ala. St. Dec. 22, 1812, § 10. Simmons v. Augustin, 3 Port. 69. Miss. St. Dec. 22, 1812, § 10; St. June 13, 1822, § 24. Jordan v. Roach, 32 Miss. 481, 616.

Estates tail can still be created, and are recognized by statute, in Maine, Massachusetts, Rhode Island, and Delaware. See statutes cited at beginning of this note. In Maryland, estates in tail general are in effect abolished by virtue of 1 Pub. Gen. Laws (1924), Art. 46, § 1, but other estates may be created. See Posey v. Budd, 21 Md. 477, 486; 1 Alexander, Brit. Stat. in Md. (2d ed.) 121, 127. It seems also that estates tail are recognized in Wyoming, Rev. Sts. (1931), § 89-3922; Jensen v. Jensen, 89 Pac. 2d 1085. And see an ambiguous reference to "Estate tail" in heading of Nev. Comp. Laws (1929),

§ 1517. They can be created in Kansas. Ewing v. Nesbit, 88 Kan. 708, 129 Pac. 1131. Gardner v Anderson, 116 Kan. 431, 227 Pac. 743. Coleman v. Shoemaker, 147 Kan. 689, 78 Pac. 2d 905. In Pennsylvania they can no longer be created, but those existing at the time of the passage of the Statute of April 27, 1855, are not disturbed. Reinhart v. Lantz, 37 Pa. 488.

In Connecticut, an estate to one and the heirs of his body was held to give neither a fee simple conditional nor an estate tail; but to give "an absolute estate in fee simple to the issue of the first donee in tail." The Statute of 1784 (Conn. Gen. Sts. 1930, § 5001), to this effect, is said to have been declaratory of the common law of the Colony. Welles v. Olcott, Kirby 118. Chappel v. Brewster, Id. 175. Hamilton v. Hempsted, 3 Day 332. See Ohio Gen. Code (1930), § 8622.

In Oregon, the Statute De Donis is not in force. A gift to A. and the heirs of his body gives him a fee simple conditional. Rowland v. Warren, 10 Ore. 129. Lytle v. Hulen, 128 Ore. 483, 275 Pac. 45. See 19 Ore. Law Rev. 367. The same is true in Iowa. Pierson v. Lane, 60 Iowa 60, 14 N. W. 90. Kepler v. Larson, 131 Iowa 438, 108 N. W. 1033. Sagers v. Sagers, 158 Iowa 729, 138 N. W. 911. Shope v. Unknown Claimants, 174 Iowa 662, 156 N. W. 850. And the law

stitute another in his own place to hold the fee of the lord;[1] or (2) by subinfeudation, grant the land to be held of himself. But the former mode could be employed only when the feoffee was to hold the same fee that the feoffor had held; and, therefore, when the feoffor conveyed a part only of his land the feoffee had to hold of him; and so, when the feoffor conveyed a life estate, or a fee with a special limitation (e. g. to A. and his heirs, tenants of the Manor of Dale), or (after the Statute *De Donis*) an estate tail, the feoffee held directly of him.[2] All reversions and possibilities of reverter were therefore always in the hands of the persons of whom land was held; for though a reversion could be alienated, it carried with it the lordship of the particular estate; and a possibility of reverter could not be alienated.[3]

has been said to be the same in Nebraska. Yates v. Yates, 104 Neb. 678, 178 N. W. 262.

In most of the United States estates tail have, at the present day, been abolished by statute expressly or impliedly. In Texas, they seem to be prohibited by the Constitution, Art. I., § 26. In New Hampshire, it is held that they have been done away with by implication from the statutes. Merrill v. Amer. Baptist Missionary Union, 73 N. H. 414, 62 Atl. 647. Idaho, Utah and Washington are the only States (to which should be added the District of Alaska) in which the Statutes and the Courts are silent with regard to estates tail; and such estates would logically seem to be there preserved; but very possibly the Courts would decline to recognize them. In Nevada, the Courts might do likewise, notwithstanding the doubtful mention of estates tail cited above. Words

which under the Statute De Donis would create an estate tail give, by statute, in some States, an estate in fee simple; in others an estate for life (or an estate tail lasting only for life) in the first donee, with remainder in fee to his children or his heirs. See Stimson, American Statute Law, § 1313; 17 Harv. Law Rev. 305–316; 13 Yale L. J. 267. Amer. Law Inst. Restatement, Property, Chap. 5, Introductory note; Uniform Property Act, § 10 (Handbook of Uniform State Laws 1938). On the effect of the Illinois Statute see Kales, Estates, §§ 402–441; 1 Ill. Law Rev. 323. In Hawaii there is neither fee tail nor fee simple conditional. Rooke v. Queen's Hospital, 12 Hawaii 375.

§ 20. [1] Bract. 81. 2 Inst. 65.

[2] 2 Inst. 65. Digby, Hist. Law Real Prop., c. 4, § 5. 1 P. & M. Hist. Eng. Law (2d ed.) 329–331.

[3] See §§ 13, 14, ante.

**§ 21. Statute Quia Emptores.** The St. Westm. III., 18 Edw. I., c. 1 (1290), known as the Statute *Quia Emptores Terrarum*, enacts that on all conveyances in fee the tenant shall not hold of the grantor, but of the grantor's lord.[1] This put an end to subinfeudation. The Statute does not affect gifts in tail or for life.[2] And, as lands in frankalmoign could not be held of anyone but the grantor,[3] land could not be granted in frankalmoign after the Statute, except by the King.[4] We have here to consider the effects of the Statute on the future interests allowed by the common law.[5]

**§ 22. The Statute in the United States.** Before dealing with this, however, it will be convenient to see how far the Statute *Quia Emptores* is in force in the United States; and a question preliminary to this inquiry is: How far does tenure exist in the United States? For it is idle to inquire whether a statute directing of whom land shall be held is in force, if land cannot be held at all. This preliminary question has been much discussed. Land was held of the Crown in the Colonial times,[1] and it does not seem that so fundamental an alteration in the theory of property as the abolition of tenure would be worked by a change of political sovereignty. Tenure still obtains between a tenant for life or years and the reversioner; and so in like manner, it is conceived, a tenant in fee simple holds of the chief lord, that is, of the State.[2]

§ 21. [1] In an article in 36 Yale L. J. 593, 605, Professor Vance questions the accuracy of this statement, but without sufficient grounds. See Appendix N, § 975, post.

[2] See § 3 of the Statute ad fin.; Y. B. Middlesex Iter. 22 Edw. I., p. 641; 2 Inst. 504, 505: Digby, Hist. Law Real Prop., c. 4, § 5, note.

[3] Lit., § 141. Perk., § 260.

[4] Lit., § 140.

[5] See § 7, ante.

**[G. R. P.]—2**

§ 22. [1] As is the case in British Colonies. See 64 Sol. J. 385. But cf. Re Simpson, [1927] 4 Dom. L. R. 817, 822.

[2] Sharswood, Law Lect. VIII. 207–232. Hoff. Leg. Out. 593. United States v. Repentigny, 5 Wall. 211, 267, 18 L. E. 627. Estate of O'Connor, 126 Neb. 182. 252 N. W. 826. Cf. 2 Bl. Com. (Sharswood's ed.) 77, note; 8 Law Series, Univ. Mo. Bull. 3. But see contra 1 Washb. Real Prop. (5th ed.)

**§ 23. Tenure in Various States.** The subject has, however, in many States been affected by legislation or decision.

**Connecticut.** "Every proprietor in fee simple of lands has an absolute and direct dominion and property in the same."[1]

**New York.** "All lands within this State are declared to be allodial, so that, subject to the liability to escheat, the entire and absolute property is vested in the owners, according to the nature of their respective estates; and all feudal tenures, of every description, with all their incidents, are abolished."[2]

**New Jersey.** The St. of Feb. 18, 1795,[3] declares that the purchaser of lands shall hold them of the chief lord, if there be any, of the fee; that all tenures are turned into free and common socage; but that this shall not take away "any rents certain, or other services incident or belonging to tenure in common socage, due or to grow due to this State, or any mean lord, or other private person, or the fealty and distresses incident thereunto;" and that the tenure of all grants made or to be made by the State shall be "allodial and not feudal," and "in free and pure allodium only."[4] The statement in 1 Washb. Real Prop. (5th ed.) * 40, that tenure does not exist in New Jersey, seems to be incorrect.

*pp. 39–42, (6th ed.) p. 59; 2 Bl. Com. (Cooley's ed.) 102, note; 33 Yale L. J. 248; 34 Harv. Law Rev. 717, 728. And the prevalent American doctrine as to possibilities of reverter after determinable fees may well be considered to imply the non-existence of tenure. See §§ 23.2, note 9, 41.1, note 2, post.

§ 23. 1 St. Oct. 1793. See St. 1821, tit. 56, c. 1, § 1, note; Gen. Sts. (1902), § 4025.

2 Rev. Sts., pt. 2, c. 1, tit. 1, § 3. Matter of People, 234 N. Y. 48, 136 N. E. 235. Kavanaugh v.

Cohoes P. & L. Corp., 114 Misc. 590, 610–624, 187 N. Y. S. 216, 229–237. This section of the Revised Statutes had been preceded by St. Feb. 20, 1787, which was identical with the New Jersey Statute, post. See Cornel v. Lamb, 2 Cowen 652; Hoff. Leg. Out. 595.

3 1 Gen. Sts. (1895), pp. 879, 880.

4 "Allodial" land is now usually employed to mean land held of no one. 2 Bl. Com. 45, note, 47, 105. See Wright, Tenures 146, 147; Gilbert, Tenures (4th ed.) 352,

**[G. R. P.]**

**Pennsylvania.** In *Wallace* v. *Harmstad*,[5] it was held that tenure does not exist in Pennsylvania. This will be considered below in connection with the Statute *Quia Emptores*.[6]

**Maryland.** In *Matthews* v. *Ward*,[7] it is said that after the Revolution "lands became allodial, subject to no tenure."[8]

**Virginia.** Tenures were abolished by St. 1779, c. 13.[9]

**§ 23.1. Ohio, Indiana, Illinois, Michigan, and Wisconsin.** These States were formed out of the Northwest Territory, which was ceded by Virginia to the United States in 1784, subsequent to the abolition of tenure. In these States, therefore, there would seem to have been originally no tenure.[1] The government of the Northwest Territory, July 14, 1795, passed an Act declaring that the common law of England and all Acts of Parliament of a general nature made in aid of the common law prior to 4 Jac. I. (which was the date of the settlement of Virginia), "and also the several laws in force in this Territory," should be in full force.[2] It is doubtful how far this republication of the common law and

Watkins's note 5; Somner, Gavelkind 109–111, 126. This is the sense in which it is employed in the New York Revised Statutes, ubi sup. Used with this meaning the expression "allodial tenure" is nonsense. But "allodial land" was also employed to mean land which, though held of a lord, was not subject to any services. "Erat alodium praedium non modo ab omni praestatione liberum, sed a quolibet servitio reali et personali immune, licet illius possessor dominum agnosceret, a quo illud tenebat in feudum honoratum." Du Cange, Glos. Alodis. See also Spelm. Glos. Aloarius, sub. fin. Cf. Du Cange, Glos. voc. cit. passim; Co. Lit. 1 b, 5 a, 65 a, Harg. note; Allen, Prerog. 196; Digby, Hist. Law Real Prop. (5th ed.), c. 1, sect. I., §§ 2, 4. In the New York Stat-

ute of 1787, and the New Jersey Statute, the word seems to be employed in this latter sense. See. Miller v. Miller, 91 Kan. 1, 6, 136 Pac. 953, 954; Stanton v. Sullivan, 7 Atl. 2d 696 (R. I.) and sub Georgia, post. But cf. 3 Kent, Com. 513, note (a).

5 44 Pa. 492.

6 See § 26, post.

7 10 G. & J. 443, 451.

8 See Hoff. Leg. Out. 594.

9 10 Hen. St. 50, 64, 65. See 2 Minor, Inst. (4th ed.) 79; 1 Lomax, Dig. 539.

**§ 23.1.** 1 See Penny v. Little, 4 Ill. 301, 304, 305; Lavalle v. Strobel, 89 Ill. 370, 380. Cf. McCool v. Smith, 1 Black 459, 468, 17 L. E. 218; Bates v. Brown, 5 Wall. 710, 714, 18 S. Ct. 535, 538, 18 L. E. 535.

2 1 Chase, St. 190, 191.

re-enactment of the English Statutes were within the power
of the Territorial Government.[3] If the Act was valid, then
tenure, and at the same time the Statute *Quia Emptores,*
were re-established in the Northwest Territory. After Ohio
was set off as a State, its Legislature, Feb. 14, 1805,[4] passed
a statute repealing the Act of the Territorial Government,
and then re-enacting it. But on Jan. 2, 1806, the Legislature
of Ohio passed an Act[5] repealing so much of the last Act as
declared that the common law of England and English Statutes should be in force. It would seem, therefore, that the
law in Ohio was relegated to its condition before the Territorial Act of 1795, and that therefore there is no tenure
in that State.[6]   On Ohio's becoming a State in 1802, all the
rest of the original Northwest Territory was included within the Territory of Indiana. The Legislature of this Territory in 1807 enacted that the common law, and the British
Statutes made in aid thereof prior to 4 Jac. I., should be considered in full force, and this provision has stood on the
Statute Book of the Territory and of the State of Indiana
ever since.[7]   If, therefore, tenure has been restored in Indiana, the Statute of *Quia Emptores* has been restored with
it. In 1809 the Territory of Illinois was set off from Indiana,
and a statute similar to that of Indiana has always continued on the Statute Book of Illinois.[8]   The Territory of
Michigan was set off from the Territory of Indiana in 1805.
In 1821 a law was enacted in very singular language; it
provided "that no Act of the Parliament of England, and
no Act of the Parliament of Great Britain, shall have any
force within the Territory of Michigan: *Provided,* That all

---

[3] 1 Chase, St. 190, note. Doe d.
Thompson v. Gibson, 2 Ohio 339.
Helfenstine v. Garrard, 7 Ohio, pt.
1, 275.   Carroll v. Olmsted, 16
Ohio 251, 260.   Knapp v. Thomas,
39 Ohio St. 377, 385.

[4] 1 Chase, St. 512.

[5] 1 Chase, St. 528.

[6] 11 Am. Jur. 94, 95.   Walker,

Am. Law, § 124.   Cf. Crawford v.
Chapman, 17 Ohio 449.

[7] 1 Burns' Ind. Statutes (1908),
§ 236.   Cf. Stevenson v. Cloud, 5
Blackf. 92; McCord v. Ochiltree, 8
Blackf. 15, 19; Short v. Stotts, 58
Ind. 29; Ledgerwood v. The State,
134 Ind. 81, 84, 33 N. E. 631, 632.

[8] Ill. Rev. Sts., c. 28, § 1.   See
the cases cited in note 7, ante.

rights arising under any such Act shall remain as if this Act had not been made; the same being adopted from the laws of one of the original States, to wit, the State of Virginia, as far as necessary and suitable to the circumstances of the Territory of Michigan."[9]  And in the same year[10] it was also enacted that estates tail shall be abolished, and all persons then seised in tail should be deemed to be seised of an allodial estate.  Whatever the intention of these statutes may have been, it seems to be now held in Michigan that if the Statute of *Quia Emptores* is not in force there, it is because there is no need of it, and that subinfeudation would not be allowed in that State.[11]  It is unnecessary to enter upon the earlier history of Wisconsin law for the Constitution of the State provides that land shall be allodial.[12]

§ 23.2. **West Virginia.**  This State was not set off from Virginia till 1862, and carried with it the law of Virginia. Tenure, therefore, has never existed in this State.

**Kentucky.**  In this State titles are now declared by statute to be allodial.[1]

**South Carolina.**  The Statute of Dec. 12, 1712,[2] § 5, declared that the only tenure of lands in South Carolina was that of free and common socage.  The statements, therefore, in 1 Washb. Real Prop. * 40, and Smith on Landl. and Ten. (Am. ed.) 6, note, that there is no tenure in South Carolina appear to be incorrect.

**Georgia.**  The Code of 1911, § 3623, reads thus: *"Allodial tenure.*  The tenure by which all realty is held in this State is under the State as original owner; it is without service of any kind, and limited only by the right of eminent domain remaining in the State."  This is a legislative declaration that tenure exists.[3]

---

9 1 Mich. Terr. Laws, 900. ·

10 1 Mich. Terr. Laws, 815.

11 Mandlebaum v. McDonell, 29 Mich. 78, 95.

12 Wis. Const. (1848), Art. 1, § 14.  Barker v. Dayton, 28 Wis. 367, 384.

§ 23.2. 1 Ky. Gen. Sts. (1873), c. 63, § 2.

2 Grimké's Laws, 99.  Rev. Sts. 1893, § 1872.

3 On the use of the expression, "allodial tenure," see § 23, note 4, ante.

**Minnesota.** The Constitution (1857)[4] declares that all land shall be allodial.

**Iowa.** In 1834 Iowa was made part of the Territory of Michigan; in 1836 it was attached to the Territory of Wisconsin; and in 1838 it was made a separate Territory. It is probable that should any case arise it will be held in Iowa, as in Michigan, that if the Statute of *Quia Emptores* is not in force in that State, it is because there is no need of it.[5]

**Arkansas.** The Constitution (1874) declares that all lands are "allodial" and prohibits "feudal tenures of every description with all their incidents."[6]

**California.** In this State all lands are said to be "allodial."[7]

It is not improbable that the courts of other States may follow that of Maryland, and declare tenure abolished without legislative aid; but as yet the Maryland case (except in Pennsylvania)[8] finds no support elsewhere.[9]

**§ 24. The Statute in various States.** In those States where tenure no longer obtains, there can be no question whether the Statute *Quia Emptores* is in force; its subject-

---

[4] Art. I., § 15. Cf. Minneapolis Mill Co. v. Tiffany, 22 Minn. 463; Dutcher v. Culver, 24 Minn. 584, 617.

[5] See Pierson v. Lane, 60 Iowa 60, 14 N. W. 90. Cf. O'Ferrall v. Simplot, 4 Iowa 381; Lorman v. Benson, 8 Mich. 18, 25; Coburn v. Harvey, 18 Wis. 147; Webster v. Morris, 66 Wis. 366, 376, note, 390, 28 N. W. 353, 362; Gilbert v. Stockman, 81 Wis. 602, 52 N. W. 1045.

[6] Art. II., § 28.

[7] Title and Trust Co. v. Garrott, 42 Cal. Ap. 152, 157, 183 Pac. 470, 472.

[8] As to Pennsylvania, see § 26, post.

[9] The fact that since the third edition of this work no case has been decided affirming the existence of tenure in America (for the slight references to tenure in Miller v. Miller, 91 Kan. 1, 6, 136 Pac. 953, 954, and Estate of O'Connor, 126 Neb. 182, 252 N. W. 826, may well be considered negligible), and the general recognition in this country of possibilities of reverter, whose existence may be considered to involve the absence of tenure, render it increasingly likely that American Courts will decide against the existence of tenure, whenever the question comes up, except in those States where there is some clear authority to the contrary. See §§ 22, ante, 41.1, note 2, post.

matter has ceased to exist. In this condition are at least
Connecticut, New York,[1] Maryland,[2] Virginia,[3] Ohio, Wiscon
sin, West Virginia, Kentucky, Minnesota, Arkansas.[4]

§ 25. In the States where there is no reason to question
the existence of tenure, there seems as little reason to question the existence of the Statute *Quia Emptores.* There is
no cause why this Statute should not have prevailed as generally as the Statute *De Donis.* Denio, J., in *Van Rensselaer* v.
*Hays,*[1] points out the absurdity of supposing that subinfeudation existed in the Colonies generally. In New Jersey the
Statute was in force, and has been expressly re-enacted;[2] Mr.
Dane says[3] that the Statute of *Quia Emptores* was "never
adopted here" (*quære* whether this means in Massachusetts).
But no authority is cited for the proposition. The alleged non-
existence of the Statute in North Carolina, Tennessee, Georgia,
Alabama, and Mississippi rests upon the same ground as
the alleged non-existence in those States of the Statute *De
Donis,* which, as we have seen,[4] wholly fails.[5] In Indiana, Illinois, Michigan, and Iowa, either there is no tenure, or, if tenure
exists, the Statute *Quia Emptores* exists also.[6] There would
seem to be, of the States in which tenure exists at the present

§ 24. [1] It has been sometimes
said that the Statute Quia Emp-
tores was not in force in New
York even before the Revised
Statutes. Jackson v. Schutz, 18
Johns. 174, 179, 180. De Peyster
v. Michael, 6 N. Y. 467, 502, 503.
But see Denio, J., in People v. Van
Rensselaer, 9 N. Y. 291, 338, and
in Van Rensselaer v. Hays, 19 N.
Y. 68, 71-75; 1 Chalm. Col. Op.
129 (Am. ed. 149); and 25 Alb.
L. J. 169.

[2] See Chancellor Kilty's English Statutes in Maryland 146;
and the Charter to Lord Baltimore, Lucas, Chart. 95. Cf.
Thomas v. Hamilton, 1 H. & McH.
190; Matthews v. Ward, 10 G. &
J. 443, 450.

[3] The Statute Quia Emptores
was in force in Virginia, 1 Chalm.
Col. Op. 121 (Am. ed. 142); but
was repealed by St. 1792, c. 147,
after tenures had been abolished,
1 Lomax, Dig. 539.

[4] See Mandlebaum v. McDonell,
29 Mich. 78, 95.

§ 25. [1] 19 N. Y. 68, 75.

[2] 1 Chalm. Col. Op. 123 (Am.
ed. 143). See § 23, ante. As to
New York and Virginia before the
abolition of tenure, see notes to
§ 24, ante.

[3] 4 Dane, Ab. 504.

[4] § 19, note 4, ante.

[5] And see Martin's English
Statutes in North Carolina (1792)
39.

[6] § 23.1, ante.

day, but two in which the Statute *Quia Emptores* is not in force,—Pennsylvania and South Carolina.

**§ 26. Pennsylvania.** By the Charter of 1681 the Crown granted to William Penn the power to grant land to be held of himself, his heirs and assigns, and not immediately of the Crown, the Statute *Quia Emptores* notwithstanding.[1] And in *Ingersoll* v. *Sergeant*[2] (1836), a very elaborately argued and carefully considered case, it was held that the Statute *Quia Emptores* was not in force, and that therefore rent reserved on a conveyance in fee simple was rent service and could be apportioned. This decision has always been deemed a landmark in the law of Pennsylvania. But in *Wallace* v. *Harmstad*[3] (1863), the Court ruled that there was no tenure in the State.[4] This ruling was unnecessary to the decision of the case, and has been far from meeting with universal acceptance. It has been severely criticised by Chief Justice Sharswood in his Law Lectures,[5] and by Mr. Cadwalader in his treatise on Ground Rents.[6] Their criticisms seem just. If *Wallace* v. *Harmstad* had professed to overrule *Ingersoll* v. *Sergeant*, the ruling, whether right or wrong, would be plain enough. But on the contrary it is said: "That ground rent is a rent service was fundamental in *Ingersoll* v. *Sergeant*, a case which has been so often recognized and followed as to have become a rule of property."[7] In fact *Wallace* v. *Harmstad* is unintelligible. To speak of rent service, or of the Statute *Quia Emptores*, in any State where tenure is nonexistent, is an absurdity; rent service and the Statute *Quia Emptores* necessarily imply tenure. They are meaningless terms without it. Considering the high authority which has always attached to *Ingersoll* v. *Sergeant*, there may be reason, in spite of *Wallace* v. *Harmstad*, to believe that tenure still

§ 26. [1] Lucas, Chart. 106, 107.
[2] 1 Whart. 337.
[3] 44 Pa. 492.
[4] Cf. Huston, Land Titles in Pa. 374, and see Stuart v. Easton, 170 U. S. 383, 393, 18 S. Ct. 650, 42

L. E. 1078, 1081–2.
[5] Pp. 207–232.
[6] Chap. 1. See Jackson & Gross, Landl. & Ten., §§ 1–11; Foulke, Treatise, § 73, note.
[7] 44 Pa. 495.

exists in Pennsylvania, and that the Statute *Quia Emptores* does not.[8]

§ **26.1. Delaware.** Delaware was granted by the Duke of York to William Penn (though it appears to have been outside of the patent granted to the Duke), but it was never incorporated into Pennsylvania. There was no exemption from the Statute *Quia Emptores* in the patent to the Duke, and the Statute was therefore in force over the land held under the patent, and presumably in Delaware.[1]

§ **27. South Carolina.** On Dec. 12, 1712, was passed an Act to put in force in the Province the English Statutes therein particularly mentioned; the tenth section of this Act declared that all the English Statutes not enumerated and made of force in the Province by the Act were impracticable in the Province. The Statute *Quia Emptores* was not mentioned in this Act, and is therefore not law in South Carolina.

§ **28.** The important result of this inquiry, for our present purpose, is that in all of the United States, with the exception of South Carolina and perhaps Pennsylvania, land, if held at all, can be held of none but the State; for in all the States, with the two exceptions, either there is no tenure, or, if there is tenure, the Statute *Quia Emptores* is in force.[1]

§ **29. Effect on Future Interests.** We recur now to the question stated above,[1] namely, the effect of the Statute *Quia Emptores* on the future interests allowed by the common law or the Statute *De Donis*.[2]

§ **29.1. Remainders and Reversions.** If tenant in fee grants estates for life or in tail and subsequently grants the

<hr>

8 See 5 Temple L. Q. 279.

§ **26.1.** 1 1 Chalm. Col. Op. 123 (Am. ed. 143). It would seem that a notion must have prevailed that the Statute Quia Emptores was not in force, for the Delaware St. of 24 Geo. II., c. 119, § 13, speaks of land escheating to the immediate landlord. At present, by the Rev. Sts. of 1852, c. 82, § 1, all land in Delaware escheats to the State.

§ **28.** 1 Where there is no tenure, the land of one dying without heirs passes to the State, not by escheat, but in the same way in which the personal property of one who dies without next of kin passes to the State. See § 205.1, post.

§ **29.** 1 § 21, ante. See § 975 et seq., post.

2 See §§ 7, 18, ante.

reversion in fee, the tenants for life or in tail hold of the grantee of the reversion after as before the Statute *Quia Emptores;* but if he grants particular estates and by the same conveyance grants the ultimate remainder in fee, the tenants of the particular estates, as well as the ultimate remainder-man, hold since the Statute of the chief lord.[1]

§ 30. **Interests Arising on Condition Broken.** These were not affected by the Statute *Quia Emptores.* The right of the feoffor to enter and substitute himself for the feoffee is not a reversionary right, nor is it dependent upon tenure.[1] The validity of conditions attached to fees has been repeatedly recognized in America.[2]

§ 31. **Possibilities of Reverter.** These rights, as their name implies, were reversionary rights; but a reversionary right implies tenure, and the Statute *Quia Emptores* put an end to tenure between the feoffor of an estate in fee simple and the feoffee.[1] Therefore, since the Statute, there can be no possibility of reverter remaining in the feoffor upon the conveyance of a fee; or, in other words, since the Statute, there can be no fee with a special or collateral limitation; and the attempted imposition of such a limitation is invalid.[2] The distinction between a right of entry for condition broken and a possibility of reverter is this: after the Statute, a feoffor, by the feoffment, substituted the feoffee for himself as his lord's tenant. By entry for breach of condition, he avoided the substitution, and placed himself in the same position to the lord which he had formerly occupied. The right to enter was not a reversionary right coming into effect on the termination of an estate, but was the right to substitute the estate of the grantor for the estate of the grantee. A possibil-

§ 29.1. [1] Anon., Dyer 362 b, pl. 19. Lit., §§ 215–217. 2 Inst. 505. Leake, Law of Property in Land (2d ed.) 29, 233. Challis, Real Prop. (3d ed.) 22.

§ 30. [1] Lit., §§ 325, 347. Co. Lit. 202. Doe d. Freeman v. Bateman, 2 B. & Ald. 168.

[2] See especially Van Rensselaer v. Ball, 19 N. Y. 100; Van Rensselaer v. Dennison, 35 N. Y. 393, 400.

§ 31. [1] See §§ 20, 21, ante.
[2] See article on Determinable Fees in American Jurisdictions, by J M. Zane, 17 Harv. Law Rev. 297; but see also §§ 39–41, post, as to the law in America.

ity of reverter, on the other hand, did not work the substitution of one estate for another, but was essentially a reversionary interest,—a returning of the land to the lord of whom it was held, because the tenant's estate had determined.[3]

§ **32. In England.** In accordance with the doctrine of the foregoing section, no possibility of reverter after a determinable[1] fee has been sustained in England since the Statute *Quia Emptores.* A fee simple subject to a conditional limitation, that is, to a shifting use or executory devise, is sometimes called a determinable fee;[2] but this is not technically exact. A determinable fee is one subject to a special limitation; that is, a limitation which marks the original bounds of the estate, and after which, in case of a fee, no other estate can be granted at common law. A conditional limitation, as the term is commonly used, cuts off the first estate and introduces another.[3] An estate to A. and his heirs, tenants of the Manor of Dale, is an instance of a determinable fee. An

[3] It has been suggested that the possibility of reverter passed to the chief lord, but as to this see § 776, post. The Statute having no application to the King, he could of course still grant determinable fees. Rents charge are not held of anyone; and if A. who has a rent charge in fee grants it for a less estate to B., B. does not hold of A.; so it would seem that the Statute Quia Emptores does not inhibit a rent charge being created de novo in fee simple determinable, nor an existing rent charge being granted in fee simple determinable; and that the law is the same as to other like incorporeal hereditaments, such as profits and easements in gross. There is next to nothing in the books on the subject; but cf. A. G. v. Cummins, [1906] 1 I. R. 406; §§ 33.12, 43, 87.1, post; and see Wright v. Gerrard, W. Jones 2;

Pinkerton v. Pratt, [1915] 1 I. R. 406.

§ **32.** [1] In deference to Mr. Challis's opinion, the employment of "qualified" as synonymous with "determinable" has been avoided. See Challis, Real Prop. (3d ed.), c. 19.

[2] E. g. in Aldred v. Sylvester, 184 Ind. 542, 561, 111 N. E. 914, 920; Stubbs v. Abel, 114 Ore. 610, 233 Pac. 852; Hess v. Kernen Bros., 169 Iowa 646, 149 N. W. 847. See 36 Harv. Law Rev. 987, 990; 23 Columbia Law Rev. 207; 3 Minn. Law Rev. 320, 335. Likewise a fee subject to a right of entry for condition broken. This error is pointed out in Brown v. Hobbs, 132 Md. 559, 104 Atl. 283; and see § 40, note 1, post.

[3] As to the case where it follows a conditional or determinable fee, see §§ 14, note 8, ante, and 114, note 3, post.

estate to A. and his heirs, but if he dies unmarried, then to B. and his heirs, is a fee simple subject to a conditional limitation. Determinable fees were good at common law, but were done away with by the Statute *Quia Emptores*. Conditional limitations were not good at common law; they were first introduced by the Statutes of Uses and of Wills.[4]

§ 33. The effect, however, of the Statute *Quia Emptores* in putting an end to determinable fees has been often overlooked, though, as has just been said, no such fee has been actually sustained in England by decision since the Statute. The *dicta* of English judges which support or assume the validity of such fees since the Statute follows.

§ 33.1. Choke, J.[1] (1467): "As if I give land to a man to have to him and his heirs in fee so long as John A'Down has issue of his body, in that case the feoffee will hold of his Lord, etc.; yet if John A'Down dies without heir of his body, etc., in that case I may well enter, etc. But not by escheat, etc., but because the feoffment is determined."[2]

§ 33.2. Counsel (1535) says:[1] "If I give land to you and to your heirs so long as such a tree shall live, that is a good fee simple determinable for the life of the tree, and I see no diversity in reason why a fee simple shall not be as well determined by the life of a man as by the life of a tree, for it is all one in reason. So it seems to me that, etc." Baldwin, Chief Justice of the Common Pleas: "You say well."[2]

§ 33.3. **Poole v. Needham**[1] (1608). Ejectment. J. was tenant in tail male, remainder in fee to T. T. granted his

---

[4] On the difference between a special limitation and a conditional limitation, and on the different meanings of the latter term, see Gray, Restraints on Alienation (2d ed.), § 22, note. Cf. Sifton v. Sifton, [1938] A. C. 656, 676; 3 Conveyancer, N. S. 213; and Amer. Law Inst. Restatement, Property, §§ 23, 24.

§ 33.1. [1] Y. B. Trin. 7 Edw. IV. 12, pl. 2.

[2] See § 35, note 3, post.

§ 33.2. [1] Y. B. Mich. 27 Hen VIII. 29, pl. 19.

[2] The report ends here with "Quod nota. Vide M. xxxix E. iii." This reference seems to be to the case of John Osborn v. The Prior of Eston, Y. B. Mich. 39 Edw. III. 29, pl. 30. Cf. Y. B. Lib. Ass. 39 Edw. III. 233, pl. 7.

§ 33.3. [1] Yelv. 149.

remainder to the Queen in fee, as long as any issue male of
J. should live. J. suffered a common recovery, under which
the plaintiff claimed, and J. died without issue. The defendant, as servant to T., entered. Judgment for the plaintiff.
The Court held that the grant of the remainder to the Queen
was void because the estate granted could never come into
possession, and that therefore the recovery barred T.'s remainder. They seem to have been of opinion that the Queen
did not take a fee simple absolute; that the fee simple determinable on the termination of the particular estate tail was
void, because there was no possibility of advantage in it; but
that if it had been a reversion that had been so granted to the
Queen, the grant would have been good, on account of the at-
tendant services, etc. T. having entered upon the plaintiff,
the plaintiff was entitled to proceed against him in ejectment
for disturbance of possession.[2] If the grant to the Queen was
void, then T.'s estate was barred by the recovery; if the grant
to the Queen passed a fee simple absolute, then T. had no
estate to be barred. The judgment for the plaintiff was therefore good *quacunque via,* and the remarks of the Court on the
Queen's having been granted a determinable fee were *obiter.*
In Noy's report of this case,[3] it is said: "And this case was
put by the justices. Land is given to A. and his heirs, so
long as B. hath issue male, etc. B. dies, his wife being big
with a son, who is afterwards born. Yet the estate of A. is
determined, and judgment was given accordingly."

§ **33.4. Liford's Case**[1] (1614). In this case it is said: "A
man may have an inheritance in fee simple in lands, as long
as such a tree shall grow, 27 Hen. VIII. 29 *b,* because a man
may have inheritance in the tree itself."[2] In 1 Roll. R. 95,
101, where the case is reported *sub nom. Stampe* v. *Clinton,*
the expression is, "If land is given as long as an oak shall
grow, it is an inheritance (*'tam diu que querke crescera ceo est*

[2] Asher v. Whitlock, L. R. 1 Q.
B. 1.   Perry v. Clissold, [1907]
A. C. 73.   Professor J. B. Ames
in 3 Harv. Law Rev. 323–325.
[3] P. 132.

§ **33.4.** [1] 11 Co. 46 b, 49 a.
[2] The citation is to Y. B. Mich.
27 Hen. VIII. 29, pl. 19.   See
§ 33.2, ante.

*inherit*')." It is not clear whether the remark is to be attributed to counsel or to the Court.

§ **33.5. Pells v. Brown**[1] (1620). Here Mr. Justice Houghton, in his argument, puts this case: "If a man give or devise lands to one and his heirs as long as J. S. hath issue of his body, he shall not, by recovery, bind him who made this gift, without making him a party by way of vouchee."

§ **33.6. Gardner v. Sheldon**[1] (1671). Vaughan, C. J., speaking to a point which he expressly declares is not material to the case, says:[2] "An estate to a man and his heirs as long as John Stiles hath any heir, which is no absolute fee simple, is doubtless as durable as the estate in fee which John Stiles hath to him and his heirs, which is an absolute fee simple."[3]

§ **33.7. Ayres v. Falkland**[1] (1697). Treby, C. J., and Powell, J., say: "A man may have a possibility of reverter where he cannot limit a remainder; as if A. gives lands to B. and his heirs during the time that such an oak shall grow, he hath a possibility of reverter, though no remainder can be limited."

§ **33.8. Idle v. Cook**[1] (1705). Powell, J., says: "A fee tail was a fee-simple at common law; for there were three sorts of fee-simples, absolute, qualified (which was to time only, *scil.* as long as such a tree stood, or as J. S. had heirs of his body); and also fee-simple conditional, which was limited as to the heirs inheritable." He then states the effect of the Statute *De Donis* on the last class. His statement is correct as to the law existing before the passage of the Statute *De Donis*, which, it will be remembered, was before the date of the Statute *Quia Emptores*.

§ **33.9. Attorney-General v. Pyle**[1] (1738). A freehold messuage was devised to the charity-school at R., the rents and profits to be applied for the benefit of the school, so long as it should "continue to be endowed with charity." Lord Hardwicke, C., said: "Where a sum of money is given to a charity,

§ **33.5.** [1] Cro. Jac. 590, 593.
§ **33.6.** [1] Vaugh. 259.
[2] P. 273.
[3] See also pp. 269, 270.
§ **33.7.** [1] 1 Ld. Raym. 325, sub

nom. Eyres v. Faulkland, 1 Salk. 231.
§ **33.8.** [1] 1 P. Wms. 70, 74, 75, 2 Ld. Raym. 1144, 1148.
§ **33.9.** [1] 1 Atk. 435.

so long as it shall continue to be endowed with charity, it is only given *quousque,* and when it ceases, if it is a gift of real estate, it shall fall into the inheritance for the benefit of the heir, if personal, into the *residuum,*" and he declared that the rents and profits of the messuage ought to be applied to the benefit of the charity-school at R., "so long as the said charity-school shall continue to be endowed with charity," and he decreed the heir of the testator "to convey the said messuage to the other defendants, the trustees of the charity." It would seem that the legal estate conveyed to the trustees was a fee simple, and that any interest of the heir was only equitable, as a resulting trust.[2]

§ 33.10. Lethieullier v. Tracy[1] (1754). Lord Hardwicke is reported by Atkins and Ambler to have said that if an estate is given to trustees until A.'s reaching twenty-one, and on A.'s attaining that age, then to him, the trustees take a determinable fee with a vested remainder to A.; but in Ambler he is previously made to call the estate of the trustees a chattel interest, and it seems incredible that Lord Hardwicke should have spoken of a vested remainder after a determinable fee.[2]

§ 33.11. Wellington v. Wellington[1] (1768). Here, on a devise upon default of issue of the testator to trustees until debts and legacies were paid and then to A., the Court of King's Bench certified that the trustees took a determinable fee, but the only point in issue was whether the trustees took a present or a future estate. There is no opinion.[2]

§ 33.12. A. G. v. Cummins.[1] The Crown granted certain quit-rents to A. and his heirs till he should be paid £5,000.

[2] See Re Randell, post, §§ 327, 603.9, post. In the Registrar's Book the order and decree are as stated in Atkins.

§ 33.10. [1] 3 Atk. 774, Ambl. 204, 3 Kenyon 40.

[2] See Butler's note to Fearne, C. R. 226; Blunt's note to Ambl. 206, 207; and the note to Warter v. Hutchinson, 1 B. & C. 742.

§ 33.11. [1] 1 W. Bl. 645, 4 Burr. 2165.

[2] See also Anon., Dyer 300 b, where the case referred to by the judges seems to have been simply one of a springing use; and Commissioners of Donations v. De Clifford, 1 Dr. & W. 245.

§ 33.12. [1] [1906] 1 I. R. 406; and see § 31, note 3, ante.

Palles, C. B., in delivering the opinion held that the Crown had a possibility of reverter in the quit-rents. He did not refer to the Statute *Quia Emptores,* and there was no need that he should, for the Statute has no application to grants by the Crown.

§ **34.** Possibilities of reverter have also been spoken of by counsel and text-writers as if they were valid interests, without paying any regard to the Statute *Quia Emptores.*[1] But the English books reveal no actual case since the passing of the Statute down to modern times, in which a determinable fee with a possibility of reverter has been held to have been

§ **34.** [1] Y. B. Mich. 27 Hen. VIII. 29, pl. 19. Walsingham's Case, 2 Plowd. 557. Edward Seymor's Case, 10 Co. 97 b. Anon., Jenk. Cent. 5. Hall v. Deering, Hardr. 148. Cardigan v. Armitage, 2 B. & C. 202. Co. Lit. 1 b, 27 a. Shep. Touch. 101. 1 Prest. Est. 431–433, 440–444, 481, 482, 508, 509; and many modern authors. See also 50 Law Quart. Rev. 33. Mr. Preston, loc. cit., has a list of instances of determinable fees, and this list is given in a revised form by Mr. Challis, Real Prop. (3d ed.) 254–260, who says it is a "list of determinable or collateral limitations, which have been actually used or proposed in books of authority to be used in the limitation of determinable fees." It is believed that § 33, ante, contains all the dicta of judges included in Mr. Challis's list. In Re Leach, [1912] 2 Ch. 422, a devise in trust for A. until he became bankrupt was said to be a determinable fee. But it might well have been construed as a fee subject to an executory limitation. 36 Yale L. J. 593, 598, note; § 32, ante. (See, however, Re Machu, 21 Ch. D. 838, as to the validity of a gift over on bankruptcy.) The practical result would have been the same on either theory. The interests in Re Leach were equitable, and the question was not of a legal possibility of reverter but of a resulting trust. See § 327.1, post. The Court, however, does not make any distinction between legal and equitable interests. The Court refers to the ordinary limitation in a marriage settlement to the settlor until the marriage as a determinable fee. And this opinion is also advanced in Challis, Real Prop. (3d ed.) 256, 3 Cambridge, L. J. 463, 464, 1 Conveyancer, N.S. 193, 206, and 54 Law Quart. Rev. 258, 262. But is it not a determinable fee only in the sense of a fee subject to an executory limitation? See Wms. Real Prop. (24th ed.) 450. Cf. Collier v. Walters, L. R. 17 Eq. 252; § 37, post. See, however, Robinson v. Wood, 27 L. J., Ch. 726, and Re Bold, 95 L. J. Ch. 201, in which cases it was decided that equitable fees might be cut short by the occurrence of an event without any gift over, and the Court seems there-

created; and the learned reader need not be reminded that little reliance is to be placed on statements, however often repeated, which have never been brought to the test of decision. "The mere statement and restatement of a doctrine, the mere repetition of the *cantilena* of lawyers, cannot make it law, unless it can be traced to some competent authority, and if it be irreconcilable to some clear legal principle."[2]

§ 35. On the other hand, in *Christopher Corbet's Case* in the Common Pleas, as reported by Sir Edmund Anderson, the Chief Justice,[1] where the question was whether a proviso for the cesser of an estate tail upon an attempt to bar the entail was void, the Chief Justice, in his opinion, remarks:[2] "Intendments should be guided by the rules of the law, and not by idle conceits, and to prove this further, 13 Hen. VII., 11 Hen. VII., 21 Hen. VI. fol. 37,[3] it is held, and the law seems plain, that if land be given to one and his heirs so long as J. S. has heirs of his body, the donee has a fee and can alien it, notwithstanding there be a condition that he shall not alien; and 11 Lib. Assize, pl. 8[4] a like case is put and held as above: and there if land be given to one and his heirs so long as J. S. or his heirs may enjoy the Manor of D., these words (so long) are utterly vain and idle, and do not abridge the estate . . . and yet it is to be admitted that one may have an estate

fore to have assumed that equitable determinable fees may exist. See §§ 783–786, post. Terminable trusts for charitable purposes are admittedly good. §§ 327.1, 603.9, post.

[2] O'Connell v. The Queen, 11 Cl. & F. 373.

§ 35. [1] 2 And. 134.

[2] Pp. 138, 139.

[3] The correct citations are Y. B. Easter 13 Hen. VII. fol. 24; Y. B. Mich. 11 Hen. VII. 6, pl. 25; Y. B. Hil. 21 Hen. VI. 33, pl. 21. The only one of importance is the first, where we find this colloquy in the Common Pleas. Vavasour, J., "A condition to the donee in tail at the Common Law, and to the feoffee of a fee simple, so long as J. at S. has issue; in these cases the condition is void." Townshend, J., "It seems the condition in both cases is good."

[4] The correct citation is Y. B. Lib. Ass. 11 Edw. III. 29, pl. 8 (1338). A case is cited there where there was a grant of a rent "as long as the grantor, his heirs and his assignees should hold the house, etc., and it was adjudged freehold, etc."

[G. R. P.]—3

in fee determinable, but never by the act and consent of the
parties, without any entry for condition broken or title defeasible; and to show briefly how this will be is now convenient,
and it will be if the lord of a villein being tenant in tail enters
on the land, etc., he and his heirs will enjoy the land so long
as the villein has issue, and then his estate will determine;
so he who recovers rent against a tenant in tail, *'que ill teign
in tail'* [out of what he holds in tail?]; or [suppose] that tenant in tail of land be attainted of treason, the King will have
a fee of the land entailed determinable on death without issue,
and has no greater estate; but these estates last mentioned
are not made by the first creation of these estates, but by
matter coming afterwards by other means."[5]

§ **36.** Mr. Sanders was the first author to distinctly recognize, or at any rate to distinctly state, that the Statute *Quia
Emptores* put an end to determinable fees.[1] He says that his
remarks are taken from an opinion of his own, "which was
subsequently well considered by two gentlemen of eminence
at the bar, and signed by them." The Commissioners on Real
Property (Sir John Campbell and Messrs. Tinney, Duval,
Hodgson, Duckworth, Brodie, and Tyrrell, all, except the
chairman, among the most eminent real-property lawyers of
their time), in their third Report, made in 1832,[2] speaking

---

[5] When a tenant in tail makes
a conveyance, e. g. a feoffment,
which operates as a discontinuance, but leaves to the issue, or
at any rate to the reversioner or
remainder-man, the right to a
formedon, the grantee has a base
fee which, while it lasts, descends
to his heirs. Leake, Law of Property in Land (2d ed.) 28, 231.
Challis, Real Prop. (3d ed.), c. 22.
As Anderson, C. J., remarks, such
an estate is not and cannot be
created by the intention of the
parties; it results by operation of
law from their intention not being fulfilled. It was argued in

Champernon's Case, Y. B. Easter 4
Hen. VI. 19, pl. 6 at fol. 21a (51
Selden Soc. 29, 34), that when a
tenant in tail had made a lease for
life inconsistent with the fee tail,
and thereby worked a discontinuance, and given himself a base fee
in reversion, he held of the principal lord, and not of the donor; but
the Court decided that he still
held of the donor. Base fees
would therefore seem not to have
been affected by the Statute Quia
Emptores.

§ **36.** [1] 1 Sand. Uses (5th ed.)
208.

[2] P. 36.

[G. R. P.]

of a devise of an estate to A. B. and his heirs, on condition
that they use the name and arms of C. D., say: "Some have
thought that the will passed a fee simple, determinable upon
the non-performance of the condition; but it was not a determinable fee in the proper sense of the expression, if (as is
perhaps the true state of the law on this subject) a determinable fee was an estate before the Statute of *Quia Emptores*,
as upon a grant to A B. and his heirs, so long as I. S. and his
issue should live, in which case the donor retained, in the
nature of a right to an escheat, a reversionary interest which
arose on the death of I. S. and the failure of his issue. But
the Statute of *Quia Emptores*, by destroying the tenure between the donor and donee, in cases where the fee was granted
subsequently to the Statute, put an end to any right of reverter on such grants;" and reference is made to the passage
in Anderson, above quoted.[3] Most of the careful recent
writers have adopted this view.[4]

§ **37.** The history of the only devise which in recent times
has been claimed in England as raising a determinable fee is
very singular. The Statute *Quia Emptores* was not referred
to, but the final decision is a strong authority that determinable fees do not now exist. *Collier* v. *M'Bean*[1] (1865)
was a bill by a vendor for specific performance. Sir John
Romilly, M. R., held that a devise to trustees to hold during the life of A. B., and also until the testator's debts and
legacies were paid, was a determinable fee. Under this construction the plaintiff did not make a good title. The Lords
Justices[2] dismissed an appeal on the ground that, if the Master

[3] And see Re Machu, 21 Ch. D.
838, commented on in Gray, Restraints on Alienation, § 22, note.

[4] Leake, Law of Property in
Land (2d ed.) 25. Marsden, Perp.
71, 72. Pollock, Land Laws (3d
ed.) 226–228. Edwards, Law of
Property (5th ed.) 32. See Mr.
Sweet's note to Challis, Real Prop.
(3d ed.) 439; 2 Wms. Vend. & P.
(4th ed.) 929, note b. For a discussion of Mr. Challis's argu-

ment that the Statute related
only to fees simple absolute, see
§§ 774–782, post. The view that
determinable fees could be created in law, as well as in equity,
after the Statute Quia Emptores,
is expressed in 50 Law Quart.
Rev. 33, and 1 Conveyancer, N. S.
193, 205–206.

**§ 37.** [1] 34 Beav. 426.

[2] L. R. 1 Ch. 81.

of the Rolls thought the title bad, it was too doubtful to be forced on a purchaser; but Sir J. L. Knight Bruce, L. J., stated his impression to be that the trustees took a fee simple, and that the title was good. In 1873 a case involving the same question under the same will came before the then Master of the Rolls, Sir George Jessel. *Collier* v. *Walters*.[3] The Master of the Rolls doubted whether he was not bound to follow the decree in the former case; but, on the matter being mentioned at his request to the Lords Justices, they were of opinion that it was open to him to hear the case unfettered by the former decisions. The result is thus given by him:[4] "When the case comes to be argued on the footing that I was not to be bound by that decision, neither counsel asserts that that decision is right, but both positively abandon it: both the leading counsel and the junior counsel, on consideration, say that they cannot support the decision of the Master of the Rolls. That is a very strong and a very peculiar circumstance. His Lordship having determined that according to the true construction of the will there was a determinable fee, neither of the counsel for the plaintiff will argue in support of that proposition at all. In fact, there is not any authority to be found for any such determinable fee. I have looked at an enormous number of cases to see if I could find such an authority, but I have been quite as unsuccessful as the counsel for the plaintiff, and I think there is no such case to be found.[5] I think, therefore, I may dismiss the interpretation of the will given by Lord Romilly as untenable."[6]

---

[3] L. R. 17 Eq. 252.

[4] P. 261.

[5] Mr. Challis, in his treatise on Real Property (3d ed.) 259, says that Bagshaw v. Spencer, 1 Ves. Sr. 142, 144, "seems to have escaped the diligence of Sir George Jessel, M. R.," but in that case Lord Hardwicke, C., held that a devise to trustees till debts were paid carried the legal fee; he held not that the devise carried a fee simple determinable, but that it carried "the whole fee." But see §§ 783–786, post.

[6] See Conner v. Waring, 52 Md. 724, 734; § 40.9 post; and Doe d. McDonnell v. McIsaac, 1 Haz. & Warb. 353, Pet. P. E. I. 236.

The subject of determinable fees is more fully discussed in App. E, §§ 774 et seq., post.

**§ 38. In the United States.** In Pennsylvania (if *Wallace* v. *Harmstad*[1] is unsound) and in South Carolina tenure exists and the Statute *Quia Emptores* is not in force. In these States, therefore, apart from the question of remoteness,[2] determinable fees may be valid. In *Scheetz* v. *Fitzwater*,[3] *Penn. R. R. Co.* v. *Parke*,[4] *Henderson* v. *Hunter*,[5] and *Slegel* v. *Lauer*,[6] it was assumed that fees simple determinable might be created.[7]

**§ 39.** In the other States there is either no tenure at all, or, where there is tenure, there is no good reason to doubt the existence of the Statute *Quia Emptores*. In neither case can there be any possibility of reverter.[1] In the United

Under the Law of Prop. Act (1925), § 1, the only legal estates which can thereafter be created are estates in fee simple absolute, except terms for years, certain statutory estates, and estates subject to a right of entry. See § 7 of the Act, as amended by the Law of Prop. Amendment Act, 1926. Legal possibilities of reverter are therefore abolished, except as to the statutory estates referred to. There does not seem to be any language in the Act authorizing the creation of a determinable equitable fee, except where a determinable fee, legal or equitable, could previously be created. As to determinable equitable fees, see § 34, note 1, at end, ante. As to interests in personalty analogous to determinable fees, see Re Chardon, [1928] Ch. 464; § 87.1, post.

§ 38. [1] 44 Pa. 492. See § 26, ante.
[2] As to this see § 312, post.
[3] 5 Pa. 126.
[4] 42 Pa. 31.
[5] 59 Pa. 335.

[6] 148 Pa. 236, 23 Atl. 996.
[7] See also Union Canal Co. v. Young, 1 Whart. 410, 427, 428; Kerlin v. Campbell, 15 Pa. 500; First Methodist Church v. Old Columbia Co., 103 Pa. 608; Courtney v. Keller, 4 Pennyp. 38; Gumbert's Appeal, 110 Pa. 496, 1 Atl. 437; Pa. Schuylkill Valley R. R. Co. v. Paper Mills, 149 Pa. 18, 24 Atl. 205; Scott v. Murray, 218 Pa. 186, 67 Atl. 47; Pitcairn v. Cemetery Co., 229 Pa. 18, 77 Atl. 1105; Riggs v. New Castle, 229 Pa. 490, 78 Atl. 1037; Penn. Horticultural Soc. v. Craig, 240 Pa. 137, 87 Atl. 678; Citizens Electric Co. v. Susquehanna Co., 270 Pa. 517, 113 Atl. 559; Speese v. Schuylkill River E. Side R. R. Co., 23 Pa. C. C. 17; Foulke, Treatise, §§ 27, 73, 74. Cf. Stuart v. Easton, 170 U. S. 383, 18 S. Ct. 650, 42 L. E. 1078.

§ 39. [1] The above statement has been left as it stood in previous editions. But even apart from authority, it is not clear on principle that in States where there is no tenure there can be no

States, there are, however, many cases which assume that such interests are possible.[2]

possibility of reverter. All reversionary rights are dependent on tenure, where tenure exists (§§ 20, 31, ante), but it does not necessarily follow that where no tenure exists there can be no reversionary rights. Before the Statute Quia Emptores, a possibility of reverter was undoubtedly a reversionary right, and it is difficult to hold that the enactment of the Statute changed the nature of the right so that it was no longer reversionary. But where no tenure exists, then either there can be no reversionary rights, or they exist without tenure. There can be reversions after estates for life and in tail in incorporeal hereditaments, which are not a subject of tenure, resulting trusts after equitable life estates in personalty, and, in America at least, reversions after legal life estates in chattels personal. § 852, post. It seems also that a rent charge, or other incorporeal hereditament, may be granted in fee simple determinable and that an existing rent charge in fee may be similarly granted, in which case there must be a reversion or possibility of reverter in the grantor. See § 31, note 3, ante. It has been held in England, as well as America, that there may be an interest in personalty, analogous to a determinable fee. See Re Chardon, [1928] Ch. 464; §§ 78, note 2, 87.1, 90, note, post. Where there is no tenure, it seems a reasonable step to allow reversionary interests in

land, including possibilities of reverter, to take effect as in the case of incorporeal hereditaments, and personalty. See 3 Minn. Law Rev. 320, 329. For the application of this course of reasoning to the American cases, see § 41.1, note 2, post.

[2] Worster v. Gt. Falls Mfg. Co., 41 N. H. 16, 22. Congregational Soc. v. Stark, 34 Vt. 243. Curtis v. Gardner, 13 Metc. 457, 461. Mayor of New York v. Stuyvesant, 17 N. Y. 34. Reed v. Stouffer, 56 Md. 236, 254. Newbold v. Glenn, 67 Md. 489, 10 Atl. 242. Hall v. Turner, 110 No. Car. 292, 14 S. E. 791. Thayer v. McGee, 20 Mich. 195, 211. Delhi School District v. Everett, 52 Mich. 314, 17 N. W. 926. Epworth Assembly v. Ludington Railway, 236 Mich. 565, 211 N. W. 99. Ford v. Detroit, 273 Mich. 449, 263 N. W. 425. Fletcher v. Fletcher, 88 Ind. 418. Wiggins Ferry Co. v. Ohio & Miss. R. Co., 94 Ill. 83. McDaniel v. Watson, 4 Bush 234. Davis v. Memphis & Charleston R. R. Co., 87 Ala. 633, 6 So. 140. Peyton, C. J. (dissenting), in Kilpatrick v. Graves, 51 Miss. 432. Johnson v. Lane, 98 Ark. 274, 135 S. W. 2d 853. White v. Kentlin, 345 Mo. 526, 134 S. W. 2d 39. Dabney v. Edwards, 5 Cal. 2d 1, 12, 53 Pac. 2d 962, 967 (but see 9 So. Cal. Law Rev. 299). Loomis v. Heublein, 91 Conn. 146, 99 Atl. 483. Sorrells v. McNally, 89 Fla. 457, 105 So. 106. Brown v. Hobbs, 132 Md. 559, 104 Atl. 283. Chouteau v. St. Louis, 331 Mo. 781, 55 S.

§ **40.** The earlier cases in which possibilities of reverter[1] have come, or were supposed to have come, before American courts (besides the Pennsylvania cases[2]) follow.[3]

§ **40.1. Wood v. Cheshire.**[1] This case states that the Superior Court in the same suit had held, at July Term, 1854, that an estate granted to a county for so long a time as the land should be used as a court-house terminated, without entry, upon the land not being so used. No such case is reported in the decisions of the Court for July Term, 1854, or anywhere else in the New Hampshire Reports.

§ **40.2. Jamaica Pond Aqueduct Co. v. Chandler.**[1] In this

W. 2d 299. Anderson v. Anderson, 119 Neb. 381, 229 N. W. 124. Matter of Terry, 218 N. Y. 218, 112 N. E. 931. Walker v. Marcellus Ry., 226 N. Y. 347, 123 N. E. 736. Sharpe v. Railroad, 190 No. Car. 350, 129 S. E. 826 (but see § 40.11, post). Magness v. Kerr, 121 Ore. 373, 251 Pac. 1012. Green v. Gresham, 21 Tex. Civ. Ap. 601, 53 S. W. 382. Stephens County v. Oil Co., 113 Tex. 160, 254 S. W. 290. Caruthers v. Leonard, 254 S. W. 779 (Tex. Civ. Ap.). See Friedman v. Steiner, 107 Ill. 125; Flaten v. Moorhead, 51 Minn. 518, 53 N. W. 807; Church v. Young, 130 No. Car. 8, 40 S. E. 691; Rowland v. Warren, 10 Ore. 129; Bolling v. Petersburg, 8 Leigh 224, 234; Carney v. Kain, 40 W. Va. 758, 812, 816, 23 S. E. 650, 657, 659; Boal v. Metropolitan Museum, 292 Fed. 303, 305 (N. Y.); Estate of Douglass, 94 Neb. 280, 143 S. E. 299; Copenhaver v. Pendleton, 155 Va. 463, 155 S. E. 802; York v. York, 275 Ky. 573, 112 S. W. 2d 140. There seems to have been a valid determinable fee, according to the prevailing American doctrine, in

Watrous v. Limbocker, 140 Kan. 154, 33 Pac. 2d 938, although the Court held that the whole devise was invalid; see 3 J. B. A. Kan. 153.

§ **40.** [1] In America the right to enter for condition broken is often loosely termed a possibility of reverter. See Sharpe v. Railroad, 190 No. Car. 351, 129 S. E. 826; Copenhaver v. Pendleton, 155 Va. 463, 479, 155 S. E. 802; Trustees of Calvary Church v. Putnam, 221 N. Y. A. D. 502, 224 N. Y. S. 651; §§ 31, 32, ante. In Amory v. Amherst College, 229 Mass. 374, 383, 118 N. E. 933, 936, a fee subject to a right of entry is called a "fee simple conditional."

[2] § 38, ante.

[3] The remarks of the author on these earlier cases, in previous editions, are given in full, except as to First Universalist Society v. Boland. References to later cases have been inserted in note 2 to the preceding section. See also §§ 40.-17, note 1, 41, 41.1, post.

§ **40.1.** [1] 32 N. H. 421. See Lyford v. Laconia, 75 N. H. 220, 226, 72 Atl. 1085, 1089.

§ **40.2.** [1] 9 Allen 159.

case a fee simple determinable was said to be created, but
all that was necessary for the decision was to find that a fee
was created; whether determinable or absolute was, as is
observed in *Chandler* v. *Jamaica Pond Aqueduct*,[2] immaterial.

§ 40.3. First Universalist Society v. Boland.[1] Deed of
land to a religious society to hold so long as it shall be by
the society or its assigns devoted to the uses, interests, and
support of certain doctrines; and when it should be diverted
from said support to any other uses then the title of the society
or its assigns should cease, and be vested in forty-one persons,
one of whom was the grantor. A church was built on the
land, and had been used for worship according to said doctrines, but the society having contracted to sell the land, the
vendee refused to accept a deed on the ground that the society
had not a good title, and a bill brought by the society for
specific performance was dismissed. The Court said that the
society had a determinable fee, and the gift over being void,
there was a possibility of reverter in the grantor.[2]

§ 40.4. Hooker v. Utica Turnpike Road Co.[1] Here it was
merely held that a turnpike company who had abandoned
their road could not recover under a penal statute for injur-
ing it.

§ 40.5. Leonard v. Burr.[1] Devise to A. of the use of land

[2] 125 Mass. 544, 547.

§ 40.3. [1] 155 Mass. 171, 29 N. E. 524.

[2] The Court intimates, p. 175, that the doctrine of tenure has no significance in this country. But is this certain? May it not still have a bearing on some questions, for instance, of escheat or of rents? See Kavanaugh v. Cohoes P. & L. Corp., 114 Misc. 590, 610–624, 187 N. Y. S. 216, 229–237. For an extended criticism of this case of the First Universalist Society, see third edition, § 40, pp. 35–38, where it is compared with Brattle Square Church v. Grant, 3 Gray 142, and the contention is made that the deed gave a fee subject to an executory devise. But see First Universalist Church, Petitioner, Mass. Land Court Dec. 209, 211. The case of the First Universalist Society v. Boland is followed in Institution for Savings v. Home for Aged Women, 244 Mass. 583, 139 N. E. 301. A similar case, better considered than most on this topic, is Yarbrough v. Yarbrough, 151 Tenn. 221, 269 S. W. 36.

§ 40.4. [1] 12 Wend. 371.
§ 40.5. [1] 18 N. Y. 96.

until Gloversville was incorporated into a village, and then
to the trustees of said Gloversville. The Court of Appeals
held that the devise over to the trustees was void, and that
A. took a determinable fee. The precise point was passed
upon, because if A. took a fee simple subject to a void executory devise, he would have an absolute estate, whereas it
was held that on the incorporation of Gloversville the land
reverted to the grantor's heirs. It is submitted that the decision was incorrect, and that in truth there was a devise to
A. in fee, subject to a bad executory devise, and that therefore A. took a fee simple absolute.[2]

§ 40.6. Gillespie v. Broas.[1] A deed of land for the use of
a county as long as the land should be used for a court-house,
and when it should cease to be so used, to revert to the grantor
and his heirs, was held not to pass "a good unincumbered
title." Here there seems to have been a determinable charitable trust, and a resulting trust.[2]

§ 40.7. State v. Brown.[1] Here, as in *Jamaica Pond Aqueduct Co.* v. *Chandler, ante,* a fee simple determinable is said
to have been created; but the only point at issue was whether
there was a fee at all.[2]

§ 40.8. Foy v. Baltimore.[1] Land was given to trustees for
the use of the Roman Catholics of Baltimore, to build a chapel
and lay out a burying-ground; and if the trustees did not
build the chapel and use the residue as a burying-ground,

[2] But see Lougheed v. Dykeman
Baptist Church, 40 N. Y. S. 586.

§ 40.6. [1] 23 Barb. 370.

[2] See § 40.8, post.

§ 40.7. [1] 3 Dutch. 13. See Hoboken Land Co. v. Hoboken, 36 N.
J. L. 540, 550.

[2] Such was the case also in
Loomis v. Heublein, 91 Conn. 146,
99 Atl. 483; Connecticut Junior
Republic v. Litchfield, 119 Conn.
106, 174 Atl. 304; Penick v. At-
kinson, 139 Ga. 649, 77 S. E. 1055;
Mendenhall v. First New Church,
177 Ind. 336, 98 N. E. 57; Des
Moines Ry. Co. v. Des Moines. 183
Iowa 1261, 159 N. W. 450; Moul-
ton v. Trafton, 64 Me. 218; Farns-
worth v. Perry, 83 Me. 447, 22
Atl. 373; Weed v. Woods, 71 N.
H. 581, 53 Atl. 1024; Piper v.
Meredith, 83 N. H. 107, 139 Atl.
294; Camden Land Co. v. West
Jersey Ry., 92 N. J. L. 385, 105
Atl. 229; First Reformed Dutch
Church v. Croswell, 210 N. Y. A.
D. 294, 206 N. Y. S. 132; Aumiller
v. Dash, 51 Wash. 520, 99 Pac. 583.

§ 40.8. [1] 4 Gill 394.

then the deed to be void and the premises to revert.  The
land was used as a burying-ground, but the chapel was built
on an adjoining parcel.  On a petition to restrain the City of
Baltimore from selling the land for taxes, brought by the
priest of the chapel and a parishioner who had buried some of
his family in the land, it was held that the petitioners had no
*locus standi,* and the majority of the Court seem to place
their decision on the ground that the land had reverted to the
grantor.[2]  But is not the true view of the case that the trustees
held the land upon a determinable charitable trust, and then
when the charitable trust came to an end, there was a resulting
trust to the grantor?[3]

§ **40.9. Conner v. Waring.**[1]  Devise to A. for life, with
power in A. to appoint among such one or more of the testator's children or their issue as A. might see fit.  A. appointed
a share to trustees in trust to permit L., a daughter of the
testator, to take the rents and profits during her life, and after
her death in trust that the share should become the estate of
her children, and in case any one of her children should die
under age without issue, its share should go to her surviving
children.  A. also appointed that in case L. died without having any children or descendants of children, her share should
go to the testator's surviving children and their representatives.  This last appointment was held in *Torrance* v. *Torrance,*[2] on a like provision under the same will, to be on an
indefinite failure of issue, and to be, therefore, void for remoteness.  L. died without ever having had issue, and the
question arose, on a bill in equity, as to the disposition of her
share.  The Court held that her trustees took a determinable
fee, that her death terminated their estate, and that the land
vested, by way of reverter, in the heirs of the testator.  The
Court obviously fell into the same mistake into which Lord
Romilly had fallen in *Collier* v. *M'Bean,*[3] which counsel could
not be found to defend, and which Sir George Jessel had so

[2] Pp. 405, 406.  See Reed v.
Stouffer, 56 Md. 236, 254.
[3] See §§ 41.1, 603.9, post.

§ **40.9.** [1] 52 Md. 724, 734.
[2] 4 Md. 11.
[3] 34 Beav. 426.

emphatically condemned in *Collier* v. *Walters*.[4] It is clear that the trustees had a fee simple absolute, which, on the contingency that had occurred, they held subject to a resulting trust in favor of the testator's heirs.[5]

§ **40.10. Second Universalist Society v. Dugan.**[1] Land was conveyed to trustees for the use of the society of Christian people called Quakers in Baltimore to keep the same for a burying-place, and to build a meeting-house, and for no other use, intent, or purpose whatsoever. The Legislature authorized the trustees to sell the land. Held, that a court of equity would not force on a purchaser a title derived from the trustees, as there might be some reversionary right in the heirs of the grantor.[2]

§ **40.11. School Committee v. Kesler.**[1] It was held that determinable fees do not exist in North Carolina. Pearson, C. J., who delivered the opinion in this case, had previously declared that an easement might be made determinable.[2] This was undoubtedly correct,[3] and was followed in *Hall* v. *Turner*,[4] but the Court in that case, speaking of *School Committee* v. *Kesler*, say:[5] "However broad may be the language quoted, we have no idea that it was the purpose of the Chief Justice to say that the limitation expressly defined by him as a base or qualified fee in *Merriman's Case* could not be made in North Carolina. Such limitations are not infrequent in this and other States (2 Wash. R. P. 4), and we are not prepared to adopt a view which leads to such a revolution in the law of limitations of real property." And this passage has since been quoted, seemingly with approval.[6]

[4] L. R. 17 Eq. 252. See § 37, ante.

[5] The heirs were undoubtedly entitled, but it was under a resulting trust and not by possibility of reverter.

§ **40.10.** [1] 65 Md. 460, 5 Atl. 415.

[2] Perhaps they were entitled under a resulting trust. See §§ 41.1, 327, 603.9, post. Cf. Insti-tute for Savings v. Home for Aged Women, 244 Mass. 583, 139 N. E. 301.

§ **40.11.** [1] 67 No. Car. 443.

[2] Merriman v. Russell, 2 Jones Eq. 470.

[3] See § 279, post.

[4] 110 No. Car. 292, 14 S. E. 791.

[5] P. 306.

[6] Keith v. Scales, 124 No. Car. 497, 514, 32 S. E. 809, 812. See al-

**§ 40.12. Carr v. Georgia Railroad.**[1] Land was conveyed to a railroad company by a deed containing the express stipulation that when the company ceased to use the land for a station, "this deed shall cease, determine and be void, and of no effect whatever, neither in law nor in equity, and the land, with all the rights, privileges, and appurtenances, shall revert to the donor or his heirs." It was held that the deed created a determinable fee, and that upon the railroad's ceasing to use the land for a station it reverted without entry.[2]

**§ 40.13. Young v. Mahoning County.**[1] Y. conveyed land to an incorporated village. Afterwards he brought an action at law against the village in the United States Circuit Court for the Northern District of Ohio to recover the land. The Court considered that a reference in the deed of the plaintiff to a statute had the effect of making the deed read as a conveyance of the land for the purpose of its being used as a burying-ground. The land had ceased to be used as burying-ground. The Court held that the deed created a determinable fee, which had come to an end, and that the plaintiff was entitled to recover. But the Circuit Court of Appeals, on a writ of error, was of opinion that the village took a fee simple absolute, subject to a trust, and reversed the judgment.

**§ 40.14. Daniels v. Wilson.**[1] Land in a village was conveyed to a county by a deed, with a proviso that the land was sold for county purposes so long as the county-seat re-

so Sharpe v. R. R., 190 No. Car. 350, 129 S. E. 826. But see remarks of Clark, C. J., in Blue v. Wilmington, 186 No. Car. 321, 327, 119 S. E. 741, 745, approving School Committee v. Kesler.

§ 40.12. ¹ 74 Ga. 73.

² In Macon v. East Tennessee, &c., R. Co., 82 Ga. 501, 9 S. E. 1127, there was a somewhat similar grant to a railroad. The Court thought the deed created a determinable fee, but said it was immaterial whether it created a determinable fee or a fee on condition subsequent. And see Jackson v. Dougherty County, 99 Ga. 185, 25 S. E. 625; Atlanta Ry. Co. v. Jackson, 108 Ga. 634, 34 S. E. 184.

§ 40.13. ¹ 51 Fed. 585, in error sub nom. Mahoning County v. Young, 59 Fed. 96.

§ 40.14.  27 Wis. 492.

mained in the village; and if at any time the county-seat was removed therefrom, "then this conveyance to be void and of no effect, and the land reverts to the" grantors. It was held, or rather assumed without contention, that this provision was good, but whether as a condition or a limitation is not clear. The counsel for the grantor treat it as the former.[2]

§ 40.15. **Daniel v. Jackoway.**[1] Land was conveyed to a county board for the use and benefit of the county, for a county site for a court-house. The Superior Court of Chancery of Mississippi held that when the land ceased to be used for a court-house, there was a resulting trust to the grantor, and ordered a reconveyance. The grantor was not held to have any legal interest. This was clearly correct.[2]

§ 40.16. **McBride v. Farmers' Gin Co.**[1] Land was conveyed to G., his heirs and assigns to hold "as long as said premises or pools situated on said premises are used for the purpose and use of the gin and mill attached," which was on adjoining land. It was held by the Court of Civil Appeals of Texas that when the use aforesaid ceased, an assignee of the grantor was entitled to the premises conveyed.[2]

§ 40.17. **North v Graham.**[1] The Court says, with regard to an alleged possibility of reverter: "An estate of this nature has so frequently been upheld by this Court that it must be held to be recognized as the settled law in this State;" but the Illinois cases referred to by the Court were not cases of

[2] See p. 494.

§ 40.15. [1] Freem. Ch. (Miss.) 59.

[2] See §§ 41.1, 327, 603.9, post. Cf. Memphis & Charleston R. R. Co. v. Neighbors, 51 Miss. 412, 418; Hopkins v. Grimshaw, 165 U. S. 342, 17 S. Ct. 401, 41 L. E. 739. In Jenkins v. Jenkins University, 17 Wash. 160, 49 Pac. 247, it is not clear whether the Court thought there was a right to enter for condition broken, or a possibility of reverter, or a resulting trust; whatever it was, it was held good.

§ 40.16. [1] 152 S. W. 1135.

[2] See First Church v. Spinks, 260 S. W. 1073 (Tex. Civ. Ap.).

§ 40.17. [1] 235 Ill. 178, 85 N. E. 267; and see Dees v. Cheuvronts, 240 Ill. 486, 88 N. E. 1011. These were gifts for charitable purposes. See § 41.1, post. Other cases where gifts for charitable or public purposes were said to create determinable fees are: Pond v. Douglas, 106 Me. 85, 75 Atl. 320; Board v. Buck, 79 N. J. Eq. 472, 82 Atl. 418; Dick v. Darden, 204 Ala. 400, 85 So. 369; Petit v. Stuttgart Inst., 67 Ark. 430, 55

determinable fees at all, but were the ordinary cases of devises in fee simple with executory devises over.[2]

§ 41. **Conclusions on Reverter in United States.** The question naturally arises: Why inquire so curiously as to the validity of a common-law possibility of reverter, since by a shifting use or an executory devise to the grantor the same result can be reached? The answer is: Shifting uses and executory devises are, past a doubt, subject to the Rule against Perpetuities; but possibilities of reverter are not. It was expressly said in *First Universalist Society* v. *Boland* that they are not; and this seems to be the almost necessary consequence of allowing determinable fees.[1] Therefore, if determinable fees are valid, interests can, by means of them, be created in a grantor and his heirs and assigns, which may not come into possession for centuries. It is submitted that theory and policy alike agree in denying the existence at the present day of possibilities of reverter.[2]

§ 41.1. In the matter of possibilities of reverter a distinction can be taken which is possibly sound. Property may be given to trustees for temporary charitable purposes, and when those purposes have been accomplished, there is a valid re-

S. W. 485; Phillips v. Board, 12 Ohio Ap. 459; Yarbrough v. Yarbrough, 151 Tenn. 221, 269 S. W. 36; Battistone v. Banusky, 110 Conn. 267, 147 Atl. 820; Bruce v. Henry Ford Hospital, 254 Mich. 394, 236 N. W. 813; Regular Predestinarian Baptist Church v. Parker, 373 Ill. 607, 27 N. E. 2d 522.

[2] In Morton v. Babb, 251 Ill. 488, 96 N. E. 279, land was conveyed by deed to A. and his heirs, but if he died without issue, the premises to revert to the grantor and his heirs. The Court seems to have thought that a definite failure of issue was meant; and it held that A. took a determinable fee. This seems to have been done to avoid the application of a supposed doctrine that you cannot have a conditional limitation after a conveyance in fee by deed. But this doctrine, which was peculiar to Illinois, has been repudiated there, and it is not likely that the case will be followed elsewhere. See § 68, post.

§ 41. [1] See § 312, post.

[2] But see the following section, and especially note 2. The matter of determinable fees is further discussed in App. E, §§ 774 et seq., post; 1 Tiffany, Real Prop. (2d ed.), § 93, Id. (3d ed.), § 220; and 17 Harv. Law Rev. 297; 23 Columbia Law Rev. 207; 33 Yale L. J. 248, 265, 266.

sulting trust to the grantor.   This doctrine, however objectionable, seems to be established.[1]  Between allowing a resulting trust on the accomplishment of a charitable purpose, and allowing the estate of the trustee to determine of itself upon the accomplishment of that purpose, the practical distinction is small, and it may be argued that if the former be allowed, so also should be the latter   Should this argument be yielded to, possibilities of reverter might be allowed where the first estate was for a charitable purpose (and it would seem immaterial whether the estate had been acquired by sale or gift). This result if accepted would explain and justify *First Universalist Society* v. *Boland* and several of the other American cases mentioned above, but it could not be invoked in favor of *Leonard* v. *Burr* or *Carr* v. *Georgia Railroad*.[2]

§ 41.1. [1] § 603.9, post.

[2] The above remarks have been left as written in the third edition.  But the weight of American authority, increased since the last edition, is to the contrary. Many of the remarks by American Courts about determinable fees are dicta; many of the cases concern terminable charitable trusts; many of them are open to criticism for loose use of terms and doubtful constructions; and there is almost no discussion of theory.   Nevertheless, the consensus of opinion, without any contrary voice except in North Carolina, may well be held to have settled the law for the United States. The Amer. Law Inst. Restatement, Property, so assumes in §§ 44, 47. It is difficult to attribute to the courts any particular theory in support of this conclusion.  Perhaps the most probable supposition is that they have assumed the non-existence of tenure, a premise clearly correct in

some States, and fairly maintainable in many others (§§ 22–23.2, ante), which renders immaterial any discussion of the Statute of Quia Emptores.  This appears to have been the ground taken by the Court in First Universalist Society v. Boland, 155 Mass. 171, 175, 29 N. E. 524, 525, the leading case in this country, and the only one in which the question of tenure is discussed in connection with determinable fees. In the absence of tenure, it may be that determinable fees can be created. See § 39, note 1, ante.  And in that case executory devises can be limited to follow such fees.  § 14, note 8, ante. As to equitable interests analogous to determinable fees, see § 327.1, post.  And as to interests in personalty analogous to determinable fees, see §§ 78, 87.1, post.  On the alleged right of the grantor of land to a corporation upon the dissolution of the corporation, see §§ 44 et seq., post.

**§ 42. Reverter under Statutes.** In several of the States, statutes have been enacted for the dedication of streets, which the courts consider as providing for the passage of the fee. In Illinois it has been held under such a statute that when the street is disused the land reverts to the grantor.[1]

**§ 42.1. Curtesy and Dower.** The Statute *Quia Emptores* affected curtesy only indirectly by affecting the tenure of the wife. The tenant by the curtesy held of the lord of whom his wife had held. The Statute did not affect dower at all, for the tenant in dower held of the heir.

§ 42. [1] Gebhardt v. Reeves. 75 Ill. 301. Helm v. Webster, 85 Ill. 116. Matthiessen Zinc Co. v. La Salle, 117 Ill. 411, 8 N. E. 81. But see Prall v. Burckhartt, 299 Ill. 19, 132 N. E. 280; Counselman v. Wisconsin Cement Co., 299 Ill. 84, 132 N. E. 289; Sowadski v. Salt Lake Co., 36 Utah, 127, 104 Pac. 111. The matter is discussed in Kales, Estates, §§ 284–299; 1 Ill. Law Rev. 312. See also Board of Education v. Edson, 18 Ohio St. 221; Thayer v. McGee, 20 Mich. 195; Patterson v. Patterson, 135 Ky. 339, 122 S. W. 169; Lithgow v. Pearson, 25 Colo. Ap. 70, 135 Pac. 759; Thomison v. Hillcrest Asso., 5 Atl. 2d 236 (Del.); Colgate v. Phila. Elec. Power Co., 20 Fed. 2d 263; Hopkins v. School District, 173 Iowa 43, 151 N. W. 443; Carter v. Davis, 141 Okla. 172, 284 Pac. 3. Contra, Pettingill v. Devin, 35 Iowa 344; Day v. Schroeder, 46 Iowa 546. And see Wright v. Walcott, 238 Mass. 432, 435, 436, 131 N. E. 291, 293; School Board v. Buford, 140 Va. 173, 124 S. E. 286; Chesapeake & Ohio Canal Co. v. Great Falls Power Co., 143 Va. 697, 129 S. E. 731. Cf. Jaenke v. Taylor, 160 La. 109, 106 So. 109. A similar situation may arise in England, under the School Sites Act (1841) and other statutes; see Law of Prop. Act (1925), § 7; A. G. v. Shadwell, [1910] 1 Ch. 92; Re Peel's Release, [1921] 2 Ch. 218, 223; Dennis v. Malcolm, [1934] Ch. 244; Re Cawston's Conveyance, [1939] Ch. 784; 86 I. J. 452; 20 Conveyancer 160. Under a common-law dedication only a right in the nature of an easement is created. The fee remains in the dedicator, and if the public use comes to an end, the fee stays as it is, the incumbrance being removed. On determinable interests under the United States mining laws, see 17 Harv. Law Rev. 301. The Supreme Court of the United States has held that such interests are incorporeal and not corporeal hereditaments, and that therefore there is no right of dower in them. Black v. Elkhorn Mining Co., 163 U. S. 445, 16 S. Ct. 1101, 41 L. E. 221. In some of the States, statutes abolishing estates tail (see § 19, note 4, ante) have been held to create what are called determinable fees. See the interesting treatment of this sub-

**§ 43. Rights in Land of Others.** Such rights are not the subjects of tenure;[1] consequently the Statute *Quia Emptores* has no application to them.

**§ 44. Escheat of Land of a Corporation.** The effect of the Statute *Quia Emptores* on the right of escheat was, of course, to give that right to the grantor's lord. It is said by Lord Coke[1] that "if land holden of I. S. be given to an abbot and his successors, in this case if the abbot and all the convent die, so that the body politique is dissolved, the donor shall have againe this land, and not the lord by escheat. And so if land be given in fee simple to a deane and chapter, or to a mayor and commonalty, and to their successors, and after such body politique or incorporate is dissolved, the donor shall have again the land, and not the lord by escheate." This statement has been often repeated as law, and has proved a sore stumbling-block to courts and writers in this country  Being unwilling to follow it, they have been constrained to call it "obsolete."[2] Let us examine the authorities cited by Lord Coke for his assertion. They are (*a*) 17 Edw. II., St. 3; (*b*) 9 Edw. III. 26; (*c*) 7 Edw. IV. 11, 12.  F. N. B. 33, cited by Lord Coke, contains nothing in point.

**§ 45.** (*a*) Statute 17 Edw. II., St. 3, *De Terris Templariorum* (1324).  This Statute recites that lands of the Templars which were holden of the King and divers other lords were, upon the dissolution of the order, "seised into the Hands of our Soveraigne Lord the King, and of divers other Lords of the Fees of them, who challenged the same Lands for the Con-

ject by Mr. Zane, 17 Harv. Law Rev. 305 et seq.

**§ 43.** [1] Y. B. Easter 27 Hen. VIII. 10, pl. 29. Bro. Ab. Escheate 9, 22. A. G. v. Sands, Hardres 488, 496. 3 Inst. 19, 21. Co. Lit. 298 a, Butler's note (2). Wms. Real Prop. (24th ed.) 527. See Dean & Canons of Winsor v. Webb, Godb. 211, and § 31, note 3, ante. The term "tenement," though it strictly means "that which is holden," is

[G. R. P.]—4

often extended loosely so as to cover incorporeal hereditaments. Co. Lit. 6 a. 2 Bl. Com. 16, 17. Shep. Touch. 91. 1 Prest. Est. 8–10. Williams, Commons 30. Rex v. Skingle, 1 Stra. 100. King v. Hollington, 3 East 113. Challis, Real Prop. (3d ed.) 42, 43.

**§ 44.** [1] Co. Lit. 13 b.
[2] Owen v. Smith, 31 Barb. 641. 2 Kent, Com. 307, note (b). See Folger v. Chase, 18 Pick. 63, 66.

sideration aforesaid, that the same Lands ought to revert to them as their Escheats." It then enacted that the lands should be given to the order of the Hospital of St. John of Jerusalem, to hold of the King and other Lords of the Fees by the same services as the Templars held them. There is nothing here to indicate that the lords claimed as donors; on the contrary, it is expressly said that they claimed by escheat, because the lands were holden of them.

§ 46. (b) Y. B. Trin. 9 Edw. III. 25, pl. 24 (1335). This is the case of *The King* v. *The Prior of the Hospital of St. John*. The advowson of the church of Sanford was in the Master of the Temple, and after the lands and tenements of the Templars had been seised into the hands of the King and the other lords, the church became void. The question was whether the King had the right to present on this vacancy, or whether it had passed to the Prior of the Hospital by the grant in the above Statute of all the lands of the Templars. Shardelowe, J., said: "There is no doubt in law but that by reason of the dissolution of the order their possession was *escheat* to the King, and in the same manner to all the other Lords that which was held of them, so that the estate that the Prior had in the advowson is of the King's grant. Wherefore, after he has parted by his deed with his right of advowson, the presentation cannot remain to him." A distinct statement that the lands passed by *escheat* to the lords of whom they were held. Not a word of their passing to the donors as distinct from the lords.[1]

§ 47. (c) Y. B. Trin. 7 Edw. IV. 10, pl. 2 (1467). *The Prior of Spalding's Case*. Trespass by the Prior for taking an estray in the Manor of Spalding. The Manor of Spalding was held by the Prior in frankalmoign of John of Gaunt as lord of the Honour of Bolingbroke. The King in Parliament granted to John of Gaunt the estrays *infra omnia feoda sua*. The Honour of Bolingbroke was forfeited by Act of Parliament to the King, and the defendant, as the King's bailiff, took an estray

§ 46. [1] See Littleton, arguendo, in Bishop of Winchester v. Prior of St. John of Jerusalem, Y. B. Easter 35 Hen. VI. 56, pl. 2.

[G. R. P.]

in the Manor of Spalding. The question at issue was whether
land held of John of Gaunt in frankalmoign could be properly said to be *infra feoda sua,* within his fee. The counsel
for the plaintiff contended that, as no services were rendered
by tenant in frankalmoign, the land could not be said to be
within the lord's fee. The judges were of a contrary opinion.
It should be remembered that land in frankalmoign can be
held only of the donor, and therefore, after the Statute *Quia
Emptores,* estates in frankalmoign could be created only by
the King.[1] So in frankalmoign lands the donor and the lord
must be the same. Thus Fairfax, *arguendo* in this case: "If
all the monks and the abbot or prior of such a house die, the
donor shall have the land by way of escheat, so he is lord, and
the land within his fee." Therefore in a case of frankalmoign
the words "donor" and "lord" are interchangeable. The only
thing in this case that makes for Lord Coke's proposition is
a remark of Choke, J.: "As to what has been said, that if
the abbot and all his monks die the donor can enter, it seems
to me that he well may: for if the gift was to the abbot and
his successors, then when the succession fails, the gift is determined, for the gift depends wholly on the succession. As if
I give land to a man to have to him and his heirs in fee so
long as John A'Down has issue of his body, in that case the
feoffee will hold of his lord, etc., yet if John A'Down dies without heir of his body, etc., in that case I may well enter; etc.
But not by escheat, etc., but because the feoffment is determined, etc.; so here when the succession fails, the gift is determined, etc., and therefore the donor may well enter, etc."
Danby, C. J.: "It seems to me that this cannot be, for notwithstanding they die, yet others can be made, etc." This
*dictum* of Mr. Justice Choke certainly supports the statement of Lord Coke. It must be borne in mind, however, that
it was made in a discussion on frankalmoign tenure, where the
donor and the lord must be the same person, and that the
statement of Choke, J., that if land is to be held so long as
John A'Down has heirs of his body, there is a possibility of

§ 47. [1] Lit., §§ 140, 141. F. N. B. 210 et seq.

reverter, which is the basis of Choke, J.'s proposition, is probably not law.[2]

§ 48. In early times conveyances to corporations were generally gifts to ecclesiastical corporations, and gifts to ecclesiastical corporations were usually in frankalmoign.[1] Upon the dissolution of a corporation, land held by it in frankalmoign escheated to the donor, for the donor was the lord. Hence, one may suspect, arose the notion that on the dissolution of any corporation all its land came back to the donor, the fact being that what made this true in case of land held in frankalmoign did not apply to land held on other tenures by corporations. At any rate, the *dictum* of Choke, J., *supra,* is the only one of the authorities cited by Lord Coke which supports his statement.

§ 49. Before the publication of Lord Coke's First Institute, 1628, he and two of his fellows of the Common Bench had said in *Dean and Canons of Winsor* v. *Webb*[1] (1613): "That if a man give lands unto Dean and Canons, and to their successors, and they be dissolved; or unto any other corporations; that the donor shall have back the lands again, for the same is a condition in law annexed to the gift; and in such case no writ of escheat lieth, yet the land is in him in the nature of an escheat." The remark does not seem to have been called for by the decision of the case, which was a prohibition to an Ecclesiastical Court to entertain a suit by a parson to recover the treble value of tithes. Moore 282, 283, pl. 435,[2] is merely an opinion of Serjeants Moore and Brograve (1590) that the suppression of a monastery gave a right of entry to the founders, and that the King should be understood founder if no other was found. It was not known of whom

---

[2] See §§ 31–41, ante; App. E, §§ 774 et seq., post. Cf. Y. B. Trin. 11 Edw. IV. 4, pl. 7; Y. B. Easter 12 Edw. IV. 2 b, pl. 7.

§ 48. [1] Third Report of Commissioners on the Law of Real Property 7. "Stipulations for definite spiritual services were very rare when compared with gifts in frankalmoign." 1 P. & M. Hist. Eng. Law (2d ed.) 241.

§ 49. [1] Godb. 211.

[2] Cited in Harg. note to Co. Lit. 13 b.

or on what tenure the land was held.   The King would clearly have been entitled by escheat.[3]

§ 50.   But the notions which Lord Coke imposed upon his brethren did not always long survive his retirement.   In *Johnson* v. *Norway*[1] (1622) arose the precise question whether, on the dissolution of a corporation, its land went to the donor or escheated to the lord.   Hobart, C. J., said: "The great doubt of the case will be upon the barre of the defendant, whether by the death of the abbot and the monks, the land escheat to the lords of whom that was holden, or whether that shall go to the donors, and to the founders, and he thought that the land shall escheat, to which Winch seemed to agree."   The report adds that the judges said they would advise of the case, and gave order to argue it again; but Lord Hale's MSS.[2] say that it was held that the land escheated. This is the only English case in which the question has been decided.

§ 51.   But although Lord Coke's doctrine rests solely on a *dictum* of a judge in the fifteenth century, and is contrary to the only English case, it has often been referred to as law.[1]

[3] See Southwell v. Wade, 1 Roll. Ab. 816, A, pl. 1.

§ 50. [1] Winch 37.

[2] Cited Co. Lit. 13 b, Harg. note.

§ 51. [1] Per Lord Hardwicke in A. G. v. Gower, 9 Mod. 224, 226. Per Lord Mansfield in Burgess v. Wheate, 1 W. Bl. 123, 165. Per Lord Denman in Mayor of Colchester v. Brooke, 7 Q. B. 339, 384. Folger v. Chase, 18 Pick. 63, 66. Bingham v. Weiderwax, 1 Comst. 509. Nicoll v. N. Y. & Erie R. R. Co., 12 Barb. 460, 465, 12 N. Y. 121, 129, 130. Robie v. Sedgwick, 35 Barb. 319, 329. Commercial Bank v. Lockwood, 2 Harring. 8, 13. Diamond State Iron Co. v. Husbands, 8 Del. Ch. 205, 68 Atl. 240. Fox v. Horah, 1 Ired. Eq. 358, 361. State v. Rives, 5 Ired. 297, 309. Life Assoc. v. Fassett, 102 Ill. 315. Coulter v. Robertson, 24 Miss. 278, 321. See Bacon v. Robertson, 18 How. 480, 483, 487; Mormon Church v. U. S., 136 U. S. 1, 47, 10 S. Ct. 792, 34 L. E. 478; Owen v. Smith, 31 Barb. 641; People v. Mauran, 5 Denio 389, 401; Woodworth v. Payne, 5 Hun 551, 553, 74 N. Y. 196, 201; Re Mt. Sinai Hospital, 128 Misc. 476, 489, 490, 219 N. Y. S. 505, 516–518; A. G. v. Clergy Society, 10 Rich. Eq. 604, 610; St. Philip's Church v. Zion Church, 23 So. Car. 297, 298–303, 314; Moultrie v. Smiley, 16 Ga. 289, 298, 299; Davis v. Memphis & Charleston R. R. Co., 87 Ala. 633, 637, 6 So. 140, 141; State Bank v. State, 1 Blackf.

Only one decision, however, has ever followed it, and it is probably among those *decantata* which when carefully examined will be found not only "obsolete and odious," but in fact to have never been law at all.[2]   The alleged right of the grantor is sometimes spoken of as a possibility of reverter, but this it cannot be, for if it were, a corporation could never make a good title to its land.[3]   If the right exists at all, it must be a right in the nature of escheat.[4]   The case of *Hastings Corporation* v. *Letton*[5] calls for notice in this connection. It was a suit by a lessor against a surety for the rent. The lessee was a corporation. The corporation (and also another corporation to which the lease had been assigned) had been dissolved. The question was whether the lease had determined; if it had, then the liability of the surety was at end; if it had not, the lease had passed to the Crown as *bona vacantia*, and the surety was still held.   If the lease had determined, as the Court held it had, there was no question of where the title

267, 282; McRoberts v. Moudy, 19 Mo. Ap. 26; Murray v. Green, 64 Cal. 363, 367, 28 Pac. 118, 120. But cf. Gibson v. Armstrong, 7 B. Mon. 481, 489, 490; People v. College of California, 38 Cal. 166; 1 Bl. Com. 484; 2 Prest. Est. 50; 1 Prest. Abs. 272; Shep. Touch. (Prest. ed.) 30; 2 Kent, Com. 307; Challis, Real Prop. (3d ed.) 35; 9 Holdsworth, Hist. Eng. Law (3d ed.) 67. And the early North Carolina cases have since been expressly overruled on this point. Wilson v. Leary, 120 No. Car. 90, 26 S. E. 630. Univ. of No. Car. v. High Point, 203 No. Car. 558, 166 S. E. 511

[2] The result reached in the text has been approved by Mr. Sweet in his note to Challis, Real Prop. (3d ed.) 467.   See also Richards v. Coal Co., 221 Mo. 149, 171, 119 S. W. 953, 959; and cf. McAlhany

v. Murray, 89 So. Car. 440, 71 S. E. 1025; Mobile Temperance Hall v. Holmes, 189 Ala. 271, 65 So. 1020.   But cf. the remarks of Professor Williston, 2 Harv. Law Rev. 163, 164; and 10 Mich. Law Rev. 121.

[3] See Mr. Sweet's note, loc. cit., where he comments on Preston's remarks.

[4] A question of escheat can hardly arise on the dissolution of most modern corporations, as the lands or their proceeds are divided among stockholders (but see remarks of Romer, C. J., in Re Wells, [1933] 1 Ch. 29, 62), or, in the case of charitable corporations, used cy pres for charitable purposes.   As to charities, see Re Slevin, [1891] 2 Ch. 236; Tud. Char. (5th ed.) 4, 148, 157–159; 14 Mass. L. Q. (No. 6) 50, 51.

[5] [1908] 1 K. B. 378.

to the land should go, the title continued in the lessor, who
had been always seised in fee. The doctrine of Lord Coke
was referred to by the Court with approval. But in truth it
had no bearing on the question involved. If a fee simple is
granted to a corporation, and the corporation is dissolved, the
estate in fee of the corporation is at end. And the question
arising is who has the right of escheat or in the nature of
escheat, a question which did not and could not arise in *Hastings Corporation* v. *Letton.*

*In Re Woking Urban Council,*[6] a canal company sold its
real estate to A., and was dissolved. It does not appear how
the real estate was acquired by the company. The question
arose whether A.'s assignees were subject to liabilities imposed on the company by the statute creating it. The Court
of Appeal held that they were not so liable. The Lord Justices said that the title reverted to the company's grantors
upon dissolution, quoting Coke, and that A.'s assignees had
acquired title under the Statute of Limitations. But the remarks as to the title reverting to the grantors were mere
*dicta.* The Court assumed, for the purposes of the case, that
the assignees had title, and stated their opinion as to the
source of such title. But there were no facts in the record
on which to found a decision that any person had acquired
title on the dissolution, or that the Statute of Limitations
had run against such person. As pointed out by Swinfen
Eady, L. J., at p. 315, the ground of the decision was that,
however the assignees got such title as they might have, they
were not subject to the liabilities. *Hastings Corporation* v.
*Letton* and *Re Woking Urban Council* were approved in a
*dictum* by Lord Sumner in *Morris* v. *Harris.*[7] But in *Re
Wells,*[8] the Court of Appeal treats *Hastings Corporation* v.
*Letton* with scant respect, and authority of that case, as supporting Lord Coke, must now be considered as seriously impaired.[9]

6 [1914] 1 Ch. 300.                Lawrence, L. J., at p. 54. agreeing with Mr. Sweet and the au-
7 [1927] A. C. 252, 259           ing with Mr. Sweet and the au-
8 [1933] 1 Ch. (C. A.) 29.        thor, as against Lord Coke; and
9 See especially the opinion of   to the same effect, 175 L. T. 83,

**§ 51.1. American Cases.** The only case which has been decided in accordance with Lord Coke's remark is *Mott* v. *Danville Seminary.*[1] Melissa B. Lamon gave a parcel of land to the Board of Trustees of the Danville Seminary, a body incorporated under a general statute. The gift was "for the building and maintaining on said grounds an institution of learning, as provided by said law authorizing said incorporation." The corporation was dissolved by decree. The Supreme Court of Illinois held that the title thereupon vested in the donor without entry. This case, as a decision, as yet stands alone.[2]

## 4. STATUTES OF USES AND OF WILLS

**§ 52. Statute of Uses.** The next change in the law of fu-

and 51 Law Quart. Rev. 347. But see also an article in 49 Law Quart. Rev. 240, and 51 Law Quart. Rev. 361, supporting Lord Coke.

In Re Albert Road, [1916] 1 Ch. 289, a leasehold owned by a company was held to be determined by the dissolution of the company, following Hastings Corporation v. Letton. Mr. Cyprian Williams, however, contends that the leases in those two cases had not determined but were bona vacantia, and that those cases were therefore incorrectly decided. He likewise dissents altogether from Lord Coke's doctrine as to the escheat of real estate held by corporations. 2 Wms. Vend. & P. (3d ed.) 932–934, (4th ed.) 929–931. See also Mr. Williams's article in 75 Sol. J. 843, 846. The opinions in Re Wells lend support to his views on both points.

**§ 51.1.** [1] 129 Ill. 403, 21 N. E. 927, 136 Ill. 289, 28 N. E. 54.

[2] See Presbyterian Church v. Venable, 159 Ill. 215, 42 N. E. 836; Miller v. Riddle, 227 Ill. 53, 81 N. E. 48; County of Franklin v. Blake, 283 Ill. 292, 119 N. E. 288; People v. Greer College, 302 Ill. 538, 544, 135 N. E. 80, 82; McGee v. Vandeventer, 326 Ill. 425, 439, 158 N. E. 127, 132; Victoria Hospital v. All Persons, 169 Cal. 455, 147 Pac. 124; Jenkins v. Jenkins University, 17 Wash. 160, 49 Pac. 247; 2 Ill. Law Rev. 196; Kales, Estates, § 302. Possibly the result reached in Mott v. Danville Seminary might be supported on a theory, entirely different from that of an escheat, that the land was held on a charitable trust which failed on the dissolution of the corporation, leaving a resulting trust to the donor's heirs. Cf. §§ 40.17, 41.1, ante. See 23 Columbia Law Rev. 207, 231; 21 Cal. Law Rev. 1, 9. In the absence of any express clause of limitation or reverter, property in such a case would usually be applied cy pres for charitable purposes.

ture estates was worked by the Statute of Uses, 27 Hen. VIII.,
c. 10 (1535). This Statute enacted that when anyone was
seised to the use of another, such other should be seised of
the same estate of which he had the use. Uses in equity could
be created by parol without livery of seisin, and there was no
restraint on their creation *in futuro*. When, therefore, by
means of the Statute of Uses, the legal estate was united to
the use, it became possible to create freeholds without livery
of seisin, and commencing *in futuro*.

§ 53. **Statute of Wills.** Uses could be devised in equity,
but when the legal estates were joined to them, they ceased to
be devisable until St. 32 Hen. VIII, c. 1 (1540), which permitted devises of land. As devises were good without livery,
so they too could be made to take effect *in futuro*.

§ 54. **Uses and Devises.** When a use or devise takes effect
on the determination of preceding estates created at the same
time, it is a remainder limited by way of use or devise.

When a use cuts short another granted estate, it is called a
shifting use.

When it cuts short the estate of the person creating it, it is
called a springing use.

Devises are not distinguished into springing and shifting.
All future devises which are not remainders are called executory devises.

Conditional limitation is a common term for a shifting use
and a shifting executory devise.[1]

§ 55. Apart from the Rule against Perpetuities, there are
no restraints on the creation of shifting and springing uses
and executory devises *in futuro*. Only three exceptions to
this have ever been suggested: (1) that a future freehold
cannot be raised by a bargain and sale; (2) that a contingent
use is bad if preceded by an estate for years; (3) that a bargain and sale cannot be to a person not *in esse*. The validity
of these three supposed exceptions will now be examined.

§ 54. [1] For another meaning of conditional limitation, see Gray, Restraints on Alienation (2d ed.), § 22, note, and § 32, ante. As to conditional limitations taking effect on the termination of a determinable fee, see § 114, note 3, post.

**§ 56. (1) Future Freehold raised by Bargain and Sale.**
There is no doubt that a feoffment may be made to a future
use, or that a man may covenant to stand seized to a future
use; and it would seem equally clear on principle that a man
may by bargain and sale create an estate to begin *in futuro*.
In a bargain and sale, as in a covenant to stand seised, the
owner of the land stands seised to his own use until the time
named in the bargain or covenant, and then the use shifts; the
use in both cases arises out of the seisin of the owner; there
is no difference in the two except in the character of the consideration.

**§ 57.** In Massachusetts it was early held, by a singular
error, that while a future estate could be raised by a covenant
to stand seised, it could not be raised by a bargain and sale.
"The conveyance, being in effect a bargain and sale, must
have all the other requisites and qualities of a bargain and
sale.  One of these qualities is, that it must be to the use of
the bargainee, and that another use cannot be limited on that
use; from which it follows that a freehold to commence *in
futuro* cannot be conveyed in this mode; as that would be to
make the bargainee hold to the use of another, until the future
freehold should vest."[1]  The fallacy is obvious; it lies in assuming that the use to the bargainee arises immediately upon
the bargain and sale; that, under the Statute, the legal estate
vests immediately in him; and that the interest of the bargainor, until the future event happens, must arise out of that
legal estate of the bargainee.  Whereas, in fact, the use does
not arise until the future event, and in the meantime the
bargainor retains his original estate.  It is surprising that the
learned Court did not perceive that the objection which it
made to a bargain and sale applied equally to a covenant to
stand seised.  The Massachusetts doctrine has not been
adopted elsewhere, and the error on which it rests has been

§ 57. [1] Welsh   v.   Foster,   12   Pick. 111; Hunt v. Hunt, 14 Pick.
Mass. 93, 96.  The same law is   374, 380, 381; Gale v. Coburn,
laid down in Wallis v. Wallis, 4   18 Pick. 397; Brewer v. Hardy,
Mass. 135;  Pray  v.  Pierce,  7   22 Pick. 376.
Mass. 381; Parker v. Nichols, 7

often pointed out.[2] Even in Massachusetts the practical inconvenience of the doctrine is done away with by the other erroneous doctrine, peculiar to that State, that a covenant to stand seised can be supported by a pecuniary consideration.[3] One error neutralizes the other. *A use* in futuro *can be raised by a bargain and sale.*

§ 58. (2) **Contingent Use Preceded by an Estate for Years.** In *Adams* v. *Savage*[1] (1703), it was said, and in *Rawley* v. *Holland*[2] (1712), it was held, that a use limited after an estate for years to a person not *in esse* was bad as a contingent remainder unsupported by a freehold.[3]

§ 59. The soundness of these two cases is very questionable. It is well settled that if a future limitation can be construed as a remainder it must be so construed, and not as a springing use; but it is a very different thing to say that a good springing use must be construed into a bad remainder, because it is preceded by an estate which is insufficient to support a remainder. To construe a limitation as a remainder, if it can be a remainder, is one thing; but to insist upon construing it as a remainder, when it cannot be a remainder, seems the very wantonness of destruction. In fact, an estate after an estate for years, though commonly called a remainder, is not strictly so: a remainder is an estate after a freehold; a remainder-man, so called, after an estate for years,

[2] Jackson v. Dunsbagh, 1 Johns. Cas. 92. Rogers v. Eagle Fire Co., 9 Wend. 611. Bell v. Scammon, 15 N. H. 381. Wyman v. Brown, 50 Me. 139 (overruling the dictum in Marden v. Chase, 32 Me. 329). Jordan v. Stevens, 51 Me. 78. Drown v. Smith, 52 Me. 141. Savage v. Lee, 90 No. Car. 320. Bunch v. Nicks, 50 Ark. 367, 7 S. W. 563. Chandler v. Chandler, 55 Cal. 267. See Parsons v. Mills, 2 Roll. Ab. 786; Gilbert, Uses (Sugd. ed.) 163; 4 Mich. Law Rev. 113; Leake, Law of Property in Land (2nd ed.) 88.

[3] Trafton v. Hawes, 102 Mass. 533. Recker v. Brown, 183 Mass. 424, 67 N. E. 353. See 3 Mass. Law Quart. 111.

§ 58. [1] 2 Ld. Raym. 854, 2 Salk. 679.

[2] 22 Vin. Ab. 189, 2 Eq. Cas. Ab. 753.

[3] See Earl of Bedford's Case, Moore 718, Pop. 3; Chudleigh's Case, 1 Co. 135 a; Penhay v. Hurrell, 2 Vern. 370; Freem. Ch. 213, 231, 235, 258; Jackson v. Jackson, Fitzgib. 146; Hayes, Limit. 72; Gilb. Uses (Sugd. ed.) 169 et seq.

has the present seisin, and the reason why at common law an estate cannot be given to a person not *in esse* after an estate for years is that there is no one to take the present seisin, and that a freehold cannot be granted *in futuro*.[1] But, by way of use, a freehold can be granted *in futuro*.

§ 60. The cases of *Adams* v. *Savage* and *Rawley* v. *Holland* have, accordingly, been much criticised.[1] But, further, they must be considered as being overruled by the cases in which it has been repeatedly held that a future contingent devise after an estate for years is a good executory devise, and not a bad remainder.[2] There is no intelligible distinction in this respect between springing uses and springing executory devises, and if *Adams* v. *Savage* and *Rawley* v. *Holland* have not been formally overruled, it is in all probability because the question has not arisen under a deed, as it has under wills.[3] The statement may therefore be ventured that *a contingent use is good although preceded by an estate for years.*

§ 61. (3) **Bargain and Sale to a Person not in Esse.** It is clear that a use, either in possession or remainder, may be raised by bargain and sale to one man, on a consideration paid by another.[1] In Gilbert on Uses[2] it is said: "If a man bargains and sells lands to one for life, then to his first son in tail, who is not yet born, it seems this is a good contingent remainder, rising out of the estate of the bargainor; but 'tis said by Judge Newdigate,[3] that by bargain and sale only,

§ 59. [1] Leake, Law of Property in Land (2nd ed.) 231. Challis, Real Prop. (3d ed.) 80, 99.

§ 60. [1] Gilb. Uses (Sugd. ed.) 167, 168, note. Hayes, Limit. 67, note, 72, note. 1 Sand. Uses (5th ed.) 147, 148. Wilson, Uses 69, 70. Challis in 1 Law Quart. Rev. 412 et seq.

[2] Gore v. Gore, 2 P. Wms. 28 (1722). Haywood v. Stillingfleet, 1 Atk. 422 (1737). Harris v. Barnes, 4 Burr. 2157 (1768). See Lord Mansfield in Goodtitle v. Burtenshaw, Fearne, C. R., Ap. 570, 571; Gilb. Uses (Sugd. ed.) 171; 22 Law Quart. Rev. 261 et seq.

[3] Cf. Challis, Real Prop. (3d ed.) 172.

§ 61. [1] Sharington v. Strotton, Plowd. 298, 307. 2 Roll. Ab. 784, pl. 6, 7. 2 Inst. 672. Buckley v. Simonds, Winch 59, 61. Case of Sutton's Hospital, 10 Co. 23, 34 a.

[2] (Sugd. ed.) 398.

[3] 2 Sid. 158.

no contingent use can be supported, it seems he means by the estate of the bargainee; but, *quære*, whether it may not, *ut ante,* but it seems a feoffment or fine is the surest way, and so to put it out of the power of the owner of the land to destroy the future uses. *Quære,* whether the consideration given by the party in uses will create a use to one not *in esse.*" To this passage the editor, Mr. Sugden, has appended a note: "It seems clear that a contingent use to a person not *in esse* cannot be raised by a bargain and sale; because of course the intended *cestui que use* cannot pay a consideration, and a consideration paid by the tenant for life would not, it is conceived, extend to the unborn son." In the same book[4] Gilbert says that a man cannot in a bargain and sale reserve to himself a power of making leases, because "no uses will rise without consideration, therefore not to the lessees; for where the persons are altogether uncertain, and the terms unknown, there can be no consideration." To this the editor adds in a note: "But although a general power of leasing cannot be reserved, yet a power may be reserved in a bargain and sale to grant a lease to a person from or on behalf of whom a valuable consideration moved at the execution of the deed."[5] In Sanders on Uses[6] it is said that "if there be a bargain and sale for the life of the bargainee, with a power for him to make leases, a lease made under that power cannot operate as an appointment of the use to the lessee."

§ 62. The statement of these eminent lawyers appears to have little support either in principle or authority. As a consideration paid by one person can raise a use, and even a future use, to another, there seems no reason why it should not raise a use to a person not *in esse.* If the *cestui que use* had to pay or promise the consideration, that would be a reason for requiring him to be *in esse;* but as the consideration can be paid or promised by a stranger, the reason fails. A man may covenant to stand seised to the use of relatives not *in esse,* e. g. to the use of the covenantor's unborn children.[1]

<hr>

[4] P. 91.

[5] See also Sugd. Pow. (8th ed.) 138, 139.

[6] 2 Sand. Uses (5th ed.) 62.

§ 62. [1] See Bolls v. Winton, Noy 122; Mildmay's Case, 1 Co.

And it would seem that if a use can be raised to an unborn person by a covenant to stand seised, it can be raised to such person by a bargain and sale.

§ **63.** The only authorities cited in support of the theory that a use to a person not *in esse* cannot be raised by bargain and sale seem to be 2 Sid. 158 and Pop. 81. The first citation is a *dictum* of Newdigate, J., in *Heyns* v. *Villars*,[1] a case in the Upper Bench during the Commonwealth (1659). He says, speaking of a bargain and sale, as distinguished from a covenant to stand seised and from a feoffment: "By this conveyance only no contingent use can be supported. See for this 4 Ma. Dy. f. 155 *a,* acc." This case referred to is *Tyrrel's Case*,[2] which established that a use cannot be raised' out of the use of a bargainee,—a proposition undoubtedly correct, but giving no support to the theory that a contingent use cannot be raised out of the seisin of the bargainor. The second authority cited is *Dillon* v. *Fraine*.[3] Popham, C. J., there says: "And I remember that when I was a counsellor at law in the time of the Lord Dyer, where a feoffment was made to the use of one for life, with remainders over, with restraint to alien, and with power given to tenant for life to make leases for one and twenty years or three lives, it was much doubted whether this power so limited to him without words in the assurance that the feoffee and his heirs shall stand seised to these uses, shall be good to make such leases or not. And therefore suppose that a man bargains and sells land to one for his life by deed indented and inrolled, and make therein a proviso, that the tenant for life may make such leases, this is to no purpose as to power to make a lease." What the Chief Justice seems to mean is this: In case of a feoffment to uses with power in A. to make leases, it is doubtful whether any use will arise to the lessees, unless it is expressly stated in the deed of feoffment that the feoffee is

175, 176 b, 177 a; Warwick v. Gerrard, 2 Vern. 7; 2 Hayes, Conv. (5th ed.) 89 et seq.; Sugd. Pow. (8th ed.) 138, 139. But cf. Bradford v. Griffin, 40 So. Car. 468, 471, 19 S. E. 76, 77, § 398.1, post; 4 Kent, Com. 496.

§ **63.** [1] 2 Sid. 157, 158.
[2] Dyer 155 a.
[3] Pop. 70, 81.

seised to the uses of the lessees under such leases as A. shall make; and so in a bargain and sale, with power in A. to make leases, no use will arise to the lessees, unless the bargain and sale is in terms to the lessees under such leases as A. shall make.[4] This is a question of the merest form, on which the matter would certainly not turn at the present day. Whatever the meaning of this obscure *dictum*, it is a slight foundation on which to build so inconvenient a doctrine, as that a use to a person not *in esse* cannot be raised by bargain and sale. It is entirely *obiter*, and occurs in a case better known as *Chudleigh's Case*,[5] abounding in the most futile conceits of school logic. Sugden in his Treatise on Powers[6] well says of another *dictum* of Popham in this case: "Indeed, had the whole Court delivered this opinion it would not at this day be entitled to much attention. All the settlements in the kingdom are made by way of use which is there styled impious."

§ 64. The origin of the notion that a bargain and sale cannot raise a use to a person not *in esse* seems to have been this: In a covenant to stand seised a general power to lease is bad, because the lessee may not be of the blood of the covenantor, and by covenant to stand seised no use can be raised to one who is not of kin or connected by marriage.[1] Hence it was assumed that a general power to lease must be bad also in a bargain and sale. The fallacy lay in forgetting that while a consideration of blood cannot come from a stranger, a money consideration can. The true doctrine is therefore believed to be that *a bargain and sale to a person not* in esse *is good*.[2]

---

[4] See Mildmay's Case, 1 Co. 175.

[5] Reported, besides ut sup., 1 Co. 120, Jenk. 276, 1 And. 309.

[6] 1 Sugd. Pow. (7th ed.) 22.

§ 64. [1] In a covenant to stand seised a power to lease to unborn relations is good. See § 62, ante.

[2] In Ocheltree v. McClung, 7 W. Va. 232, 242–247, it was considered that a use to persons not in esse might be raised by a bargain and sale. It is not clear how far the decision rested on the special language of the Virginia Statute. But in the first edition the case of Smith v. Smith, 1 Jones 135 (1853), was overlooked. In this case it was held that upon a bargain and sale to A. an appointment under a general power given to B. was bad. The decision is rested largely upon the remarks of Sugden and Sanders cited and referred to ante. Cf. Taylor v. Eatman, 92 No. Car. 601. See also Kepler v. Castle, 281 Ill. 444, 117

§ 65. The practical importance of this last discussion lies in the fact that when an intended conveyance has failed to take effect as a feoffment through lack of livery or a statutory substitute for livery, it may take effect, if it be for a consideration of blood, as a covenant to stand seised, or if it be, or be alleged to be,[1] for a valuable consideration, as a bargain and sale.[2] It is most undesirable to hamper the effect of this sensible and beneficent rule of law by an unnecessary theory that a use to persons not *in esse* cannot be raised by a bargain and sale. For if such theory be groundless, then every conveyance will operate according to the intention of the parties, unless in the very rare case that there is neither a consideration of blood, nor a valuable consideration, nor a recital of a valuable consideration.[3]

§ 66. If the three questions discussed in §§ 56–65, *ante*, have been correctly answered in the affirmative, then there is no restraint on the creation of future estates in land, either

N. E. 1029; Legout v. Price, 318 Ill. 425, 149 N. E. 427; Kales, Estates, § 475; 22 Ill. Law Rev. 894.

§ 65. [1] "The recital of a consideration is conclusive for the purpose of supporting the deed against the grantor and his heirs." Trafton v. Hawes, 102 Mass. 533, 541. So, accordingly, Fisher v. Smith, Moore 569; Wilkes v. Leuson, Dyer 169 a; Salisbury v. Clarke, 61 Vt. 453, 17 Atl. 135; Fuller v. Missroon, 35 So. Car. 314, 14 S. E. 714; Davis v. Jernigan, 71 Ark. 494, 76 S. W. 554; Kuuku v. Kawainui, 4 Hawaii 515; Gilb. Uses (Sugd. ed.) 96. See Jackson v. Serbring, 16 Johns. 515; Gault v. Hall, 26 Me. 561. The case of Singleton v. Bremar, 4 McCord 12, is perhaps contra.

[2] Elphinstone, Interp. of Deeds 40 et seq. Pray v. Pierce, 7 Mass. 381. Russell v. Coffin, 8 Pick. 143, 151. Hunt v. Hunt, 14 Pick. 374, 380–382. Havens v. Sea Shore Land Co., 47 N. J. Eq. 365, 20 Atl. 497. See, in Thatcher v. Omans, 3 Pick. 521, Handy v. McKim, 64 Md. 560, 4 Atl. 125, Perry v. Price, 1 Mo. 553, and Lambert v. Smith, 9 Ore. 185, the converse case, where a deed purporting to be a bargain and sale was allowed to operate as a feoffment. See also 4 Mich. Law Rev. 111, where there is a collection of cases in which a deed expressed in one form was allowed to operate in another.

[3] See Bryan v. Bradley, 16 Conn. 474; Eckman v. Eckman, 68 Pa. 460. Cf. 4 Mich. Law Rev. 121.

by way of use or by will, other than the Rule against Perpetuities.

## 5. LATER LEGISLATION

§ 67. **American Statutes.** In several of the United States freehold estates may be created *in futuro* either by express provision of statute[1] or by inference from statutes dispensing with the necessity of livery of seisin.[2] And although in several of the States (e. g. New York, Michigan, and Wisconsin[3]) uses have never existed or have been abolished, which of itself would greatly limit the creation of estates *in futuro*, yet wherever this has been done it is believed that freehold estates can, by statute, be created *in futuro*, so that the abolition of uses occasions no practical inconvenience.[4]

§ 68. A possible exception to this is Ohio. The Statute of Uses is not in force in that State.[1] And it has never been expressly enacted that freeholds can be created *in futuro*.

§ 67. [1] 1 Stimson, Amer. Stat. Law, § 1421.

[2] See Abbott v. Holway, 72 Me. 298; Gorham v. Daniels, 23 Vt. 600; Savage v. Lee, 90 No. Car. 320; Rowland v. Rowland, 93 No. Car. 214; Sabledowsky v. Arbuckle, 50 Minn. 475, 52 N. W. 920; Bunch v. Nicks, 50 Ark. 367, 7 S. W. 563; Miller v. Miller, 91 Kan. 1, 136 Pac. 953; Puukaiakea v. Hiaa, 5 Hawaii 484; 2 Washb. Real Prop. (6th ed.) 554, note.

[3] See 1 Greenl. Cr. 302, note; 1 Stimson, Amer. Stat. Law, § 170.

[4] Ferguson v. Mason, 60 Wis. 377, 19 N. W. 420. See Kuuku v. Kawainui, 4 Hawaii 515; 34 Harv. Law Rev. 353, 354; 39 Harv. Law Rev. 466; and 64 Sol. J. 405. In England, the Statute of Uses has been abolished by the Law of Prop. Act (1925), § 207.

[G. R. P.]—5

Whether the Statute of Enrolments, 27 Hen. VIII., c. 16, is in force in America generally, quære. It is in force in New Brunswick. Doe d. Hanington v. McFadden, Bert. 153. See, however, 64 Sol. J. 405. But not in Massachusetts. Trafton v. Hawes, 102 Mass. 533, 541. Nor in New York. Jackson v. Dunsbagh, 1 Johns. Cas. 91, 97. Nor in California. Chandler v. Chandler, 55 Cal. 267, 271. See 4 Tiffany, Real Prop. (3d ed.), § 958, p. 14. It has been abolished in England by Stat. 15 Geo. V., c. 5, Sch. 10.

§ 68. [1] Doe d. Thompson v. Gibson, 2 Ohio 339. Helfenstine v. Garrard, 7 Ohio, pt. 1, 275. Williams v. First Presbyterian Soc., 1 Ohio St. 478, 497. Carroll v. Olmsted, 16 Ohio 251, 260. See § 23.1, ante.

But land passes there by deed without livery of seisin,[2] and the courts of Ohio will not improbably hold, as have those of Maine and other States,[3] that when livery of seisin is no longer necessary the objection to the creation of a freehold *in futuro* falls with it.[4]

§ **68.1.** In Illinois the Supreme Court has said,[1] and later directly ruled, that a fee cannot be limited upon another fee either by deed[2] or by will.[3] The learned court soon corrected this slip so far as executory devises were concerned,[4] and more recently with regard to limitations by deed.[5]

[2] Borland v. Marshall, 2 Ohio St. 308, 313, 314.

[3] See note 2 to preceding section.

[4] See 1 Univ. Cinn. Law Rev. 136.

§ **68.1.** [1] McCampbell v. Mason, 151 Ill. 500, 38 N. E. 672.

[2] Palmer v. Cook, 159 Ill. 300, 42 N. E. 796.

[3] Ewing v. Barnes, 156 Ill. 61, 40 N. E. 325.

[4] Glover v. Condell, 163 Ill. 566, 45 N. E. 173. Strain v. Sweeny, 163 Ill. 603, 45 N. E. 201.

[5] Harder v. Matthews, 309 Ill. 548, 141 N. E. 442. See third edition, § 68 a, note; Kales, Estates, §§ 443–462; 18 Ill. Law Rev. 485; and Richman v. Hopkins, 45 Fed. 2d 737 (C. C. A.).

The Circuit Court of the United States for the Northern District of Georgia held, in Printup v. Hill, 107 Fed. 789, that by the law of that State, before the passage of the Code, no shifting use could be created by deed. This decision and a dictum in Greer v. Pate, 85 Ga. 552, 11 S. E. 869, rest upon a misconception of the case of Cook v. Walker, 15 Ga. 457, where it was held in accordance with the doctrine generally received in the United States that if a fee is granted with a conditional limitation over in case the grantee does not dispose of the land by deed or will, such conditional limitation is void. This doctrine, whether right or wrong (as to which see Gray, Restraints on Alienation, §§ 56 et seq., 11 Law Series, Univ. Mo. Bull. 3, 47), furnishes no objection to the validity of shifting uses generally. Executory devises would be equally objectionable. Under the present Civil Code of Georgia (1911), § 3658, a fee can be limited on a fee either by deed or by will. Davis v. Hollingsworth, 113 Ga. 210, 38 S. E. 827. See as to a similar blunder made with regard to personal property, App. F, §§ 846, 847, post.

Still more remarkable is a dictum in Simmons v. Cabaune, 177 Mo. 336, 76 S. W. 618, that a fee cannot be limited on a fee even by will, that is, that there can be neither shifting use nor

[G. R. P.]

## 6. EQUITABLE ESTATES

**§ 69.** Of future uses before the Statute of Uses, and of future trusts since, there has been no restraint on the creation, save the Rule against Perpetuities.[1]

### B. LANDS OF COPYHOLD TENURE

**§ 70. Copyhold.** (1) In lands held in copyhold there may be reversions and remainders; and the remainders may be either vested or contingent.[1] (2) Copyholds may be surrendered on condition.[2] (3) In some manors an estate to A. and the heirs of his body gives a fee simple conditional at common law; in others the principle of the Statute *De Donis* has been adopted by the custom, and A. takes an estate tail.[3] (4) It is not clear how far future estates other than remainders can be limited in a surrender,[4] and to avoid the doubt, when freehold and copyhold lands are settled, although a legal estate is given in the freeholds, the copyholds are ordinarily given to trustees to hold upon trusts corresponding to the legal estates in the freeholds.[5] (5) The Statute of Uses does not apply to copyholds.[6] (6) When copyholds are surrendered to the use of a will, an executory devisee is entitled to admittance.[7] The Statute *Quia Emptores* has no application to copyholds, and, therefore, a determinable fee with a possi-

executory devise in Missouri. This clearly is not now law in Missouri. Sullivan v. Garesche, 229 Mo. 496, 129 S. W. 949. Deacon v. St. Louis Tr. Co., 271 Mo. 669, 691, 197 S. W. 261, 266. See 11 Law Series, Univ. Mo. Bull. 3, 14-23.

**§ 69.** [1] But see § 325.1, post.

**§ 70.** [1] Wms. Real Prop. (23d ed.) 535.

A contingent remainder in copyhold land is not destroyed by the forfeiture or surrender of the particular estate; the freehold in the lord is said to support it, until the time when the particular estate would have expired; but if the contingent event does not happen before the expiration of such time the remainder fails. Fearne, C. R. 319, 320. Scriv. Cop. (7th ed.) 65, 66. Wms. Real Prop. (23d ed.) 535.

[2] Scriv. Cop. (7th ed.) 107, 108.

[3] Wms. Real Prop. (23d ed.) 558-561. Challis, Real Prop. (3d ed.) 27, 300.

[4] See 1 Scriv. Cop. (4th ed.) 159-188.

[5] 3 Dav. Prec. Conv. (3d ed.) 597.

[6] Wms. Real Prop. (23d ed.) 531, (24th ed.) 312.

[7] Glass v. Richardson, 2 De G. M. & G. 658.

bility of reverter seems possible in a limitation of copyholds.[8]
And a possibility of reverter is certainly allowed after a fee
simple conditional.[9]

## II. PERSONAL PROPERTY

### A. CHATTELS REAL

**§ 71. Old Common Law.** As there is no seisin of a chattel
real, an estate for years can be granted to begin *in futuro*,
the grantee in the meantime having an *interesse termini*.[1]
Thus an estate can be granted to A. for five years, then to B.
for five years, and then to C. for five years, the grants to B.
and C., etc., being, not remainders, but grants to commence
*in futuro*, independent of the preceding grant or grants.[2]  An
underlease or assignment of a term may be created to take
effect *in futuro*.

**§ 71.1.** A grant to A. for life of an existing term for years
gives him the whole term.  This is for the technical reason
that an estate for life is greater than any estate for years,
that, therefore, when an estate for life in a term for years
is granted, the whole term passes; and that no more passes, is
only because there is no more to grant.[1]  But a grant of a
leasehold by the termor to hold after the death of a stranger
who takes no interest in the land, is good, for though there
is a presumption of law that a life estate cannot be less than
a term for years, there is no presumption that a particular
man will not die within the term.[2]

**§ 71.2.** In England the doctrine that a grant for life of a
term for years passes the entire term has been maintained to

---

[8] See Doe d. Blomfield v. Eyre,
3 C. B. 557, 5 C. B. 713; § 783,
post.

[9] Doe d. Simpson v. Simpson, 4
Bing. N. C. 333, 5 Scott 770. Doe
d. Blesard v. Simpson (in Cam.
Scacc.), 3 Man. & G. 929. Pemberton v. Barnes, [1899] 1 Ch.
544. See § 14, ante. Copyholds
are abolished in England by the
Law of Prop. Act (1925), § 128,

and conditional fees in copyhold
are turned into equitable estates
tail.  See 160 L. T. 359.

§ 71. [1] See Barwick's Case, 5
Co. 93 b, 94 b; Weld v. Traip, 14
Gray 330; § 320.1, post.

[2] See Wright v. Cartwright, 1
Burr. 282.

§ 71.1. [1] See App. F, §§ 807 et
seq., post.

[2] See App. F, §§ 810, 811, post.

the present day; and for this reason in making settlements in England leaseholds are always put in trust.[1]

§ **71.3. American Law.**　In America, however, it is probable that chattels real will be dealt with like chattels personal, and interests for life in them allowed to be created by deed as well as by will.[1]

§ **72. Conditions in Leases.**　A condition may be attached to a lease, on breach of which the lease may be terminated without entry;[1] and the entire leasehold estate may be assigned on a condition of which the assignor may take advantage.[2]

§ **73. No Future Use of a Term.**　The Statute of Uses does not apply to leaseholds, and therefore there can be no future use raised out of a term for years.[1]

§ **74. Executory Devises of Terms.**　The validity of executory bequests of leaseholds, though once doubtful,[1] was established by *Manning's Case*[2] and *Lampet's Case,*[3] for although a generation of judges grumbled at these decisions, they have never been overruled, and the law is now perfectly settled.[4] Thus, by will, a leasehold may be made to shift upon the

§ **71.2.** [1] See App. F, § 812, post; Wms. Settlements 223, 224. But in New South Wales and New Zealand it is provided by statute that "any estate or interest that can be created by will in any chattel real may also be created by deed." N. S. W. Conveyancing Act (1919), § 15. N. Z. Prop. Law Act (1908), § 5. See 64 Sol. J. 421.

§ **71.3.** [1] See App. F, §§ 816, 856. post, and 1 Mo. Law Rev. 119. In Maryland it has been held that a life interest can be created by deed in a leasehold estate renewable forever, and the Court expressed a strong opinion that a life interest could be created by deed in any leasehold estate. Cul-

breth v. Smith, 69 Md. 450, 16 Atl. 112. Cf. Arthur v. Cole, 56 Md. 100. And now in Missouri a life interest given by deed in a term of ninety-nine years has been held good. Landers Inv. Co. v. Brown, 300 Mo. 348, 254 S. W. 14.

§ **72.** [1] See § 12, note, ante. [2] Doe d. Freeman v. Bateman, 2 B. & Ald. 168.

§ **73.** [1] Leake, Law of Property in Land (2d ed.) 92. Of course a term can be raised by the Statute of Uses out of a freehold estate.

§ **74.** [1] See §§ 148–151, post. [2] 8 Co. 94 b. [3] 10 Co. 46 b. [4] See 2 Swanst. 464, 465.

death of the person to whom it is first given, or upon any contingent event.[5]

§ 75. **Equitable Interest in Terms.** There is no restraint on the creation of equitable interests in terms for years. Thus leaseholds may be given to trustees, in trust for A. for life, and then in trust for B.

§ 76. **Gifts to A. and His Heirs.** As is the case with all chattels, if an interest, legal or equitable, in a term for years, be given to A. and his heirs or to A. and the heirs of his body, A. takes the entire interest[1] which on his death goes to his executors.

### B. CHATTELS PERSONAL

§ 77. **English Law.** The English law will first be stated, and then the American law. Taking the English law, the first thing to be noted is that as, according to the prevailing opinion, a parol gift of a chattel is not good without delivery, there can be no gift of a chattel by parol to begin *in futuro*.[1]

[5] For the theory upon which the courts went in reaching this result, see App. F, § 815, post. For the case of a devise of a term to A. for life without any gift over, see App. F, §§ 819, 820, post.

§ 76. [1] Brouncker v. Bagot, 1 Mer. 271.

§ 77. [1] The leading authorities for the common view are: Bract. 16 a; Jenk. 109; Irons v. Smallpiece, 2 B. & Ald. 551; Shower v. Pilck, 4 Ex. 478; Noble v. Smith, 2 Johns. 52. The case in which this view was first clearly announced was Irons v. Smallpiece, ubi sup. That decision was hardly in accordance with the weight of the authorities at the time. See Y. B. Mich. 2 Edw. IV. 25, pl. 28; Perk., §§ 57, 59; Wortes v. Clifton, 1 Roll. R. 61; Hudson v. Hudson, Latch 214; Ward v. Turn-

er, 2 Ves. Sr. 431, 442. And its soundness has been seriously questioned. Wilbraham v. Snow, 2 Wms. Saund. 47 a. London & Brighton R. Co. v. Fairclough, 2 M. & G. 674, 691, note. Lunn v. Thornton, 1 C. B. 379, 381, note. Ward v. Audland, 16 M. & W. 862, 870. Flory v. Denny, 7 Exch. 581, 583. Oulds v. Harrison, 10 Exch. 572, 575. Winter v. Winter, 4 L. T. R. 639, 9 W. R. 747. Martin v. Reid, 31 L. J. C. P. 126, 127. Douglas v. Douglas, 22 L. T. R. 127. Re Ridgway, 15 Q. B. D. 447. Poullain v. Poullain, 79 Ga. 11, 4 S. E. 81. But though in Re Harcourt, 31 W. R. 578, Pollock, B., refused to follow Irons v. Smallpiece, the Court of Appeal, in Cochrane v. Moore, 25 Q. B. D. 57, in an elaborate opinion, reaffirmed the doctrine of Irons v. Smallpiece. See 6 Law Quart.

But if the conveyance is by deed or for value, it can be made to take effect at any time, present or future.

§ 78. Chattels personal may be bailed for a term of years, but it is believed that a grant for life passes the entire interest, and that any gift over is void at law.[1]  Therefore, in settling property, chattels personal, like leaseholds, are settled in trust, the equitable interest shifting on the death of a *cestui que trust* or other future event.  Chattels personal may be granted on condition, and upon breach the grantor can revest the property in himself without a redelivery.[2]

§ 79. The Statute of Uses does not apply to chattels personal any more than to chattels real.

§ 80. **Executory Bequests.**  It has been settled since *Manning's* and *Lampet's Cases*[1] that an executory bequest of leaseholds is good at law, but it has been said that "it may be doubted whether the doctrine of executory bequests is appli-

Rev. 446; 7 Holdsworth, Hist. Eng. Law (3d ed.) 505–509. And the common notion is now so prevalent that it is not likely that it will be departed from. See § 96, post.

§ 78. [1] Wms. Pers. Prop. (18th ed.) 439.  This is the prevailing view in the English textbooks. But there appears to be no judicial decision in support of it, and see 2 Bl. Com. 398, and App. F, § 829, post.

[2] See § 72, ante.

Can there be under English law an interest in a chattel personal analogous to a fee simple determinable in land?  If the law in England is that there can be no legal future interest in a chattel personal created by deed, and that all legal future interests created by will are executory (see §§ 85–86.1, post), there can be no legal interest in a chattel personal analogous to a determinable fee with a possibility of reverter. Even if a legal possessory interest for life, followed by a vested remainder or reversion, should be allowed, it may be doubtful whether a legal right of possession, of indefinite duration, yet not amounting to absolute ownership, would be recognized.  On the other hand, objections to determinable fees founded on questions of tenure, or the Statute Quia Emptores, have no application to personalty.  Determinable fees apparently can be created in incorporeal hereditaments, where no tenure exists.  See § 31, note 3, ante.  Cf. § 39, note 1, ante. In equity, such an interest in personalty has been allowed.  Re Chardon, [1928] Ch. 464; § 87.1, post.  See also O'Mahoney v. Burdett, L. R. 7 H. L. 388, § 785, post; 39 Yale L. J. 771, 772, 785.

§ 80 [1] 8 Co. 94 b. 10 Co. 46 b. § 74, ante.

cable in law to any other chattels than chattels real."[2]   The
authorities are as follows:  In Year Book, Trinity 37 Hen. VI.
30, pl. 11 (1459), a testator made A. and B. his executors, and
bequeathed a graile or mass-book to B. to have and use for the
term of his life, and after his death the remainder to A. in
the same manner for the term of his life, and after his death
the remainder to the parishioners of a church forever.  Prisot,
Chief Justice of the Common Pleas, said that the property
was in the executors "and not in the devisees, for they will
have only the occupation and *'manurance'* for the term of
their two lives, and so no property in them."  Bro. Ab. Devise 13, under this case says:  "In the time of Hen. VIII.
and Edw. VI. it is agreed to be good law that the occupation
can so remain, but if the thing itself was devised to the use
the remainder is void, for a gift or devise of a chattel for
an hour is forever, and the donee or devisee can give, sell, and
dispose of it, and the remainder dependent on it is void,
which note, for it is *'valde bone diversitie.'* "[3]   In Owen, 33,
under the heading of Trinity Term, 7 Eliz. (1565), is this:
"Note by Dyer [C. J. of the C. P.] that the Lord Fitz-James,
late Lord Chief Justice of England, did devise his land to
Nicholas Fitz-James in tail, with divers remainders over, and
in the same devise he devised divers jewels and peeces of
plate, viz. the use of them to the said Nicholas Fitz-James,
and the heires males of his body.  In this case it was the opinion of the Court that the said Nicholas had no property in
the said plate, but onely the use and occupation.  And the
same law where the devise was that his wife should inhabit
in one of his houses which he had for terme of years during
her life, because the wife takes no interest in the terme, but
onely an occupation and usage, out of which the executors
cannot eject her during her life; but Walsh held the contrary."

2 Wms. Pers. Prop. (18th ed.)
440.  As to the nature of executory bequests, see § 795, post.

3 See  Welcden  v.  Elkington,

Dyer 358 b, 359 a, Plowd. 519,
521, 522; Paramour v. Yardley,
Plowd. 539, 542, Bro. New Cas.,
§ 334; Anon., Dyer 7 a.

**§ 81. Uses of Chattels.** From these meagre indications it would appear that originally no legal right of property could be created by will in a chattel, either real or personal, other than an absolute interest, but that the use or occupation of a chattel might be given to A. for life, and that although A. thereby acquired no property, he yet gained a right of occupation.[1]

**§ 82.** In *Mallet* v. *Sackford*[1] (1607), a term was devised to A. for life, and on A.'s death over. The Court were divided in opinion whether the gift over was void; and in this case apparently, according to 1 Roll. Ab. 610, the Court said: "If a man devise a chattel personal to one for life, the remainder to another, it is a void remainder." But two years later, in *Manning's Case*,[2] it was held that upon a devise of a term to A. for life, and on A.'s death to B., B. took a legal estate by executory devise; and that it was immaterial whether the gift was of the term or of the use of the term. This was confirmed in *Lampet's Case*.[3] From the way these decisions were received it is clear that the doctrine was an innovation. Was the innovation to be extended to chattels personal?

**§ 83.** It had been pointed out by counsel, and agreed to by the Court of King's Bench in *Paramour* v. *Yardley*,[1] that there might be an occupation of a chattel personal distinct from the property, but that the devise of the occupation of a term was the same as a devise of the land itself. Accordingly it would not be strange to find preserved, as to chattels personal, the distinction between a bequest of the use of a chattel and a bequest of the chattel itself, which distinction had disappeared as to chattels real. Such is in fact the case. In the Court of Common Pleas, *Anon.*[2] (1641), "A prohibition was prayed unto the Council of the Marches of Wales, and the case was thus: A man being possessed of certain goods devised them by his will unto his wife for her life, and after

§ 81. [1] See Paramour v. Yardley, Plowd. 539, 542.

§ 82. [1] Cro. Jac. 198.

[2] 8 Co. 94 b.

[3] 10 Co. 46 b.    § 74, ante.

§ 83. [1] Plowd. 539, 542.

[2] March 106.

her decease to J. S., and died.   J. S. in the life of the wife
did commence suit in the Court of Equity, there to secure his
interest in remainder, and thereupon this prohibition was
prayed.   And the Justices, viz. Banks, Chief Justice, Crawley,
Foster (Reeve being absent), upon consideration of the point
before them, did grant a prohibition, and the reason was because the devise in the remainder of goods was void, and
therefore no remedy in equity, for *Æquitas sequitur legem.*
And the Chief Justice took the difference, as in 37 H. 6, 30,
Br. Devise 13, and Com. *Welkden & Elkington's Case,* betwixt
the devise of the use and occupation of goods, and the devise
of goods themselves.   For where the goods themselves are devised, there can be no remainder over; otherwise, where the
use or occupation only is devised.   It is true that heirlooms
shall descend, but that is by custom and continuance of them,
and also it is true that the devise of the use and occupation
of land is a devise of the land itself, but not so in case of
goods, for one may have the occupation of the goods, and another the interest, and so it is where a man pawns goods and
the like.   For which cause the Court all agreed that a prohibition should be awarded."   There are three things shown
from this case as to the then understanding of the law:   (1)
That a devise of chattels, after a devise of them for life, was
bad; while a devise of them subject to a devise of the use of
them was good.   (2) That the same rule prevailed in equity
as in law.   (3) That the interest which the devisee of the use
of a chattel had, though not a right of property, was a legal
right of possession like that of a pawnee.

§ 84.   But, in a series of decisions in the last half of the
seventeenth century, it was held that, in equity, if a chattel
personal be bequeathed to A. for life, and on A.'s death to B.,
the bequest of the chattel to A. will be considered as a bequest
of the use to him; that the property will be considered to
belong to B.; and that A. will have only the use.[1]   In *Vachel*

§ 84. [1] Vachel v. Vachel, 1 Ch.     38, 59 (1688).   Shirley v. Ferrers,
Cas. 129 (1669).   Catchmay v.        1 P. Wms. 6, note (1690).   Clarges
Nicholas, Cas. temp. Finch 116        v. Albemarle, 2 Vern. 245 (1691).
(1673).   Smith v. Clever, 2 Vern.    Anon., Freem. Ch. 206 (1695).

v. *Vachel* and *Catchmay* v. *Nicholas* the opinions of common-
law judges were sought, and were in accordance with the
judgments delivered, so we may assume that the common law
was considered to agree with equity on this point.

§ **85. Later English Law.** It may safely be considered as
settled at the present day that on a bequest of a personal
chattel to A. for life, and on A.'s death to B., A.'s right to
enjoy it during his life, and B.'s right to have it on A.'s
death, will both be somehow protected; but the manner of
doing so is not entirely clear. There seems to be three modes
in which it may be done. *First*, A. may be considered as having a right to possession at law, and the immediate vested
right of property as being in B. This appears to be the theory of the cases cited in the preceding sections. *Second*, A.
may be considered as having the legal right of property,
which on his death shifts to B. This appears to have been
Lord Thurlow's opinion,[1] and it is the opinion of the modern
English text-writers.[2] For most questions[3] it is immaterial
which of these two theories is adopted. On either hypothesis,
both A. and B. have legal rights, and are entitled to legal
remedies.

§ **86.** *Third.* The whole interest may pass to A. at law,
who will hold the chattel in trust for himself for life, and on
his death for B. This was possibly Mr. Fearne's view;[1] but

Hyde v. Parrat, 1 P. Wms. 1, 2 Vern. 331 (1695). Tissen v. Tissen, 1 P. Wms. 500 (1718). See Boucher v. Antram, 2 Ch. Rep. 65, Pollexf. 37; Upwell v. Halsey, 1 P. Wms. 651; Randall v. Russell, 3 Mer. 190, 195; Re Swan, [1915] 1 Ch. 829. In the last case, Sargent, J., said, "I see no reason why the first taker should not be deemed as to the possession of the articles to be a trustee for the remainderman, subject to her own life interest" or "it may well be that the first taker is in the position of a bailee of

the articles" (p. 835). But these remarks were dicta, made apparently on the assumption that the first taker had a life interest. She had actually an absolute interest subject to an executory bequest.

§ **85.** [1] See Foley v. Burnell, 1 Bro. C. C. 274, 278.
[2] See App. F, § 831, post.
[3] But not for all, see § 86.1, post.

§ **86.** [1] Fearne, C. R. 401, 414. See Anon., Freem. Ch. 137; and cf. Sabbarton v. Sabbarton, Andrews 333, 335, Cas. temp. Talb.

the case of *Hoare* v. *Parker*[2] is perhaps inconsistent with such
a theory, for there the person interested in chattels, after the
death of the one who had enjoyed them during her life,
brought trover for them, to maintain which he must have had
a legal right to possession. The case is, however, so imperfectly reported, that it furnishes a dangerous ground for
argument. The weight of authority certainly preponderates
in favor of one of the two former views. The question is
important, for if the last view be sound, the owner for life,
having the whole legal estate, may transfer the chattel to a
purchaser for value without notice, who will hold it free from
the claim of one interested in remainder, for, under the last
view, this claim is *ex hypothesi* equitable only.

§ 86.1. Although, as has been said,[1] it is immaterial in
most cases which of the first two theories is adopted; yet
there are two classes of questions (as will be shown hereafter)
in which the adoption of the one or the other theory is vital,
questions of remoteness, and questions on reversionary interests where there is a life interest given without any gift
over.[2] The first theory is that of the older decisions, indeed
it may be said (with one exception[3]) of all the decisions. The
second is that of the modern English textbooks. The former
theory is believed to be correct. There is no reason why the
use of a chattel personal belonging to B. should not be given
to A. for life, the property remaining vested in B. The modern theory arose, apparently, from a mistaken analogy to
chattels real. There is a legal presumption that a life estate
is larger than any term for years, but there is no legal presumption that an interest for life in a picture will last longer
than the picture itself, and therefore there is no technical

55, 245; Doo v. Brabant, 4 T. R.
706, 710.

[2] 2 T. R. 376.

§ 86.1. [1] § 85, ante.

[2] See App. F, §§ 838–842, post.

[3] Re Tritton, 81 L. T. R. 301,
6 Morell 250, stated App. F, §
833, post. See Re Thynne, [1911]

1 Ch. 282. Cf. 7 Holdsworth,
Hist. Eng. Law (3d ed.) 476, 477.
In the case of Re Backhouse,
[1921] 2 Ch. 51, cited by Professor Holdsworth, the ultimate
limitation would have been contingent and therefore too remote
if the property had been realty.
See § 251, post.

objection to regarding the right to a chattel of which the use
has been given to another for life, as vested in the owner.
In other words, if a chattel is bequeathed to A. for life and
then to B., B. ought to be regarded as having a vested interest in the nature of a remainder in the chattel and not an
executory interest. Appendix F is mainly devoted to an examination of these two views.[4]

§ 87. **Equitable Interests.** There is no restraint on the
creation of equitable interests in chattels personal.

§ 87.1. **Equitable Determinable Interests.** Here may be
noticed the case of *Re Chardon*.[1] Money was bequeathed to
trustees to pay the income to a cemetery company "during
such period as they shall continue to maintain" two graves.
If the company failed so to do, the income was to be disposed
of under the residuary bequest. Romer, J., held the provisions of the will valid. With reference to the interest of the
company, he said: "While it is true that it is not equivalent
to an absolute interest it is very much like, and analogous to,
a determinable fee in real estate. Where land was limited to
A. and his heirs until a certain event should happen, a determinable fee was created, though the question whether since
the statute *Quia Emptores* a determinable fee can be created
is a matter upon which lawyers are not agreed. But if the
determinable fee in real estate can no longer be created, it is
because of the statute of *Quia Emptores,* and most assuredly
the statute *Quia Emptores* had nothing to do with personal
estate." The learned judge pointed out that the company's
interest did not offend the Rule against Perpetuities, because
that Rule concerns the commencement of interests and not
their duration;[2] and that there is no rule that it is impossible
to separate the legal from the equitable title for a longer period than that fixed by the Rule against Perpetuities.[3] The

---

[4] See also 7 Holdsworth, Hist.
Eng. Law (3d ed.) 469–478; 24
Law Quart. Rev. 431; 29 Harv.
Law Rev. 501, 731.

§ 87.1. [1] [1928] Ch. 464. And
see 1 Jarm. Wills (7th ed.) 251,
and Tud. Char. (5th ed.) 701.

[2] §§ 209, 232, post.

[3] Most of the cases cited in
§ 232, notes 8, 9, 11, 12, post, are
instances of trusts lasting longer
than that period. See 16 Conveyancer 43, and § 121.7, note 4,
post.

residuary interest, in the event of the company's interest coming to an end, he held to be vested.[4]

However it may be as to a legal interest in personalty analogous to a determinable fee, with a possibility of reverter,[5] it seems that there may be an equitable interest, of a similar character, in personalty followed by a resulting trust. The objection to determinable fees is grounded on the effect of the Statute *Quia Emptores* upon tenure.[6] That statute has nothing to do with personalty, not merely because it applies by its terms only to lands, but because it is wholly concerned with tenure and there is no tenure of personalty. Conditional or determinable fees apparently can be created in incorporeal hereditaments, where no tenure exists,[7] and there seems to be no reason why analogous interests in personalty should not be created, at least in equity.[8] The fact that such interests are equitable is no objection to their validity. The recent English authorities apparently recognizing equitable determinable fees, are not very satisfactory on the question of the propriety of allowing determinable fees at all, but they assume without discussion, and it seems correctly, that an equitable determinable fee is not more objectionable than a

[4] See §§ 327.1, 603.9, post. The facts do not fully appear in the report, and are best stated in Tud. Char. (5th ed.) 701–703. It is there suggested that the gift after the termination of the trust for the company was contingent, and therefore too remote, because it did not on the true construction of the will fall into the residue. See also 1 Jarm. Wills (7th ed.) 252. The learned judge appears to have decided the case on the supposition that the gift over upon the termination of the trust fell into the residue. Even if this was an error, any gift over would be void for remoteness, and there would then be an ulti-

mate resulting trust. Therefore the correctness of the decision as to the immediate trust would not be affected. See 54 Law Quart. Rev. 238.

[5] See § 78, note 2, ante.

[6] § 31, ante.

[7] § 31, note 3, ante. Cf. § 39, note 1, ante. And see the cases on annuities to a man and his heirs. Stafford v. Buckley, 2 Ves. Sr. 170, 180. Re Rivett-Carnac, 30 Ch. D. 136, 141. 2 Jarm. Wills (7th ed.) 1105, 3 Jarm. Wills (7th ed.) 1783. Challis, Real Prop. (3d ed.) 62.

[8] See O'Mahoney v. Burdett, L. R. 7 H. L. 388, § 785, post; Re Bold, 95 L. J. Ch. 201.

legal determinable fee.[9]  Terminable trusts for charity of both
realty and personalty are everywhere allowed.[10]

§ 88. American Law.[1] Wills. Coming to the United States,
future limitations in wills will first be taken up, and then
those in deeds.  In America a future limitation by will of a
chattel personal passes a legal interest.  This has not only
been said in many cases in which the parties' equitable rights
were in controversy, but has been expressly determined in
suits at law.[2]  Even in North Carolina, where, as will be

[9] See Re Leach, [1912] 2 Ch.
422; § 34, note 1, ante, and references in that note, and § 327.1,
post. The trust in Re Chardon
is said in 44 Law Quart. Rev. 419,
and 166 L. T. 296, to infringe on
the Rule against Perpetuities because of its indefinite duration;
see also 44 Law Quart. Rev. 415;
and 16 Conveyancer 43, 56. But
in view of the cases of trusts
lasting longer than the period of
that Rule (note 3 to this section), the principle on which this
criticism is founded is not clear.
The cases about trusts for the
maintenance of graves, and other
non-charitable objects, which contain language of doubtful im-
port about perpetuities, lay down
no principle applicable to the
present case. The true ground of
decision in those cases is that
such trusts are unenforceable for
lack of definite beneficiaries, or,
if the instrument is construed as
giving to the trustee a mere power to use the property for the
purpose designated, such power is
too remote under the Rule against
Perpetuities.   30 Columbia Law
Rev. 60.  § 909, post.  In Re
Chardon, there was no trust for
the maintenance of graves, and

no question of a mere power.
The trustees held subject to a
valid trust to pay to the Cemetery Company, so long as the
latter complied with the condition.  The Cemetery Company
took subject to the condition or
special limitation, but not upon
trust.  For further discussion of
Re Chardon, see 53 Law Quart.
Rev. 24; 54 Law Quart. Rev. 258.
Cf. Re Tyler, [1891] 3 Ch. 252;
§§ 311, 603.3, post.

[10] §§ 327.1, 603.9, post. See also cases of resulting trusts on the
dissolution of unincorporated as-
sociations, § 896.2, post.

§ 88. [1] On the whole subject of
future interests in chattels personal, see an article in 39 Yale
L. J. 771, by Professor Simes; 1
Simes, Fut. Int., §§ 202–224; and
1 Mo. Law Rev. 119.

[2] Smith v. Bell, 6 Pet. 68, 78,
8 S. Ct. 322, 326, 8 L. E. 322.
Griggs v. Dodge, 2 Day 28.  Taber
v. Packwood, Id. 52.  Moffat v.
Strong, 10 Johns. 12, 18.  Smith
v. Van Ostrand, 64 N. Y. 278.
State v. Warrington, 4 Harring.
55.  Dashiell v. Dashiell, 2 Har. &
G. 127.  Royall v. Eppes, 2 Munf.
479.  Bartlett v. Patton, 33 W.
Va. 71, 10 S. E. 21.  Keating v.

seen, a future limitation of a chattel personal by deed is bad, a future limitation by will of such chattel is good.[3]

Reynolds, 1 Bay 80. Henry v. Means, 2 Hill 328 (So. Car.). Rogers v. Randall, 2 Speers 38. Marshall v. Rives, 8 Rich. 85. Russell v. Kearney, 27 Ga. 96. Paulk v. Smith, 56 Ga. Ap. 53, 192 S. E. 68. Lott v. Meacham, 4 Fla. 144. Adie v. Cornwell, 3 T. B. Monr. 276. Moore v. Howe, 4 T. B. Monr. 199. Thrasher v. Ingram, 32 Ala. 645. See Sampson v. Randall, 72 Me. 109; Albee v. Cummings, 12 Cush. 382, 387; Thomas v. Castle, 76 Conn. 447, 56 Atl. 854; Westcott v. Cady, 5 Johns. Ch. 334; Deihl v. King, 6 S. & R. 29; Culbreth v. Smith, 69 Md. 450, 16 Atl. 112; Hill v. Hill, Dudl. Eq. 71, 83, 84; Horry v. Glover, 2 Hill Ch. 515, 523, Riley Ch. 53; Evans v. Adams, 180 So. Car. 214, 185 S. E. 57; Philips v. Crews, 65 Ga. 274; Waldo v. Cummings, 45 Ill. 421; Trogdon v. Murphy, 85 Ill. 119; McCall v. Lee, 120 Ill. 261, 11 N. E. 522; Bowling v. Dobyns, 5 Dana 434; Jackson v. Sublett, 10 B. Monr. 467; Maulding v. Scott, 13 Ark. 88; Damon v. Dickson, 7 Hawaii 694; State v. Welsh, 175 Mo. Ap. 303, 162 S. W. 637; Lanciscus v. Louisville Trust Co., 201 Ky. 222, 256 S. W. 424; Pratt v. Skiff, 289 Ill. 268, 124 N. E. 534; Belleville Bank v. Aneshaensel, 298 Ill. 292, 131 N. E. 682; King v. Stevens, 146 Ark. 443, 225 S. W. 656; Warfield v. Bixby, 51 Fed. 2d 210. It was so held in Virginia, in several cases, as early as 1736. Edmonds v. Hughes, 1 Jeff. 2. Waddy v.

Sturman, Id. 5. Jones v. Langhorn, Id. 37. Spicer v. Pope, Id. 43.

It has been said of future limitations of personal property that "although allowed," they "are certainly not to be favored; it is with reluctance that they have been sanctioned by our courts; and they will lean against the creation of them, either by deed or will." Brewster v. McCall, 15 Conn. 274, 291. And see Kirkpatrick v. Davidson, 2 Ga. 297, 301, 302. But the correctness of such a general proposition may be doubted. See Banks v. Marksberry, 3 Lit. 275, 279; Welsch v. Belleville Bank, 94 Ill. 191, 204. As to consumable chattels, see § 824, post.

[3] Jones v. Zollicoffer, No. Car. Term Rep. 212. Burnett v. Roberts, 4 Dev. 1. Knight v. Wall, 2 Dev. & B. 125. Knight v. Leak, Id. 133. Threadgill v. Ingram, 1 Ired. 577. Carter v. Spencer, 7 Ired. 14. In Jones v. Zollicoffer, it was expressly held that a purchaser without notice from the person having the life interest could not hold as against those entitled under the executory bequest; and see Burnett v. Roberts, ubi sup.; and Braswell v. Morehead, Busb. Eq. 26. Cf. also Russell v. Kearney, 27 Ga. 96.

In Alabama it has been held that if one to whom a chattel has been bequeathed for life assigns it by what purports to be an absolute conveyance, the right of those having the future interest

**§ 89.** That a future limitation by will gives a legal and not merely an equitable interest appears to be universally held to be law in America. The sole exception, if it be an exception, is *Homer* v. *Shelton.*[1] In that case personal property was bequeathed to A., with an executory bequest over, should A. at his death leave only one child. The question in dispute was whether A. was entitled to possession of the property without giving security. The Court held that as A. was the absolute owner of the property, he was entitled to the possession of it without giving security; but that he would hold it "in trust, subject to the limitation over." It is certainly not clear that the Court meant to decide that the executory bequest gave an equitable interest only. As was natural in a court having then no equitable jurisdiction, equitable terms such as "trust" were loosely employed. It does not seem that the decision would have been affected by the fact of the gift over being legal rather than equitable. The result of holding an executory bequest of a chattel personal to give only an equitable interest would, as has been said,[2] be very important; for, if such were the case, the legatee for life could pass the property to a *bona fide* purchaser, free from any claim under the executory bequest. Until a more express decision than *Homer* v. *Shelton,* it will not be safe to assume that the courts of Massachusetts mean to depart from what is now everywhere else the accepted doctrine in America.[3]

**§ 90.** After an absolute bequest of personalty, any future

is discontinued, and turned into a chose in action. Broome v. King, 10 Ala. 819. Price v. Talley, 18 Ala. 21. But this seems to be the employment of a nomenclature and ideas foreign to the modern law of personal property. See Pickett v. Doe d. Pope, 74 Ala. 122; and § 90, post.

**§ 89.** [1] 2 Met. 194, 206, 207.
[2] See § 86, ante.
[3] And is probably also the law in England. §§ 85, 86, ante. See, however, Chisholm v. Starke, 3 Call 25; and in Glover v. Condell, 163 Ill. 566, 45 N. E. 173, a future limitation of personalty is called an equitable interest. See also 8 Iowa Law Bull. 104; 39 Yale L. J. 771, 790–797; 1 Simes, Fut. Int., §§ 217–218; Amer. Law Inst. Uniform Property Act, §§ 3, 21 (Handbook, Uniform State Laws, 1938).

limitation must be an executory bequest;[1] whether, after a
bequest of personalty for life, a future limitation is to be
regarded as in the nature of a remainder according to the
first theory mentioned above,[2] or as an executory bequest, is
not, except on the question of remoteness,[3] important, for the
future interest is, on either theory, a legal one.

§ 90.1. But if a chattel personal is bequeathed to one for
his life, and nothing is said in the will as to its destination,
then it becomes necessary to decide between the two theories.
If the legatee has the absolute interest, then as there is no
gift over, the chattel must pass on the legatee's death to the
legatee's executor as part of his estate. It is so held in Delaware.[1] But if the legatee has only the use and occupation
of the chattel, then on the legatee's death, it reverts to the
testator's executor. This, which is believed to be the correct
view,[2] is the prevailing one in the United States.[3]

§ 90. [1] On the erroneous notion
which has sometimes found expression, that there can be no
executory limitation after an absolute bequest of personalty, see
App. F, §§ 846, 847, post.

Chattels personal can be granted or bequeathed on condition.
§ 78, ante. See Green v. Old
People's Home, 269 Ill. 134, 109
N. E. 701; 1 Simes, Fut. Int.,
§ 213; 39 Yale L. J. 771, 786–788.
With regard to interests in personalty analogous to determinable fees, see §§ 78, note 2, 87.1,
ante. As in the United States
vested future legal interests in
personalty (§§ 117.1–117.3, post)
and determinable fees in realty
(§§ 39–41, ante) are generally
recognized, and the tendency is
to treat interests in personalty
like interests in realty, legal interests in personalty analogous to
determinable fees will probably

be recognized. See Boal v. Metro-
politan Museum, 292 Fed. 303,
305, aff'd 298 Fed. 894; 1 Simes,
Fut. Int., § 212; 39 Yale L. J. 771,
785–786; § 327.1, note 3, post.
Cf. Amer. Law Inst. Uniform
Property Act, § 3 (Handbook of
Uniform State Laws, 1938).

[2] §§ 85, 86.1, ante.

[3] As to which see §§ 117–117.3,
post; App. F, §§ 838–841, 851.

§ 90.1. [1] See App. F, § 852,
post.

[2] See § 86.1, ante.

[3] See cases cited, App. F. § 852,
last note, post. The question
does not seem to have arisen in
England with regard to chattels
personal. In the case of a term
for years it has been held that
there is a reversion to the testator's executor. Eyres v. Faulkland, 1 Salk. 231, although this
seems contrary to the theory as
to chattels real maintained in

[G. R. P.]

**§ 91. American Law. Deeds.** It is the common opinion in the United States that a future limitation of a chattel personal as a legal interest can be created by deed as well as by will. Thus, upon the gift of a chattel to A. for life, and after his death to B., B. takes a legal interest.[1] So upon the gift of a chattel to A., but if he dies without leaving issue at his death then to B., B. has a legal interest.[2] So, if he dies

England. See § 71.1, ante; App. F, §§ 842, 856, post.

The notes to § 90 in the first edition of this book were pronounced by the author in the third edition to be incorrect.

**§ 91.** [1] Tucker v. Stevens, 4 Des. 325. M'Call v. Lewis, 1 Strob. 442. Nix v. Ray, 5 Rich. 423. (Cooper v. Cooper, Brevard MSS. Rep.; 1 Rice, So. Car. Dig. 207, contra, is overruled.) Sharman v. Jackson, 30 Ga. 224. Keen v. Macey, 3 Bibb 39. Price v. Price, 5 Ala. 578. Williamson v. Mason, 23 Ala. 488. See Sampson v. Randall, 72 Me. 109, 112; Fuller v. Fuller, 84 Me. 475, 481, 24 Atl. 946, 948; Bradley v. Mosby, 3 Call 50; Kirkpatrick v. Davidson, 2 Ga. 297, 301; Owen v. Cooper, 46 Ind. 524; McCall v. Lee, 120 Ill. 261, 11 N. E. 522; Aikin v. Smith, 1 Sneed 304; Lyde v. Taylor, 17 Ala. 270; Jones v. Hoskins, 18 Ala. 489; Harris v. McLaran, 30 Miss. 533, 568, 569; Durfee v. Meadowcroft, 193 Mass. 267, 79 N. E. 268; Uniform Property Act, § 3 (Handbook of Uniform State Laws, 1938).

[2] Hill v. Hill, Dudl. Eq. 71. See Powell v. Brown, 1 Bail. 100;

Welch v. Kinard, Speers Eq. 256, 262; Henderson v. Kinard, 29 So. Car. 15, 6 S. E. 853. In Betty v. Moore, 1 Dana 235, 237, there was a gift by parol of the absolute interest in a slave on condition that if the donee should die without children, the slave should revert to the donor. This conditional or reversionary gift was held void, although an executory devise to the same effect would have been good. In Wilson v. Cockrill, 8 Mo. 1, the testator gave certain slaves to A., her executors, administrators, and assigns, and other slaves to B., his executors, administrators, and assigns. but should either die without heirs, "then the property of the one so dying shall absolutely vest in the other." A. and B. were children of the testator. A. died without issue; the gift over to B. was held void. It is not easy to follow the reasoning of the Court. If the decision means that an executory gift by deed of personalty is bad, although it might be good by will, this case and Betty v. Moore, ubi sup., seem to be the only cases in the United States, outside of North Carolina, to support such a distinction. See App. F, § 847, post.

in the lifetime of C.[3]   And in like manner, upon a gift by
deed of a chattel personal to take effect on the death of the
donor, the donee, on the death of the donor, becomes entitled
to possession as legal owner.[4]

§ 92. In North Carolina alone is the opposite doctrine
held. There, upon a gift of a chattel personal by deed to A.
for life, and upon A.'s death to B., or to A. with an executory
limitation over to B. upon a definite failure of A.'s issue for
life, the gift to B. is void.[1]   And so if, in a gift of a chattel
personal by deed to A., the chattel is reserved to the grantor
for his life, the gift to A. is void.[2]

§ 93. In 1823 the Legislature of North Carolina enacted[1]
that "Every limitation by deed or writing of a slave or slaves,
which limitation, if contained in a last will and testament,
would be good and effectual as an executory devise or bequest, shall be and is hereby declared to be a good and effectual limitation in remainder of such slave or slaves, and any

[3] Security Co. v. Hardenburgh, 53 Conn. 169, 2 Atl. 391.

[4] Dukes v. Dyches, 2 Strob. Eq. 353, note.   Dawson v. Dawson, Rice Eq. 243, 261.   Jaggers v. Estes, 2 Strob. Eq. 343, 378, 397. (Vernon v. Inabnit, 2 Brev. 411, and the dictum in Ingram v. Porter, 4 McCord 198, contra, are overruled.)   Robinson v. Schly, 6 Ga. 515.   McGlawn v. McGlawn, 17 Ga. 234.   Horn v. Gartman, 1 Fla. 73.   Banks v. Marksberry, 3 Lit. 275.   Caines v. Marley, 2 Yerg. 582.   Johnson v. Mitchell, 1 Humph. 168, 173.   Adams v. Broughton, 13 Ala. 731.   Gullett v. Lamberton, 6 Ark. 109.   Nalley v. First Nat. Bank, 135 Ore. 409, 293 Pac. 721.   See Hope v. Hutchins, 9 G. & J. 77; Culbreth v. Smith, 69 Md. 450, 16 Atl. 112.

§ 92. [1] Cutlar v. Spillar, 2 Hayw. 130. Gilbert v. Murdock, Id. 182.   Dowd v. Montgomery, 2 Car. Law Rep. 100.   Smith v. Tucker, 2 Dev. 541.   Hunt v. Davis, 3 Dev. & B. 42. Harrell v. Davis, 8 Jones 359.

[2] Graham v. Graham, 2 Hawks 322.   Foscue v. Foscue, 3 Hawks 538.   Sutton v. Hollowell, 2 Dev. 185.   Morrow v. Williams, 3 Dev. 263.   Hunt v. Davis, 3 Dev. & B. 42.   Foscue v. Foscue, 2 Ired. Eq. 321.   Outlaw v. Taylor, 168 No. Car. 511, 84 S. E. 811.   Speight v. Speight, 208 No. Car. 132, 179 S. E. 461.   The case of Duncan v. Self, 1 Murph. 466, contra, is overruled; and Timms v. Potter, 1 Hayw. 234, apparently contra, is explained in Gilbert v. Murdock, 2 Hayw. 182.   See Vass v. Hicks, 3 Murph. 493; Hughes v. Cannon, 2 Humph. 589; 14 No. Car. Law Rev. 196.

§ 93. [1] Rev. Sts., c. 37, § 22.

limitation made or reserved to the grantor, vendor, or donor, in any such deed or writing, of a slave or slaves, shall be good and effectual in law: *Provided* such limitation, had it been made to another person, would be good and effectual according to the preceding clause: *Provided, also,* that all such deeds or writing shall be proved, witnessed, and registered."[2] The Statute applies only to slaves; as to all other chattels personal the law remained and remains as it was before the Statute;[3] and the courts of North Carolina presume the law in other States to be like their own common law.[4]

§ 94. It might perhaps have been thought that in North Carolina, although an executory gift by deed passed nothing at law, yet the first taker might be held a trustee for those to whom the gift over was made;[1] but this does not appear to have been ever held; and, on the contrary, it was decided in *Butler* v. *Godley*[2] that on a deed of a slave to A. in trust for himself for life, and afterwards in trust for B., A.'s interest was absolute, and B. took nothing in equity.[3]

§ 95. In the United States, outside of North Carolina, a gift *inter vivos* of a chattel personal, after a life interest

[2] For cases under this Statute, see Tillman v. Sinclair, 1 Ired. 183; Bonner v. Latham, Id. 271; Baldwin v. Joyner, 7 Ired. 123; Sutton v. Craddock, 1 Ired. Eq. 134; Murphy v. Merritt, 3 Jones 37; Parish v. Merritt, Id. 38; Holton v. McAllister, 6 Jones 12. The Statute was held not to apply to the case of a gift of a slave for life, with no limitation over. Newell v. Taylor, 3 Jones Eq. 374, but this was remedied by the Revised Code of 1854, c. 37, § 21, which provided that "Every kind of estate in slaves, be the same vested or contingent, or for life or for years, which is allowed to be created and limited by any last will or testament, may be created and limited by way of reservation, remainder, reversion, or otherwise, by any written conveyance of slaves."

[3] Lance v. Lance, 5 Jones 413. Dail v. Jones, 85 No. Car. 221.

[4] Griffin v. Carter, 5 Ired. Eq. 413. Brown v. Pratt, 3 Jones Eq. 202.

§ 94. [1] See Hill v. Hill, Dudl. Eq. 71, 83.

[2] 1 Dev. 94.

[3] See Harrell v. Harrell, 5 Jones Eq. 229. Upon the gift of a chattel personal by deed to A. in trust for the grantor for life, but upon the grantor's death in trust for himself, A., after the grantor's death, was held entitled at law to the property. Lewis v. Lewis, 1 Jones 444.

(whether such gift is to be regarded as vested or executory[1])
has always been held valid; and (except in the cases of *Betty*
v. *Moore* and *Wilson* v. *Cockrill*[2]) the same has been held
when the first gift does not purport to be for life, but to be of
an absolute interest, and the gift over must therefore be, of
course, executory.[3]

§ **96.** It being the generally accepted doctrine that a parol
gift of a chattel personal can be effected only by delivery,[1] it
has often been held that a parol gift to take effect on the
death of the donor is bad.[2]   The reason does not apply when
a parol gift of a chattel personal to A. for life, with a limitation on A.'s death to B., is accompanied by a delivery of the
chattel to A.; but it has nevertheless been held in *Kirkpatrick*
v. *Davidson*[3] and *Deer* v. *Devin*[4] that such a future limitation
on a parol gift is void.[5]   But in *Brummet* v. *Barber*,[6] a future
limitation on a gift, with delivery, of a chattel, evidenced by
a writing not under seal, was held good; and this seems the
sounder view; and in *Knight* v. *Donahoo*,[7] a parol gift, with
delivery, of a chattel for life and remainder was held good for
both the life interest and the interest in remainder.[8]

§ **97.** We have seen[1] that it has sometimes been held that

§ **95.** [1] See § 86.1, ante.

[2] See these cases stated, § 91, note 2, ante. See also Young v. Young, 80 N. Y. 422, 440; Welsch v. Belleville Bank, 94 Ill. 191, 205; Bunch v. Nicks, 50 Ark. 367, 376, 7 S. W. 563, 566. Cf. App. F, §§ 846, 847, post.

[3] See § 90, ante.

§ **96.** [1] See § 77, ante.

[2] Young v. Young, 80 N. Y. 422. Pitts v. Mangum, 2 Bail. 588. M'Ginney v. Wallace, Riley 290. Jaggers v. Estes, 2 Strob. Eq. 343, 378, 397. Bennett v. Cook, 28 So. Car. 353, 6 S. E. 28. Payne v. Lassiter, 10 Yerg. 507. Williams v. Thornton, 160 Tenn. 229, 22 S. W. 2d 1040.

[3] 2 Ga. 299.   See Maxwell v. Harrison, 8 Ga. 61, 67; Yarborough v. West, 10 Ga. 471.

[4] 1 Humph. 66.

[5] And see to the same effect Fitzhugh v. Anderson, 2 Hen. & M. 289, 302; London v. Turner, 11 Leigh 403, 412; Hallum v. Yourie, 1 Sneed 369; Mowry v. Thompson, 189 Minn. 479, 250 N. W. 52.

[6] 2 Hill 543, 549 (So. Car.).

[7] 3 B. Monr. 277. Cf. Betty v. Moore, 1 Dana 235.   And see Durfee v. Meadowcroft, 193 Mass. 267, 79 N. E. 268.

[8] And see further 2 Simes, Fut. Int., § 298.

§ **97.** [1] See § 90.1, ante.

on a bequest for life of a chattel personal with no gift over, there was no reversionary interest; but also that the better-supported doctrine seems to be that a reversionary interest is as valid as an executory bequest. So it has been held that on a gift *inter vivos* of a personal chattel to A., an executory limitation over to the donor is good.[2]

## III. SUMMARY

§ 98. **Rule against Perpetuities Only Restraint on Creation of Future Interests.** The result of the investigation pursued in the present chapter is this: Originally the creation of future interests at law was greatly restricted, but now, either by the Statutes of Uses and of Wills, or by modern legislation, or by the gradual action of the courts, all restraints on the creation of future interests, except those arising from remoteness, have been done away.[1] This is true in the United States, save in North Carolina. In England and North Carolina it is true, with the exception that legal future interests in personalty cannot be there created *inter vivos*. This practically reduces the law restricting the creation of future interests to the Rule against Perpetuities.

[2] Higgenbotham v. Rucker, 2 Call 313. Johnson v. Johnson, 104 Ky. 714, 47 S. W. 883. See Betty v. Moore, 1 Dana 235, 237; Wilson v. Cockrill, 8 Mo. 1, 7; § 91, note 2, ante. Cf. the common case of a chattel mortgage, observed upon in Hill v. Hill, Dudl. Eq. 71, 76.

§ 98. [1] See Glover v. Condell, 163 Ill. 566, 592, 45 N. E. 173, 181; and § 68.1, ante.

## CHAPTER III

## VESTED AND CONTINGENT INTERESTS

**§ 99. Importance of Distinction.** Thus far has been considered what future interests in property can be created. Before discussing the application of the Rule against Perpetuities to them, a distinction should be pointed out between vested and contingent interests. To do so is the object of this chapter. The distinction is of great importance as concerns the Rule against Perpetuities, for a true[1] vested interest is never obnoxious to the Rule, while a contingent interest not only may be, but often is. The vesting of interests in real and in personal estate will be considered separately.

### I. REAL ESTATE

**§ 100. Remainders.** Originally the word *vestire* meant to put in possession of land; to deliver the seisin.[1] When, instead of granting the fee to one person, a particular estate was given to one and the remainder to another, the remainder-man was vested with a portion of the fee. Mr. Hawkins seems quite correct in saying that the word "vested" had originally no reference to the absence of contingency. A remainder was said to be vested, because the remainder-man had a portion of the fee of which livery of seisin had been made.[2] Indeed,

§ 99. [1] See §§ 110.1, 205.2, post.

§ 100. [1] Du Cange, sub. voc. 2 P. & M. Hist. Eng. Law (2d ed.) 32, 85.

[2] Hawkins, Wills (3d ed.) 263. Cf. Carney v. Kain, 40 W. Va. 758, 822, 23 S. E. 650, 661. See § 972, post.

In the common law freehold interests in land by way of remainder or reversion are called estates. This is a peculiarly English conception. In other systems of law such interests take effect by way of substitution. Markby, Elements of Law, §§ 330, 331. 2 Holdsworth, Hist. Eng. Law, (3d ed.) 350. 13 Jour. Comp. Leg. (2D S.) 47. 16 Jour. Comp. Leg. (3D S.) 18. §§ 757, 762, 768, 971, post. They are analogous to shifting uses and executory devises in the English law.

Freehold estates could be created only by livery of seisin, therefore freehold estates could not be created in futuro, but a continuous ownership of land

at first there seem to have been no contingent remainders.[3]

§ 101. **Vested and Contingent Remainders.** Since contingent remainders have been recognized, the line between them and vested remainders is drawn as follows: A remainder is vested in A., when, throughout its continuance, A., or A. and his heirs, have the right to the immediate possession, whenever and however the preceding freehold estates may determine.[1] A remainder is contingent if, in order for it to come into possession, the fulfilment of some condition precedent other than the determination of the preceding freehold estates is necessary.[2]

might be cut up into a particular estate and remainder, and by giving livery of seisin to the first tenant, the estates in remainder were created. Lit., § 721. Co. Lit. 49 a, 143 a. But the ownership must be continuous. Challis, Real Prop. (3d ed.) 104. In a vested remainder "the gift is immediate; but the enjoyment must necessarily depend on the determination of the estates of those who have a prior right to the possession." Wms. Real Prop. (24th ed.) 412. According to the common law, only vested interests were called estates; contingent remainders were only possibilities of estates. See 7 Holdsworth, Hist. Eng. Law (3d ed.) 101–102; Challis, Real Prop. (3d ed.) 76. But in recent usage the term estates is often employed to include contingent remainders and other contingent interests.

On the idea of remainders in the earliest times see 2 P. & M. Hist. Eng. Law (2d ed.) 21; Professor Maitland in 6 Law Quart. Rev. 25, 26.

3 Wms. Real Prop. (24th ed.) 425. 3 Holdsworth, Hist. Eng. Law (3d ed.) 104, 134, 137. Scrutton, Land in Fetters 115. 3 Enc. Laws of Eng. (2d ed.) 515. 62 Sol. J. 485. See § 134, post.

§ 101. 1 See Johnson v. Edmond, 65 Conn. 492, 499, 33 Atl. 503, 505; Starnes v. Hill, 112 No. Car. 1, 9, 16 S. E. 1011; Storrs v. Burgess, 29 R. I. 269, 273, 67 Atl. 731, 732; §§ 8–10, ante. As to whether a postponement of possession, imposed on the owner of an equitable interest, when the postponement is not for the benefit of any person other than the equitable owner, prevents the vesting of the interest for the purposes of the Rule against Perpetuities, see §§ 120, 121 note, post.

2 Professor Kales has considered the nature of vested and contingent remainders in his treatise on Future Interests in Illinois, §§ 68–113 (second edition, entitled Estates in Illinois, §§ 27–29, 307–368) and in the following articles: 22 Law Quart. Rev. 250, 383; 24 Law Quart. Rev. 301; 20 Harv. Law Rev. 192; 8 Columbia Law Rev. 245; 3 Ill. Law Rev. 373, 379; 5 Ill. Law Rev. 381,

§ **102.** A remainder is none the less vested because it may terminate before the remainder-man comes into possession; thus if land be given to A. for life, remainder to B. for life, B. may die before A., yet the remainder is vested, for during its continuance, namely, the life of B., it is ready to come into possession whenever and however A.'s estate determines. This result is not affected by the fact that the termination of the remainder is contingent; that is, that it is subject to a condition subsequent. For instance, if land is devised to A. for life, remainder to B. and his heirs, but if B. dies unmarried then to C. and his heirs, B.'s remainder is vested, although it is possible that he may die unmarried in A.'s lifetime.

§ **103.** The law favors the vesting of estates, and therefore prefers to construe conditions as subsequent rather than pre-

386; 8 Ill. Law Rev. 225; 28 Yale L. J. 656. See comments on Professor Kales's views in 5 Mich. Law Rev. 497; 20 Harv. Law Rev. 243; 15 Columbia Law Rev. 680, 686.

In several passages (e. g. Estates, § 309), Professor Kales states as essential characteristics of contingent remainders that they are destructible and inalienable. Two remarks suggest themselves: First. Contingent remainders are often said to be destructible, but the expression is not strictly accurate. If a contingent remainder-man fails to come into possession, it is not because his estate is destroyed, but because he has never had an estate, only the potentiality of an estate. When a remainder is said to be destructible, what is meant is that it needs a particular estate to support it, and that this estate is destructible. To call the remainder destructible avoids an inconvenient periphrasis, and the use of the word with this meaning is so common, that it would be pedantic not to employ it. But to use the word when distinguishing vested from contingent remainders tends to bring about that confusion of conditions precedent and conditions subsequent which has been such a fruitful source of error, and had therefore best be avoided. And see § 286, post. Second. A contingent remainder is at common law inalienable; a vested remainder is not. But this incident, which is common to all interests on conditions precedent, does not affect the question whether a remainder is vested or contingent. In most jurisdictions contingent remainders have become alienable (Amer. Law Inst. Restatement, Property, § 162), but that does not prevent their continuing to be contingent remainders.

cedent;[1] so that when a condition attached to a remainder
might take effect after it had come into possession, the condition will be deemed subsequent and the remainder vested,
although the contingency may happen before the end of the
particular estate, and so the remainder may never come into
possession, as in the case put in the preceding section.

§ 104. **Disputed Case.** One class of cases, however, presents some difficulty, that, namely, in which the contingency,
if it happens at all, must happen at or before the termination
of the particular estate, and the coming into possession of the
remainder. Suppose, for instance, a gift to A. for life, remainder to B. and his heirs, but if B. dies before the termination of the particular estate, then to C. and his heirs. Here,
if the condition ever affects B.'s estate at all, it will prevent it

§ 103. [1] See Duffield v. Duffield,
1 Dow & Cl. 268, 311. This rule,
like all rules of construction, has
at the present time less influence
with the courts than it once had.
See Crapo v. Price, 190 Mass. 317,
319, 320, 76 N. E. 1043, 1044.
As to whether the courts have
not gone too far in disregarding
rules of construction, cf. Gray,
Nature and Sources of the Law,
§ 700, (2d ed.), pp. 173–176; 51
Harv. Law Rev. 254, 307, 308.

Estates are construed as vested, not only by holding a condition subsequent rather than precedent, but often also by holding
that there is no condition at all.
Thus a devise to a widow for life
if she did not marry again, but if
she did, then to A., was held to
give an estate to the widow till
she married or died, and a vested
remainder to A. Luxford v.
Cheeke, 3 Lev. 125. Kern v. Kern,
293 Ill. 238, 127 N. E. 396. So
in the case, which is of daily occurrence in practice, where an
estate is given to A. for life, and
on his death to B., the remainder
to B. is vested, and B. will take
although the particular estate
should determine before A.'s
death, by forfeiture or otherwise.
Doe d. Poor v. Considine, 6 Wall.
458, 18 L. E. 869, and cases cited.
Wms. Real Prop. (24th ed.) 411. 1
Simes, Fut. Int., § 74. The decisions
to the contrary in New Hampshire,
Hall v. Nute, 38 N. H. 422, and
Hayes v. Tabor, 41 N. H. 521,
were inexplicable aberrations of
an able and learned but eccentric
court. They were without any
precedent, see 6 Albany L. J.
361; and they have now been
overruled in New Hampshire.
Kennard v. Kennard, 63 N. H.
303. Wiggin v. Perkins, 64 N. H.
36, 5 Atl. 904. Parker v. Ross, 69
N. H. 213, 45 Atl. 576. Cf. Bates
v. Gillett, 132 Ill. 287, 24 N. E.
611. But see Starnes v. Hill, 112
No. Car. 1, 16 S. E. 1011; Richardson v. Richardson, 152 No.
Car. 705, 68 S. E. 217.

from coming into possession; it will never divest it after it has once come into possession. Remainders subject to conditions of this sort might have been regarded in three ways.

§ 105. (1) If the law looked on vested and contingent interests with an impartial eye, it would seem that such remainders should be held contingent. A condition which may prevent an estate's coming into possession, but which can never divest it after it has come into possession, is a condition in its nature precedent rather than subsequent. But the preference of the law for vested interests has prevented this view's being adopted.[1]

§ 106. "New York Rule." (2) Such a condition might be regarded in all cases as a condition subsequent, the circumstance that the contingency must happen, if at all, at or before the end of the particular estate being regarded as immaterial. The effect of this construction would be to make a remainder vested at any time, if there was, at that time, a person ready and entitled to take possession as remainderman, should the particular estate then determine, although, should the particular estate determine at some other time, such person might not be entitled to the remainder. Upon this theory, if there was a devise to A. for life, remainder to his surviving children, the remainder would be at any particular moment vested in the children who would survive A. should he at that moment die.

§ 107. The New York Revised Statutes seem to have defined a vested remainder in this sense: "Future estates are either vested or contingent. They are vested, when there is a person in being, who would have an immediate right to the possession of the lands upon the ceasing of the intermediate or precedent estate. They are contingent, whilst the person to whom, or the event upon which, they are limited to take effect remains uncertain."[1] It is doubtful whether this piece

§ 105. [1] Cf. 5 Mich. Law Rev. 507.

§ 107. [1] N. Y. Rev. Sts., pt. 2, c. 1, tit. 2, § 13. The phraseology of the Statute was altered by Laws of 1896, c. 547, § 30, and now reads: "A future estate is either vested or contingent. It is vested when there is a person in being, who would have an im-

of legislative definition was intended to change the common
law;[2] but the courts have decided, and it would seem correct-

mediate right to the possession
of the property, on the determination of all the intermediate
or precedent estates. It is contingent while the person to whom
or the event on which it is limited to take effect remains uncertain." N. Y. Real Prop. Law,
§ 40.

[2] Chancellor Kent says this
definition "appears to be accurately and fully expressed." 4
Kent, Com. 202. On Chancellor
Kent's authority the Supreme
Court of Alabama said that if a
devise is made to a woman for
life, and on her death to her
children then living, the children
take a vested remainder; but the
decision would, it seems, have
been the same had the remainder
been held contingent. Kumpe v.
Coons, 63 Ala. 448. See Gindrat
v. Western R., 96 Ala. 162, 11 So.
372. But in Smaw v. Young, 109
Ala. 528, 20 So. 370, the Court
acknowledged that in Kumpe v.
Coons they had been misled by
Chancellor Kent, and that the decision could not be sustained on
principle, although a majority of
the Court thought it must be followed as having settled a rule of
property. But the common-law
definition of a contingent remainder has now been restored by Ala.
Code of 1928, § 6905. See Lyons
v. Bradley, 168 Ala. 505, 513, 53
So. 244, 247. The Supreme Court
of New Hampshire adopted view
(2), which is stated in § 106,
ante, in Cole v. Society, 64 N. H.
445, 457, 458, 14 Atl. 73, 75, 76;

but see Hayward v. Spaulding, 75
N. H. 92, 71 Atl. 219; Dana v.
Sanborn, 70 N. H. 152, 46 Atl.
1053. See also Kennard v. Kennard, 81 N. H. 509, 129 Atl. 725.
So the Supreme Court of Vermont in Wheeler v. St. Johnsbury, 87 Vt. 46, 87 Atl. 349; and
the Supreme Court of Indiana in
Wood v. Robertson, 113 Ind. 323,
15 N. E. 457; but the latter case
is not followed in Indiana on this
point, see Hackleman v. Hackleman, 146 N. E. 590, petition for
rehearing denied, 169 N. E. 539.
The Supreme Court of Illinois
adopted definition (2) in some
cases (see Kales, Fut. Int. in
Ill., §§ 94–113, and Estates,
§§ 357–368), but these cases have
been overruled by Golladay v.
Knock, 235 Ill. 412, 85 N. E. 649;
see, however, Mettler v. Warner,
243 Ill. 600, 90 N. E. 1099. See also
35 Ill. Law Rev. 241. Chancellor
Kent was also followed into the
same error by Mr. Justice Swayne
in Croxall v. Shererd, 5 Wall. 268,
288, 18 L. E. 572, a case in which
land is said to have been "settled
in apparently some sort of tail;"
but where a contrary ruling would
not have affected the decision (p.
290). This definition (2) was approved in Iowa, Archer v. Jacobs,
125 Iowa 467, 475, 101 N. W.
195, 197; Shafer v. Tereso, 133
Iowa 342, 110 N. W. 846; but
these cases have been expressly
overruled on this point, and the
New York rule not followed, in
Birdsall v. Birdsall, 157 Iowa 363,
132 N. W. 809; and see Fulton v.

ly, that it has done so.³   And it is conceived that the adoption
of this view necessitates the decisions of the Court of Appeals,
which at first appear rather startling, that since the abolition
of the Rule in *Shelley's Case* a remainder to heirs, after a
life estate to the ancestor, is vested.⁴

Fulton, 179 Iowa 948, 162 N. W.
253; 10 Iowa Law Bull. 89, 96.
Cf. however, Flanagan v. Spalti,
225 Iowa 1231, 282 N. W. 347.
Cf. Re Haslett, 116 Fed. 680;
Starnes v. Hill, 112 No. Car. 1, 12,
13, 16 S. E. 1011, 1014; Forsythe
v. Lansing, 109 Ky. 518, 59 S. W.
854.   The case of Farnam v.
Farnam, 53 Conn. 261, 2 Atl. 325,
would seem, at first view, to have
been decided on this theory; but
in a later case in the same volume, Andrews v. Rice, 53 Conn.
566, 5 Atl. 823, there was a gift
by will to trustees in trust to pay
the income to the testator's daughter for life, and on her death to
divide the principal into as many
equal shares as the testator
might have grandchildren or
their issue then living, the issue
of any deceased grandchild to be
counted as one share, and the testator gave a share to each of said
grandchildren, and a share to the
issue then surviving of each deceased grandchild, and it was held
that the grandchildren had a contingent interest.   The decision in
Farnam v. Farnam must therefore be considered as turning upon the special terms of the will
in that case.   See White v.
Smith, 87 Conn. 663, 89 Atl. 272.

³ See Lawrence v. Bayard, 7
Paige 70; Coster v. Lorillard, 14
Wend. 265, 301, 302; Mead v.
Mitchell, 17 N. Y. 210, 213; Con-

nelly v. O'Brien, 166 N. Y. 406, 60
N. E. 20; Stringer v. Young, 191
N. Y. 157, 83 N. E. 690; Trowbridge v. Coss, 126 N. Y. A. D.
679, 110 N. Y. S. 1108, 195 N. Y.
596, 89 N. E. 1114; Doscher v.
Wyckoff, 132 N. Y. A. D. 139, 116
N. Y. S. 389; Matter of Watson,
262 N. Y. 284, 186 N. E. 787.

⁴ Sheridan v. House, 4 Keyes
569, 4 Abb. Ct. Ap. 218.   Moore
v. Littel, 41 N. Y. 66, reversing
40 Barb. 488. House v. Jackson,
50 N. Y. 161.   See also Rome
Bank v. Eames, 4 Abb. Ct. Ap.
83, 98; Chism v. Keith, 1 Hun
589; Drake v. Lawrence, 19 Hun
112; Matter of Brown, 29 Hun
412; Lockman v. Reilley, Id. 434;
Ramsay v. De Remer, 65 Hun
212, 20 N. Y. S. 143; Doctor v.
Hughes, 225 N. Y. 305, 310, 122
N. E. 221; Estate of Barnes, 155
Misc. 320, 279 N. Y. S. 117; Re
Bolton's Will, 257 N. Y. A. D.
760, 15 N. Y. S. 2d 696. But see
Hennessy v. Patterson, 85 N. Y.
91, 104; Carmichael v. Carmichael, 4 Keyes 346, 1 Abb. Ct.
Ap. 309; and 6 Albany L. J. 361.
Cf. Purdy v. Hayt, 92 N. Y. 446,
454, 456; Hall v. La France
Engine Co., 158 N. Y. 570, 53 N.
E. 513; Richards v. Hartshorne,
110 N. Y. A. D. 650, 97 N. Y. S.
754; Matter of Wilcox, 194 N. Y.
288, 87 N. E. 497; Clowe v.
Seavey, 208 N. Y. 496, 502, 102
N. E. 521, 523.   Mr. Stewart

**§ 108. Common Law Rule.** (3) Neither of these views is that of the common law. Whether a remainder is vested or contingent depends upon the language employed. If the conditional element is incorporated into the description of, or into the gift to, the remainder-man, then the remainder is contingent; but if, after words giving a vested interest, a clause is added divesting it, the remainder is vested. Thus on a devise to A. for life, remainder to his children, but if any child dies in the lifetime of A. his share to go to those who survive, the share of each child is vested, subject to be divested by its death.[1] But on a devise to A. for life, remain-

Chaplin, in his treatise on Suspension of Alienation (3d ed.), §§ 570–582, argues against the view that the Revised Statutes changed the common law on vesting; but see Fowler, Real Prop. Law of N. Y. (3d ed.) 242–248; Walsh, Law of Prop. (2d ed.), § 247; Walsh, Fut. Estates in N. Y. 29–37; 1 Simes, Fut. Int., §§ 83–92; Professor Fraser in 4 Minn. Law Rev. 307, 323; and cf. also 6 Columbia L. T. 96; 1 Columbia Law Rev. 279; 9 Columbia Law Rev. 587, 687; 19 Corn. L. Q. 112; 8 Fordham Law Rev. 166. The New York Statute has been copied in Minnesota, Mason's Gen. St., § 8043; see Ashbaugh v. Wright, 152 Minn. 57, 188 N. W. 157. In Michigan, 3 Comp. Laws (1929), § 12933; see Porter v. Osmun, 135 Mich 361, 98 N. W. 859; Lowry v. Lyle, 226 Mich. 676, 684, 198 N. W. 245, 247. And in Wisconsin, St. (1933), § 230.13; see Scott v. West, 63 Wis. 529, 24 N. W. 161; Re Moran's Will, 118 Wis. 177, 96 N. W. 367 (in which last case the distinction between the statutory definition and the common-

law conception of a contingent remainder is pointed out); and McMichael v. Peterman, 140 Wis. 589, 123 N. W. 262. Cf. Los Angeles County v. Winans, 13 Cal. Ap. 234, 109 Pac. 640.

Cf. also Den d. Hopper v. Demarest, 1 Zabr. 525; 2 Zabr. 599, under a statute, construing a remainder to heirs after a life estate to A. as a remainder to A.'s children; Croxall v. Shererd, 5 Wall. 268, 288, 18 L. E. 572; Fields v. Lewis, 118 Ga. 573, 45 S. E. 437; Kales, Fut. Int. in Ill., §§ 271–273, and Kales, Estates, §§ 410–411; 1 Ill. Law Rev. 323.

**§ 108.** [1] Littlejohns v. Household, 21 Beav. 29. Thaw v. Ritchie, 136 U. S. 519, 546, 10 S. Ct. 1037, 34 L. E. 531. Parker v. Ross, 69 N. H. 213, 45 Atl. 576. Blanchard v. Blanchard, 1 Allen 223. Lenz v. Prescott, 144 Mass. 505, 11 N. E. 923. (See Gibbens v. Gibbens, 140 Mass. 102, 3 N. E. 1.) Carpenter v. Perkins, 83 Conn. 11, 74 Atl. 1062. Re Rogers' Trust Estate, 97 Md. 674, 55 Atl. 679. Walker v. Alverson, 87 So. Car. 55, 68 S. E. 966. Jeefers v. Lampson, 10 Ohio St. 101. Moores

der to such of his children as survive him, the remainder is contingent.[2]

v. Hare, 144 Ind. 573, 43 N. E. 870. (See Wood v. Robertson, 113 Ind. 323, 15 N. E. 457.) Ducker v. Burnham, 146 Ill. 9, 34 N. E. 558. Hinrichsen v. Hinrichsen, 172 Ill. 462, 50 N. E. 135. Mettler v. Warner, 243 Ill. 600, 90 N. E. 1099. Lachenmyer v. Gehlbach, 266 Ill. 11, 107 N. E. 202. Strickland v. Strickland, 271 Ill. 614, 111 N. E. 592. Corson v. Thornburn, 323 Ill. 338, 154 N. E. 144. Nicol v. Morton, 332 Ill. 533, 164 N. E. 5. Danz v. Danz, 373 Ill. 482, 26 N. E. 2d 872. L'Etourneau v. Henquenet, 89 Mich. 428, 50 N. W. 1077. Callison v. Morris, 123 Iowa 297, 98 N. W. 780. (But see Saunders v. Wilson, 207 Iowa 526, 220 N. W. 344, and 14 Iowa Law Rev. 80.) Mercantile Bank v. Ballard, 83 Ky. 481. Forsythe v. Lansing, 109 Ky. 518, 59 S. W. 854. Caples v. Ward, 107 Tex. 341, 179 S. W. 856. See Den d. Hopper v. Demarest, 1 Zabr. 525, 2 Zabr. 599; Clark v. Cox, 115 No. Car. 93, 20 S. E. 176.

[2] Doe d. Planner v. Scudamore, 2 B. & P. 289. Whitby v. Von Luedecke, [1906] 1 Ch. 783. Re Samuda's Trusts, [1924] 1 Ch. 61. Re Ramadge's Settlement, [1919] 1 Ir. R. 205. Robinson v. Palmer, 90 Me. 246, 38 Atl. 103. (See Spear v. Fogg, 87 Me. 132, 32 Atl. 791.) Olney v. Hull, 21 Pick. 311. Nash v. Nash, 12 Allen 345. Thomson v. Ludington, 104 Mass. 193. Brown v. Williams, 5 R. I. 309. Alverson v. Randall, 13 R. I. 71. R. I.

Hosp. Trust Co. v. Harris, 20 R. I. 408, 39 Atl. 750. Andrews v. Rice, 53 Conn. 566, 5 Atl. 823. Van Tilburgh v. Hollinshead, 1 McCart. 32. Delbert's Appeal, 83 Pa. 462. List v. Rodney, Id. 483. Mergenthaler's Appeal, 15 W. N. C. (Pa.) 441. Coggins' Appeal, 124 Pa. 10, 16 Atl. 579. Craige's Appeal, 126 Pa. 223, 17 Atl. 585. Raleigh's Estate, 206 Pa. 451, 55 Atl. 1119. Vashon v. Vashon, 98 Va. 170, 35 S. E. 457. Howbert v. Cawthorn, 100 Va. 649, 42 S. E. 683. Allison v. Allison, 101 Va. 537, 44 S. E. 904. Whitesides v. Cooper, 115 No. Car. 570, 20 S. E. 295. (See Bowen v. Hackney, 136 No. Car. 187, 200, 48 S. E. 633, 997.) Faber v. Police, 10 So. Car. 376. McElwee v. Wheeler, Id. 392. Bouknight v. Brown, 16 So. Car. 155. Stephens v. Evans, 30 Ind. 39. Golladay v. Knock, 235 Ill. 412, 85 N. E. 649 (see § 107, note 2, ante). Smith v. Chester, 272 Ill. 428, 112 N. E. 325. Ryan v. Beshk, 339 Ill. 45, 170 N. E. 699. Johnson v. Jacob, 11 Bush 646. Emison v. Whittlesey, 55 Mo. 254. De Lasses v. Gatewood, 71 Mo. 371. Buxton v. Kroeger, 219 Mo. 224, 117 S. W. 1147. Los Angeles County v. Winans, 13 Cal. Ap. 234, 109 Pac. 640. Hall v. Wright, 17 Cal. Ap. 502, 120 Pac. 429. D'Abbadie v. Bizoin, Ir. R. 5 Eq. 205, 210. 4 Kent, Com. (12th ed.) 203, note 1. Wms. Real Prop. (24th ed.) 428. Cf. Sulley v. Barber, 59 L. T. R. 824. See also Amer. Law Inst. Restate-

**§ 109.** There are three kinds of vested remainders which call for a word of special mention: (1) Remainders to a class. (2) Remainders after estates tail. (3) Remainders in default of appointment.

**§ 110. (1) Remainders to a Class.**[1] Sometimes a remain-

ment, Property, §§ 249, 250, 253.

Mr. Williams's definition of a vested remainder is an estate which "is always ready, from its commencement to its end, to come into possession the moment the prior estates, be they what they may, happen to determine." Real Prop. (24th ed.) 412. Judge Holmes, in his note to Kent's Commentaries, loc. cit., criticises this definition of Mr. Williams as if it were equivalent to that contained in the New York Revised Statutes, and common in textbooks, which declares, in substance, that a remainder is vested at any moment, if at that moment there is a remainder-man ready to take possession should the particular estate then determine, although, should that estate determine at another time, some other remainder-man might be entitled to the same remainder. Judge Holmes shows clearly the unsoundness of this definition. But is this Mr. Williams's definition? His meaning would rather seem to be the correct one, that a remainder is vested in a man if he is ready and entitled during the continuance of the remainder to take the land whenever and however the preceding estate determines.

The ambiguity and error in the definition of vested remainders have arisen in part from considering them abstracted from the persons to whom they belong. A vested remainder is, ex vi termini, vested in somebody, and if the subject is approached from the side of the remainder-man, some of the difficulty disappears.

In the simple typical cases given in the text it is easy to apply the rule of the common law, but as the vesting or contingency of a limitation depends upon the language employed, the determination whether it is vested or contingent is a matter, often a difficult matter, of construction; but as such it has no place in this treatise, which does not profess to deal with questions of construction. The fullest statement of the English cases is in 2 Jarm. Wills (7th ed.) 1325 et seq. See also Theob. Wills (9th ed.) 509 et seq., and Hawkins, Wills (3d ed.) 265–288. In 1 Tiffany, Real Prop. (2d ed.), §§ 137–139, 168–171, (3d ed.), §§ 137–139, there is an excellent statement of the law and an accurate citation of many American cases in point.

**§ 110.** [1] A class is a number of persons having a common characteristic. By a gift to a class is meant a gift to persons, the share of each of whom is deter-

der is given to a class of persons, e. g. to children, the number
of members in which may be increased between the time of
creating the remainder and the termination of the particular
estate; for instance, on a devise to A. for life, remainder to
the children of A. and their hèirs as tenants in common.
Here, although it is certain that each child born, or its heirs,
will have a share in the estate, that share will be diminished
by the birth of every other child of A. Each child, nevertheless, on its birth is said to have a vested remainder. The
remainder is said to "open" and let in the after-born children.[2] So when the remainder is to an individual and a class,
as to A. and the children of B.[3]

§ 110.1. The placing of this class of remainders under the
head of vested remainders is to some extent artificial. Such
a remainder is vested, in so far as it is certain that whenever

mined by the number of the class
to which he belongs. § 369, note 1,
post.

[2] Doe d. Comberbach v. Perryn,
3 T. R. 484, 494, 495. Carver v.
Jackson, 4 Pet. 1, 90. Pingrey v.
Rulon, 246 Ill. 109, 92 N. E. 592.
Thomas v. Thomas, 247 Ill. 543,
93 N. E. 344. Archer v. Jacobs,
125 Iowa 467, 101 N. W. 195.
Smith v. Neill, 104 N. J. Eq. 339,
145 Atl. 537. Milner v. Gay, 145
Ga. 858, 90 S. E. 65. Strawback-
er v. Strawbacker, 132 Neb. 614,
27 N. W. 772. Fearne, C. R. 312–
314, Butler's note (e). 3 Jarm.
Wills (7th ed.) 1642. 1 Simes,
Fut. Int., § 76. Amer. Law Inst.
Restatement, Property, § 157,
Comments 1–n. See A. G. v.
Crispin, 1 Bro. C. C. 386; Devisme
v. Mello, Id. 537; Lee v. Lee, 1
Dr. & Sm. 85, 86; Baldwin v.
Rogers, 3 De G. M. & G. 649, 656,
657; Browne v. Hammond, H. R.
V. Johns. 210, 212, note (a); Mc-

Arthur v. Scott, 113 U. S. 340,
380, 5 S. Ct. 652, 28 L. E. 1015;
Minot v. Purrington, 190 Mass.
336, 77 N. E. 630; Boston S. D.
& Trust Co. v. Nevin, 212
Mass. 232, 237, 98 N. E. 1051,
1053; Richardson v. Warfield,
252 Mass. 518, 522, 148 N. E.
141, 143; Latta v. Lowry, 11
Ont. 517. Will of White, [1914]
Vict. 412. In Tennessee, by the
local law, which it is admitted is
contrary to the common law, a
remainder to a class does not
vest in the living members of the
class. Sanders v. Byrom, 112
Tenn. 472, 79 S. W. 1028. Jordan
v. Jordan, 145 Tenn. 378, 408, 239
S. W. 423, 431. This makes the
remainder contingent. But see
now Jennings v. Jennings, 165
Tenn. 295, 54 S. W. 2d 961; Tenn.
Code (1932), § 7598; 12 Tenn.
Law Rev. 115.

[3] See Cooke v. Bowen, 4 Y. &
C. 244.

[G. R. P.]

and however the preceding estate determines there will be one or more persons who will surely come into possession of the land, but in so far as it is not certain what the number of those persons will be, or in other words as the number and consequent size of the shares is contingent, the remainder cannot be truly said to be in all respects vested. The imperfect character of the vesting in this class of cases is brought out by the application of the Rule against Perpetuities. Interests which are truly and in all respects vested, never come within the Rule, but when there is a gift in remainder to a class which has become vested in a living pèrson, if the number of persons who will finally constitute the class may not be determined until a remote period, the remainder is void. For instance, suppose a devise to A. for life, remainder to his eldest son (unborn) for life, remainder to the grandchildren of B. B. is living and has had one grandchild, C., born to him. C. is said to have a vested remainder, but as the number of the grandchildren in whom the remainder is ultimately to vest in possession, and consequently the size of the shares, cannot be determined till too remote a period, the whole devise to the grandchildren is invalid as too remote. This is apparently an exception to the rule that vested interests are never too remote, but in truth remainders of this sort, although called vested, are not really so; at a certain point, and on the point which the Rule against Perpetuities touches, they are, in fact, contingent.[1]

§ 110.1. [1] See §§ 205.2, 205.3, post. The reason why a remainder to a class which might increase was called "vested" was undoubtedly, as suggested to the author by his learned friend, Roland R. Foulke, Esq., because "vested" had originally no reference to the absence of contingency, but only to seisin, and when there was a remainder-man in esse, the requirements of seisin were satisfied. When "vested" came to be opposed to "contingent," its application to a remainder to an increasable class was inappropriate. If we were making a new Rule against Perpetuities it might be well to disuse the term "vested" altogether and to substitute "not subject to a condition precedent;" but the usage is so fixed that it seems best not to depart from it, but to show that such a remainder, notwithstanding its name, is subject to the Rule against Perpetuities. See §§ 201, 205.2, post.

**§ 111. (2) Remainders after Estates Tail.** On the passage of the Statute *De Donis*[1] remainders after estates tail took effect whenever and however the particular estates determined, and were therefore vested. But in the course of time, when, by recoveries or fines, estates tail and the remainders dependent on them could be barred, a remainder after an estate tail was not only postponed until the failure of the issue of the tenant in tail, but also became dependent on the contingency of the tenant in tail not suffering a recovery or levying a fine. The remainder, however, is still deemed vested.[2] The barring of the estates by the tenant in tail is considered as in the nature of a condition subsequent divesting the whole series of estates, as well the particular estate tail as all the subsequent remainders.[3]

Sections 110 and 110.1, with the preceding portion of this note, have been left as written by the author in the third edition. Their language, however, seems to require some qualification. Remainders to a class, some members of which are in existence and have fulfilled the required conditions, are not merely called vested, but are treated as vested (though subject to be partially divested) for all purposes except the application of the Rule against Perpetuities. See, as to the indestructibility of such interests, Breckenbury v. Gifford, 2 Ch. D. 417; Abbiss v. Burney, 17 Ch. D. (C. A.) 211, 218, § 325, post; 51 Harv. Law Rev. 1329, 1333; as to alienability, Leach v. Stephens, 159 Ga. 193, 125 S. E. 192; as to acceleration, Jull v. Jacobs, 3 Ch. D. 703; Yeaton v. Roberts, 28 N. H. 459; 3 Simes, Fut. Int., § 759; and in general, Fearne, Cont. Rem. 239 (IV), 240; Amer. Law Inst. Restate-

ment, Property, § 157, Comments 1 and m. It seems, therefore, not so accurate to say that the law as to the application of the Rule against Perpetuities to such remainders shows that they are really contingent, as to say that such remainders are vested, but are treated for the purposes of the Rule against Perpetuities as if they were contingent. Professor Leach has argued powerfully that, on principle, remainders to a class should be treated as vested for the purposes of the Rule against Perpetuities also. See 51 Harv. Law Rev. 1329; and § 375, note 4, post.

§ 111. [1] St. Westm. II., 13 Edw. I., c. 1 (1285).

[2] § 447, post.

[3] Mr. Josiah W. Smith in his treatise on Executory Interests, § 192, says that a remainder after an estate tail is vested because a failure of issue "is considered certain to happen some time or other;" it is submitted that the

§ **112. (3) Remainders in Default of Appointment.** If in a settlement or will a power to appoint is given, and a remainder limited in default of appointment, the remainder is not rendered contingent by the fact that the execution of the power may destroy it.[1] When the remainder would be

reason given in the text is the sounder. Hawkins, Wills (3d ed.) 263.

§ 112. [1] Cunningham v. Moody, 1 Ves. Sr. 174, 177. Doe d. Willis v. Martin, 4 T. R. 39. Doe d. Tanner v. Dorvell, 5 T. R. 518. Woodman v. Woodman, 89 Me. 128, 35 Atl. 1037. Grosvenor v. Bowen, 15 R. I. 549, 10 Atl. 589. Bonnell v. Bonnell, 47 N. J. Eq. 540, 20 Atl. 895. Lantz v. Massie, 99 Va. 709, 40 S. E. 50. Williman v. Holmes, 4 Rich. Eq. 475. Heilman v. Heilman, 129 Ind. 59, 28 N. E. 310. Railsback v. Lovejoy, 116 Ill. 442, 6 N. E. 504. Ducker v. Burnham, 146 Ill. 9, 34 N. E. 558. Harvard College v. Balch, 171 Ill. 275, 49 N. E. 543. Kirkpatrick v. Kirkpatrick, 197 Ill. 144, 64 N. E. 267. Burke v. Burke, 259 Ill. 262, 102 N. E. 293. Rutherfurd v. Farrar, 118 S. W. 2d 79 (Mo. Ap.). Osbrey v. Bury, 1 Ball & B. 53. Heron v. Stokes, 2 Dr. & W. 89, 99, 100. Fearne, C. R. 226-232. Sugd. Pow. (8th ed.) 452, 453. Farwell, Pow. (3d ed.) 310. 1 Simes, Fut. Int., § 80. Amer. Law Inst. Restatement, Property, § 157, Comments p and r. Leonard Lovie's Case, 10 Co. 78 a, 85 a, contra, is overruled. See Walpole v. Conway, Barnard. Ch. 153, 157; Smith v. Camelford, 2 Ves. Jr. 698. Cf. §§ 258, 535, post. In Johnson v. Battelle, 125 Mass.

453, 454, a remainder after a power is said to be "contingent on its not becoming necessary to exercise that power," and in Taft v. Taft, 130 Mass. 461, 464, 465, where the life tenant had a power to appoint by deed or will it is said that "the gift of the remainder to the plaintiffs is contingent upon the event that some estate remains at the death of the defendant not disposed of by her will. They thus take contingent remainders." But these remarks were dicta entirely unnecessary to the decision of the cases; the attention of the Court apparently was not called to the question whether the remainders were vested or contingent; and it seems hardly likely that the Massachusetts court, if the point is presented for decision, will hold contrary to the whole course of modern authority.

In Minot v. Treasurer, 207 Mass. 588, 93 N. E. 973, a statute passed in 1909 declared that where the donee of a power omitted to exercise it, a disposition of property should be deemed to take place as though the persons becoming entitled to the possession of such property had succeeded thereto by a will of the donee taking effect at the time of such omission, and should be subject to a succession tax.

contingent in the absence of the power, of course the presence of the power does not render it vested.[2]

§ **112.1.** That the existence of a power does not make a remainder in default of appointment contingent seems to be settled law everywhere.[1]

§ **113. Reversions.** All reversions are vested interests. From their nature they are always ready to take effect in possession whenever and however the preceding estates determine.[1]

§ **113.1.** When a reversion is assigned, it continues to be a vested interest with the assignee. In this way must be explained the case of *Egerton* v. *Massey*.[1]    A testatrix devised

By a deed of 1844, N. had a life estate with power of appointment. N. died after the passage of the Statute, without exercising the power. It was held that the imposition of a succession tax on the property passing to the persons taking on default of appointment was not an unconstitutional violation of their vested rights. This refers to the vested rights mentioned in § 118, note 3, post, and has no reference to the question whether their interests were vested or contingent as those terms are used in the matter mentioned here. Cf. a similar case in Binney v. Commissioner, 293 Mass. 96, 199 N. E. 528, reversed on other grounds in 299 U. S. 280, 57 S. Ct. 206, 81 L. E. 239.

See Moore v. Weaver, 16 Gray 305; Welsh v. Woodbury, 144 Mass. 542, 545, 11 N. E. 762, 764; Dana v. Dana, 185 Mass. 156, 160, 70 N. E. 49, 51; Peabody v. Tyszkiewicz, 191 Mass. 317, 77 N. E. 839; Lawrence v. Beardsley, 74 Conn. 1, 49 Atl. 190. But cf. Spaan v. Anderson, 115 Iowa 121,

88 N. W. 200.

[2] See an article by the author, 25 Harv. Law Rev. 22 et seq., commenting on Woodcock v. Renneck, 4 Beav. 190, 1 Phil. 72, and Lambert v. Thwaites, L. R. 2 Eq. 151.

§ **112.1.** [1] See note 1 to § 112, ante. As an original question, this is very doubtful. but on the matter of remoteness, it is immaterial whether the remainder is vested or contingent. For assuming, as we do, that it would be vested in the absence of the power, it will either (1) if the power is not exercised, vest within the required limits, or (2) if the appointment under the power is in fee, it will be excluded altogether, or (3) if the appointments under the power are of estates less than a fee, it will vest subject to the estates well appointed.

§ **113.** [1] Where possibilities of reverter are allowed. as to which see §§ 31 et seq., ante, they are vested interests. (See § 113.3, post.)

§ **113.1.** [1] 3 C. B. N. S. 338. A similar point arose in Craig v.

land to A. for life, remainder to the children of A. and their
issue living at A.'s death, and in default of such issue to B.
in fee; and she gave the residue of her estate to A. A. conveyed all her estate in the land to J., and died without ever
having been married. It was held that, on the conveyance
to J., A.'s life estate merged in her residuary interest, and
that the contingent remainder to B. was destroyed. There
was here a life estate, and a contingent remainder with a
double aspect. If A. left issue at her death, the issue would
take; if she did not leave issue at her death, then B. would
take. Although these contingencies included every possibility, for A. must die either with or without leaving issue at
her death, yet until the fee vested either in the issue or in
B., it would, had there been no residuary gift, have remained
in the heir of the testatrix as a reversion.[2] This reversion
would have been destroyed by the condition subsequent of
A.'s dying leaving issue, and also by the condition subsequent of A.'s dying without leaving issue; but until the one
or the other of these conditions happened the reversion would
have remained a vested interest in the heir. Such would have
been the case had there been no gift of the residue. How did
such gift affect the question? Four different views have been
taken of such a case. (1) The gift of the fee contained in the
residue has most of the characteristics of a remainder. It is a
future estate, taking effect, if at all, at the termination of the
particular estate and created by the same instrument.[3] But

Warner, 5 Mackey 460; Bond v.
Moore, 236 Ill. 576, 86 N. E. 386;
Barr v. Gardner, 259 Ill. 256, 102
N. E. 287; Belding v. Parsons,
258 Ill. 422, 101 N. E. 570; Benson v. Tanner, 276 Ill. 594, 115
N. E. 191; Friedman v. Friedman,
283 Ill. 383, 119 N. E. 321; Cole
v. Cole, 292 Ill. 154, 126 N. E.
752; Fisher v. Easton, 299 Ill.
293, 132 N. E. 442; Archer v. Jacobs, 125 Iowa 467, 101 N. W.
195; Bennett v. Morris, 5 Rawle
9. See McCreary v. Coggeshall,
74 So. Car. 42, 53 S. E. 978; Gray
v. Shinn, 293 Ill. 573, 127 N. E.
755; Caraher v. Lloyd, 2 Com.
L. R. 480, 508 (Aust.); 4 Ill. Law
Rev. 355; Kales, Estates, §§ 95,
306; 1 Tiffany, Real Prop. (3d ed.),
§ 333; 34 Harv. Law Rev. 508,
515; 10 Iowa Law Bull. 89, 93;
29 Law Quart. Rev. 290, 296.

[2] See § 11, ante.

[3] It seems immaterial that the
residuary clause passes other
property. A gift of the residue
of the testator's real estate was

this residuary devise cannot be a vested remainder, for there
cannot be a vested remainder after a contingent remainder in
fee.[4]  (2) To obviate the difficulty in such a case of having a
vested remainder after contingent remainders in fee, Mr.
Preston suggested that such prior estates might be, not contingent remainders, but executory devises.[5]  *Egerton* v. *Massey*,
however, negatives such a theory, for these prior estates were
held in that case to have been destroyed, which could not have
happened had they been executory devises.  (3) Again, it
has been suggested that the interest of an heir after the
devise of a contingent fee will not pass by a devise, either
specific or residuary.[6]  But this, too, is negatived by *Egerton*
v. *Massey*.  (4) The true view would seem to be that although
a residuary devise is made by the same instrument which
creates a particular estate, it is not part of one gift with it,
and is therefore not a remainder.  The gift of a "residue"
implies that the former gift is completed.  If Stiles grants a
life estate to Doe, and afterwards conveys the residue of the
estate to Roe, Roe has a grant of a reversion, and not a remainder; and although in a will the residuary gift is contained in the same instrument as the particular devise, yet the
effect of the whole is to be regarded as the establishment of a
particular estate with a reversion, and an independent transfer of that reversion, so established, to the residuary devisee.[7]

specific, not only before the Wills
Act of 1837 (the will passed upon in Egerton v. Massey was
made in 1786), but is so even
since that act. Hensman v. Fry-
er, L. R. 3 Ch. 420. Lancefield v.
Iggulden, L. R. 10 Ch. 136. See
1 Prest. Est. 502; 2 Prest. Abs.
99.

4 Loddington v. Kime, 1 Salk.
224, 1 Ld. Raym. 203, 3 Lev. 431.
(See Doe d. Brown v. Holme, 3
Wils. 237, 240; Shaw v. Weigh, 2
Stra. 798, 804.) Doe d. Gilman v.
Elvey, 4 East 313. Fearne, C. R.
225. But see Hayes, Limit. 81 et

seq.; Leake, Law of Property in
Land (1st ed.) 338, note (d); 1
Tiffany, Real Prop. (3d ed.),
§ 333; 1 Simes, Fut. Int., §§ 55,
75; 29 Law Quart. Rev. 290, 296;
34 Harv. Law Rev. 508, 515. Notwithstanding the old cases, the
discussion seems to leave the
point open to doubt.

5 1 Prest. Est. 84, 502; and see
4 Jur., N. S., pt. 2, 108, 121, 133,
157; Kales, Estates, § 95.

6 9 Jur., pt. 2, 50.

7 See 9 Jur., pt. 2, 50, 52. Cf.
28 Am. Jur. 388.

It is noticeable that the judges in *Egerton* v. *Massey* always speak of the vested interest in which the life estate merged as a reversion and not as a remainder.[8]

§ **113.2.** When an estate is given on a condition, the condition is always both precedent and subsequent; it is precedent as to the estate which is given on the condition, it is subsequent as to the estate which now exists and will continue to exist if the condition is not fulfilled. The vesting of an estate is not affected by the fact that it may be divested by a condition subsequent. In *Egerton* v. *Massey,* as far as the condition affected the reversion it was not a condition precedent, but a condition subsequent, and, therefore, the case of *Egerton* v. *Massey* and the statement in § 113, *ante,* that all reversions are vested, is, it is submitted, correct. There cannot be a vested remainder after a contingent remainder in fee simple.[1] Why is it that after a contingent remainder in fee simple the reversion is vested, but a remainder is contingent? The reason is this. A remainder is created by the livery of seisin of the particular estate; if it is not ready to come into possession whenever and however the previous estates determine, it is a contingent remainder. A contingent remainder is, in truth, not an estate, but a possibility of an estate;[2] the second remainder's becoming an estate depends upon the condition precedent of the first contingent fee simple limited not vesting; while a reversion is independent of the ownership created by the livery, it is an actual estate, and, therefore, any condition affecting it is a condition which, as to it, is subsequent.[3]

§ **113.3. Possibilities of Reverter.** Where possibilities of

[8] See Johnson v. Edmond, 65 Conn. 492, 499, 33 Atl. 503, 505. But see also 34 Harv. Law Rev. 514, 517.

§ 113.2. [1] Loddington v. Kime, 1 Salk. 224, 1 Ld. Raym. 203, 3 Lev. 431. But see note 4 to preceding section.

[2] See § 100, note 2, ante; Chal-lis, Real Prop. (3d ed.) 76.

[3] See discussions of Egerton v. Massey in 1 Simes, Fut. Int., §§ 55, 75, and Amer. Law Inst. Restatement, Property, § 277, and the Appendix relating to that section in the tentative draft No. 9 of that Restatement, which cast much doubt on the status of the case in America.

reverter after determinable fees are allowed,[1] they are vested interests. In England, this is generally assumed to be the law.[2] In America, when the question of vesting has been expressly discussed, the possibility of reverter has been said to be vested.[3]

The American Law Institute, in its Restatement of the Law of Property, in § 154, on "Reversionary Interests," says that possibilities of reverter are not vested interests, and includes under the designation of "possibilities of reverter" various future interests other than possibilities of reverter following determinable fees. There seems to be something inconsistent in the notion of a reversion's being subject to a condition precedent. A reversion is a part of the grantor's old estate which is left in him. An interest subject to a condition precedent, on the other hand, is only a possibility of acquiring in the future a new estate.[4] The interests, other than those following determinable fees, which are called in the Restatement "possibilities of reverter," and are said not to be vested, can be construed either as conditions subsequent, or as vested reversions subject to be divested. Such interests, as well as possibilities of reverter after determinable fees, are, to be sure, contingent in the sense that they may never take effect.

§ 113.3. [1] As to this see §§ 31 et seq., ante.

[2] See Re Chardon, [1928] Ch. 464; 54 Law Quart. Rev. 258. None of the numerous criticisms of that case are founded on a contention that the ultimate reversionary interest was not vested. See § 87.1, ante.

[3] See Lougheed v. Dykeman Baptist Church, 40 N. Y. S. 586. The contrary is stated in Copenhaver v. Pendleton, 155 Va. 463, 155 S. E. 802. But in that case the only question discussed was as to the alienability of the future interest; and the Court confused possibilities of reverter with rights of entry for breach of condition subsequent (see pp. 478, 479). No question of remoteness was mentioned and the Court seems to assume that all possibilities of reverter are valid.

[4] See § 113.2 at end, ante. Nothing seems to turn on the use by the Institute of the term "Reversionary Interest." A possibility of reverter is a sort of reversion, as is recognized by Professor Powell in an article, 14 Ind. L. J. 397, discussing the Restatement, in which he says that a possibility of reverter is a "reversion subject to a condition precedent" (p. 414). Professor Powell took a principal part in framing the Restatement of the Law of Property.

But it does not follow they are subject to a condition precedent.[5]

The point that reversionary interests which may never
take effect might be subject to the Rule against Perpetuities,
has not been raised in any reported case, except the cases on
possibilities of reverter after determinable fees. Possibilities
of reverter after determinable fees (where allowed at
all) have always been treated as valid, irrespective of
the time when they may take effect.[6] It is true that the
American cases holding such interests good need not necessarily be based on the premise that a possibility of reverter
is a vested interest; yet they are most satisfactorily supported
on that ground. Moreover, it is not possible to eliminate any
reversionary interest, however it may be described, by the
application of the Rule against Perpetuities, inasmuch as the
Rule only applies to future interests and cannot affect
the duration of present interests in accordance with the
terms in which they are limited.[7] And it is hard to imagine
any question, other than that of their validity under the Rule
against Perpetuities, in which the point as to vesting of possibilities of reverter could be involved. There seems, therefore, to be no practical object in contending that such interests are other than vested, against the commonly received view.

§ 114. Other Future Interests in Real Estate. No other
future interests are vested. An interest to commence at a
future time certain, e. g. an executory devise to go into effect
ten years after the testator's death, is not usually called contingent; but neither is it vested. It is an executory limitation.[1] Thus: (1) Rights to enter for condition broken are

[5] Cf. §§ 108, 111, ante. To the
effect that all reversions are
vested, see remarks in 1 Simes,
Fut. Int., § 47; 54 Law Quart. Rev.
258, 264. Cf. §§ 11, note 1, 31,
ante.

[6] See § 312, post.

[7] See 2 Tiffany, Real Prop. (3d
ed.), § 404; and §§ 205, note 2,
312, post. The cases show that
there is no existing rule limiting

the duration of determinable fees.

§ 114. [1] Fearne, C. R. 1, Butler's note. Broadly speaking,
however, all executory interests
may be called contingent. See
§§ 201, note 2, 792–801 post. For
the purpose of the Rule against
Perpetuities, and indeed for most,
if not all, practical purposes, there
is no difference between executory interests that are contingent

not vested till breach of the condition. (2) Rights less than ownership in land of others to begin *in futuro* are not vested interests until they begin.[2] (3) Springing and shifting uses and (4) Executory devises are not vested interests until they take effect in possession or are turned into vested remainders.[3]

in a strict sense and those that are not so.

[2] Of course, after a right less than ownership has begun, there may be a vested future estate in it. See Challis, Real Prop. (3d ed.) 51, 327; Wms. Real Prop. (24th ed.) 514, 521, 527.

[3] An instance in which an executory devise is turned into a vested remainder would be the following: A devise to A. in fee, but if he dies unmarried, then to B. for life, and on B.'s death to C. in fee. Here B. and C. have both executory devises; but on A.'s death, unmarried, B.'s estate is turned into an estate in possession, and C.'s estate into a vested remainder. See Craig v. Stacey, Ir. Term R. 249; Storrs v. Burgess, 29 R. I. 269, 275, 67 Atl. 731, 733.

In the peculiar case of a limitation (not reversionary) following a fee simple conditional or determinable (see §§ 13, 14, ante), the limitation is regarded as contingent, although it is subject to no other condition than the occurrence of the event which operates to determine the previous estate. Such a limitation seems to be an exception to the general rule that interests not subject to any condition precedent or postponement, except the expiration of the previous estate, are vested. The anomalous character of such limitations is due to the doctrine (which must be regarded, under modern conditions at least, as purely artificial) that there can be no remainder after a conditional or determinable fee. See § 14, note 8, ante. If it were not for that doctrine, limitations of the sort in question would be treated as vested remainders. But as such limitations could not take effect as remainders, the courts, after the Statutes of Uses and Wills, allowed them to take effect as executory devises conditioned, in the eye of the law, not on the expiration of the preceding estate, but on the occurrence of a particular event, which happened also to operate to determine the preceding estate. See Gardner v. Sheldon, Vaughan 259, 270; Buist v. Dawes, 4 Rich. Eq. 421, 426. Such a limitation is apparently also an exception to the general rule that every executory limitation cuts short some preceding estate (see § 54, ante); but if the possibility of reverter after the determinable fee is vested, as is believed to be the case, then the executory limitation cuts short the possibility of reverter. See § 113.3, ante. Cf. § 11, note, ante. The distinction between a future interest which is regarded as a vested estate in the property, and a mere possibility of acquiring an estate at a future

**§ 115. Escheat.** An exception to the statement at the beginning of the preceding section is the right to take by escheat. If this is a right at all, and it would certainly seem to be, it is a vested right.[1]

**§ 115.1. Curtesy and Dower.** The estate of a wife in dower, or of a husband, after the birth of issue, in curtesy, cannot be called either vested or contingent interests. They are executory limitations.[1]

**§ 116. Equitable Interests.** There are, strictly speaking, no equitable reversions or remainders. The so-called reversions are resulting trusts, and a remainder implies the presence of seisin and tenure, which are conceptions foreign to equitable interests. But to determine whether equitable interests are vested, or contingent or executory limitations, the same principles are to be applied as with legal interests.[1]

## II. PERSONAL PROPERTY

**§ 117. Executory Interests.** After an absolute interest in personalty, just as after a fee simple in realty, every future limitation is executory and not vested; and as the only succession allowed in personalty is to executors or administrators, a gift to A. and his heirs, or to A. and the heirs of his body, or to A. simply, is taken to be an absolute gift to A. passing to his executors, and every limitation after such a gift is executory and not vested.[1]

---

time, is peculiar to the Common Law. In the Civil Law, all future interests take effect by substitution, cutting short the preceding estate, like executory limitations at the Common Law. §§ 100, note 2, ante, 205, note 2, post. And see Challis, Real Prop. (3d ed.) 74, 76; Wms. Real Prop. (24th ed.) 412.

§ 115. [1] See §§ 204, 205.1, post. The right of the Crown or State to personal property when the owner dies without next of kin is perhaps a right to succeed as ultimus heres, and not a new right. § 205.1, note 2, post.

§ 115.1. [1] See § 114, ante.

§ 116. [1] See 70 Sol. J. 423. The rule that a limitation which can be construed as a contingent remainder cannot be construed as an executory devise does not apply to equitable interests. See §§ 324, 325, post. On this rule see App. J, § 918 et seq., post.

§ 117. [1] See App. F, §§ 805, 835, post.

**§ 117.1. Interests after Terms.** An interest for years can
be created in a chattel, either real or personal, and therefore
when a limitation is ready to come into possession, whenever
and however such interest for years determines, that limitation is vested.

**§ 117.2. Interests after Gifts for Life.** The difficulty arises
when a chattel is given for life. Suppose a chattel personal,
for instance a picture, is given to A. for life and on his death
to B. Is the limitation to B. executory or vested? Marsden
in his treatise on the Rule against Perpetuities[1] says it is
"executory, and does not vest within the meaning of the Rule
against Perpetuities until A.'s death. . . . The result,
therefore, is that a future or executory limitation of personalty vests or takes effect within the meaning of the Rule when
it takes effect in possession." Unquestionably this is in accordance with the theory of the modern English conveyancers,
but the older and, it is submitted, the sounder view is that
A. has the use and occupation of the chattel only, and that B.
has a vested interest, being ready to come into possession,
whenever A.'s use and occupation is determined.[2] Whether
the one or the other theory is correct is tested by a gift of
a chattel to a living person, after a gift for life to an unborn
person. Suppose, for instance, a picture is given to A. for
life, on his death to his eldest son for life, and on the death of
such eldest son to B., a living person, and his executors, A.
at the time of the gift having no children. If the gift to B.
in this case is executory, it is too remote; if it is vested, then
it is good. All authority is in favor of its being good.[3]

§ 117.2. [1] Pp. 43, 44.
[2] See §§ 71–97, ante.
[3] Routledge v. Dorrill, 2 Ves.
Jr. 357, 362, 363, 366, 367. Evans
v. Walker, 3 Ch. D. 211. Re Roberts, 19 Ch. D. 520. Loring v.
Blake, 98 Mass. 253. Seaver v.
Fitzgerald, 141 Mass. 401, 6 N. E.
73. McAlister v. Eliot, 83 N. H.
225, 140 Atl. 708. Re Gageby's
Estate, 293 Pa. 109, 141 Atl. 842.

Salisbury v. Salisbury, 92 Kan.
644, 141 Pac. 173. See Re Samuda's Trusts, [1924] 1 Ch. 61, in
which gifts of personalty were
treated exactly like those of realty, with respect to vesting; and
also Crosby v. Crosby, 64 N. H.
77, 5 Atl. 907; Lennig's Estate,
31 W. N. C. (Pa.) 234, 236; 24
Law Quart. Rev. 431; 39 Yale
L. J. 771, 800; Uniform Law of

§ 117.3. There is more room for serious doubt in the case of chattels real. The theory always announced with regard to these is that bequests of life interests in them carry the whole interest, because a life estate is larger and therefore cannot be less than a term for years.[1] If this theory is carried out consistently, then every limitation of a term for years following a gift of the term for life is executory, and may be too remote, when a like limitation of realty would be vested and valid. But it seems likely that this piece of legal reasoning will be unable to bear the stress of application to an actual case.[2]

§ 118. Meanings of "Vested." The term "vested" has been hitherto considered as it is used in questions of remoteness; but it has also another meaning, which is so frequently given to it, that it cannot be styled improper. Such double meaning is, however, very unfortunate, as it has led to much confusion.[1] This other meaning of "vested" is "transmissible."

Property Act, § 3, Handbook of Commissioners on Uniform State Laws (1938) 260, 262; App. F, §§ 838–852, post.

The notion which at one time prevailed in Massachusetts that a different rule of construction was to be applied in determining whether a so-called remainder in personalty was vested, from that which was to be applied with regard to a remainder in real estate, was founded on a dictum in Dingley v. Dingley, 5 Mass. 535, 537. See Denny v. Allen, 1 Pick. 147; Emerson v. Cutler, 14 Pick. 108; Nash v. Cutler, 16 Pick. 491. It is now completely overthrown. Shattuck v. Stedman, 2 Pick. 468. Winslow v. Goodwin, 7 Met. 363. Childs v. Russell, 11 Met. 16. Wight v. Shaw, 5 Cush. 56. Bowditch v. Andrew, 8 Allen 339. Gibbens v. Gibbens, 140 Mass. 102, 3 N. E. 1.

In the first edition it was said that future limitations of personalty after life interests were executory, but were to be treated on questions of remoteness as if they were real estate. This worked well enough in practice as an empirical rule of thumb, but the view now presented in the text is much more satisfactory and is believed to be sound. There is no restraint on the creation of equitable interests in chattels. § 87, ante. And questions of vesting are decided as if the limitations were legal limitations of realty. Cf. § 116, ante.

§ 117.3. [1] See §§ 71.1, 71.2, ante; App. F, §§ 807 et seq., post.

[2] See App. F, §§ 816, 820, 856, post.

§ 118. [1] See Johnson v. Edmond, 65 Conn. 492, 499, 33 Atl. 503, 505; Carney v. Kain, 40 W. Va. 758, 809, 23 S. E. 650, 656;

Thus, if an estate is given to A. and his heirs, but if he dies unmarried then to B. and his heirs, here, in the first sense, B.'s interest is not vested, for it is subject to a condition precedent; in the second sense it is vested, for it is transmissible to B.'s heirs.[2] The Rule against Perpetuities does not concern itself with this secondary meaning of the word "vested." Thus, if an estate is devised to A. and his heirs, with an executory devise over to B. and his heirs in case A. or his heirs ever cease to bear the name of the testator, the executory devise to B. is vested in the secondary sense, be-

Leach, Cases on Future Interests, 259, 260. Indeed this ambiguity of meaning has been perhaps a chief factor in the production of the notion that presently alienable interests are never too remote. See Chap. VII., post.

[2] See Barnes v. Allen, 1 Bro. C. C. 181, 182; Taylor v. Frobisher, 5 De G. & Sm. 191, 197, 198; Storrs v. Burgess, 29 R. I. 269, 67 Atl. 731; Kelso v. Dickey, 7 W. & S. 279; M'Donald v. M'Mullen, 2 Mills, Const. 91, 94; Dickson v. Dickson, 23 So. Car. 216; Hudson v. Leathers, 141 So. Car. 32, 49, 139 S. E. 196, 201; 1 Roper, Leg. (4th ed.) 550; Marsden, Perp. 42; and a series of cases in Massachusetts, Dunn v. Sargent, 101 Mass. 336; Merriam v. Simonds, 121 Mass. 198, 202; Minot v. Tappan, 122 Mass. 535; Daniels v. Eldredge, 125 Mass. 356; Belcher v. Burnett, 126 Mass. 230; Russell v. Milton, 133 Mass. 180, 181; Whipple v. Fairchild, 139 Mass. 262, 30 N. E. 89; Minot v. Purrington, 190 Mass. 336, 77 N. E. 630; Clarke v. Fay, 205 Mass. 228, 91 N. E. 328.

The introduction of this meaning of "vested" into the law may perhaps have been as follows: In certain classes of legacies, to be paid when the legatee reaches twenty-one or some other age named, the courts construe the gift as an absolute one to the legatee, his executors and administrators, and the direction with regard to payment as given solely for the benefit of or on account of the legatee; that is, they regard the legacy as certain to become payable in any event,—payable when the legatee reaches twenty-one (or other age), if he so long lives; but if he dies before that time, payable to his executors or administrators. Such a legacy was called vested, because it was certain to take effect in the legatee or his representatives. Now the fact that such a legacy was vested was brought out in practice by the circumstance that the executor of the legatee took it, and the incident of transmissibility thus came to be regarded as the essential characteristic of a vested interest, and gave rise to the secondary meaning of the term "vested." See Hawkins, Wills (3d ed.) 264, 265.

cause it is transmissible from B. to his heirs; but it is nevertheless too remote, for in the primary sense it is not vested, but contingent,—that is, it is subject to a condition precedent.[3]

[3] Another use of the term "vested interest" should be noticed. "When it is said that the Legislature ought not to deprive parties of their 'vested rights,' all that is meant is this: that the rights styled 'vested' are *sacred* or *inviolable,* or are such as the parties ought not to be deprived of by the Legislature. Like a thousand other propositions which sound speciously to the ear, it is either purely identical and tells us nothing, or begs the question in issue." 2 Aust. Jur. (3d ed.) 887, 888. See Lewis, Use of Political Terms 32–34. This use of "vested" has passed from the domain of politics to that of law, by reason of the provisions in the 14th Amendment to the Constitution of the United States, and in most of the State Constitutions, that no one shall be deprived of his property "without due process of law," or "but by the law of the land." These provisions have generally been construed by the courts to prevent any general or special legislation taking away "vested rights," and have therefore called forth a somewhat more precise determination of the term. The cases will be found collected in Cooley, Const. Limit., c. 11, and in other works on American constitutional law. They do not concern us here.

[G. R. P.]—8

## CHAPTER IV

## POSTPONEMENT OF ENJOYMENT AND THE RULE AGAINST PERPETUITIES

§ 119. **Restraints on Alienation.** The tying up of property, the taking of it out of commerce, can be accomplished either, first, by restraining the alienation of interests in it, or, secondly, by postponing to a remote period the arising of future interests. To guard effectually against this evil, as the law considered it, both these methods had to be provided against. The law provided against the first by the doctrine that all interests should be alienable; it provided against the second by the doctrine that all interests must arise within certain limits,—that is, by the Rule against Perpetuities.[1] These two doctrines, though having originally a common purpose, have had a separate development.[2] The attempts to combine them have led to much confusion.[3]

§ 119.1. Neither the common law nor equity allows restraints on the alienation of property, save in the case of property settled or devised to the separate use of married women or on charitable uses.[1] The restraints imposed on estates tail by the Statute *De Donis* have long ceased to operate. It is true that life estates and estates for years may be made terminable on an attempt at alienation; but no interest, real or

§ 119. [1] On the history of the development of these two doctrines, see Chap. V., post, especially §§ 140 et seq., and Gray, Restraints on the Alienation of Property (2d ed.).

[2] See 14 Law Quart. Rev. 234, 240, note; 41 Law Quart. Rev. 52, 59; 3 Holdsworth, Hist. Eng. Law (3d ed.) 86.

[3] See §§ 2–3, ante, 140–141.6,

234–237.4, 245.2, 268–278.4, 432–437.2, 567, 590, 591, 597–603.8, 736, 737, 743, 744, 748, 750, post. The distinction between the rules governing restraints on alienation and the Rule against Perpetuities is stated in Becker v. Chester, 115 Wis. 90, 91 N. W. 87.

§ 119.1. [1] On the application of the Rule to Charitable Uses, see Chap. XVIII., post.

**[G. R. P.]**

personal, legal or equitable, can be held by any person, except a married woman, in such a way that he or she can enjoy the income or benefits thereof but cannot alienate it or subject it to his or her debts.[2]

**§ 120. Postponement of Enjoyment.** A result of the invalidity of restraints on alienation calls for attention in connection with the Rule against Perpetuities. When a person is entitled absolutely to property, any provision postponing its transfer or payment to him is void.[1] Thus, suppose property is given to trustees in trust to pay the principal to A. when he reaches thirty. When any other person than A. is interested in the property, when, for instance, there is a gift over to B. if A. dies under thirty, the trustee will retain the property for the benefit of B.; but when no one but A. is interested in the property, when, should he die before thirty, his heirs or representatives would be entitled to it, when, in short, the direction for postponement has been made for A.'s supposed benefit, such direction is void, in pursuance of the general doctrine that it is against public policy to restrain a

[2] In most of the United States restraints against alienation can be attached to equitable life interests given to men or to unmarried women. Trusts of this sort are known as spendthrift trusts. In several States, e. g. New York, such restraints are more or less permitted by statute. See the whole matter discussed in Gray, Restraints on the Alienation of Property; Griswold, Spendthrift Trusts; 1 Scott, Trusts, §§ 150–159; 1 Bogert, Trusts, § 222; 43 Yale L. J. 1211, 1222; 53 Harv. Law Rev. 296. See also Amer. Law Inst. Restatement, Trusts, §§ 151–154. On the application of the Rule against Perpetuities to provisions restraining anticipation by married women and to spendthrift trusts, see §§ 432–438, post; and as to its application to provisions postponing the right to enjoy equitable fees or absolute interests in those States, like Illinois and Massachusetts, where such postponement is allowed, see §§ 121.2 et seq., post.

**§ 120.** [1] Mr. Foulke, Treatise, § 486, says that a postponement of enjoyment is not a restraint on alienation. But the postponement of enjoyment restrains the owner of the absolute property from exercising the right, he would otherwise possess, of transferring the immediate right to its enjoyment, and may therefore, it seems, be properly called a restraint on alienation.

man in the use or disposition of property in which no one but himself has any interest.[2]

§ 121. As such provisions are void, no question of remoteness can be raised with regard to them. If such a direction to pay or convey to a legatee at a period beyond the limit of the Rule against Perpetuities were a condition precedent to the right to enjoy, and were, apart from the Rule, valid, it might be bad as violating the Rule; but as it is invalid, apart from the Rule, the objection of remoteness does not apply to it.[1]

[2] Josselyn v. Josselyn, 9 Sim. 63. Saunders v. Vautier, 4 Beav. 115, Cr. & Ph. 240. Curtis v. Lukin, 5 Beav. 147, 155, 156. Rocke v. Rocke, 9 Beav. 66. Swaffield v. Orton, 1 De G. & Sm. 326. Re Young's Settlement, 18 Beav. 199. Gosling v. Gosling, H. R. V. Johns. 265. Re Jacob's Will, 29 Beav. 402. Coventry v. Coventry, 2 Dr. & Sm. 470. Christie v. Gosling, L. R. 1 H. L. 279, 282. Magrath v. Morehead, L. R. 12 Eq. 491. Hilton v. Hilton, L. R. 14 Eq. 468, 475. Re Johnston, [1894] 3 Ch. 204. Re Thompson, 44 W. R. 582. Sanford v. Lackland, 2 Dill. 6. Huber v. Donoghue, 49 N. J. Eq. 125, 23 Atl. 495. Bennett v. Chapin, 77 Mich. 526, 43 N. W. 893. Rector v. Dalby, 98 Mo. Ap. 189, 71 S. W. 1078. McCreery v. Johnston, 90 W. Va. 80, 110 S. E. 464. See Talbot v. Jevers, L. R. 20 Eq. 255; Weatherall v. Thornburgh, 8 Ch. D. 261; Re Ussher, [1922] 2 Ch. 321; Re Smith, [1928] Ch. 915; Re Parry, 60 L. T. R. 489; Weatherhead v. Stoddard, 58 Vt. 623, 630, 5 Atl. 517, 519; Tarrant v. Backus, 63 Conn. 277, 28 Atl. 46; Conn. Trust Co. v. Hollister, 74 Conn. 228, 232, 50 Atl. 750, 751; Warner v. Keiser, 93 Ind. Ap. 547, 177 N. E. 369; Story v. First National Bank, 115 Fla. 436, 156 So. 101; Re Carter, 21 N. Z. 227; Will of Wright, [1917] Vict. 127; Re Lord's Will, [1933] Tasmanian 37. The case of Peard v. Kekewich, 15 Beav. 166, cannot, it would seem, be supported. See Gray, Restraints on Alienation (2d ed.), §§ 106–112, 124, 297, 298. The doctrine in question is sometimes called the rule in Saunders v. Vautier.

This principle, however, does not apply in jurisdictions where the doctrine of Claflin v. Claflin, 149 Mass. 19, 20 N. E. 454, prevails. See § 121.2, post. On the question whether in those jurisdictions such a provision for postponement of payment is a condition precedent to the right to enjoy, such as to prevent the absolute vesting of the interest for the purpose of the Rule against Perpetuities, see §§ 121.5, 437.1, post.

§ 121. [1] Farmer v. Francis, 2 Bing. 151, 9 Moore 310, 2 S. & St. 505. Murray v. Addenbrook, 4 Russ. 407. Bland v. Williams,

## § 121.1. When a direction for postponement is a condition precedent to the enjoyment of a right, it would come, if other-

3 Myl. & K. 411. Doe d. Dolley v. Ward, 9 A. & E. 582. Jackson v. Marjoribanks, 12 Sim. 93. Greet v. Greet, 5 Beav. 123. Davies v. Fisher, Id. 201. Milroy v. Milroy, 14 Sim. 48. Harrison v. Grimwood, 12 Beav. 192. Tatham v. Vernon, 29 Beav. 604. Knox v. Wells, 2 H. & M. 674. Saumarez v. Saumarez, 34 Beav. 432. Edmonson's Estate, L. R. 5 Eq. 389. Wilson v. Cobley, [1870] W. N. 46. Fox v. Fox, L. R. 19 Eq. 286. Mappin v. Mappin, [1877] W. N. 207. Re Bevan's Trusts, 34 Ch. D. 716. Rogers's Estate, 179 Pa. 602, 36 Atl. 1130. Wright v. Hill, 140 Ga. 554, 79 S. E. 546. Re Levy, 7 N. S. W. 885. See Taylor v. Frobisher, 5 De G. & Sm. 191; Oddie v. Brown, 4 De G. & J. 179; Baxter's Trusts, 10 Jur., N. S. 845; Kimball v. Crocker, 53 Me. 263; Lane v. Lane, 8 Allen 350; Odell v. Odell, 10 Allen 1, 13, 14; Wahl's Estate, 20 Phila. 32, 26 W. N. C. (Pa.) 249; Lewis, Perp., c. 22, and Suppl. 170, 171; 1 Jarm. Wills (7th ed.) 274, 338; Marsden, Perp., c. 11; Harg. Thel. Act, § 83. The case of Bute v. Harman, 9 Beav. 320, is wrongly reported. See Boreham v. Bignall, 8 Hare 131, 133, note (d); Southern v. Wollaston, 16 Beav. 166.

If the right to possession of a vested interest is postponed for the benefit of other persons, in order to provide for the possibility of their acquiring an interest in the property concerned, the vested interest is not absolute and in-

defeasible; and the rule in Saunders v. Vautier does not apply. See Gott v. Nairne, 3 Ch. D. 278; 2 Jarm. Wills (7th ed.) 860. The provisions allowing such other persons to take are of course within the scope of the Rule against Perpetuities. See Canda v. Canda, 113 Atl. 503, 509, 510 (N. J.).

In the third edition, §§ 121 a–121 b contained a discussion of the case of a gift to a class which may be increased by the admission of new members; and that case was also referred to in §§ 121 g and 442 a, post. These sections have been omitted for the reason that the correctness of the treatment of such cases in those sections is open to doubt. It was assumed in the discussion there that the rule in Saunders v. Vautier was applicable to the interests of the members of such a class; although its application was subject to the qualification that postponement of enjoyment was allowable where it was for the benefit of other persons. Such a course of reasoning, however, appears to be unnecessary and of questionable validity. The rule in Saunders v. Vautier applies only to indefeasible interests. Where membership of a class is liable to vary, the interest of the class as a whole may be said to be indefeasible; although there seems to be something fictitious in the notion of present ownership by a body which is conceived as including persons not yet in

wise valid, within the regulation of the Rule against Perpetuities. Such direction may take the form of a restraint on
alienation, as where property is given to A. and his heirs in
trust for B. and his heirs, with a proviso that the trust shall
not be terminated for a certain number of years. As has
been said, such a proviso being bad anyway, the time during
which the trust is declared not determinable is immaterial.
The Rule against Perpetuities has nothing to do with the
matter. It is only future interests otherwise valid that come
within the scope of the Rule.[1]

§ 121.2. **Claflin v. Claflin.** An American doctrine, first
adopted in Massachusetts in 1889, calls for notice. In *Claflin*
v. *Claflin*,[1] the Supreme Judicial Court of Massachusetts decided that if property is held by trustees for the sole absolute
interest of A., but there is a proviso that they shall not transfer it to him until he reaches twenty-five, he cannot demand
it till he arrives at that age.[2]

existence. See §§ 110, 110.1,
ante, 205.2, post. But the interest of each member of the class
is subject to be partially divested,
as long as the class remains liable to be increased; and such an
interest, it is submitted, cannot
properly be treated as indefeasible for the purpose of the application of the rule in Saunders v.
Vautier. The question of the validity of a postponement of the
enjoyment of an interest cannot
arise until it is determined that
the interest is indefeasible; and
this is a matter of construction.
The case which was apparently
intended to be stated, in § 121 b
of the third edition, is similar to
that involved in Kevern v. Williams, 5 Sim. 171, discussed in the
chapter on Construction, §§ 638–
639, post.

On the application of the Rule
against Perpetuities to accumula-

tion, see Chapter XX., post.

§ 121.1. [1] See Re Levy, 7 N.
S. W. 885.

§ 121.2. [1] 149 Mass. 19, 20 N.
E. 454.

[2] Claflin v. Claflin is discussed
in Gray, Restraints on Alienation
(2d ed.), §§ 124 l–124 p. See also Griswold, Spendthrift Trusts,
§§ 512–514; 1 Bogert, Trusts,
§ 218; 4 Bogert, Trusts, § 1002; 3
Scott, Trusts, § 337.3; 10 Iowa
Law Bull. 275, 294, 317; 37 Yale
L. J. 1070, 1076, 1081; and 43
Yale L. J. 393.

The doctrine of Claflin v. Claflin is law in Illinois. Lunt v.
Lunt, 108 Ill. 307. Howe v.
Hodge, 152 Ill. 252, 38 N. E. 1083.
Wagner v. Wagner, 244 Ill. 101,
91 N. E. 66. Guerin v. Guerin,
270 Ill. 239, 110 N. E. 402. Sheley
v. Sheley, 272 Ill. 95, 111 N. E.
591. See Rhoads v. Rhodes, 43
Ill. 239 (Gray, Restraints on

**§ 121.3.** Suppose, then, that in Massachusetts, by will, property is given to trustees for the sole absolute interest of

Alienation (2d ed.), § 124); Armstrong v. Barber, 239 Ill. 389, 82 N. E. 246; Wallace v. Foxwell, 250 Ill. 616, 95 N. E. 985; Kales, Estates, §§ 658–661, 678–681, 732–741; 5 Ill. Law Rev. 318, 386. Also in Connecticut, De Ladson v. Crawford, 93 Conn. 402, 106 Atl. 326. Colonial Trust Co. v. Brown, 105 Conn. 261, 135 N. E. 555. And apparently in California, Estate of Yates, 170 Cal. 254, 149 Pac. 555; New Jersey, Camden Safe Deposit & Trust Co. v. Scott, 121 N. J. Eq. 366, 189 Atl. 653; Oregon, Lent v. Title & Trust Co., 137 Ore. 511, 3 Pac. 2d 755; Tennessee, Tramell v. Tramell, 162 Tenn. 1, 32 S. W. 2d 1025, 35 S. W. 2d 574; Texas, Lanius v. Moore, 100 Tex. 550, 101 S. W. 1076; and Iowa, Meek v. Briggs, 87 Iowa 610, 54 N. W. 456; Dickerson v. Morse, 200 Iowa 115, 200 N. W. 601; although in the last state the result is perhaps affected by a statute; see § 736, post; 10 Iowa Law Bull. 275, 294, 317. In Kentucky, the law as to postponement of enjoyment might be influenced by the statute on "suspension of alienation" and a local doctrine as to restraints on alienation. See § 737, post. But the courts in that state seem to have allowed postponement of enjoyment on general grounds. See Carpenter v. Carpenter's Trustee, 119 Ky. 582, 84 S. W. 737; Nunn v. Peak, 130 Ky. 405, 113 S. W. 493; Miller's Executors v. Miller's Heirs, 172 Ky. 519, 189 S. W. 412; Brown v. Owsley, 198 Ky. 344, 248

S. W. 889. In several other States there is language, in cases not exactly to the same point, showing a tendency towards this doctrine. Compare, for instance the numerous cases where American courts have refused to end trusts in which all interests were vested, and all beneficiaries have requested termination. See 4 Bogert, Trusts, § 1002; Griswold, Spendthrift Trusts, §§ 511–528; 3 Scott, Trusts, §§ 337, 338; Matter of Hamburger, 185 Wis. 270, 201 N. W. 267; Fowler v. Lanpher, 193 Wash. 308, 75 Pac. 2d 132. And cf. Springfield Safe Dep. Co. v. Friele, 304 Mass. 224, 23 N. E. 2d 138. The doctrine of Claflin v. Claflin has been approved by the Supreme Court of the United States in a case from the District of Columbia. Shelton v. King, 229 U. S. 90, 33 S. Ct. 686, 57 L. E. 1086. And by the U. S. Circuit Court of Appeals in Tennessee. Stier v. Nashville Trust Co., 158 Fed. 601. See also Blossom v. Anketell, 275 Fed. 947 (Mich.).

On the other hand, while there is some obscurity in the Pennsylvania cases, yet Shallcross's Estate, 200 Pa. 122, 49 Atl. 936 (although the language with respect to the Rule against Perpetuities is inaccurate), makes it clear that the Supreme Court in that state contemplates no departure from the common law. And see Re Schwartz's Estate, 254 Pa. 88, 98 Atl. 780; Mereto's Estate, 311 Pa. 374, 166 Atl. 893.

The law in Missouri is not

the first son of A. (A. being now a bachelor), but there is a
proviso that the property shall not be transferred to such son
until he reaches twenty-five. A. marries, has a son born, and
dies soon after. The son is now of age. What is to happen?

§ 121.4. The suggestion that the right to enjoy is a right
independent of the vested property, and that such right to
enjoy, being on a remote condition precedent, can never come
into effect, though the vested interest exists, or in other words,
that a man may have a vested interest which he can never
by any possibility enjoy, is too absurd for consideration.[1]

§ 121.5. **Relation to Rule against Perpetuities.** It would
seem that one of two courses could be taken. We have a proviso for postponement of possession to which (on the assumption that *Claflin* v. *Claflin* is law) the only objection is that
the proviso is too remote. Now, we may say—

*First.* That the proviso is void as introducing a remote
modification and is to be rejected. The son will then be entitled to immediate possession of the property. This is the
mode in which the English equity courts have treated the
analogous case of clauses against anticipation attached to a
married woman's estate.[1]

*Second.* That the proviso does not violate the Rule against
Perpetuities; that the Rule is concerned only with the *beginning* of interests; that as the son's interest vests within the
prescribed limits the Rule is satisfied and has nothing more
to do with the matter; but that then another question arises,
with which the Rule against Perpetuities has nothing to do,

clear. In the earlier cases there
was some, though slight, ground
for thinking that the principle of
Claflin v. Claflin was adopted (see
Gray, Restraints on Alienation
(2d ed.), § 53, and cases there
cited); but in Rector v. Dalby,
98 Mo. Ap. 189, 197, 71 S. W.
1078, the Kansas City Court of
Appeals refused to follow that
case, and declared the opposite
view "to be supported not only
by a greater weight of authority,
but also by that of sounder reason." Now, however, see Evans
v. Rankin, 329 Mo. 411, 44 S. W.
2d 644.

The doctrine of Claflin v. Claf-
lin is apparently approved in the
Amer. Law Inst. Restatement,
Trusts, § 337, Comments j and k.

§ 121.4. [1] But see 43 Yale L.
J. 393, 397, note.

§ 121.5. [1] See §§ 432 et seq.,
post.

viz.: Can the possession of a vested interest be postponed? *Ex hypothesi* it can, and therefore the proviso is good. In other words: The Rule against Perpetuities settles the time within which interests must vest; but, when once vested, they are all, present and future alike, subject to the same restraints against alienation, and with this the Rule against Perpetuities has nothing to do.[2] This is the view which Jessel, M. R., in *Re Ridley*,[3] thought correct, though his language was not always the clearest, and though he felt bound by the earlier cases to decide against his judgment. It is respectfully submitted that this is the correct view, and that the other theory is one more instance of the confusion wrought by confounding the Rule against Perpetuities with the rules against restraints on alienation.[4]

**§ 121.6. Duration of Postponement.** Suppose that a devise takes this form. Property is given to A. and his heirs on trust to pay the income to B. and his heirs, with a proviso that the trust is not to be determined until A. wishes it. Apparently the Massachusetts court would apply the doctrine of *Claflin* v. *Claflin* and would refuse to compel the trustee to convey against his will.[1] But how if it is provided that

[2] This is quoted with approval in Armstrong v. Barber, 239 Ill. 389, 402, 88 N. E. 246, 250. See Mettler v. Warner, 243 Ill. 600, 90 N. E. 1099; Guerin v. Guerin, 270 Ill. 239, 110 N. E. 402; O'Hare v. Johnston, 273 Ill. 458, 113 N. E. 127; De Ladson v. Crawford, 93 Conn. 402, 106 Atl. 326; Tramell v. Tramell, 162 Tenn. 1, 32 S. W. 2d 1025, 35 S. W. 2d 574; 2 Tiffany, Real Prop. (3d ed.), § 408; 4 Ill. Law Rev. 281, 282. The powers given to a trustee under a trust which remains indestructible for a period longer than that of the Rule against Perpetuities may perhaps be invalid under that Rule. But a trust may be valid, although the powers given to the trustees are invalid. §§ 509.2–509.8, post. And see 30 Columbia Law Rev. 60, 70, 71.

[3] 11 Ch. D. 645.

[4] See §§ 436–437.2, 442, post.

§ 121.6. [1] See Young v. Snow, 167 Mass. 287, 45 N. E. 686; Danahy v. Noonan, 176 Mass. 467, 57 N. E. 679; Hale v. Herring, 208 Mass. 319, 94 N. E. 396; Boston Safe Deposit & Trust Co. v. Collier, 222 Mass. 390, 111 N. E. 163; Watson v. Watson, 223 Mass. 425, 111 N. E. 904; Perabo v. Gallegher, 241 Mass. 207, 135 N. E. 113; Forbes v. Snow, 245 Mass. 85, 93, 140 N. E. 418, 421; Abbott v. Williams, 268 Mass. 275, 167 N. E. 357.

the trust shall not be terminated until A. or his heirs wish it,
or until some other possibly remote contingency happens?[2]

§ **121.7.** The fact is that the Massachusetts court in *Claflin* v. *Claflin* introduced a novel idea into the law, that of the
inalienability of absolute interests, just as the Court of King's
Bench in *Pells* v. *Brown*[1] introduced a novel idea into the
law, that of the indestructibility of future interests.[2] And
as the Rule against Perpetuities had to be invented to control
the indestructible future interests created by *Pells* v. *Brown*,
so some rule must be invented to control the inalienable interests created by *Claflin* v. *Claflin*. It is perhaps likely that
the same period as that prescribed by the Rule against Perpetuities will be taken,[3] although it would seem quite open to

[2] Cf. Van Epps v. Arbuckle, 332
Ill. 551, 164 N. E. 1.

§ **121.7.** [1] Cro. Jac. 590 (1620).

[2] It is worth while in this connection to note the remarks of
Treby, C. J., in Scattergood v.
Edge, 12 Mod. 278, 287: "These
executory devises had not been
long countenanced when the
judges repented them; and if it
were to be done again, it would
never prevail," and the more pic-
turesque language of Powell, J.,
in the same case (p. 281), that
the notion that an executory devise was not barred by a recovery "went down with the judges
like chopped hay."

[3] The question arose and was
argued in Wirth v. Wirth, 183
Mass. 527, 67 N. E. 657, but the
case went off on another point,
the Court "not intimating any
opinion upon any other of the
matters in dispute." See Winsor
v. Mills, 157 Mass. 362, 364, 32
N. E. 352, 353, where Knowlton,
J., says, "Where such a restraint
[on alienation of a fee simple] is

held permissible for a limited
time, it would be deemed unreasonable and contrary to the policy of the law to allow it to continue beyond the period fixed by
the rule against perpetuities."

In Colonial Trust Co. v. Brown,
105 Conn. 261, 135 Atl. 555, a
trust was created to pay annuities to living persons and their
children for their lives, with a
vested remainder. The trustee
was given power to sell real estate within five years, except two
properties which he was expressly forbidden to sell. The five
years had expired. The Court
held the trust valid, because all
interests vested within lives in
being, although the trust might
not terminate until the death of
persons not in being. See § 232,
post. It further held that the
prohibition against selling was
invalid as a restraint on alienation lasting for a longer period
than lives in being and twenty-
one years, and that the trustee
could sell under an order of Court.

the court to adopt some other period, if found more convenient.[4]

On this point the Court said: "The rule against perpetuities and that against restraints on alienation are in reality entirely distinct, the former being concerned only with the vesting of estates in right, and the latter with the limitation which may be imposed upon the enjoyment of the property. But by analogy the same rule has been adopted for determining the length of time during which the alienation of lands may be lawfully restrained as is used in determining the period within which an estate must vest in order to be valid." (P. 279.)

See opinion of Master in Canda v. Canda, 113 Atl. 503, affirmed on other grounds in 92 N. J. Eq. 423, 112 Atl. 727; and also Kales, Estates, §§ 658, 737; 1 Bogert, Trusts, § 218; Griswold, Spendthrift Trusts, §§ 294-296; 51 Harv. Law Rev. 638, 667; 54 Harv. Law Rev. 839, 841 et seq.; 5 Mo. Law Rev. 361.

Cf. Roberts v. Jones, 30 N. E. 2d 392 (Mass.), in which the Court declared invalid an agreement restraining the alienation or partition of land held in common, on the ground that it restricted alienation for an unreasonable time. The Court said, "the agreement imposing such a restraint upon the alienation of an estate in fee simple for a period beyond that fixed by the rule against perpetuities is contrary to public policy and cannot be enforced."

The agreement perhaps contained options to purchase which were too remote; but the decision was apparently not based on that ground. As has been often recognized by the Massachusetts Court, agreements restricting alienation or partition are not within the scope of the Rule against Perpetuities. The language quoted, in view of the remainder of the opinion and the authorities cited, may be taken to mean that the Court adopts as the measure of a reasonable restraint on the alienation of a legal fee (at least in the circumstances of the present case) the same period as that adopted in the application of the Rule against Perpetuities. See 54 Harv. Law Rev. 1081.

[4] See Armstrong v. Barber, 239 Ill. 389, 403, 88 N. E. 246, 250. In Southard v. Southard, 210 Mass. 347, 96 N. E. 941, a trust was created in 1856 to continue until certain mortgages were paid out of accumulated income. In 1910 the Court ordered the trust terminated. They said: "The inhibition from making any conveyance of an estate in fee simple until the mortgages had been previously satisfied from income rendered the property inalienable for an unreasonable period and the trust should be terminated." Nothing was said as to what was a reasonable period, or about any analogy to the Rule against Perpetuities. Cf. an able article by

§ **121.8.** In calculating the period are we to begin from the testator's death, or from the beginning of the future interest? Professor Kales[1] thinks we should begin with the testator's death. Following the analogy of restraints on anticipation of future interests of married women:—if we adopt the present doctrine of the English courts, this may be right; but if we adopt the view of Jessel, M. R.,[2] which, it is submitted, is correct, we should start from the beginning of the future estate. If the latter view is sound, then every post-

Mr. G. L. Clark, 10 Mich. Law Rev. 31, 37 et seq.

The reasonable period for a restraint on alienation, or a postponement of possession, of an absolute equitable interest, seems to be the life of the equitable owner. It is doubtful whether a restraint or postponement of possession would be sustained, after the death of the equitable owner, for a period of twenty-one years, or during the life of some other person. In Old Colony Trust Co. v. Clarke, 291 Mass. 17, 23, 195 N. E. 758, 761, the Court declined to give effect to a provision against liability to creditors as against the creditors of the owner of an equitable fee, after his death. If Fleming's Estate, 219 Pa. 422, 68 Atl. 960, is to the contrary, it is wrong. See State Street Trust Co. v. Kissell, 302 Mass. 328, 19 N. E. 2d 25; Griswold, Spendthrift Trusts, § 93; 1 Scott, Trusts, § 158.1; Foulke, Treatise, § 241. If the postponement of possession is good only within the term of one particular life, the analogy of the rule on this point to the Rule against Perpetuities is imperfect.

The rule in question is some-times called a rule against indestructible trusts. This name is not inappropriate as applied to the principle discussed in this chapter that the equitable owner of property, in which no one else has any interest, has the right to terminate the trust, subject in some jurisdictions to a limited delay. But there is no general rule that a trust cannot be created which will remain indestructible for longer than the period of the Rule against Perpetuities. See §§ 232–245, post; Colonial Trust Co. v. Brown, 105 Conn. 261, 278, 135 Atl. 555, 562 (stated in preceding note); Re Chardon, [1928] Ch. 464, § 87.1, ante; 1 Bogert, Trusts, § 218; 16 Conveyancer 43; 9 Minn. Law Rev. 314, 327; 43 Yale L. J. 393, 398; and Amer. Law Inst. Restatement, Trusts, §§ 62, Comment k, 365, Comment a.

§ **121.8.** [1] 19 Harv. Law Rev. 604, note. 20 Harv. Law Rev. 202.

[2] In Re Ridley, 11 Ch. D. 645, 651. See §§ 436–442, post; Griswold, Spendthrift Trusts, §§ 294–296; 1 Scott, Trusts, § 62.10; 54 Harv. Law Rev. 839, 843; Amer. Law Inst. Restatement, Trusts, § 562, Comment k.

ponement of enjoyment confined to the life of the first taker of a vested interest would be good.[3]

[3] Section 121 j, in previous editions of this work, discussed what appeared to be a local doctrine in Kentucky as to postponement of enjoyment, similar to the doctrine of Claflin v. Claflin. The section thus designated is omitted in the present edition, for the reason that the Kentucky courts now seem to have adopted in effect the doctrine of Claflin v. Claflin, and there appears to be no ground to suppose that a peculiar situation exists in that State as to postponement of enjoyment of equitable interests. See §§ 121.2, note 2, ante, 737, note 1, post.

## CHAPTER V

## ORIGIN AND HISTORY OF THE RULE AGAINST PERPETUITIES

### 1. No Question of Remoteness in Early Times

#### Possibility on a Possibility

**§ 123. Before 1535.** Before the enactment of the Statute of Uses[1] (1535) and the Statute of Wills[2] (1540), no question of remoteness in the creation of estates and interests seems to have come before the courts. It is true that freehold estates could not be granted *in futuro* except by way of remainder; but this arose from the necessity of livery, not from any idea of remoteness. It is also true that existing incorporeal hereditaments, e. g. reversions, rents, etc., could not be granted *in futuro;* but this again was not on the score of remoteness.[3] And to the interests which could be created *in futuro,* such as rents, chattels real, uses in equity, we never hear of an objection that they were too remote.[4]

**§ 124.** There was a mode before the Statutes of Uses and Wills in which a freehold estate could be created *in futuro.* By the custom of gavelkind, and by the customs in many localities, e. g. in London, land was devisable. Land passed under a will without livery, and it was repeatedly held that a power to executors to sell the testator's land was good; that until the sale the land was in the heir or devisee; but that upon the execution of the power the estate passed to the vendee, by virtue of the will, without livery, and even without a deed, from the executors.[1] The right of the executors to thus create an estate, when they had no estate themselves,

§ 123. [1] St. 27 Hen. VIII., c. 10.
[2] St. 32 Hen. VIII., c. 1.
[3] See § 17, ante.
[4] See Everwike v. Prior of Bridlington, Y. B. Mich. 22 Edw. III. 19, pl. 96; Fitz. Ab. Condicion. 11,

12; Y. B. Hil. 10 Hen. VII. 12, pl. 3; Lewis, Perp., c. 29.

§ 124. [1] Lit., §§ 169, 585, 586. Y. B. Mich. 19 Hen. VI. 23, pl. 47. Co. Lit. 113 a.

was felt to be a singular one;[2] but no objection appears to
have been made on the score of remoteness, although the will
sometimes provided that the sale should be made by the executors, and, should they all die, then by the executors of the
executors.[3] So in *Farington* v. *Darrel*,[4] Martin, J., says: "It
has been adjudged that if one devises that his executor or
the executor of his executor may sell his land, and at the time
of this devise the executors of the executor were not *in rerum
natura*, yet their sale has been held good and sufficient." To
which Paston, J., replies: "That may well be; for they were
*in esse* at the time that the first executors died."[5]

§ 125. **"Possibility upon a Possibility."** It has been a
common notion that to a certain extent remoteness of limitation was prevented in the early times by means of a supposed
rule that no future interest could be limited to the unborn
child of an unborn person, because such a limitation would
be a possibility upon a possibility.[1] But the idea that there

[2] Babington, C. J., in Farington
v. Darrel, Y. B. Trin. 9 Hen. VI. 23,
pl. 19, at fol. 24, says: "Est mar-
veilous Ley de raison: mes ceo est
le nature d'un devis, et devise ad
este use tout temps en tiel forme;
et issint on aura loyalment frank-
tenement de cesty qui n'avoit
rien, et en mesne le maniere come
on aura fire from flint, et uncore
nul fire est deins le flint: et ceo
est pour performer le darrein vol-
onte de le devisor." Same case,
Y. B. Mich. 11 Hen. VI. 12, pl. 28,
at fol. 13. So Y. B. Mich. 19 Hen.
VI. 23, pl. 47, at fol. 24 b.

[3] Rex v. Croyden (Gowdchep's
Case), Y. B. Easter 49 Edw. III.
16, pl. 10.

[4] Y. B. Trin. 9 Hen. VI. 23, pl. 19,
at fol. 24.

[5] See Y. B. Liber Ass. 28 Edw.
III. 145, pl. 3; 2 Harg. Jurid.
Arg. 28, 29. Such a power
would now be held too remote.

"Supposing the second executor
not to have been born at the testator's death, the estate to arise
under an execution of the power
might by possibility not take effect until the expiration of fifty
years or more after the decease
of the first executor, the life in
being." 1 Chance, Pow., § 307. It
does not appear that executory
devises raised in any other way
than by powers given to executors
were ever held valid. Thus in the
Prior of St. Bartholomew's Case,
Dyer 33 a, which was determined
in 1537, before the Statute of
Wills, it was held by the Court
of Common Pleas that a shifting
executory devise, on breach of
condition by the first devisee, was
bad, because the heir only could
enter for breach of condition.
The land was devisable by custom. See Lewis, Perp. 77, 78.

§ 125. [1] Mr. Charles Sweet, in

cannot be a possibility on a possibility seems to have been a conceit invented by Chief Justice Popham.[2] The idea is expressed in different forms. Thus, it is said, a lease could not "commence upon a contingent which depended upon another contingent."[3] "A possibility which shall make a remainder good, ought to be a common possibility and *potentia propinqua*."[4] "A possibility cannot increase upon a possibility."[5] "Sometimes one possibility shall not beget another."[6] "The law will never intend a possibility upon a possibility."[7] But in none of these shapes does it meet with any countenance in the earlier cases.[8]

§ 126. The authorities referred to for this doctrine in the places above cited are as follows: Y. B. Liber Ass. 12 Edw. III. 34, pl. 5. A. let land to B. on condition that if A. or his heirs paid B. or his heirs ten pounds within a certain time, it should be lawful for them to re-enter; and if they did not pay within the term, and B. paid A. ten pounds on a certain subsequent day, that then B. should have the fee "*sans plus en la condition*." Neither A. nor B. paid. A. entered after both terms (*apres l'un terme et l'auter*), and B. ousted him. A. brought an assize, but took nothing by his writ. There is only a short note of the case. It would seem that A. failed because the condition did not

15 Law Quart. Rev. 71, 29 Law Quart. Rev. 304, 1 Jarm. Wills (6th ed.) 287 note (h) and addenda, and 12 Columbia Law Rev. 199, while utterly condemning the notion that a limitation of a possibility upon a possibility is void, yet maintains that the rule in question existed, based on another reason. This matter is discussed in §§ 191–199, 287 et seq.; App. K, §§ 931 et seq., post.

2 Rector of Chedington's Case, 1 Co. 153 a, 156 b. Cholmley's Case, 2 Co. 50 a, 51 a. Stafford's Case, 8 Co. 73 b, 75 a. Lampet's Case, 10 Co. 46 b, 50 b. Blamford v. Blamford, 3 Bulst. 98, 108. Co. Lit. 184 a. "If anyone turns to the passage in Coke upon Littleton where it is discussed, I hope he will understand it better than I do. I confess I do not understand it now, and never did." Per Lindley, L. J., in Whitby v. Mitchell, 44 Ch. D. 85, 92. See §§ 133, 288, post.

3 1 Co. 156 b.
4 2 Co. 51 a.
5 8 Co. 75 a.
6 3 Bulst. 108.
7 Co. Lit. 184 a.
8 See Wms. Real Prop. (24th ed.) 435.

provide that, on failure to pay by B., A. might enter. Whatever the ground of the decision, there is not the slightest reason to suppose it to have been that a contingent "depended upon another contingent."[1]

**§ 127. William v. Florence.**[1] Osbern and Florence his wife levied a fine of land, and the conusee conveyed the land to Osbern and Florence for life, remainder to Geoffrey the son of Osbern in tail, remainder to Austin the brother of Geoffrey in tail, remainder to the heirs of Osbern. In an action against Florence, after the death of her husband, for possession of the land, she made default; and then came one John, saying that Florence had only a life estate, that Geoffrey and Austin had both died without issue, and that he was entitled after the death of Florence as the heir of Osbern, and praying that he might be allowed to come in and defend. The demandant replied that Geoffrey the son of Osbern was alive, and Austin his brother. Ash, of counsel for John, said: "Your plea is not properly pleaded, if you do not say that Geoffrey to whom the remainder was limited is alive." To which Pole, for the demandant, replied: "You have simply alleged that the remainder was given in tail to Geoffrey the son of Osbern and Austin his brother, and that they are dead, and to that we say that Geoffrey the son of Osbern is alive, and Austin, and it is enough for me to traverse what you have said in the same words as you have used to me." The counsel for John rejoined: "I acknowledge that Geoffrey the son of Osbern is alive and Austin his brother also, but I say that their being so ought not to oust me, for I say that they were not born at the time of the fine levied, but were born long time after the fine." Pole then said: "You have acknowledged that they are alive who bear the same name and surname as those to whom you have said the remainder was given, and before by your plea you made no mention of them." To which John's counsel rejoined: "By our plea we have not undertaken to plead of any others than those to whom the remainder was given

§ 126. 1 1 Co. 156 b.   § 127. 1 Y. B. Mich. 10 Edw. III. 45, pl. 9.

[G. R. P.]—9

in tail, and that cannot be to others than those who were alive at the time of levying the fine, but as to your pleas of the others, that by their being alive I shall not be received, now for the time it is enough for me to say that their being alive does not oust me from being received." The reporter adds: "And afterwards he was received." The fact seems to be that the land was conveyed, after the life estates, in remainder to two persons—Geoffrey and his brother Austin—who were then living. A limitation to two persons, one of the name of Geoffrey and the other his brother of the name of Austin, neither of whom had been born, might suggest itself as a hypothetical case to a lawyer of the sixteenth century, but it is inconceivable that a baron of the fourteenth should ever have actually settled his estate in that fashion. This Geoffrey and Austin died, and another Geoffrey and Austin were born, very likely of the same parents; but these latter could not be the persons for whom the remainder was intended, for they were not even born when it was created.[2]

§ **128.** In Y. B. Mich. 18 Edw. III. 39, pl. 34, an estate was given to a man and his sister and the heirs of their bodies; in Y. B. Trin. 24 Edw. III. 29, pl. 17, an estate was given to two men and their wives and the heirs of their bodies; in Y. B. 44 Edw. III., Fitz. Ab. Taile, pl. 13, an estate was given to brothers and a sister and the heirs of their bodies; and in Y. B. Trin. 7 Hen. IV. 16, pl. 9, the case was put of a devise to two men, or to a man and his mother, or to a man and his daughter, and the heirs of their bodies; and in all these cases it was held that the grantees had separate inheritances, because, as the reason is given in the last case, the will of the donor should

---

[2] See Cholmley's Case, 2 Co. 50 a, 51 b; Wms. Real Prop. (24th ed.) 435, 436. Perhaps no second Geoffrey and Austin were really born and the question raised may have been one of pleading. John's objection is that the demandant's pleading is improper because it does not allege that the Geoffrey and Austin to whom the remainder was limited are alive, and though there be a Geoffrey and Austin alive as alleged, they may not be the Geoffrey and Austin to whom the remainder was limited, and for the failure to allege that they are, John says the pleading is bad.

[G. R. P.]

be preserved,—there is nothing about a possibility on a possibility.[1]

§ **129.** In *Farington* v. *Darrel*,[1] Babington, C. J., to illustrate the position that the validity of a devise must be determined at the death of the testator, says that if a devise is made to chantery or college, and there is no such chantery or college, the devise is void, though a chantery or college of that name be afterwards founded. Here the gift purports to be to an existing corporation; if there is no such corporation the gift fails; and of course it cannot be claimed by a subsequently established corporation, not because there could not be a gift to such a corporation, but because it was not, in fact, the corporation for which the gift was intended.[2]

§ **130.** Y. B. Hil. 2 Hen. VII. 13, pl. 16. The passage referred to here is a remark of Serjeant Keble. He says: "The remainder to the right heirs of J. at S. is good, because it can be a good remainder by common intendment; but if the King grants to an abbey, and there is none such, the grant is void notwithstanding that it is made afterwards. And in the case of the heirs of J. at S., suppose when the remainder is created that there is no J. at S., and afterwards a J. at S. is born, it [the remainder] is void, notwithstanding J. at S. dies and has heirs at the time of the remainder." This remark of Serjeant Keble lends no aid to the notion of the invalidity of a possibility upon a possibility. If the remainder, instead of being to the heirs of J. at S., had been to J. at S. himself, and there was no such person as J. at S. alive, the learned Serjeant would have considered the remainder just as invalid; this is clear from the case he puts of the abbey. He means that a gift to a person *tanquam in esse* will not take effect if there is no such person living, for there is no one answering the description of the donee.[1]

§ **131.** In *Lane* v. *Cowper*[1] (1575), Wray, Chief Justice of

§ **128.** [1] Co. Lit. 184 a.
§ **129.** [1] Y. B. Trin. 9 Hen. VI. 23, pl. 19, at fol. 24.
[2] 1 Prest. Abs. 128. See Corpus Christi College Case, 4 Leon. 223.

§ **130.** [1] Per Lord Coke in Simpson v. Southwood, 1 Roll. R. 253, 254. 1 Prest. Abs. 128.
§ **131.** [1] Moore 103, 104.

the Queen's Bench, and Gawdy, J., "took the diversity, to wit, that a person not *in esse* at the beginning can take a remainder by purchase, if he is *in esse* before the end of the particular estate, so that the limitation of the remainder is in general words, as 'to the right heirs of J. S.,' or 'to him who shall first come to St. Pauls,' 'to the wife that shall be,' and the like.  But if the limitation be in special words, as to 'Jane, the first wife of J. S.,' where he has no wife at the time, or to 'the Mayor and Commonalty at Islington,' where there is none such at this time, then although before the end of the particular estate J. S. takes one Jane to wife, or Islington is incorporated by the name of the Mayor and Commonalty, yet they will not take the remainder."  Here again the gift is void, because made to persons or corporations *tanquam in esse* who are not *in esse*.[2]

§ 132.  The above sections 126–131 contain all the cases referred to as authorities for the theory that a possibility upon a possibility is invalid, but *Manning* v. *Andrews*[1] (1576) also deserves attention.  In that case there was a feoffment before the Statute of Uses to the use of W. and his wife J. for their lives, and after their death to the use of the heir of the bodies of W. and J. for life, then to the use of the heir of the same heir, and in default of such issue to the use of the heirs of the body of W. and J. for the life or lives of every such heir or heirs, and, for default of such heirs, to the heirs of the body of W., and in default, etc., to the heirs of W.  Condition, that if "any of the said heirs" should attempt to alienate his interest, the use limited to such heir should be void during his life, and the feoffees should be seised to the use of the heir apparent of the offender.  After the feoffment W. had issue T. and died.  T. had issue F. and P.  After the Statute of Uses, T., and afterwards F., levied a fine to the defendant. The feoffees entered to revive the use to P., who was F.'s heir apparent, and then P. entered.  Jeffrey, J., thought that an entry by the feoffees was necessary, and that they were

2 See Jeffrey, Serj., arguendo, in        Cf. 7 Holdsworth, Hist. Eng. Law
Mutton's Case, 2 Leon. 223, Dal.        (3d ed.) 99.
91; Brent v. Gilbert, Dal. 111, 112.        § 132. 1 1 Leon. 256.

debarred from entering by the fine. Wray, C. J., and Southcote, J., agreed that no entry by the feoffees was necessary;
but the Chief Justice seems to have thought that P. was
debarred from entry by the fine. Southcote, J., held that P.'s
entry was effectual to vest the estate in him; and neither of
the other judges seems to have had any doubt that the shifting
use over on alienation was valid,—they differed only on the
effect of the fine.[2] The case is important as showing that the
notion of the impossibility of limiting an estate to the issue
of an unborn person had no existence at that time.

§ 132.1. The existence of a rule at common law, that after
an estate for life to an unborn child a remainder to such
child's children is void, has been of late so positively asserted
that it is worth while to quote the language of the judges in
*Manning* v. *Andrews,* to show that no such rule was known
to them. Gawdy, J., said "that every issue begotten betwixt
William and Joan should have an estate for life successive,
and a remainder in tail expectant as right heir of the body of
William, and this estate tail shall not be executed in possession by reason of the mesne remainder for life limited to the
heir of the body of William and Joan, and although that these
mesne remainders are but upon a contingent, and not *in esse,*
yet such regard shall be had to them, that they shall hinder
the execution of the estates for life, and in tail in possession."
Wray, C. J., said: "If a devise be made to one for life, and
then to his heir for life, and so from heir to heir *in perpetuam*
for life, here are two estates for life, and the other devisees
have fee, for estates for life cannot be limited by general
words from heir to heir, but by special words they may."

§ 133. Lord Coke has admitted that as a general proposition the statement that there cannot be a possibility upon a
possibility is bad law. "Coke moves another matter in this
case on Popham's opinion, Co. 1, Rector de Chedington, that
a possibility on a possibility is not good, for here in our case
is a possibility on a possibility . . . yet it seems that it is

[2] See 1 Sugd. Pow. (7th ed.) post. See 15 Law Quart. Rev. 73,
15, 16. Cf. also Wood v. Sanders, note.
1 Ch. Cas. 131, Pollexf. 35, § 161,

good, for if Popham's opinion should be law, it would shake the common assurances of the land . . . but I agree that in divers cases there shall not be possibility upon a possibility, and he puts the diversities put in *Lampet's Case,* 10 Co. 50 *b.*"[1]

§ **134.** The true reason why before the time of the Statutes of Uses and Wills no objection of remoteness appears to have been made to any limitations is that in fact no need of any such restriction on the creation of future estates was felt. Incorporeal hereditaments would seldom be created to begin

§ **133.** [1] See Blamford v. Blamford, 3 Bulst. 98, 108, better reported in 1 Roll. R. 318, 321.

As the notion of a possibility on a possibility had no roots in the law, so it flourished but a short time. In 1681, Lord Chancellor Nottingham, in the great Case of the Duke of Norfolk, said: "that there may be a possibility upon a possibility and that there may be a contingency upon a contingency is neither unnatural or absurd in itself; but the contrary rule given as a reason by my Lord Popham in the Rector of Chedington's Case, 1 Co. 156 b, looks like a reason of art; but in truth has no kind of reason in it, and I have known that rule often denied in Westminster Hall." 3 Ch. Cas. 29. See Mayor of London v. Alford, Cro. Car. 576, 577; Love v. Windham, 1 Sid. 450, 451; Thellusson v. Woodford, 4 Ves. 227, 327.

On the revival of the doctrine as the parent of the alleged rule that, at common law, a remainder to the child of an unborn person could not be limited after a remainder for life to its father, see §§ 191 et seq., post.

Except as the doubtful parent of the alleged rule that life estates cannot be limited to successive generations, no one can now be found to defend it. Fearne, C. R. 251, Butler's note. Cole v. Sewell, 4 Dr. & W. 1, 32. Egerton v. Brownlow, 4 H. L. C. 1, 54. Re Ashforth, [1905] 1 Ch. 535, 543. Third Real Prop. Comm. Rep. 29. 1 Prest. Abs. 128. 1 Leake, Law of Property in Land (1st ed.) 335. Sugd. Pow. (8th ed.) 393, 394. Wms. Real Prop. (24th ed.) 435. 3 Enc. Laws of Eng. (2d ed.) 518. Whitby v. Mitchell, 42 Ch. D. 494, 44 Ch. D. (C. A.) 85. Re Frost, 43 Ch. D. 246. 6 Law Quart. Rev. 410, 424. 14 Law Quart. Rev. 234. 25 Law Quart. Rev. 385, 393. 30 Law Quart. Rev. 353. Cf. Challis, Real Prop. (3d ed.) 118; 7 Holdsworth, Hist. Eng. Law (3d ed.) 93–99, 212, 235; 25 Iowa Law Rev. 1.

As to the later growth of the idea that future limitations of remainders are governed by this supposed rule, and as to the present condition of the law upon the subject, see §§ 284–298.8, post, which should be consulted here.

*in futuro.* Terms for years were generally short, present interests. Executory devises under powers given to executors could arise only in those comparatively rare localities where land was devisable. Contingent remainders were probably for a long time unknown to the law.[1] It had been adjudged, however, before 1430 that a remainder to the heirs of a living person was good.[2] But contingent remainders, though allowed as legal, were seldom employed, even after the Statute of Uses. Mr. Joshua Williams says that in all marriage settlements prior to the reign of Queen Mary, who came to the throne in 1553, "the remainders appear to be uniformly vested, the estates tail being given to living parties, and not to sons or daughters unborn."[3] From *Chudleigh's Case*[4] it appears that in 1556 a feoffment was made to uses giving estates tail to the successive (unborn) children of living persons, substantially in the form of a modern English settlement; and 1556 is also the date of the earliest settlement traced by Mr. Williams in which contingent remainders to unborn persons occur.[5] Even had contingent remainders been more frequent, the ease with which the tenant for life could, by feoffment, fine, or recovery, destroy the particular estate necessary to support a contingent remainder would have prevented their becoming practically inconvenient, however remote.[6]

## 2. INTRODUCTION OF CONDITIONAL LIMITATIONS

**§ 135. First Recognition.** As has been shown,[1] executory devises had long been recognized as possible in localities

§ 134. [1] § 100, ante.

[2] Anon., cited in Farington v. Darrel, Y. B. Trin. 9 Hen. VI. 23, pl. 19, at fol. 24. Y. B. Hil. 32 Hen. VI. Fitz. Ab. Feoff. & Faits, pl. 99.

[3] 1 Jurid. Soc. Papers 47.

[4] 1 Co. 120 a.

[5] 1 Jurid. Soc. Papers 47.

[6] Williams on Seisin 190, 191. See Mr. Cyprian Williams's conjecture, 3 Enc. Laws of Eng. (2d ed.) 518, 519, that originally no remainders to uncertain persons were allowed, and that when they were introduced, they were confined to remainders after a vested estate of freehold; and the same author's article, 14 Law Quart. Rev. 234, 238. See also 62 Sol. J. 485. On any objection to the remoteness of rights of entry on common-law conditions, see §§ 299 et seq., post.

§ 135. [1] § 124, ante.

where lands were devisable, but it was not until after the passage of the Statutes of Uses (1535) and of Wills (1540) that contingent future limitations of freeholds, other than remainders, became valid generally.

§ **136.** Springing uses seem to have been first recognized in *Anon.*[1] (1538), where a covenant to stand seised to the use of B. on the performance of an act by B. was held to raise the use on the happening of the contingency.[2]

§ **137.** In *Anon.*[1] (1552), there was a feoffment to the use of W. and his heirs until A. paid a sum of money, and then to A. and his heirs.[2] It was assumed by all that this was a good shifting use.[3]

§ 136. [1] Bro. Ab. Feoff. al Uses, 340, pl. 50 (30 Hen. VIII.).

[2] See Gilb. Uses (Sugd. ed.) 164, note. So Wood's Case, in the Court of Wards (1560), cited 1 Co. 99 a; and see Mutton's Case, Dyer 274 b, 2 Leon. 223, Dal. 91, Moore 96, 376, 1 And. 42 (1573); Woodliff v. Drury, Cro. El. 439, sub nom. Woodlet v. Drury, 2 Roll. Ab. 791, pl. 1 (1595); Mills v. Parsons, Moore 547 (1595); Blackbourn v. Lassels, Cro. El. 800 (1600); Wood v. Reignold, Cro. El. 764, 854 (1601); Lewis, Perp. 57, 58.

§ 137. [1] Bro. Ab. Feoff. al Uses, 339, pl. 30 (6 Edw. VI.).

[2] The question discussed was whether the estate could vest in A. without an entry on the part of the feoffees to uses. This point was often afterwards mooted. See Brent's Case, 2 Leon. 14, Dyer 340 a; Manning v. Andrews, 1 Leon. 256; Chudleigh's Case, 1 Co. 120 a, 1 And. 309, Pop. 70, Jenk. 276; and the other cases cited 1 Sugd. Pow. (7th ed.) 10–39. It is now generally conceded that no entry by the feoffees is necessary. The matter does not concern us here.

[3] See Brent v. Gilbert, Dal. 111 (1574); Brent's Case, 2 Leon. 14, Dyer 340 a (1575); Manning v. Andrews, 1 Leon. 256 (1576); Bracebridge's Case, 1 Leon. 264, sub nom. Harwell v. Lucas, Moore 99 (1578); Stonley v. Bracebridge, 1 Leon. 5 (1583); Smith v. Warren, Cro. El. 688 (1599); Anon., Moore 608; Anon., 13 Co. 48 (1609) (s. c., semble, Jenk. 328): Sympson v. Sothern, Cro. Jac. 376, 2 Bulst. 272, sub nom. Simpson's Case, Godb. 264, sub nom. Simpson v. Southwood, 1 Roll. R. 109, 137, 253 (1615); Allen's Case, Ley 55 (1617); Lewis, Perp. 58–60.

Bostock's Case, Ley 54 (1616). In the Court of Wards. Fine to the use of Edward Bostock for life, remainder to the use of his heirs male on the body of his wife Margery begotten, with remainders over. "And if the said Edward should fortune to die (living the said Margery), that then the said fine should be . . . to the use of the said Margery,

**§ 138.** In *Anon.*[1] (1555) and *Wilford* v. *Wilford*[2] (1555), there were executory devises, but in neither case does their validity appear to have been drawn in question.[3] In *Oclie's Case*[4] (1567) the validity of an executory devise is said to have been decided. Later cases in which executory devises were recognized as valid are given in the note.[5]

**§ 139.** No question as to the remoteness of a conditional limitation of a freehold estate in freehold or copyhold land, either by way or use of devise, appears to have ever come before the courts until *Snow* v. *Cutler*[1] in 1664. The doctrine of remoteness was brought to the attention of the courts in other ways. In most of the cases of conditional limitations they were not in fact such as are forbidden by the modern Rule against Perpetuities, but in *Manning* v.

for term of life, and after her decease to the uses aforesaid." Edward Bostock died, leaving Margery his widow, and an infant son. Held, by Coke, C. J., Hobart, C. J., and Tanfield, C. B., that the King was not entitled to wardship or marriage of the son during the life of Margery. Mr. Lewis, Perp. 150, 151, speaks of this case as "a clear adjudication of the validity of a shifting use." But the use to Margery, though somewhat inartificially expressed, was not a shifting use at all, but simply an ordinary vested remainder for life, limited by way of use. Such evidently was the opinion of the Court. They say, "The estate of Margery is an immediate estate for life."

§ 138. [1] Dyer 124 a. This case seems to be the same as Hinde v. Lyon, reported 2 Leon. 11, 3 Leon. 64, 70, as having been decided in 1578. See Challis, Real Prop. (3d ed.) 170.

[2] Dyer 128 a.

[3] See also Boulton's Case (1564), cited by counsel from Egerton's Reports in Pells v. Brown, 2 Roll. R. 216, 217, Palm. 131, 132.

[4] Cited in Pells v. Brown, 2 Roll. R. 216, 220.

[5] Wellock v. Hammond, Cro. El. 204, 2 Leon. 114 (1590); see Boraston's Case, 3 Co. 19 a, 20 b; Hoe v. Garrell (1591), cited in Pells v. Brown, 2 Roll. R. 216, 220, Palm. 131, 136. Fulmerston v. Steward (1596), cited in Pells v. Brown, Cro. Jac. 590, 592, Palm. 131, 135, 2 Roll. R. 216, 218. Purslowe v. Parker, 2 Roll. Ab. 253, pl. 2, Id. 793, pl. 2 (1600), cited sub nom. Pinsloe v. Parker, 2 Roll. R. 218, 219, sub nom. Mullineux's Case, in Palm. 136. Pay's Case, Cro. El. 878, sub nom. Payne v. Ferrall, Noy 43 (1602). See Lewis, Perp. 80, 81.

§ 139. [1] 1 Lev. 135, 1 Keb. 752, 800, 851, 2 Keb. 11, 145, 296, T. Raym. 162, sub nom. Snow v. Tucker, 1 Sid. 153. § 165, post.

*Andrews*[2] the limitation was what would now be considered too remote. Perhaps this was also the case with *Fulmerston* v. *Steward*.[3] In *Pay's Case*[4] there was a devise to A. from Michaelmas following the testator's death for five years, and then to B. and his heirs. It was held by all the judges of the Court of Queen's Bench, without argument, that the springing executory devise (or remainder, as it was called) to B. was good. It will be observed that this executory devise might possibly not have vested in B. and his heirs within the life of any person living at the death of the testator, although it must have vested at Michaelmas following the testator's death.[5]

### 3. MEANING OF "PERPETUITY"

**§ 140. In Early Times.** Estates in fee simple were at one time to a considerable extent inalienable, but the Statute *Quia Emptores,* 18 Edw. I., c. 1 (1289), enabled tenants in fee simple to alienate their land at pleasure; and provisions expressly introduced into conveyances for the purpose of restraining alienation were held invalid.

[2] 1 Leon. 256, stated in §§ 132, 132.1, ante.

[3] Cited in Pells v. Brown, Cro. Jac. 590, 592, Palm. 131, 135, 2 Roll. R. 216, 218. The doubt as to Fulmerston v. Steward arises from the lack of agreement in the reports. As stated by Croke, Sir Richard Fulmerston devised to Sir Edward Cleere and his wife, and the heirs of Sir Edward, certain lands in Elden, "upon condition they should assure lands in such places to his executors and their heirs to perform his will; and if he (sic) failed, then he devised the said lands in Elden to his executors and their heirs." The limitation to the executors was held a good executory devise. Palmer states the devise as being "sur condition que Cleere faiera divers acts, et sur condition que si Cleere ou his heirs ne perform le condition, que son estate cessera, et les executors averont le terre, et ceo convey al ascun de son nosme." Rolle gives the devise to Sir Edward and his heirs, as on condition "that if he does not perform," etc. If the condition was one that the heirs of Sir Edward could perform (which is doubtful on the reports), the limitation over would now be considered too remote. If, on the other hand, it was to be performed, if at all, in his lifetime, it would be valid.

[4] Cro. El. 878, sub nom. Payne v. Ferrall, Noy 43.

[5] See § 176 et seq., post.

**§ 141.** The Statute *De Donis,* Westm. I., 13 Edw. I., c. 1
(1285), which created estates tail, enacted that they could
not be barred by fine, but in *Taltarum's Case,* Y. B. Mich. 12
Edw. IV. 19, pl. 25 (1472), the judges, who, for some reason or
other, were always favorable to the transfer of land, held
that estates tail could be barred by a recovery; and at last,
by the Statutes of Fines, 4 Hen. VII., c. 24 (1489) and 32
Hen. VIII., c. 36 (1540), the same effect was allowed to fines
levied with certain formalities.

**§ 141.1.** As early at least as the fifteenth century, it was
settled that alienation of a fee simple could not be restrained
indirectly by means of a condition or limitation any more
than it could be directly.[1] But in an estate tail a condition
that the tenant should not make a feoffment, or a clause of
cesser upon his making a feoffment, was good. As, however,
not only would an estate tail be barred, but all conditions
and limitations annexed to it would be destroyed by a common recovery or by a fine under the Statute, they became
practically valueless unless a tenant in tail could be restrained from suffering a recovery or levying a fine. This
could not be done directly, but attempts began to be made
towards the end of the sixteenth century to attach to an

---

§ 141.1. [1] Gray, Restraints on
Alienation (2d ed.), § 19. And so
it was said by Popham, C. J., in
Chudleigh's Case, 1 Co. 120 a, 138
(1595). "If a feoffment be made
to the use of A. for life, and after
to the use of every person who
should be his heir, one after another, for the term of the life of
every such heir only; in this case
if this limitation should be good,
the inheritance would be in nobody; but this limitation is
merely void, for the limitation of
an use to have a perpetual freehold is not agreeable with the
rule of law in estates in possession." Whether this dictum is
law, and whether it means that
A. takes a fee, or that A. takes
a life estate, and his heir a remainder in fee (which, by the
Rule in Shelley's Case, would give
A. the fee), or that A. took a
life estate and his heir a life estate with resulting use in remainder to the feoffor in fee, are
matters which will be dealt with,
in the discussion of the question
whether the validity of a remainder to an unborn child and the
invalidity of a following remainder to its child depends upon the
Rule against Perpetuities or upon
some independent rule. See §§ 298
et seq., App. K, § 937, post.

estate tail conditions against going about to levy a fine or suffer a recovery. These attempts were not successful.[2]

§ 141.2. In the Essay on the Use of the Law (commonly but perhaps wrongly attributed to Lord Bacon), published in 1629, it is said: "There is started up a device called perpetuity; which is an entail with an addition of a proviso conditional tied to his estates, not to put away the land from the next heir; and, if he do, to forfeit his own estate. Which perpetuities, if they should stand, would bring in all the former inconveniences of entails that were cut off by the former mentioned statutes."[1]

§ 141.3. Three of these cases came before the courts during the last few years of the sixteenth century: *Germin* v. *Ascot*,[1] *Cholmeley* v. *Humble*,[2] in 1595, and *Corbet's Case*,[3] in 1599. In the first two of these cases the condition was held invalid as "repugnant"; so it was in the last also, but here the word "perpetuities" occurs twice. The reporter says, "Divers matters were moved by the justices in their argument concerning the general case of perpetuities," and Glanville, J., said that "Richill, who was a judge in the time of Rich. II., and Thirning, who was chief justice of the Common Pleas in the time of Henry IV., intended to have made perpetuities, and, upon forfeiture of the estate tail of one of their sons, to have given the remainder and entry to another."[4]

§ 141.4. Contingent Remainders Destructible. These attempts of a feoffor, donor, or testator, to prevent alienation for an indefinite period, having failed, it occurred to some ingenious person that it was perhaps possible to keep control over the ownership of property for a time by granting an estate for life with contingent remainders, for, as contingent remainders were not transferable, no alienation of the fee could take place until they vested. This device

---

[2] Gray, Restraints on Alienation (2d ed.), §§ 75–77.

§ 141.2. [1] 7 Bacon's Works (Spedding's ed.) 491.

§ 141.3. [1] Moore 364.

[2] Moore 592.

[3] 1 Co. 83 b.

[4] See 7 Holdsworth, Hist. Eng. Law (3d ed.) 205; 1 Tiffany, Real Prop. (3d ed.), § 398.

would not work at common law, because, although contingent remainders were not transferable, they were destructible[1] by the life tenant; but it was hoped that advantage might be taken of the Statute of Uses, and that contingent remainders limited by way of use would be held indestructible.   This question was presented in *Chudleigh's Case*,[2] "commonly called the Case of Perpetuities," to all the judges, but they held that contingent remainders limited by way of use were as destructible as if limited at common law.

§ 141.5.  In *Corbet's Case* and *Chudleigh's Case*, the term "perpetuity" seems to have been used for the first time in our law, and it will be seen that there were two kinds of perpetuities:  *First*, An estate tail with a condition or clause of cesser intended to prevent alienation.  *Second*, A future contingent interest limited by way of use.

The Court quashed both these kinds of perpetuities, the first by declaring that the condition or clause of cesser was invalid, and the second by declaring that contingent interests limited by way of use were destructible.[1]

§ 141.6.  The judgment as to the first kind of perpetuities has stood unshaken; it has always been law and is law to-day.[1]  But we shall see that the ingenuity of conveyancers, aided by the inadvertence of the judges, created a class of future interests which the courts held to be indestructible; that thereupon it became necessary to make a new rule for the restraint of indestructible future interests; and that this rule is the Rule against Perpetuities.[2]

§ 141.4. [1] On the meaning of "destructible" when it is said that a contingent remainder is destructible, see § 101, note 2, ante.

[2] 1 Co. 120 a.

§ 141.5. [1] See 1 Jarm. Wills (7th ed.) 253 et seq.; 15 Law Quart. Rev. 71; 35 Law Quart. Rev. 258; 12 Columbia Law Rev. 203; 22 Iowa Law Rev. 437–441;

25 Iowa Law Rev. 707; Scrutton, Land in Fetters 123; 3 Enc. Laws of Eng. (2d ed.) 519; 11 Enc. Laws of Eng. (2d ed.) 66.

§ 141.6. [1] See Gray, Restraints on Alienation (2d ed.), § 77.

[2] Cf. Mr. Williams's suggestive note to his article in 14 Law Quart. Rev. 234, 240.

On the difficulties arising from

## 4. CONDITIONAL LIMITATIONS AT FIRST HELD DESTRUCTIBLE LIKE CONTINGENT REMAINDERS

§ 142. **Early Cases.** No difference on the score of destructibility was at first felt to exist between remainders limited by way of use and conditional limitations. In *Brent v. Gilbert*[1] (1574), there was a feoffment to the use of A. and of such woman as should be his wife at his death, for their lives, with remainders over. A. levied a fine, married B., and died. The feoffees entered. It was held by the Court of Queen's Bench that the entry of the feoffees revived the use to B. In *Brent's Case*[2] (1575), the statement of facts was the same, except that the limitation was not to the use of A. and of such woman as should be his wife at his death, but to the use of A. and such woman as he shall marry, and except also that it appeared that A., before levying the fine, made a feoffment in which the feoffees joined. In the Common Pleas, Dyer, C. J., Manwood, and Monson, JJ. (Harper, J., dissenting) held that if the entry of the feoffees was necessary to revive the use, they were debarred from entry; and Dyer, C. J., and Manwood, J., thought such entry was necessary. There is no indication that the opinions of the judges would have been altered if B. had had a remainder instead of a shifting use. Indeed it is said that B. "shall take by way of remainder."[3]

§ 143. In *Woodliff v. Drury*,[1] decided in 1595, not long after *Chudleigh's Case*, there was a feoffment to the use of the feoffor "and A. his *feme* that should be after their marriage, and of the heirs of their bodies," and the feoffor married A. It was held in the Queen's Bench that A. would take by this limitation of the use. All the justices said: "By the marriage the new use shall arise and vest, if there be no act in the mean-

confounding these two kinds of perpetuities, see §§ 278 et seq., post.

§ 142. [1] Dal. 111.
[2] 2 Leon. 147, Dyer 340 a.
[3] 2 Leon. 16. See Dillon v. Fraine, Pop. 70, 76; 1 Sugd. Pow.

(7th ed.) 13–15; and cf. Hoe v. Garrell (1591), cited in Pells v. Brown, 2 Roll. R. 216, 220, Palm. 131, 136.

§ 143. [1] Cro. El. 439, sub nom. Woodlet v. Drury, 2 Roll. Ab. 791, pl. 1.

time to destroy that future use (as it was in Chudley's Case),"
thus showing that no distinction had then occurred to the
Court between remainders limited by way of use and conditional limitations. They were supposed to be alike destructible.

§ **144.** The first indication of the idea that a conditional
limitation of a freehold interest was indestructible appears in
*Smith* v. *Warren*[1] (1599). In that case a fine was levied to
the use of the conusee and his heirs on condition that he would
pay an annuity to the conusor, and on default of payment the
land should be to the use of the conusor for his life, and one
year over. The conusee made a feoffment in fee; the annuity
was not paid, and the conusor entered on the feoffee's lessee.
The Court of Common Pleas held that the feoffment had not
destroyed the use to the conusor, "for it is a charge or burden upon the land, which goes along with the land, in whose-
soever hands it comes. And being limited to the conusor
himself, Glanville [J.] conceived it to be a condition unto him;
but if it had been to a stranger, to have arisen upon such
a condition, the non-performance thereof had been a springing
[or, as we should now say, shifting] use unto him; for now
it is merely a tie and charge upon the land, which is not destroyed by the feoffment; and although it be a future use, it
may be well raised upon non-performance of the condition;
as it was adjudged in *Bracebridge's Case.*"[2] The springing
use here was preserved under circumstances in which, according to *Chudleigh's Case,* a remainder limited by way of use
would have been destroyed. The fact that the use arose as a
penalty for breach of a condition in favor of the grantor seems
to have had some influence—it is hard to say precisely what
—on the decision.

§ **145. Purslowe v. Parker**[1] (1600). Devise of rents out
of land; if the heir pay the "said annuities," he to have the

---

§ 144. [1] Cro. El. 688.

[2] This is not Bracebridge v.
Cook, Plowd. 416, as stated in the
margin, but Bracebridge's Case, 1
Leon. 264.

§ 145. [1] 2 Roll. Ab. 253, pl. 2,
Id. 793, pl. 2, cited sub nom.
Pinsloe v. Parker, 2 Roll. R. 218,
219, sub nom. Mullineux's Case,
Palm. 136.

land; if he do not pay them, then the executors to have it. The heir made a feoffment of the land, and the annuities were not paid. It was held by the Court of Queen's Bench that the feoffment had not destroyed "the contingent remainders," "for there is a diversity between a contingent remainder which depends on a limitation and contingent uses, for the feoffment in this case has not done away the limitations which are to persons known with certainty, between whom there is a privity as in this case."[2]   In the account given, 2 Roll. R. 219, the distinction is still more clearly stated to be between a limitation to persons certain which is not destroyed by a feoffment, and a limitation to a person uncertain which is destroyed. No difference between remainders limited by way of use and conditional limitations is taken.[3]

§ 146. **Wood v. Reignold**[1] (1601).  A. covenanted, in contemplation of marriage with B., to stand seised of land to the use of himself and his heirs until marriage, and then to the use of himself and B. and the heirs of his body.  A. then let the land for years to C., married B., and died.  Popham, C. J., and Gawdy and Clench, JJ., were of opinion that the lease bound the springing use but did not destroy it.  Fenner, J., thought the use was neither destroyed nor bound.  This was because the making of a lease did not destroy or affect the seisin of the freehold.  Remainders limited by way of use are not destroyed by a lease.  This was held six years later by the same court in *Bould* v. *Wynston*.[2]  It was assumed that if A. had made a feoffment instead of a lease, the shifting use would have been destroyed.  "If a freehold be conveyed to one upon consideration, the future use shall not rise; for

[2] 2 Roll. Ab. 793.
[3] This notion that contingent interests are destructible when the contingency has reference to persons, but are not destructible when the contingency has reference to events, emerges here for the sole time in the law. Arch-

er's Case, 1 Co. 66 b, which is cited, is no authority for such a distinction.

§ 146. [1] Cro. El. 764, 854.
[2] Cro. Jac. 168, sub nom. Bolls v. Winton, Noy 122, 2 Roll. Ab. 793 (1607).  But see Barton's Case, Moore 742, contra.

there is not any person seised to that use when it should arise."[3]

§ 147. *Smith* v. *Warren*[1] is the only early case which favors any distinction on the score of destructibility between remainders and conditional limitations; and no suggestion that the invalidity of a future limitation of real estate is dependent upon its remoteness appears until much later.[2]

### 5. EXECUTORY DEVISES OF TERMS INTRODUCED

§ 148. **Early Devises.** As has been said, it was in the discussion of executory devises of chattels real that the Rule against Perpetuities had its origin and took its shape.[1] Although chattels real were always devisable at common law, no attempt to limit an executory devise of them is to be found in the books till about the time of the Statute of Wills. But there is a case where a future bequest of the use of a chattel personal was held good.[2] A distinction was taken between the bequest of a chattel personal to A. for life, which passed the absolute interest to A., and admitted no executory bequest; and a gift of the use of a chattel personal to A. for life, which gave A. the occupation only, and left the title in the executor. But in *Paramour* v. *Yardley*,[3] it is said that a devise of the occupation of a term was the same as a devise of the land itself, so that this distinction could not be availed of for the establishment of executory devises of leaseholds. It now remains to trace the history of their gradual introduction. It will be remembered that the Statute of Uses did not apply to leaseholds, and that therefore the only conditional limitations of chattels real in England were executory devises.

§ 149. In *Anon.*[1] (1536), a term was devised to A. and the

3 Per Fenner, J., Cro. El. 765.

§ 147. 1 Cro. El. 688, § 144, ante.

2 See Chilcott v. Hart, 23 Colo. 40, 54, 45 Pac. 391, 396.

§ 148. 1 Whatever may have been the case as to chattels personal, future limitations of chat-

[G. R. P.]—10

tels real were regarded as executory and not in the nature of remainders. See App. F, §§ 807 et seq., post. But cf. § 856, post.

2 Y. B. Trin. 37 Hen. VI. 30, pl. 11. See §§ 80, ante, 826, post.

3 Plowd. 539, 542, 543.

§ 149. 1 Dyer 7 a.

heirs of her body, the remainder, if she died without issue within the term, to B. The Court of Common Pleas held that a term could not be "limited in remainder." The limitation would now undoubtedly be held bad, because after an indefinite failure of issue; but the objection made at the time was apparently to an executory devise of a term under any circumstances. In *Anon.*[2] (1543), a slight advance seems to have been made on this. It was there said that if a term was devised to one for life, the remainder over, the remainder over is good; but if the devisee for life aliens, the remainder-man is without remedy.[3]

§ **150.** In *Cecil's Case*[1] (1566), an executory limitation of a term by deed was held bad, as it would be in England at the present day;[2] but in *Anon.*[3] (1568), Weston, Walsh, and Harper, JJ., are reported to have said: "The remainder of a term devised to one for term of life is good by devise, but not by estate executed in the lifetime." The reporter, however, who was then Chief Justice of the Court, adds, "Yet, *quære* the first."

§ **151.** Ten years afterwards, in *Welcden* v. *Elkington*[1] (1578), it was distinctly held that an executory devise of a term on the death of the first taker was good and could not be destroyed by any act of the first taker; and in the thirty years following, the same or a similar point was frequently decided in the same way.[2] The current of opinion, however,

[2] Bro. Ab. Chat. 140, pl. 23 (33 Hen. VIII.).

[3] So Anon., Dyer 74 b, pl. 18 (1552). And see North v. Butts, Dyer 139 b (1556).

§ 150. [1] Dyer 253 b.

[2] And see Green v. Edwards, Cro. El. 216, 1 Leon. 218, 1 And. 258, Moore 297. See §§ 807 et seq., post.

[3] Dyer 277 b.

§ 151. [1] Plowd. 516, Dyer 358 b; and see Curson v. Karvile (1562) and Wallis v. Arden (1571), both cited in Cole v. Moore, Moore 806, 807.

[2] Paramour v. Yardley, Plowd. 539 (1579). Amner v. Luddington, 2 Leon. 92, 3 Leon. 89, Godb. 26, 1 And. 60 (1584). Vincent Lee's Case, 3 Leon. 110, sub nom. Lee v. Lee, Moore 268 (1584). Hannington v. Ryder, 1 Leon. 92, sub nom. Haverington's Case, Owen 6, sub nom. Hannington v. Richards, Golds. 59, 65, sub nom. Rudiard v. Hannington, 1 And. 162, Moore 249, pl. 393

was not unbroken. In *Anon.*[3] (1587), there are *dicta* by Anderson, C. J., and Rhodes, J., that an executory devise of a term after a life interest therein is void, and such a devise was held bad by the Court of Common Pleas in *Rayman* v. *Gold*[4] (1592). In *Woodcock* v. *Woodcock*[5] (1600), the judges of the Court of Common Pleas expressed opinions that such a devise was void. Walmsley, J., said: "There are divers judgments against my opinion, but upon what reasons I understand not." In *Mallet* v. *Sackford*[6] (1607), the Court of Queen's Bench was divided on the question. Coke, C. J., and Walmsley, J., thought such executory devise not to be good. Warburton and Daniel, JJ., thought that it was good.[7]

§ **152. Held Indestructible.** But in *Manning's Case*[1] (1609) and *Lampet's Case*[2] (1612), it was solemnly adjudged that after a devise of a term for life, an executory devise over was good, and not destructible by the first taker; and although these decisions have been grumbled at,[3] they have never been overruled.[4] *Lampet's Case*[5] is the first case in which "perpe-

(1587). Handall v. Brown, Moore 748 (1603). Cole v. Moore, Moore 806 (1607).

[3] 3 Leon. 195, 4 Leon. 192.

[4] Moore 635.

[5] Cro. El. 795.

[6] Cro. Jac. 198, 1 Roll. Ab. 610, pl. 4, 5. See § 82, ante.

[7] See Rector of Chedington's Case, 1 Co. 153 a, sub nom. Lloyd v. Wilkinson, Moore 478.

§ **152.** [1] 8 Co. 94 b.

[2] 10 Co. 46 b, sub nom. Lampitt v. Starkey, 2 Brownl. 172.

[3] E. g. by all the judges of the Common Pleas and barons of the Exchequer (except Tanfield, C. B.). They said, "that the first grant or devise of a term made to one for life, remainder to another, hath been much controverted, whether such a remainder might be good, and whether all may not be de-

stroyed by the alienation of the first party; and if it were now first disputed, it would be hard to maintain; but being so often adjudged, they would not now dispute it." Child v. Baylie, Cro. Jac. 459, 461 (cf. W. Jones 15). Per Hide, Twisden, and Browne. JJ., "Though we do not hold it fit to call in question the judgment in Matthew Manning's Case, yet do not think it safe to stretch the law against the ordinary rules of law further than in that case it is done." Pearse v. Reeve, Pollexf. 29, 30.

[4] 2 Harg. Jurid. Arg. 41 et seq. Lewis, Perp. 83–89. See §§ 818 et seq., post. Even after Manning's Case it was held in Price v. Atmore, 1 Bulst. 191, 4 Leon. 246, sub nom. Price v. Almory, Moore 831, that if the executory

tuity" is mentioned in connection with an executory devise. Lord Coke, C. J., in arguing against the proposition that an executory devisee cannot release his interest to the first taker of the term, says that "it would be inconvenient that such manner of perpetuity should be made of a chattel, when of an inheritance neither by act executed by the common law, nor by limitation of an use, nor by devises in last wills, any perpetuity can be established."

## 6. FIRST SUGGESTIONS AT THE BAR OF THE RULE AGAINST PERPETUITIES

§ **153. Before 1620.** In *Anon.*[1] (1536), a limitation of a term after an indefinite failure of issue had been held bad; but the objection apparently was not to the remoteness of the executory devise, but to any executory devise of a term whatever.[2] And in *Forster* v. *Brown*[3] (1604), on a devise of a term to A. and the heirs of his body, but if A. died without issue, then to B., it seems to have been held, although the case is obscurely reported, that the gift over was bad. But in *Tatton* v. *Mollineux*[4] (1610), which was decided by Lord Ellesmere, C., assisted by Warburton and Croke, JJ., it was said: "If the remainder of such a term be limited over, the particular donee in tail or for life cannot sell it to the prejudice of the remainder; but such a remainder will be preserved by the common law, as has been adjudged in the Court of Common Pleas,[5] and also in Chancery, as divers decrees are there made." And so in *Retherick* v. *Chappel*[6] (1612), it was held, on the authority of *Manning's Case,* that, on a devise of a term to A. so long as he should have issue, and if he died without issue, then to B., the remainder to B. was good.[7]

devisee of a term died during the life of the first taker, his executor would not take his interest. But see Welcden v. Elkington, Plowd. 516, 525, in marg., and cases cited.
[5] 10 Co. 46 b, 52 a.
§ 153. [1] Dyer 7 a.
[2] See § 149, ante.

[3] Moore 758.
[4] Moore 809, Pollexf. 24.
[5] Probably Manning's Case, § 152, ante, which had been decided the previous year, is meant.
[6] 2 Bulst. 28.
[7] But see Bennet v. Lewknor, 1 Roll. R. 356, where it is said that this point was not argued in

§ 154. Thus far there had been no distinction taken between an executory devise of a term after a life interest and
after an indefinite failure of issue. Both limitations were at
first thought alike bad; and now *Manning's Case* was supposed to make them alike good. In *Bennet* v. *Lewknor*[1]
(1616), the distinction between them was first clearly insisted
on. Here there was a devise of a term to A. and his heirs
male, with an executory devise over on failure of such heirs
to a person living at the testator's death. The only report
of the case contains nothing but the arguments of counsel in
the Exchequer and a statement that the case was adjourned.[2]
Serjeant Finch, who argued against the executory devise, gave
three reasons for its invalidity. 1. That by intendment the
estate of A. was to continue forever. 2. "If it is a good remainder, then there will be a possibility on a possibility."
3. "If it is a good remainder, then there will be a perpetuity
of a chattel where there cannot be of a freehold, and there
will be no means to dock it." Here we first meet the idea of
remoteness as an objection to a limitation struggling to find
expression.

§ 155. **Child v. Baylie.**[1] This case, which came before the
King's Bench in 1618, was as follows: A devise of a term to
A. and his assigns, provided, that if A. died without issue
living at his death, then the term should go to B.[2] A. as-

---

Retherick v. Chappel; and cf.
Child v. Baylie, Cro. Jac. 459, 461,
462, Palm. 333, 335, 336; and
Wallis v. Arden (1571) cited in
Cole v. Moore, Moore 806, 807,
808.

§ **154.** [1] 1 Roll. R. 356.

[2] In the reports of Child v. Baylie, Cro. Jac. 459, 460, Palm. 48,
50, 333, 334, W. Jones 15, it is
said that the Court held the executory devise void; but in the report of that case in 2 Roll. R. 129,
130, it is said that this was only
the remark obiter of one of the
barons.

§ **155.** [1] Cro. Jac. 459, Palm. 48,
333, W. Jones 15, 2 Roll. R. 129,
See Duke of Norfolk's Case, 3 Ch.
Cas. 1, 34.

[2] This is the correct form of the
devise. It is so given in Croke,
and in Palm. 48. In the report of
the case in the Exchequer Chamber, Palm. 333, the proviso is
said to be that if A. dies within
the term, without issue then living, which is substantially the
same. In W. Jones it is given
thus: "If A. dies without issue
during the life of B." In 2 Roll.
R. alone is it given simply, "If A.

signed the term and died without leaving issue at his death;
and B. brought ejectment against the assignee. This case
raised clearly the question whether the reason why a gift of
a term after a general failure of issue was bad was to be found
in its remoteness. If remoteness was the reason, then the gift
here to B. was good, because it must take effect on the death
of A., and that was not more remote than the gift which had
been held good in *Manning's Case*. In the Court of King's
Bench no attention was paid by counsel or court to the fact
that the gift over was in case A. died without issue living at
his death. It was treated as if the gift had been on failure of
issue generally;[3] and the gift to B. was held bad because the
gift was to A. and his assigns; because a term cannot be entailed; because it was the gift of a possibility on a possibility;[4]
and because if the gift to B. was good it could not be barred
by A., and thus future interests in chattels would be less
destructible than they were in freeholds, "and if the law
will not suffer such perpetuities of inheritances, then much
less will it suffer perpetuities of chattels."[5]

§ 156. The evils arising from the Statute *De Donis* creating inalienable estates tail were familiar to the courts, and
after their predecessors had, by the doctrine of *Taltarum's
Case*, broken down the "perpetuities" of estates tail,[1] the only
perpetuities which they had had occasion to consider, they
were resolved not to have them surreptitiously introduced by
entailing long terms, to which the device of common recoveries could not be applied. Having been warned by the
history of estates tail, they timely took the matter in hand,

dies without issue during the
term." The words "living at the
death" must have been in the devise, for the argument in the Exchequer Chamber turns largely upon them. And in the Duke of
Norfolk's Case, 3 Ch. Cas. 1, 34,
Lord    Chancellor    Nottingham
caused the record to be examined,
and found that Croke's report was
correct.

[3] 2 Roll. R. 129, Palm. 48, Cro.
Jac. 459.

[4] This is sometimes called a
"remote possibility;" but the context shows that by "remote" is
meant "improbable," not "distant
in point of time."

[5] 2 Roll. R. 129, ad fin.

§ 156. [1] See § 141, ante.

and in *Bennet* v. *Lewknor*,[2] as devises after failure of issue
could not be docked, they seem to have held such devises void
*ab initio*.   If there was present to the mind of the Court of
King's Bench in *Bennet* v. *Lewknor* and *Child* v. *Baylie* any
idea that a limitation might be objectionable because it was to
begin at too distant a day, such idea was still extremely vague.

§ **157.** The case of *Child* v. *Baylie* was carried to the Exchequer Chamber in 1623.[1]  There the attention of the Court
was called by counsel to the fact that the limitation over to
B. was not on the death of A. without issue generally, but
on the death of A. without issue living at his death.   But
the judges[2] held "for the case in question, where there was a
devise to one and his assigns, and if he died without issue
then living, that it would remain to another, it is a void devise; and it is all one as the devise of a term to one and his
heirs of his body, and if he die without issue, that then it
shall remain to another, it is merely void; for such an entail
of a term is not allowable in law, for the mischief which otherwise would ensue, if there should be such a perpetuity of a
term."[3]  It is clear that "perpetuity" is not used here in the
sense of remoteness, for obviously there is a great difference
between the two devises in the matter of remoteness.[4]   Of
*Retherick* v. *Chappel*[9] the Court say, "And though there be
such a judgment given in the King's Bench as allows the re-

---

[2] § 154, ante.
  § **157.** [1] Cro.  Jac.  459,  460,
Palm. 333, W. Jones 15.
  [2] Tanfield, C. B., dissented;
Palm. 334, adds, "totis viribus."
W. Jones 15, says Denham, B.,
also dissented; but the other reporters do not agree with this:
Palm. 335, Cro. Jac. 461.
  [3] Cro. Jac. 461.
  [4] It might be fairly urged that
the ground taken by the Court
would require them to hold that
if a term is given for life to one,
and on his death to another, as
in Manning's Case, 8 Co. 94 b,

§ 152, ante, the gift over to such
other is bad; and they admit this.
They say, "The first grant or devise of a term made to one for
life, remainder to another, hath
been much controverted, whether
such a remainder might be good,
and whether all may not be destroyed by the alienation of the
first party; and if it were now
first disputed, it would be hard
to maintain; but being so often
adjudged, they would not now dispute it."  Cro. Jac. 461.
  [5] 2 Bulst. 28.  See § 153, ante.

mainder to be good, yet time has discovered the inconvenience that such limitations have introduced in the republic."[6]

§ **158.** The case of *Child* v. *Baylie* is important as showing that none of the twelve judges of England, except Chief Baron Tanfield,[1] were then disposed to recognize the question of remoteness as having anything to do with the validity of a limitation. But it is also important because Davenport (afterward Chief Baron of the Exchequer), in his argument before the Court of Exchequer Chamber for the validity of the gift over, was the first person to enunciate clearly the principle on which the Rule against Perpetuities rests. He said: "There is no danger of perpetuity by such a conveyance. For he took a diversity when the contingency is such as can or ought [*doet*] to happen in the life of the devisee.[2] There a remainder limited on such an estate in case of a devise of a chattel is good, as in our case, if he should die without issue of his body living at the time of his death, so that it does not exceed his life. But if the contingency be such as is foreign [*forrein*], or is to commence *in futuro* after the death of the first devisee, there, because such limitation tends to make a perpetuity, a remainder limited on it is bad, as, if he should die without issue or without heir, that then it shall remain over. And on this diversity they strongly [*fortment*] rely."[3]

### 7. SLOW JUDICIAL RECOGNITION OF REMOTENESS AS THE ESSENTIAL POINT IN JUDGING FUTURE LIMITATIONS

§ **159. Pells v. Brown.** After the decision of *Child* v. *Baylie* in the King's Bench, but before the argument in the Exchequer Chamber, came in 1620 the case of *Pells* v. *Brown* in the King's Bench.[1] A testator seised in fee devised the land

[6] Palm. 335, 336.

§ **158.** [1] Except also, possibly, Baron Denham, see note to the preceding section.

[2] It is printed "devisor," but clearly "devisee" is meant. It is corrected by an old hand into "devisee" in Judge Story's copy of Palmer, now in the Library of the Law School of Harvard University.

[3] Palm. 334. On this case, see also App. K, § 940, post.

§ **159.** [1] Cro. Jac. 590, 2 Roll. R. 196, 216, Godb. 282, sub nom. Pills v. Brown, Palm. 131, sub. nom. Petts v. Browne, J. Bridg. 1.

to A. and his heirs, and if A. died without issue, living B.,
then to B. and his heirs. A. suffered a recovery and died without issue, living B. It was held by Montagu, C. J., Chamber-
layne and Houghton, JJ., that B. was not barred. Doderidge,
J., dissented on the ground that if the executory devise to B.
was not destroyed by the recovery, "it would be a mischievous
kind of perpetuity which could not by any means be destroyed."[2] His brethren replied: "There is no such mischief
that it should maintain perpetuities, for it is but in a particular case, and upon a mere contingency, which peradventure
never may happen, and may be avoided by joining him in the
recovery who hath such a contingency."[3] The devise to B. was
in fact not too remote within the Rule against Perpetuities as
now established, but no question of remoteness was mooted in
the case. It was assumed that the gift to B. was good; the
question discussed was whether it was destructible. The remark of the Court that the objection of perpetuity might be
avoided by joining B. in the recovery shows that "perpetuity"
was not used as meaning a remote interest, but as meaning an
inalienable interest. Although no question of remoteness was
presented in *Pells* v. *Brown*, it is hard to overestimate its influence on the subsequent history of conveyancing. Had it
been held that conditional limitations could be destroyed like
contingent remainders, the need of a rule against remoteness
might never have been felt; even if some such rule had finally
been evolved, it would probably have been in other than its
present form. But when conditional limitations were declared
indestructible, the need of distinguishing between those which
could be allowed and those which must be condemned as too
remote was sure, sooner or later, to present itself to the
courts.[4]

[2] Cro. Jac. 592.
[3] Cro. Jac. 593.
[4] See 2 Harg. Jurid. Arg. 32 et
seq. Lewis, Perp. 128–134. Lord
Kenyon's "nervous expression" in
Porter v. Bradley, 3 T. R. 143,
that the case of Pells v. Brown
"is the foundation, and as it were

the Magna Charta, of this branch
of the law," refers not, however,
to its deciding that an executory
devise is indestructible, but to its
deciding that the failure of issue
intended was definite and not indefinite. See Marsden, Perp. 198.
   In the case of Gay v. Gay, or

**§ 160. Further Cases.** After, however, as before the case of *Pells* v. *Brown* it was the consideration of chattels real to which the Rule of Perpetuities owed its growth. Down to

Jay v. Jay, Style 258, 274 (1651), in the Upper Bench, there was a devise of a copyhold to A. and his heirs, but if A. died during the life of his mother then to B. and his heirs. "Rolle, Chief Justice, said, it is an inconvenience to devise such a contingent estate. Nicholas [J.] doubted, for he said it would shake many wills, if it might not be." (P. 275.) The judgment is not reported. Latch, of counsel, is said to have "confessed that in the case of Pell and Brown, 17 Jac. rot. 44, the contrary was adjudged; but that there did appear such apparent inconvenience in it, that upon it the Court was afterwards divided, and 21 Jac., in the Serjeant's Case,* it was made a flat quære, and ever since it hath been disputable, whether a contingent devise be good or not, and in Jacob and Telling's Case it is not determined, and Hanbury and Cookrell's Case is not adjudged, but if it be, it is on my side; and Mich. 37 & 38 C. B. rot. 1149, it was adjudged upon solemn argument at the Bar, and on the Bench, contrary to the judgment in Pell and Brown's Case, if lands be devised to one and his heirs, and if he die without issue, that the land shall be to another and his heirs, this is no estate tail; for it cannot stand with the rules of law to devise such an estate, for it is but a possibility, and if it should be more, it must be a fee upon a fee, and so a perpetuity, and it cannot be known within what bounds it shall end, either in case of years or life or other contingencies, and the comparison of Lamport's [Lampet's] Case is not like to this case, for that was of a term." (Pp. 274, 275.) These statements attributed to Latch find no support in the printed books, and both counsel and reporter bear rather an evil name for accuracy. See per Twisden, J., in Foxwith v. Tremain, 1 Mod. 296; Palmer, Preface; O. Bridg. Pref., p. ix; Wallace, Reporters (4th ed.) 262, 288. It is clear, however, that the judges felt anxious about the consequences of the decision in Pells v. Brown, that executory devises were indestructible. The notion that an executory devise was not barred by a recovery "went down with the judges like chopped hay." Per Powell, J., Scattergood v. Edge, 12 Mod. 278, 281. "These executory devises had not been long countenanced when the judges repented them; and if it were to be done again, it would never prevail." Per Treby, C. J., 12 Mod. 287.

* "It is true, it was made a question afterwards in the Serjeant's Case; but what then? We all know that to be no rule to judge by; for what is used to exercise the wits of the serjeants is not a governing opinion to decide the law." Per Lord Chancellor Nottingham, in the Duke of Norfolk's Case, 3 Ch. Cas. 1, 31, 32.

and including the great *Case of the Duke of Norfolk*,[1] in the year 1681, there were, besides *Gay* v. *Gay*,[2] mentioned in the note to the preceding section, only two cases in which the validity of executory devises of freeholds came in question,—*Snow* v. *Cutler* and *Taylor* v. *Biddal*. They are discussed below.[3] The decisions on executory devises of terms, on the other hand, were numerous. The principle announced by Davenport in *Child* v. *Baylie*,[4] that the validity of an estate on condition precedent depended not on the character but on the time of the contingent event, although ultimately to prevail, was, as we have seen, at first rejected by almost the entire bench, and won its way but slowly to judicial recognition.

**§ 161.** Two classes of executory devises of terms came before the courts,—those after a life interest and those after a failure of issue. In the latter class of cases, where the failure of issue was indefinite, the executory devises were held bad.[1] In *Wood* v. *Sanders*[2] (1669), a term was assigned in trust for A. for sixty years if he lived so long; then to B. for sixty years if she lived so long; then the trustees to assign to C. in case he survived A. and B. If C. died in the lifetime of A. and B., leaving issue who were living at the death of A. and B., then the trustees to assign to the one who should then be C.'s eldest son; if C. died without issue before such assignment, then to D. and the heirs of his body, and in default of such issue, then to E. C. died before A. and B. without issue, and E. was appointed his administrator. Then A. and B. died, and D. entered and afterwards died without issue. Lord Keeper Bridgman, assisted by Twisden, Rainsford, and

§ 160. 1 3 Ch. Cas. 1.
2 Style 258, 274.
3 §§ 165, 172, post.
4 See § 158, ante.
§ 161. 1 Sanders v. Cornish, Cro. Car. 230 (1631). Backhouse v. Bellingham, Pollexf. 33 (1664); see § 361, post. Wood v. Sanders, 1 Ch. Cas. 131, Pollexf. 35 (1669). Love v. Wyndham, 1 Mod. 50, 2 Keb. 637, 1 Sid. 450,

1 Lev. 290, 1 Ventr. 79, 2 Ch. Rep. 14 (1670). Burges v. Burges, 1 Ch. Cas. 229, 1 Mod. 115, Pollexf. 40, Finch 91 (1674); see § 166, post. Knight v. Knight, Pollexf. 42, Finch 181 (1674). Warman v. Seaman, Pollexf. 112, 2 Ch. Cas. 209, Finch 279, Freem. Ch. 306 (1675).
2 1 Ch. Cas. 131, Pollexf. 35.

Wilde, JJ., held that as C.'s interest had never vested, D.'s administrator was entitled to the trusts of the term. The case is very shortly reported. Its decision is inconsistent with any theory of a gift of a possibility upon a possibility being bad. Here the gift to D. was held good; and yet it took effect only in case C. died, only in case he died in the lifetime of A. and B., and only in case he died in the lifetime of A. and B. without issue. On the other hand the case falls short of deciding that remoteness is the only objection to the creation of a future interest. It was apparently still the opinion of the Court that if a term was given to A. and the heirs of his body, and A.'s interest vested, no gift over was good even though it was made contingent on the extinction of A.'s issue during a life in being.[3] And this is confirmed by *Boucher* v. *Antram*.[4] There a legacy was given to A. "for her to have the use of it during her life, and her child or children to have it after her decease, but if she happens to die, leaving no child surviving her," then to B. It was held by Lord Keeper Bridgman that the gift to B., "it being a personalty, is in the nature of a perpetuity," and was void.[5]

§ 162. The other class of executory devises of terms which came up for consideration were gifts after life interests. In accordance with *Manning's Case*[1] such gifts continued to be held good.[2] In *Cotton* v. *Heath*[3] (1638), a case was referred out of Chancery to Jones, Croke, and Berkeley, Justices of the King's Bench. A. devised a term to his widow for eighteen years, then to C. for life, and then to the eldest issue male of C. for life. The judges resolved without question,[4] and the Lord Keeper Coventry agreed,[5] that "although C. has not any issue male at the time of the devise and death of the devisor,

---

[3] See Howard v. Norfolk, 2 Ch. Rep. 229, 239, 2 Swanst. 454, 467, 468.

[4] 2 Ch. Rep. 65, Pollexf. 37 (1671).

[5] See also Pearse v. Reeve, Pollexf. 29.

§ 162. [1] 8 Co. 94 b. See § 152, ante.

[2] E. g. Veizy v. Pinwell, Pollexf. 44.

[3] 1 Roll. Ab. 612, pl. 3, Pollexf. 26.

[4] Pollexfen says that the certificate was signed by two of the judges.

[5] See Pollexf. 26.

yet if he has issue male before his death, this issue male shall
have it as an executory devise, because although it is a contingency on a contingency, and the issue not *in esse* at the time
of the devise, yet inasmuch as it is limited to him only for life,
it is good, and all one with *Manning's Case;*" and further,[6]
that a feoffment by C. after the birth of issue male did not
destroy the executory devise.

§ **163.** Twenty-three years later, however, in 1661, Lord
Chancellor Clarendon, assisted by Twisden and Browne, JJ.,
held, in *Apprice* v. *Flower*,[1] that after the devise of a term
to A., a devise of it to the unborn children of A. was void,
because it "tended to raise and create a perpetuity contrary
to the rules of law." As such limitations were the ordinary
form in which freehold land was settled and devised, the
objection would seem to have been the indestructibility of
chattel interests. In accordance with *Apprice* v. *Flower* it
was said by Hyde, Twisden, and Browne, JJ., in *Pearse* v.
*Reeve*[2] (1661) : "Though we do not hold it fit to call in question the judgment in *Matthew Manning's Case,* yet do not
think it safe to stretch the law against the ordinary rules
of law, further than in that case it is done; and, therefore, if
the devisor by his will doth limit the remainder of it to his
children, or to the issue of his body, whereby his intention
appears to limit it in a kind of perpetuity to his issue or to
his children, we hold such limitation to be void." And in
*Goring* v. *Bickerstaffe*[3] (1662), before Lord Chancellor Clarendon, assisted by Foster, C. J., Bridgman, C. J., and Hales,
C. B.,[4] the Court "did all agree in one uniform opinion, that
the limitation of a term to several persons in remainder, one
after another, if those persons were in being, and particularly
named, could not tend to a perpetuity; otherwise, if the persons were not in being, and that a man might declare the trust
of a possibility in remainder, but that the limitation of a

6 See Pollexf. 26.

§ **163.** 1 Pollexf. 27, 1 Ch. Rep.
175.

2 Pollexf. 29.

3 Freem. Ch. 163, 1 Ch. Cas. 4,
Pollexf. 31.

4 So in Pollexfen; in Chancery
Cases, Wyndham, J., is given instead of Bridgman, C. J.

trust of such possibility to the heir of the limiter was a void limitation."[5]

§ **164.** In *Sackvile* v. *Dobson*[1] (1663), however, there was a limitation of the trust of a term to husband and wife, and the longest liver of them, for life, and after to the eldest issue of them, none being then born. It was held that though a gift to an unborn person, after two limitations to persons living, was void, yet a gift to an unborn person after one such limitation was good, and that the limitation to husband and wife was but one limitation, and therefore the gift over in this case was good.[2]

§ **165.** In the series of cases on chattels real must be intercalated the case of *Snow* v. *Cutler*[1] (1664). A., having the reversion of copyhold land after his wife's death, devised it to the heirs of his wife's body, if he or they should attain fourteen years. A. died without leaving issue by his wife. She married again and had a son who reached fourteen. She then died. The question was whether the son was entitled. The judges seem to have been in great doubt. Kelyng, C. J., and Twisden, J., thought the devise good. Wyndham and Morton, JJ., *contra*. The objection of the two latter seems to have been that the devise was in form a present devise to a person not *in esse*. Thus Wyndham says: "A present devise to an infant *in ventre sa mere* is void; *contra* if it be said 'when he shall be born;' so to J. S. when he shall marry my daughter, this is executory and good; so had our devise been to the heir, when he shall be born, [it] had been good; but this being to the heirs of the wife, it's intended present, and so void."[2] But the judges are said to have been all agreed that an executory devise "may well be allowed to take place within the compass of a life, but not after a dying without issue, for that would make a perpetuity."[3] This is the clearest state-

---

[5] Freem. Ch. 166.

§ **164.** [1] 1 Ch. Cas. 33.

[2] The case seems to have been decided on a misunderstanding of Goring v. Bickerstaffe.

§ **165.** [1] 1 Lev. 135, 1 Keb. 752, 800, 851, 2 Keb. 11, 145, 296, T. Raym. 162, sub nom. Snow v. Tucker, 1 Sid. 153.

[2] 1 Keb. 802.

[3] 1 Lev. 136.

ment given up to this time of the proposition that the validity of an executory devise depends upon the question whether it must happen within a lifetime.[4]

§ **166.** Returning now to the cases of terms for years, the next is *Burges* v. *Burges*[1] (1674). There a term was settled in trust for A. for life, then for his wife for life, then for their first and other sons successively and the heirs of their bodies, and then for their daughters. Lord Keeper Finch, while holding that the limitation to the daughters was void,[2] yet "would allow one contingency to be good, viz. that to the first son, though the first son was not *in esse* at the time of his decease."[3] In *Oakes* v. *Chalfont*[4] (1674), Lord Keeper Finch went a step further, and held that the limitation of a term after limitations to unborn children was good, if the children took life interests only, and the limitation over was to a person *in esse*.

§ **167.** In the case of *Goring* v. *Bickerstaffe*[1] (1662), we found the first distinct enunciation of the proposition that the number of executory limitations of a term is immaterial if they are all to persons in being.[2] But in *Love* v. *Wyndham*[3] (1670), this was more emphatically expressed. In that case there was a devise of a term to A. for life, then to B. for life, but if B. should die without issue to C. It was held that an indefinite failure of issue was meant, and this being so, of course the devise to C. was void. The case is noteworthy on account of some remarks of Twisden, J. They are differently reported. In 1 Mod. 54, thus: "If a tenant of a term devise it

---

[4] Kelyng, C. J., is reported to have said, "Where the intent is exprest to be in future, it is an executory devise; and if an ordinary contingency be thereupon limited, which may determine within one life or such time, it's good." 2 Keb. 300.

**§ 166.** [1] 1 Ch. Cas. 229, 1 Mod. 115, Pollexf. 40, Finch 91.

[2] See § 161, ante.

[3] 1 Mod. 115.

[4] Pollexf. 38, sub nom. Chalfont v. Okes, 1 Ch. Cas. 239.

**§ 167.** [1] Freem. Ch. 163, 1 Ch. Cas. 4, Pollexf. 31. See § 163, ante.

[2] See passage cited in § 163, ante.

[3] 1 Mod. 50, 2 Keb. 637, 1 Sid. 450, 1 Lev. 290, 1 Ventr. 79, 2 Ch. Rep. 14. See § 226, post; and also Huntbatch v. Lee, 3 Keb. 750 (1676), obscurely reported.

to B. for life, the remainder to C. for life, the remainder to D. for life; I have heard it questioned, whether these remainders are good or not? But it hath been held, that if all the remaindermen are living at the time of the devise, it is good: if all the candles be light at once it is good. But if you limit a remainder to a person not in being, as to the first-begotten son, etc. and the like, there would be no end if such limitations were admitted, and therefore they are void: and some judges are of the same opinion to this hour." In 1 Sid. 451: "Note by Twisden, J., that the law is now settled, and if a term be devised to one for life, remainder to another for life, remainder to a third for life, etc., and so to twenty, one after the other, that it is a good devise to them all, notwithstanding the objection of possibilities upon possibilities, if all the persons were *in esse* at the time of the devise, because all the candles are lighted at once. But if the devise be to one for life, who is not then *in esse* (as to the first son), there no limitation of a term can be after that. And of this opinion seemed all the court."[4]

§ 168. **Summary of Early Cases.** The law up to this time may be summed up thus: Any number of life interests could be given in succession to persons in being.[1] Limitations to unborn persons might be good.[2] But the remoteness in time of a contingency was not the sole test of the validity of an interest conditioned on it. The nature of the contingency was also involved. Thus a gift of chattels after an indefinite failure of issue was bad, although confined to a failure within the lifetime of persons in being. This had been held in *Child* v. *Baylie*,[3] and had never been overruled. It was reserved for Lord Nottingham, in the great *Case of the Duke of Norfolk*, against the opinion of the heads of all the law courts, to establish for the first time, but on a foundation which has never been shaken,[4] the doctrine that the validity of a con-

[4] The case of Taylor v. Biddal is the next in chronological order, but it will be most conveniently considered later. See § 172, post.

§ 168. [1] Goring v. Bickerstaffe, Love v. Wyndham, §§ 163, 167,

ante.

[2] See Burges v. Burges, § 166, ante, but under what restrictions was far from clear. §§ 162–164.

[3] §§ 155–158, ante.

[4] "From that time to the pres-

tingent interest depends upon its distance in time, and not upon the character of the contingency.

### 8. RULE AGAINST PERPETUITIES ESTABLISHED

**§ 169. Duke of Norfolk's Case.**[1]    That case was as follows: Land was conveyed by the Earl of Arundel to trustees for a long term, in trust for B. his second son and the heirs male of his body, but if A., the Earl's eldest son, should die without issue male in the life of B., or if the earldom should descend upon B., then the trust to be for C., the third son.[2] A. died without issue in the life of B., and the question arose in Chancery whether the executory devise to C. was good. Lord Chancellor Nottingham called in the assistance of Pemberton, C. J., North, C. J., and Montagu, C. B. The judges were all of opinion that the executory devise to C. was bad as tending to a perpetuity; but the Lord Chancellor was of an opposite opinion, and made a decree in favor of C. A bill of review was filed, and in 1683 Lord Keeper North reversed the Chancellor's decree; but, on appeal to the House of Lords, the decree of the Lord Keeper was, in 1685, reversed, and Lord Nottingham's decree affirmed.[3] The question in this case was whether, after a limitation of a term to one and the heirs of his body, there could be a limitation over. The judges were of opinion that there could not be. The Chancellor held the limitation over good, provided the contingency on which the limitation over was to take effect must happen within a life in being. He said that no one now disputed that a contingent limitation of a term to take effect within, or at the end of, the life of one to whom an interest for life was limited in the term was good, and it was absurd to make any distinction because the first taker was declared to hold to himself and the heirs of

ent, every judge has acquiesced in that decision." Per Lord Kenyon, Long v. Blackall, 7 T. R. 100, 102.

§ 169. [1] 3 Ch. Cas. 1, Pollexf. 223, sub nom. Howard v. Norfolk, [G. R. P.]—11

2 Ch. Rep. 229, 2 Swanst. 454. See 23 Va. Law Rev. 538.

[2] The conveyance was drawn by Sir Orlando Bridgman. See 3 Ch. Cas. 27.

[3] 3 Ch. Cas. 53.

his body, if the limitation over was only on a contingency
which could not happen after his death; that it was obvious
that there was no more a perpetuity in the one case than in the
other; and, in short, that if the future estate must vest within
a lifetime, it was immaterial what was done with the term before it vested.   This case overruled *Child* v. *Baylie*, and put
the law on a rational basis.   It has not been shaken since.   In
favor of the plaintiff the supposed doctrine that you could not
have a possibility upon a possibility was invoked, but it met
with no favor in any quarter.   "There may be a possibility
upon a possibility, and a contingency upon a contingency, and
in truth every executory devise is so, and therefore the contrary rule given by Lord Popham in the *Rector of Chedington's Case* is not reason.   These things were agreed by all."[4]
Lord Nottingham was pressed with this case: "Suppose a
contingency which must take effect, if at all, within one hundred years, but may not take effect any sooner.   What then?
Where will you stop?"   "Where?" he answered; "why, everywhere, where there is not any inconvenience, any danger of a
perpetuity; and whenever you stop at the limitation of a fee
upon a fee, there will we stop in the limitation of a term of
years."[5]   "But what time? and where are the bounds of that
contingency?   You may limit, it seems, upon a contingency
to happen in a life.   What if it be limited, if such a one die
without issue within twenty-one years or a hundred years, or
while Westminster Hall stands?   Where will you stop, if you
do not stop here?   I will tell you where I will stop: I will
stop wherever any visible inconvenience doth appear; for the
just bounds of a fee simple upon a fee simple are not yet determined, but the first inconvenience that ariseth upon it will
regulate it."[6]

§ 170.   The *Duke of Norfolk's Case* marks the close of the
first stage in the history of the Rule against Perpetuities.   It
was now a settled point that a future interest might be limited

[4] 2 Ch. Rep. 237.   See to the
same effect, 3 Ch. Cas. 29, 30; and
on the nature of a perpetuity, 3
Ch. Cas. 31.
[5] 3 Ch. Cas. 36.
[6] 3 Ch. Cas. 49.

to commence on any contingency which must occur within lives in being. Whether this period could be extended remained to be determined. Before considering the series of decisions on this point, one matter must be noticed. Notwithstanding the first decision in the *Duke of Norfolk's Case,* it is said in *Massenburgh* v. *Ash*[1] (1684) that "it was agreed by the counsel and so declared by the Court," "that the general rule that has hitherto obtained was, that you might limit a term to as many persons as you would, one after another, that were *in esse* at the time of the limitation; and one step further, to a person not *in esse;* but that there could be but one contingent remainder of a term for years." This seems to be the last case in which the number of contingent interests is suggested to be of importance; and in *Gulliver* v. *Wickett*[2] (1745) (a case, it is true, of freeholds, not leaseholds), we find Lee, C. J., saying, "The number of contingencies are not material, if they are all to happen within a life in being, or a reasonable time afterwards."

9. Extension of the Rule so as to cover the Minority of a Grantee or Devisee

§ **171. Minorities.** The first extension of the period within which future interests might be created was to make it cover the time necessary for the birth of posthumous children, and also the minority of an executory devisee unborn at the death of the testator. In *Snow* v. *Cutler,*[1] there had been a devise to the heirs of the body of the testator's wife, if he or they should attain fourteen years. The Court was divided on the question whether the devise was good. It seems, however, that the objection of those who thought it invalid was to the form rather than to the substance, and that if the devise had been "to the heir when he shall be born," they would have deemed it good.

§ 170. [1] 1 Vern. 234.
[2] 1 Wils. 105.
§ 171. [1] 1 Lev. 135, 1 Keb. 752, 800, 851, 2 Keb. 11, 145, 296, T.
Raym. 162, sub nom. Snow v. Tucker, 1 Sid. 153. See § 165, ante.

§ **172.** In *Taylor* v. *Biddal*,[1] it appeared by special verdict
in ejectment that A. devised land to his sister B., the wife
of C., until D., the son of B. and C., should reach twenty-one,
and then to D: and his heirs, but if he should die under
twenty-one, then to the heirs of the body of C. and to their
heirs "as they should attain their respective ages of twenty-
one years."[2] D. died under twenty-one, then B. died, leaving
a daughter, E., the defendant, the sole surviving issue of herself and C. Then C. died, leaving E. of full age.[3] E. claimed,
therefore, either as heir of the body of C., or if the devise to
such heir was void, then as heir of her brother D. The plaintiff's lessor was the heir of A. The case was argued in the
Common Bench in 1678.[4] The reports agree that the Court
held that D.'s estate was vested, and E. entitled as his heir,
even if the executory devise over to her was void.[5] As to the
executory devise, Freeman[6] says the Court was of opinion it
was bad; but the report in 2 Modern[7] makes Chief Justice
North declare it good. As Mr. Hargrave[8] remarks, it is hard
to reconcile the language attributed to the Chief Justice in
2 Modern with his opinion in the *Duke of Norfolk's Case;*[9]
but, notwithstanding, it appears to be the fact not only that
the Court thought the executory devise good, but that they gave
judgment for the defendant on that ground. For Lord Hardwicke and the other judges of the King's Bench, in certifying
to the Court of Chancery in 1736 that a devise to grandchil-
ren when they reach twenty-one was good,[10] said: "We do not

§ **172.** [1] 2 Mod. 289, Freem. K.
B. 243.

[2] These last words are omitted
in Freeman's Report, but in Carter's Report (vide infra) the words
are: "As they or any of them
shall accomplish the age of twenty-one years."

[3] See 2 Mod. 293.

[4] Another ejectment had been
brought before the death of C.
The arguments are reported under
the name of Taylor v. Wharton,
Carter 182 (1667), but no judg-

ment is given. In Freeman, the
second ejectment is reported as
having been argued at Hilary
Term, 1677. The year then began in March. According to our
present reckoning the case was
argued, as stated, in 1678.

[5] Freem. K. B. 244, 2 Mod. 292,
ad fin.

[6] P. 244.

[7] P. 293.

[8] 2 Harg. Jurid. Arg. 36.

[9] § 169, ante.

[10] Stephens v. Stephens, Cas.

find any case wherein an executory devise of a freehold hath been held good, which hath suspended the vesting of the estate until a son unborn should attain his age of twenty-one years, except the case of *Taylor* v. *Bydall,* adjudged upon a special verdict in the Court of Common Pleas, Hil. 29 & 30 Car. 2, and reported in 2 Mod. 289. That resolution appeared in every view of it to be so considerable in the present case, that we caused the record to be searched, and find it to agree in the material parts thereof with the printed report; and therefore, however unwilling we may be to extend executory devises beyond the rules generally laid down by our predecessors, yet upon the authority of that judgment, and its conformity to several late determinations in cases of terms for years, and considering that the power of alienation will not be restrained longer than the law would restrain it, viz. during the infancy of the first taker, which cannot reasonably be said to extend to a perpetuity; and that this construction will make the testator's whole disposition take effect, which otherwise would be defeated; we are of opinion that the devise before mentioned may be good by way of executory devise." And in *Lovell* v. *Lovell,*[11] where a question arose whether on a gift to A. till B. reaches twenty-one, and then to B., B. takes a vested interest, and *Taylor* v. *Biddal* was cited, Lord Hardwicke, C., said: "*Taylor* versus *Biddal* is upon an executory devise; for I had a very particular reason to look into this case in *Stephens* versus *Stephens,* and therefore sent for the record out of the treasury; not truly stated in the report of the case, for the other point mentioned in the book could not arise, being determined only upon an executory devise."

§ **173.** In *Luddington* v. *Kime*[1] (1697), Powell, J., having expressed an opinion that on a devise to A., and if he should have a posthumous son born, to such son, the limitation to the son would be a good executory devise, "Treby, Chief Justice, doubted much of that, and was of opinion that the

temp. Talb. 228, 232. See § 175, post.

[11] 3 Atk. 11, 12.

§ **173.** [1] 1 Ld. Raym. 203, 207.

time allowed for executory devises to take effect ought not to be longer than the life of one person then *in esse*."[2]

§ **174. Gore v. Gore.**[1] Devise of land to A. for five hundred years, and after the determination of the term to the first and other sons of B., the testator's son. B. was then a bachelor. Lord Macclesfield sent the case to the Court of King's Bench, who in 1722 certified that the executory devise to the first son of B. was bad, "because it is not to take place within that compass of time which the law allows." The case against the devise was argued (1) by Mr. Bootle, who impugned it on the ground that if B.'s first son was posthumous, the estate would not vest until after a life in being; and (2) by Mr. Peere Williams, who contended that the devise might not vest till the end of the term for five hundred years. Sir John Strange says that the judges thought the devise bad on the first ground, "because it might subsist forty weeks after the death of" B., "and they were not for going a day farther than a life in being."[2] Mr. Peere Williams in his report[3] quotes the certificate of the judges as if they decided the case for the reason urged by him, "it was too remote (viz.) after five hundred years;" but the words "(viz.) after five hundred years" are no part of the certificate, which he afterwards[4] gives *verbatim* in full. Whatever the grounds, Lord Macclesfield was not pleased with the certificate, and afterwards Lord King, becoming Chancellor, sent it back to the Court of King's Bench. On the argument Lord Raymond, C. J., expressed himself not satisfied with the previous certificate;[5] but before the case was decided Lord Raymond was succeeded by Lord Hardwicke.[6] The case was argued again, and the Court sent, in 1734,[7] another certificate, in which they declared that the executory devise was good; and Lord Talbot, who was now Chancellor, decreed accordingly. Lord Raymond, C. J., and

[2] Such a limitation would now be held a good contingent remainder. See Reeve v. Long, 3 Lev. 408.

§ **174.** [1] 2 Stra. 958, 2 P. Wms. 28, 9 Mod. 4, 10 Mod. 501, W. Kel. 254, 2 Barnard. K. B. 209,

229, 355.

[2] 2 Stra. 958.
[3] 2 P. Wms. 63.
[4] P. 64.
[5] W. Kel. 259.
[6] 2 Barnard. K. B. 355.
[7] 2 P. Wms. 64.

Page, J., "doubted whether there was any other rule which the Court could go by in judging upon such a devise, than to consider whether it tended to a perpetuity or not."[8]

§ 175. In 1736, in the case of *Stephens* v. *Stephens*,[1] Lord Hardwicke and the other judges of the King's Bench certified, and Lord Chancellor Talbot decided, that an executory devise to a child of a person living at the testator's death on such child's reaching majority was good. The judges came reluctantly to this conclusion, but conceived themselves bound by *Taylor* v. *Biddal*.[2] Lord Mansfield, in *Doe* v. *Fonnereau*,[3] said: "In *Stephens* v. *Stephens* the Court took a large stride of twenty-one years after a life in being. The argument was, that this would not create a perpetuity. Former cases had said a limitation might be made to take effect on the death of a person *in esse*, or the birth of a posthumous child; and alienation was not restrained for any longer time in *Stephens* v. *Stephens*, for, if a devise could hold to a posthumous child, there could be no alienation till he should attain the age of twenty-one." The step had perhaps been taken before *Stephens* v. *Stephens*, but that case may be said to have firmly settled the law, that a future gift to the child of a living person upon such child's reaching majority is not too remote. The point has never been questioned since.[4]

10. EXTENSION OF THE RULE SO AS TO COVER A TERM IN GROSS

§ 176. **Term of Years in Gross.** The period within which future devises could be created was therefore extended beyond lives in being to cover the minorities of the devisees. Could it be further extended? and if so, to what limit? In *Pay's Case*[1] (1602), there was a devise to A. from Michaelmas following the testator's death for five years, and then to B. in

---

[8] 2 Barnard. K. B. 212.

§ 175. [1] Cas. temp. Talb. 228, W. Kel. 168, 2 Barnard. K. B. 375.

[2] 2 Mod. 289, Freem. K. B. 243. See § 172, ante.

[3] 2 Doug. 487, 508.

[4] The inconsistency of this extension with legal principle and analogy is discussed, §§ 187, 188, post.

§ 176. [1] Cro. El. 878, sub nom. Payne v. Ferrall, Noy 43. See § 139, ante.

fee. It was held, without argument, that the devise to B.
was good. The objection of remoteness was not raised, nor at
that early day was it likely to be raised.

§ 176.1. **Massingberd v. Ash**[1] (1685). A term was assigned in trust for A. and his wife during their lives and the
life of the survivor, but if there should be issue male of their
bodies living at the death of the survivor, then to their eldest
son, but if he died before twenty-one years of age, then to the
second and other sons, there being a limitation over on the
death of any son under twenty-one to the next son; but if
there should be no such issue living at the death of the survivor of A. and his wife, or if all such issue should die before
reaching twenty-one, then to B. A. and his wife had issue
one son who died after A., but in the lifetime of the wife.[2]
A case was sent from Chancery to the Court of Common Pleas,
the judges of which certified that the devise to B. was good;
and the Lord Keeper Guilford decreed accordingly. The devise to B. was in the alternative, either on the death of the
issue before A. and his wife, or upon their death after their
parents under twenty-one. The former alternative had taken
place, and the devise to B. was clearly good, without raising
the question whether it would have been good had the issue of
A. and his wife outlived their parents and died under twenty-
one; but the counsel and judges seemed to have considered
the case as involving the question whether a limitation of an
estate to begin within twenty-one years after a life in being
was good; and the judges held it good.[3] The Lord Keeper,
however, seems to have put the case rather on *Wood* v. *Sanders*,[4] and the death of the issue in the parent's life.[5] This
case differs from *Stephens* v. *Stephens*[6] in that although the
period of postponing a devise is a minority it is not the minority of the devisee.

§ 176.1. [1] 2 Ch. Rep. 275, sub
nom. Massenburgh v. Ash, 1 Vern.
234, 257, 304.

[2] See 2 Ch. Rep. 278, 282. The
statement in 1 Vern. 234, that the
son died after the wife, is, it
seems, wrong.

[3] 2 Ch. Rep. 282, 283.

[4] 1 Ch. Cas. 131, Pollexf. 35. See
§ 161, ante.

[5] 1 Vern. 305.

[6] See § 175, ante.

§ **177.** In *Davies* v. *Speed* (1692), in which case a springing use after the indefinite failure of A.'s issue was of course
held too remote, Lord Holt, C. J.,[1] said that a springing use
to commence at the end of four years would be good, as would
also one to begin after the death of A. without issue, if he die
without issue within twenty years. But this was *obiter
dictum.*[2]

§ **178.** The case of *Lloyd* v. *Carew*,[1] finally decided in
1698, is the foundation of that part of the Rule against Perpetuities which allows a future interest to be created beyond
the termination of a life in being without regard to the minority of any person. There was a conveyance to A. and his wife
for life, remainder to her children successively in tail, remainder to A. in fee, provided that if at the death of the survivor
of A. and his wife there should be no issue of theirs then living, and if the heirs of the wife should, within twelve months
after such death without issue, pay to the heirs of A. £4,000,
then the estate should go to the heirs of the wife forever. A.
and his wife both died without leaving issue living at the death
of the survivor, and the heir of the wife tendered the £4,000.
The question was, whether the executory devise to the heir of
the wife was good. In favor of the executory devise it was
argued "that it was within the reason of the contingent limitations allowed in the *Duke of Norfolk's Case;* . . . that
the *ultimum quod sit* of a fee upon a fee is not yet plainly
determined; that there could not in reason be any difference
between a contingency to happen during life or lives in being,
and within one year after; and the reason of allowing them to
be good, if confined to lives in being, or upon their decease,
was, because no inconvenience could follow, and the same rule
will hold to a year after; and that the true rule to set bounds
to them is, when they prove inconvenient and not otherwise."
Against the executory devise it was urged that the life of one

§ 177. [1] As reported in 2 Salk.
675, and Holt 730.
[2] In the other reports of the
case, 4 Mod. 153, 12 Mod. 38,
Skin. 351, Carth. 262, the remark
is not given. The decision was
affirmed in the House of Lords,
Show. P. C. 104.
　§ 178. [1] Prec. Ch. 72, 106, Show.
P. C. 137.

or more persons in being was "the furthest the judges have ·
ever gone in allowing contingent limitations upon a fee, and
if they should be extended to contingencies to happen within
twelve months after the death of one or more person or persons in being, they may as well be extended to contingencies
to happen within one thousand years; and so all the inconveniences of a perpetuity will be let in."[2]  Sir John Somers, C.,
assisted by Treby, C. J., and Rokeby, J., held that the executory devise was bad.  But the Chancellor's decree was reversed on appeal by the House of Lords, Jan. 13, 1698.  It
is worthy of notice that at this time, with the exception of the
Chancellor, there was no law lord in the House.[3]

§ 179.  In *Marks* v. *Marks*[1] (1718), an executory devise to
arise on the payment of a sum of money within three months
after the death of a person living at the death of the testator
was held good by Lord Chancellor Parker, assisted by Sir
Joseph Jekyll, M. R.  The Master of the Rolls said: "Though
before the case of *Lloyd* v. *Carew,* it seems to have obtained
for law, that no executory devise of a fee upon a fee should
be allowed of, unless upon a contingency to happen during
the life of one or more persons in being at the time of the
settlement . . . yet since that case which went through the
House of Lords, and is reported Shower's Cases in Parliament,
137, the law is now settled, that in case of a contingency that
cannot in the nature of it precede the death of a person, a reasonable time may be allowed subsequent to the decease of that
person for performance of the condition; and a fee limited
thereupon is good.  In that case, a year was held no unreason-

[2] Prec. Ch. 73, 74.

[3] 16 Lords' Journals 192 a,
193 b.  The Earl of Macclesfield
mentioned as being in the House
was not the Chancellor of that
name, who was not raised to the
peerage till the reign of George I.
This peer belonged to an earlier
creation, which became extinct in
1702.  The statement of Lord
Brougham in Cadell v. Palmer, 1

Cl. & F. 372, 422, that the House
of Lords, in deciding Lloyd v.
Carew, were assisted by "the then
Chief Justice of the Common
Pleas," is wrong.  It was the
Chancellor, whose decree was re-
versed, that was assisted by Chief
Justice Treby.

§ 179. [1] 10 Mod. 419, 1 Stra.
129, Prec. Ch. 486.

able time; *a fortiori* not three months, which is the present case."[2]

## § 180. Length of Term in Gross.

Although *Lloyd* v. *Carew*, followed by *Marks* v. *Marks*, settled that a future interest might be created within a "reasonable time" after the expiration of lives in being, the question of what that "reasonable time" was remained undetermined for more than a century. In *Massingberd* v. *Ash*,[1] decided in 1685, thirteen years before *Lloyd* v. *Carew*, the judges of the Court of Common Pleas had declared of certain limitations that "being limited and confined to fall within the compass of twenty-one years" they were good.[2] In *Scatterwood* v. *Edge*,[3] decided in 1699, the year after the House of Lords had overruled Lord Somers's decree in *Lloyd* v. *Carew*, there was a devise to A. for eleven years, and subject thereto to the first issue male of B. and the heirs male of his body, provided they should take upon themselves the surname of E. B., at the time of the devise, had no issue. As Lord Thurlow remarks,[4] the case of *Scatterwood* v. *Edge* "is so ill reported, that it is not easy to discover what points were determined." Blencowe, J., thought the devise to the issue male of B. good. Treby, C. J., and Neville and Powell, JJ., thought it bad. The opinion of the two latter on the point of remoteness is not clear; but that of the Chief Justice, at any rate, is emphatic. "There are bounds," he says, "set to them [executory devises], viz. a life or lives in being; and further they shall never go, by my consent, at law, let Chancery do as they please,"[5]—an obvious reflection on *Lloyd* v. *Carew*, where the decree rendered in accordance with his ad-

[2] 10 Mod. 422.

§ 180. [1] 2 Ch. Rep. 275, sub nom. Massenburgh v. Ash, 1 Vern. 234, 257, 304. See § 176.1, ante. The cases of Massingberd v. Ash, Maddox v. Staines, 2 P. Wms. 421, sub nom. Staines v. Maddock, 3 Bro. P. C. (Toml. ed.) 108 (see Fitzg. 318), and Stanley v. Leigh, 2 P. Wms. 686, were inserted in

the first edition under the preceding head, §§ 173, 175, but they come properly under this.

[2] 2 Ch. Rep. 282, 283.

[3] 1 Salk. 229, sub nom. Scattergood v. Edge, 12 Mod. 278 (see Gore v. Gore, 2 Barnard. K. B. 209).

[4] In Doo v. Brabant, 3 Bro. C. C. 393, 398.

[5] 12 Mod. 287.

vice had been overruled by the House of Lords.  The case was affirmed in the King's Bench on error.  Lord Holt is declared there to have said that "the time in which an executory devise was to arise was not then settled."[6]

§ 181.  In *Maddox* v. *Staines*,[1] there was a bequest to A. for life, and on his death, to his children, but if they died under age, then to B.  It was held by Sir Joseph Jekyll that the executory bequest to B. was good.  Lord Chancellor King affirmed the decree, and his decree was affirmed by the House of Lords.  In *Stanley* v. *Leigh*,[2] a devise of a term with similar limitations was elaborately discussed by Sir Joseph Jekyll, M. R., and a gift over on death under twenty-one of persons not in being at the testator's death was held good.  The Master of the Rolls defined "a perpetuity, as it is a legal word or term of art," as "the limiting an estate either of inheritance or for years, in such manner as would render it unalienable longer than for a life or lives in being at the same time, and some short or reasonable time after."  In *Maddox* v. *Staines* and *Stanley* v. *Leigh*, as in *Massingberd* v. *Ash*,[3] the minority in question was not, it should be observed, the minority of the executory devisee but of a third person.  In *Gore* v. *Gore*,[4] the judges of the King's Bench, in their second certificate, given in 1734, said "that a convenient time after the life was to be allowed, according to the case of *Lloyd* v. *Cary*."

§ 182.  Following these is a series of cases in which the courts are generally passing upon or considering executory devises arising upon the devisee attaining his majority, but in which they express themselves in general terms.  Thus in

---

[6] Gore v. Gore, W. Kel. 254, 259, 2 Barnard. K. B. 209, 212. See also Gore v. Gore, 2 Barnard. K. B. 229, 230.  The statement in Salkeld's report of Scatterwood v. Edge, attributed to all the judges, that every executory devise is "a perpetuity as far as it goes, that is to say, an estate unalienable, though all mankind join in the conveyance," has often been cited with approval, and has more than one wrong decision to answer for. See § 269, post.

[1] P. Wms. 421, sub nom. Staines v. Maddock, 3 Bro. P. C. (Toml. ed.) 108 (see Fitzg. 318).

[2] 2 P. Wms. 686.

[3] § 176.1, ante.

[4] 2 Stra. 958. See § 174, ante.

*Goodtitle* v. *Wood*[1] (1740) : "The rule has in many instances
been extended to twenty-one years after the death of a person
in being." So in *Marlborough* v. *Godolphin*[2] (1759) : "It
is true that by executory devise an estate may be locked up for
a life and lives in being and twenty or twenty-one years
after." So Lord Mansfield in *Goodman* v. *Goodright*[3] (1759) :
"The allowed compass of a life or lives in being, and twenty-
one years after, which is the line now drawn, and very sensibly
and rightly drawn."[4] So again Lord Mansfield in *Buckworth*
v. *Thirkell*[5] (1785) : "I remember the introduction of the rule
which prescribes the time in which executory devises must
take effect to be a life or lives in being and twenty-one years
afterwards."[6] Lord Mansfield was called to the bar in 1730.
In *Jee* v. *Audley*[7] (1787), Sir Lloyd Kenyon, M. R., said :
"The limitations of personal estate are void, unless they necessarily vest, if at all, within a life or lives in being and twenty-
one years or nine or ten months afterwards. This has been
sanctioned by the opinion of judges of all times, from the time
of the *Duke of Norfolk's Case* to the present; it is grown
reverend by age, and is not now to be broken in upon." And
the same learned judge, when Chief Justice of the Court of
King's Bench, in *Long* v. *Blackall*[8] (1797), said : "It is an
established rule that an executory devise is good if it must
necessarily happen within a life or lives in being and twenty-
one years, and the fraction of another year, allowing for the
time of gestation." And in *Thellusson* v. *Woodford*[9] (1799),

§ 182. [1] Willes 211, 213

[2] 1 Eden 404, 418.

[3] 2 Burr. 870, 1 W. Bl. 188.

[4] 2 Burr. 879. See Doe v. Fonnereau, 2 Doug. 487, 502, 507,
note. That Lord Mansfield had
the case of a minority in his mind
is shown by his remark during
the argument of this case as giv-
en by Mr. Hargrave, ex relatione
Mr. Filmer. "That point is well
settled; and a life and twenty-
one years after is the utmost extent for an executory devise; and

is no more than the common law
allows in legal limitations, which
restrains the heir from aliening
till twenty-one." 2 Harg. Jurid.
Arg. 102, 103.

[5] 3 B. & P. 652, note, 10 J. B.
Moore 235, note.

[6] 3 B. & P. 654, note.

[7] 1 Cox 324.

[8] 7 T. R. 100, 102. See s. c. 3
Ves. Jr. 486, 489. Thellusson v.
Woodford, 11 Ves. 112, 150.

[9] 4 Ves. 227, 11 Ves. 112.

Mr. Justice Buller said: "The rule allowing any number of lives in being, a reasonable time for gestation, and twenty-one years, is now the clear law, that has been settled and followed for ages;[10] and we cannot shake that rule without shaking the foundations of the law."[11]

§ 183. In none of these cases, however, was the attention of the Court drawn to the distinction between a term in gross and the minority of the devisee, and in most of them the circumstances, and in many of them the language of the expressions themselves, show that the judges were thinking only of minorities. And in *Thellusson* v. *Woodford,* Lord Alvanley, M. R., said that the period of twenty-one years had never "been considered as a term, that may at all events be added to such executory devise or trust. I have only found this *dictum;* that estates may be unalienable for lives in being and twenty-one years, merely because a life may be an infant, or *en ventre sa mère.*"[1]  And Macdonald, C. B., in delivering the opinion of the judges in the House of Lords, said: "The established length of time, during which the vesting may be suspended, is during a life or lives in being, the period of gestation, and the infancy of such posthumous child."[2]

§ 184. In *Beard* v. *Westcott,*[1] there were devises over after limitations which were too remote, and on a contingency of the death under twenty-one of the unborn children of persons living at the testator's death. Two objections were made to the devises over: in the first place, that they were after remote limitations;[2] and, secondly, that the contingency had no reference to the minority of persons who took under such devises. Sir William Grant, M. R., sent the case to the Court of Common Pleas, which in 1810[3] certified that the limitations over

[10] The "ages" were less than a hundred years.

[11] 4 Ves. 319.

§ 183. [1] 4 Ves. 337.
[2] 11 Ves. 143.

§ 184. [1] 5 Taunt. 393, 5 B. & Ald. 801, T. & R. 25.
[2] As to the validity of this ob-

jection, see § 252 et seq., post, where the case is more fully stated.

[3] The date of the certificate is given, 5 Taunt. 407, as 28 November, 1812, but it is printed at length in Gilbert's Uses (Sugd. ed.) 272-274, note, and is there dated 28 November, 1810; and this

were good.[4] Sir William Grant doubted how far this term of twenty-one years could be thus taken, and ordered the Court to be again attended with the case on this particular question;[5] and in 1813 the Court returned a certificate to this additional query, that the case was not affected by the fact that the gifts over might take effect "at the end of an absolute term of twenty-one years after a life in being at the death of the testator, without reference to the infancy of the person intended to take."[6] Lord Eldon, not being satisfied with these certificates, sent the case in 1822 to the Court of King's Bench.[7] The case sent called particular attention to the fact that the period of twenty-one years did not correspond to the infancy of the person intended to take the gift over;[8] and the question was elaborately argued by Mr. Sugden for the plaintiff and Mr. Preston for the defendant. The Court sent a short certificate that the limitations over were bad.[9] Upon the hearing in Chancery it was urged on their behalf that it could not be collected from the certificate "whether the circumstance that the limitations were to take effect at the end of a term of twenty-one years, without reference to the infancy of the person intended to take, created such a suspense of the vesting as to render the limitations void;" but the Lord Chancellor said it was "impossible that the Court of King's Bench should not have considered that point," and confirmed the certificate, adding: "The inclination of my opinion is that the Court of King's Bench is right."[10] Mr. Justice Bayley, however, who signed the certificate, afterwards delivered the opinion of the judges in *Cadell* v. *Palmer*,[11] and in that opinion said that the foundation of the certificate of the Court of King's Bench "was that a previous limitation, clearly too remote, and which was so considered by the Court of Common

last must be correct, because Sugden's edition of Gilbert was published in 1811. See also Cadell v. Palmer, 1 Cl. & F. 372, 394.

[4] See this first certificate of the Court of Common Pleas criticised by Sugden in his edition of Gilbert on Uses 274, 275, note.

[5] 5 Taunt. 407, 408.
[6] 5 Taunt. 413.
[7] 5 B. & Ald. 801.
[8] 5 B. & Ald. 805.
[9] 5 B. & Ald. 814, 815.
[10] T. & R. 25.
[11] 1 Cl. & F. 372.

Pleas, made those limitations also void which the Common Pleas had held good. The subsequent limitations were considered as being void, not from any infirmity existing in themselves, but from the infirmity existing in the preceding limitation; and because that was a limitation too remote, the others were considered as being too remote also. Whether the Court of King's Bench gave any positive opinion on that, I am unable to say. I think the Court of King's Bench would have taken much more time to consider that point than they did, and have given it greater consideration than it received, if they had intended to differ from the certificate that had been given by the Court of Common Pleas; but when it became totally immaterial, in the construction they were putting upon the will, to consider whether they were or were not prepared to differ from the Court of Common Pleas, it is not to be wondered at that that point was not so fully considered as it might otherwise have been."[12]

§ 185. **Twenty-one Years allowed.** Mr. Justice Bayley may or may not have been right in his recollection of the ground of the certificate of the Court of King's Bench given eleven years before. But it seems clear that Sir William Grant and Lord Eldon were both inclined to agree with Lord Alvanley's opinion, expressed in *Thellusson* v. *Woodford*,[1] that a gross term of twenty-one years could not be taken in fixing the limits of remoteness; and the point was not settled until the case of *Bengough* v. *Edridge*;[2] s. c. in *Dom. Proc. sub nom. Cadell* v. *Palmer*.[3] This case was argued in the fullest manner before Sir John Leach, V. C., and on appeal to the House of Lords, by Mr. Preston and Mr. Sugden. The Vice-Chancellor held,[4] in 1826, that the term of twenty-one years could be taken without reference to the minority of anyone.[5] In the House of Lords, in 1832, the judges were summoned, and eleven attended,[6] and declared that the term

[12] 1 Cl. & F. 420, 421.

§ 185. [1] 4 Ves. 227, 337. See § 183, ante.

[2] 1 Sim. 173.

[3] 1 Cl. & F. 372, 7 Bli., N. s. 202, 10 Bing. 140.

[4] 1 Sim. 267.

[5] See Sugd. Law of Property 314.

[6] 1 Cl. & F. 411.

of twenty-one years need have no reference to the minority of
a devisee, nor, indeed, to any minority at all.  The Lords, in
accordance with this, affirmed the decree.  Lord Brougham, C.,
moving the affirmance of the decree, said that the decision of
the House in *Lloyd* v. *Carew*[7] "settled the rule."

### 11. EXTENSIONS OF THE RULE NOT TO BE JUSTIFIED ON PRINCIPLE

**§ 186. Extensions accidental.** *Cadell* v. *Palmer*, of course,
closed all controversy in England, nor does any question ever
seem to have been made in America of the propriety of allowing a gross term.  Certainly the allowance of a gross term of
some length is highly convenient.  But the result seems to
have been arrived at by accident rather than by any process
of judicial reasoning.  In the *Duke of Norfolk's Case*,[1] it was
held that any limitation is good which must take effect within
lives in being.  Soon after this an attempt was made to extend
the period beyond lives in being, but two of the most eminent lawyers of the time (indeed, with the exception of Sir
John Holt, *longo intervallo* above their contemporaries), Lord
Somers and Chief Justice Treby (assisted by Mr. Justice
Rokeby), decided, in *Lloyd* v. *Carew*, that it could not be
done.  They were, however, overruled by a body of laymen.[2]
Then came the case of *Stephens* v. *Stephens*,[3] where there was
a gift on majority to the unborn child of a living person.  The
Court allowed the gift unwillingly, upon the authority of
*Taylor* v. *Biddal*[4] (a case decided before the *Duke of Norfolk's
Case*, and of which the reports are inconsistent), and because
there was no real restraint on alienation.[5]  And finally came
*Cadell* v. *Palmer*,[6] where a gross term of twenty-one years was
allowed on the strength of *Lloyd* v. *Carew*.[7]

[7] Show. P. C. 137.  See § 178, ante.

§ 186. [1] 3 Ch. Cas. 1.  See § 169, ante.

[2] Prec. Ch. 72, 106, Show. P. C. 137.  See § 178, ante.

[G. R. P.]—12

[3] Cas. temp. Talb. 228.  See § 175, ante.

[4] 2 Mod. 289, Freem. K. B. 243.

[5] § 172, ante.

[6] 1 Cl. & F. 372.

[7] Lord Brougham, who gave the

**§ 187.** The true theory of the Rule against Perpetuities, so far as any artificial rule can be said to have a theory, is

opinion in Cadell v. Palmer, subsequently more than once pointed out the illogical process by which the allowance of a gross term of twenty-one years was arrived at. Cadell v. Palmer "went, in my opinion, no further than at least one case of great authority, and decided in this House, though it may have gone further than the original reason of the rule authorized." Tollemache v. Coventry, 2 Cl. & F. 611, 624. "The Courts, and even this House, . . . have sanctioned what even plainly appeared to be erroneous principles, introduced and long assumed as law, rather than occasion the great inconvenience which must arise from correcting the common error, and recurring to more accurate views. Accordingly, when Cadell v. Palmer was argued in this House, I advised that your Lordships should abide by the received extension which had for a great length of time been given to the period within which an executory devise might be held good." Phipps v. Ackers, 9 Cl. & F. 583, 598. "The rule of law is the term in gross of twenty-one years after the life or lives in being; that was clearly laid down by your Lordships upon my recommendation, after hearing the learned judges in the case of Cadell v. Palmer, and it is quite unnecessary to go back to the foundation of the law; I have a strong opinion, which I believe is joined in by the profession at

large, that it arises out of an accidental circumstance, out of a confusion, I may say, a misapprehension in confounding together the nature of the estate with the remedy at law by fine and recovery, which could not be applied till a certain life came to twenty-one years." Dungannon v. Smith, 12 Cl. & F. 546, 629, 630. The rule that you can take a gross term "most clearly arises from a mistake. The law never meant to give a further term of twenty-one years, much less any period of gestation. The law never meant to say that there shall be twenty-one years added to the life or lives in being, and that within those limits you may entail the estate; but what the law meant to say was this: until the heir of the last of the lives in being attains twenty-one, by law a recovery cannot be suffered, and consequently the discontinuance of the estate cannot be affected, and for that reason, says the law, you shall have the twenty-one years added, because that is the fact and not the law, namely, that till a person reached the age of twenty-one he could not cut off the entail. For that reason and in that way it has crept in by degrees; Communis error facit jus; and that rule never was applied more accurately than in Cadell v. Palmer." Cole v. Sewell, 2 H. L. C. 186, 233. See Lord St. Leonards, in Sugd. Law of Prop-

**[G. R. P.]**

that no future interest must begin beyond lives in being. The
question to be asked of any estate on condition precedent is:
"When must the contingency happen, if at all?" But the
mistake which is constantly recurring, and which has caused
so much confusion, is that judges and legislators have considered, not when will the future estate begin, but how long
will it be before an absolute fee can be conveyed.[1] That mistake occurred here; the judges did not consider when the future interest would begin; they considered how long it would
be before a fee simple could be conveyed, and they said: "An
executory devise may be postponed, it is conceded, to the end
of a life estate. There can be no harm in extending the time
till the person who takes the land on the termination of the
life estate reaches twenty-one, for until he becomes of age
he could not convey the land, even if there were no executory
devise." This step the judges took, though unwillingly, in
*Stephens* v. *Stephens.* And this is all for which they are
really responsible. The allowance of a gross term can be
traced to the unlearned peers overruling the sages of the law
in *Lloyd* v. *Carew.*

§ **188.** How unjustifiable was the step taken in *Stephens*
v. *Stephens* is easily shown. Every reason which could be
then urged for extending the period for creating an executory devise to a minority after a life in being could now be
used for extending it to a minority after an absolute term of
twenty-one years. Suppose a devise is made to such of the
great-grandchildren of the testator living twenty-one years
after his death as reach twenty-one. Until such great-grandchild
reaches twenty-one he cannot convey his share: what harm,
then, in extending the time till he reaches twenty-one? But
such reasoning would not be considered valid now; it ought
not to have been considered valid then. To take account of
the disability of infancy in considering the validity of limitations is entirely contrary to the analogy of the law. An
estate in fee simple or in tail may pass from infant to infant
for centuries without being at any time alienable or barrable.

erty 315, 316; and Gilb. Uses      § **187.** [1] See §§ 278 et seq., post.
(Sugd. ed.) 260 et seq., note.

In fact, the Rule, in its present shape, by which an arbitrary term of twenty-one years is taken, is less inconsistent with legal principle and analogy than it was to make the validity of the extension of the period for creating future interests depend upon the actual presence or absence of minority in a devisee.[1]

## 12. ANY NUMBER OF LIVES IN ESSE ALLOWED

§ 189. **Several Lives.** Notwithstanding the statements in *Goring* v. *Bickerstaffe*[1] and *Love* v. *Wyndham*[2] that any number of lives in being might be taken to compose the period during which the creation of future estates would be lawful, Treby, C. J., is said, in *Luddington* v. *Kime*,[3] to have been of opinion "that the time allowed for executory devises to take effect ought not to be longer than the life of one person then *in esse*." But in *Scatterwood* v. *Edge*,[4] the Court of Common Pleas is said to have agreed in holding that "the compass of a life or lives" was a reasonable time, "for let the lives be never so many, there must be a survivor, and so it is but the length of that life." And Lord Hardwicke, in *Hopkins* v. *Hopkins*,[5] said: "It is not (in my opinion) material to restrain it to the life of tenant for life of the land, provided it be restrained to the life of a person in being."[6]

§ 190. Finally, in 1798, came the great case of *Thellusson* v. *Woodford*.[1] A testator gave a large fortune to accumulate until all of his sons and grandsons and grandsons' children who were living at his death were dead, and then to be paid over. He left three sons and six grandsons him surviving. Lord Loughborough, assisted by Lord Alvanley, M. R., and Buller and Lawrence, JJ., held the gift over good, and the

§ 188. [1] But see 51 Harv. Law Rev. 1329, 1331.

§ 189. [1] Freem. Ch. 163, 166. See § 163, ante.

[2] 1 Mod. 50, 54, 1 Sid. 450, 451. See § 167, ante.

[3] 1 Ld. Raym. 203, 207.

[4] 1 Salk. 229. See § 180, ante.

[5] 1 Atk. 580, 596.

[6] See Low v. Burron, 3 P. Wms. 262, 265, 2 Harg. Jurid. Arg. 135, note (w); and Humberston v. Humberston, 1 P. Wms. 332, 2 Vern. 738, Prec. Ch. 455, Gilb. Eq. 128.

§ 190. [1] 4 Ves. 227, 11 Ves. 112.

House of Lords, on the unanimous opinion of the judges, affirmed the decree. The eccentricity of the will and the large
amount involved excited great interest in the case. The arguments were of the most elaborate character,[2] and the judges
did not conceal their dislike of the will, but no one of the
many eminent lawyers who took part in the decision seems
to have felt any doubt in the case.[3]

### 13. THE CONNECTION OF THE RULE AGAINST PERPETUITIES WITH THE INVALIDITY OF REMAINDERS FOR LIFE TO SUCCESSIVE GENERATIONS[1]

**§ 191. Successive Remainders for Life.** One point remains
to be considered. It is sometimes said that there is a rule of
the common law that you cannot limit legal remainders for
life to successive generations, and that from this rule the Rule
against Perpetuities is derived. The opposite is believed to be
the case, and that the former rule is simply an instance of the
latter. No suggestion of the rule that you cannot limit life
estates in remainder to successive generations makes its appearance until the eighteenth century, long after the Rule
against Perpetuities was firmly established. It has been alleged that the doctrine that you cannot limit a remainder
to the issue of an unborn person is an instance of the doctrine
that you cannot have a possibility upon a possibility. But
this notion of a possibility upon a possibility was an innova-

[2] The three days' argument of
Mr. Hargrave against the validity
of the executory devise was published by him in the second volume of his Juridical Arguments.
It is an agreeable duty to recognize the debt which every student
of the history of the Rule against
Perpetuities owes to it.

[3] Lord Eldon in his opinion said:
"It is well known that the late
Chief Justice of the Court of
King's Bench [Lord Kenyon]
could hardly be brought to think
any of the questions in this case
fit for argument." 11 Ves. 144.
See further on this matter, Re
Villar, [1928] Ch. 471, and §§ 216
et seq., post.

The history of the development
of the law of future interests,
and especially of the Rule against
Perpetuities, is not the least valuable part of Mr. Lewis's valuable
work.

**Subdiv. 13.** [1] See §§ 125–134,
ante; §§ 284–298.8, App. K, § 931,
post, which should be consulted in
connection with this subdivision.

tion in the law, and was repudiated in the *Duke of Norfolk's Case*.[1] The only instance of an invalid possibility on a possibility, as given by Lord Coke, which is a remainder to the issue of an unborn person, is a remainder to the heirs of J. S. He says that if J. S. is born and dies during the particular estate, the remainder is void. But such a remainder takes effect, if at all, at the termination of the particular estate, and would be held good at the present day.[2] In fact, to say that you cannot give a remainder to the issue of an unborn person is not correct. On a gift to a man now unmarried for life, a remainder to his grandchildren is good. The true expression of the rule, even supposing it to be distinct from the Rule against Perpetuities, is that you cannot give successive contingent remainders for life. And that even such limitations were not considered bad until after the establishment of the Rule against Perpetuities, appears from the case of *Manning v. Andrews*.[3]

§ 192. That for a long time no question with regard to remoteness arose on remainders is not surprising. Remainder there could be none after an estate in fee simple; a remainder after a fee tail could be barred at will; a contingent remainder after a life estate could practically be barred by a fine, and no contingent remainder was good after an estate for years. The reason why so many cases of remoteness arose concerning executory devises and other conditional limitations is that they were indestructible. The destructibility of legal remainders prevented any question arising concerning their remoteness.[1]

§ 193. The first case in which any question of the validity of successive remainders for life came before the courts was

§ 191. [1] 3 Ch. Cas. 1, 29. See §§ 125–133, ante.

[2] See Routledge v. Dorril, 2 Ves. Jr. 357, 366.

[3] 1 Leon. 256, stated § 132, 132.1, ante. But see 7 Holdsworth Hist. Eng. Law (3d ed.) 209, 210.

§ 192. [1] The device of giving the freehold to trustees to preserve contingent remainders, and thereby preventing the tenant for life from destroying the contingent remainders, was not invented till the middle of the seventeenth century. Garth v. Cotton, 1 Dick. 183, 188, 191, 1 Ves. Sr. 524. 1 Jurid. Soc. Papers 53–55.

*Humberston* v. *Humberston*,[1] in 1717, more than thirty years
after the doctrine of remoteness had been settled in the *Duke
of Norfolk's Case.*[2] "One Matthew Humberston (reported to
have been formerly a Christ-Hospital Boy) devised his estate,
which was very considerable, to the Draper's Company and
their successors, in trust to convey the premises to his godson
Matthew Humberston for life, and afterwards upon the death
of the said Matthew to his first son for life, and so to the first
son of that first son for life, etc., and if no issue male of the
first son, then to the second son of the said Matthew Humberston for life, and so to his first son, etc., and in failure of such
issue of Matthew, then to another Matthew Humberston for
life, and to his first son for life, etc., with remainders over to
very many of the Humberstons (I think about fifty), for their
lives successively, and their respective sons, when born, for
their lives, without giving an estate in tail to any of them, or
making any disposition of the fee." Lord Cowper, C., said
that an attempt to make a perpetuity for successive lives was
vain. There is not a word about a possibility on a possibility.[3]

§ **194.** In *Hopkins* v. *Hopkins*[1] (1739), Lord Hardwicke
said that he did not see how an estate could be devised to
trustees and their heirs to hold until the birth of a son of a
daughter of A., which daughter was unborn at the testator's
death, and then to such son;[2] but there is nothing said about
a possibility on a possibility, nor any indication that a different rule would apply in case of a remainder than in case of
an executory devise; and indeed the gift to the daughter's

§ 193. [1] 1 P. Wms. 332, 2 Vern.
738. Prec. Ch. 455. Gilb Eq. 128.
[2] 3 Ch. Cas. 1.

[3] Mr. Sweet is of opinion that
the Lord Chancellor used "perpetuity" in the sense of an unbarrable estate tail. 1 Jarm. Wills
(7th ed.) 255, note (r). This may
well be. On the bearing of this
suggestion upon Mr. Sweet's theory that the invalidity of re-

mainders to successive generations is a result from the barrable character of estates tail, see
App. K, §§ 943, 944, post.

§ 194. [1] West 606, 1 Atk. 580,
1 Ves. Sr. 268. Co. Lit. 271 b,
Butler's note VII. 2. See Abbiss
v. Burney, 17 Ch. D. 211, 70 L. T.
146.

[2] West 629, 1 Atk. 596.

son, if good, would have been an executory devise, and not a remainder.³

**§ 195. No such Rule independent of the Rule against Perpetuities.** The first suggestion to be found in the books that the doctrine of the invalidity of successive remainders for life is an independent original rule, and that the provisions of law concerning remoteness in conditional limitations have been copied from it, is to be found in Lord Keeper Northington's judgment in *Marlborough* v. *Godolphin*.¹ In that case, decided by the Lord Keeper in 1759, there was a devise to trustees for the use of several persons for life, remainder to the use of their first and other sons successively in tail male, with a direction to the trustees on the birth of each of such sons to revoke the use to him, and limit the use to him for life, remainder to his first and other sons successively in tail male. Lord Keeper Northington held the direction void. He said: "It is agreed that the Duke of Marlborough could not have done this by limitation of estate; because, though by the rules of law an estate may be limited by way of contingent remainder to a person not *in esse* for life, or as an inheritance, yet a remainder to the issue of such contingent remainder-man as a purchaser is a limitation unheard of in law, nor ever attempted, as far as I have been able to discover. Why the law disallowed these kind of limitations I will not take upon me to say; because I have never met, in the compass of my reading, with any reason assigned for it: and I shall not hazard any conjecture of my own; for technical reasons upheld by old repute, and grown reverend by length of years, bear great weight and authority; but a new technical reason appears with as little dignity as an usurper just seated in his chair of state. So far, however, is plain, that the common law seemed wisely to consider that the real property of this state ought, to a degree, to be put in commerce, to be left free to answer the exigencies of the possessors and their families, and therefore admitted no perpetuities by

³ See Lewis, Perp. 413–415.

§ **195.** ¹ 1 Eden 404, in Dom. Proc., sub nom. Spencer v. Marl-

borough, 3 Bro. P. C. (Toml. ed.) 232.

way of entails; and though it allowed contingent remainders, it afforded them no protection.[2] . . . It was said in the argument on this case, that it is determined that a person may, by executory devise, make an estate unalienable for one life in being, and twenty or twenty-one years after, but that the time not to be exceeded is nowhere defined, therefore that I might as well extend it *beyond* that period, as others have *to* it. It is true that by executory devise an estate may be locked up for a life or lives in being, and twenty or twenty-one years after. And that is in conformity to the course of limitations, and the methods of conveyance at law; for a limitation may be to one for life, with remainder to a person unborn in tail or in fee. If there are trustees to support contingent remainders, the remainder cannot be barred by the tenant for life, nor can it be conveyed by the remainder-man till he attains the age of twenty-one. Therefore the sages of the law have properly allowed a perpetuity as far in executory devises, which are accommodated to the exigencies in families, as in legal limitations. . . . I have thus far considered this case upon its general tendency to a perpetuity, beyond what I conceive the rules of law allow."[3]

§ 196. The case was carried to the House of Lords, and there affirmed in accordance with the unanimous opinion of the judges.[1] In the argument of the counsel for the respondent it is said:[2] "If the grantor should, after the first vested estate of freehold, limit a contingent estate or use for life to a person unborn, and then follow it with contingent remainders in tail to the sons or children of such unborn tenant for life, such contingent limitations of the inheritance would be void. This arises from the policy of the law against perpetuities, that the vesting of the inheritance or ownership may not be suspended beyond the compass of a life or lives in being, or beyond the age of twenty-one of the first unborn tenant in tail, during whose infancy the law itself will restrain his

[2] 1 Eden 415, 416.

[3] 1 Eden 418, 419. See, too, the argument for the plaintiff, pp. 408–411.

§ 196. [1] 3 Bro. P. C. (Toml. ed.) 232.

[2] 3 Bro. P. C. (Toml. ed.) 245.

power of alienation." Lord Northington seems to have regarded the rule against limiting successive life estates in remainder as an independent doctrine. He admits that he searched for the reason in vain, which is not strange, for no trace of such independent doctrine is to be found. He is the first to mention it. It is submitted that the statement of the counsel in the House of Lords, that the doctrine is a corollary of the Rule against Perpetuities, is not only more reasonable, but is historically correct.

**§ 197.** Lord Northington did not base the doctrine against successive life estates on any theory of the illegality of a possibility upon a possibility. We first find that doctrine referred for its origin to this theory in 1765, eighty years after it might have been hoped that such theory had, in the *Duke of Norfolk's Case*,[1] received its quietus. *Chapman* v. *Brown*[2] turned on special circumstances, but, with reference to a limitation to an unborn person for life, remainder to his issue in tail, Lord Mansfield, C. J., said: "A possibility cannot be devised upon a possibility;"[3] and Wilmot, J., said: "You cannot limit a non-

§ 197. [1] 3 Ch. Cas. 1.
[2] 3 Burr. 1626, 3 Bro. P. C. (Toml. ed.) 269.
[3] 3 Burr. 1634.
It is to this remark of Lord Mansfield that the revival of the notion that a "possibility upon a possibility" was bad, was probably due, but the reputation of Lord Mansfield as a commercial lawyer should not blind us to the fact that he was not equally great in the law of real property. For instance, his decision on the Rule in Shelley's Case in Perrin v. Blake, 1 W. Bl. 672, is now universally admitted to have been wrong. Again, his views of disseisin by election in Taylor d. Atkyns v. Horde, 1 Burr. 60, met a strong opposition from the profession. Butler's note to 1 Co.

Lit. 330 b. Thus: "It is hardly possible to conceive on what principle of tenure the decision of Taylor v. Horde can be supported. And on recent occasions the courts have allowed that Lord Mansfield's doctrine in that case cannot be sustained," 1 Prest. Conv. 60; "it is lamentable to see how the law [of seisin and disseisin] is sometimes applied in practice to subjects which involve this learning; taking modern notions of convenience, and not principle, as the guide. The judgment in Taylor v. Horde has confounded the principles of law, and produced a system of error." 2 Prest. Abstr. (2d ed.) 289; cf. Challis, Real Prop. (3d ed.) 405, 406; Lightwood, Possession of Land 43, 54. So, of Lord Mans-

entity upon a nonentity, a possibility upon a possibility."[4] How little these phrases were understood as indicating the existence of any other reason than remoteness for the invalidity of such limitations is shown by the argument of counsel for the defendants in error before the House of Lords, where the case was carried and affirmed. They said that the intent of the testator "could not take effect; as it would establish a limitation of a possibility upon a possibility, and manifestly tend to a perpetuity, by a suspension of the inheritance from vesting, and consequently render the estate unalienable for a longer time than the policy of the law allows, which has not yet been suffered to continue longer than a life or lives in being, and twenty-one years beyond."[5]

field's decision in Buckworth v. Thirkell, 3 Bos. & P. 652, note, that an executory devise does not cut off curtesy and dower, it has been said that very few cases in modern practice have provoked so much discussion or been the subject of so much animadversion. 1 Scribner, Dower (2d ed.) 305.

[4] 3 Burr. 1635.

[5] 3 Bro. P. C. (Toml. ed.) 275.

In the first and second editions of Fearne on Contingent Remainders nothing seems to be said of remainders to an unborn child of an unborn person, for in the remarks on the "Nature of the Contingency upon which a remainder may be limited," he does not seem to have had them in mind; but in the third edition, published in 1776, on page 391 (and in subsequent editions), in the part treating of executory devises, he says: "Here, indeed, it may not be improper to remark, once for all, that any limitation in future, or by way of remainder of lands of inheritance, which in its nature

tends to a perpetuity, even although there be a preceding vested freehold, so as to take it out of the description of an executory devise, is by our courts considered as void in its creation;" and he then goes on to give the case of a remainder to an unborn person followed by a remainder to his children. Mr. Sweet, in a note to 1 Jarm. Wills (7th ed.) 344, note (1), thinks that "perpetuity" here probably refers to an unbarrable estate tail, but it seems more likely from the context that Mr. Fearne is referring to the Rule against Perpetuities.

In 2 Cas. & Op. 432, on Mr. Baker's will, in 1768, an opinion of Mr. Booth states, p. 435: "It is an error to say that an unborn son cannot be made tenant for life, . . . but a limitation to that unborn son's first son is a possibility upon a possibility; and that may be, and is by most lawyers thought to be, what the law will not endure." In the opinion of Mr. Yorke, on the same will,

§ **198.** In *Long* v. *Blackall*[1] (1797), Lord Kenyon, C. J., expressed himself more clearly even than Lord Northington. He said: "The rules respecting executory devises have conformed to the rules laid down in the construction of legal limitations, and the courts have said that the estate shall not be unalienable by executory devises for a longer term than is allowed by the limitations of a common-law conveyance. In marriage settlements the estate may be limited to the first and other sons of the marriage in tail, and until the person to whom the last remainder is limited is of age the estate is unalienable. In conformity to that rule the courts have said, so far we will allow executory devises to be good. To support this position I could refer to many decisions: but it is sufficient to refer to the *Duke of Norfolk's Case,* in which all the learning on this head was gone into; and from that time to the present every judge has acquiesced in that decision. It is an established rule that an executory devise is good if it must necessarily happen within a life or lives in being and twenty-one years, and the fraction of another year, allowing for the time of gestation." This statement of Lord Kenyon, unsupported as it is by the facts, seems to be the chief ground of the common notion that the Rule against Perpetuities was borrowed from a rule forbidding the limitation of life estates in remainder to successive generations.

§ **199.** In *Thellusson* v. *Woodford,*[1] Mr. Justice Lawrence said: "The Court has no criterion to judge of the inconven-

p. 440, it is said: "By way of executory devise, or springing use, the inheritance may be suspended from vesting during a life or lives in being, or during the infancy of the first unborn tenant in tail; but it can be suspended no longer. In like manner a contingent remainder must vest during the life or immediately upon the death of the devisee of the particular estate which precedes it, such devisee being *in esse* at the time when the will speaks; but it cannot be made to wait or expect the vesting of another estate, prior in limitation, and equally contingent with itself. The law does not allow a contingency to depend upon a contingency, or one possibility to be thus raised upon another."

§ **198.** [1] 7 T. R. 100. See s. c. 3 Ves. Jr. 486, 489, and Thellusson v. Woodford, 11 Ves. 112, 150.

§ **199.** [1] 4 Ves. 227, 11 Ves. 112.

ience arising from the restriction of property by executory
devise except from contrasting it with the restraint which
the common law allows to be put on the alienation of real
property."[2]   And Lord Alvanley, M. R.,[3] and Chief Baron
Macdonald[4] say that Lord Nottingham, in the *Duke of Norfolk's Case,* declared that the rule as to the remoteness of
executory devises was based on the rule which governed legal
remainders.[5]   No such meaning can, however, be properly
attributed to Lord Nottingham.   What he says is that the
same rule must govern the executory devise of a term as
governs the executory devise of a fee: "Whenever you stop
at the limitation of a fee upon a fee, there we will stop in the
limitation of a term of years."   But what rule shall govern
the executory devise of a fee is, he says, "not yet determined."[6]   The chronological examination of the cases shows
that the Rule against Perpetuities did not arise by way of
analogy to any previous rule with regard to remainders, but
that as questions of remoteness came up with regard to different classes of limitations they were considered, and the
Rule against Perpetuities finally shaped as the rule which
was to govern all cases.[7]

### 14. The Rule against Perpetuities in America

§ 200. **Rule Part of Common Law.**   The Rule against Perpetuities, as part of the Common Law, has been carried to
all the English colonies where the principles of that Law prevail.[1]   Considering the unformed condition of the doctrine of

[2] 4 Ves. 314.

[3] 4 Ves. 331.

[4] 11 Ves. 135.

[5] See Sir Edward Sugden's language, cited § 287, post.

[6] 3 Ch. Cas. 36, 49, 2 Swanst.
468.

[7] The case of Whitby v. Mitchell, 42 Ch. D. 494, 44 Ch. D. 85,
which held that there is a rule
governing the creation of contingent remainders, independent of

the Rule against Perpetuities, and
the discussion which it has provoked, are dealt with, §§ 298 et
seq., post.   For an extended historical discussion of the supposed
rules against double possibilities
and successive remainders for life,
and their connection with the case
of Whitby v. Mitchell and the
Rule against Perpetuities, see 25
Iowa Law Rev. 1, 707.

§ 200. [1] See Yeap Cheah Neo v.

remoteness at the time when the American Colonies were planted, it would have been quite possible for it to have developed there in a different shape from that which it assumed in England. But as a matter of fact the rule seems, in the absence of statute,[2] to be always adopted throughout the United States in its modern English form.[3]

§ 200.1. The practical importance of tracing the history of the Rule against Perpetuities lies in the proof it affords that the Rule is not confined, as has been sometimes contended, to interests arising under the Statutes of Uses and Wills, but that it was developed by cases on executory devises of chattels which were common-law interests, and that it should govern all kinds of future contingent limitations.[1]

Ong Cheng Neo, L. R. 6 P. C. 381; Nelan v. Downes, 23 Com. L. R. 546 (Aust.). But cf. Cooper v. Stuart, 14 Ap. Cas. 286, 293.

[2] The statutory modifications of the Rule against Perpetuities are given in App. B and C, post. They are generally in the direction of greater stringency.

[3] See Becker v. Chester, 115 Wis. 90, 132, 91 N. W. 87, 102; Chilcott v. Hart, 23 Colo. 40, 45 Pac. 391. Cf. Mayor of New York v. Stuyvesant, 17 N. Y. 34. See § 224, post.

Ashton v. Ashton, 1 Dall. 4 (1760), in the Supreme Court of Pennsylvania, seems to be the first reported case in America in which a question of remoteness was involved.

§ 200.1. [1] See §§ 284–303, 312, 314–316, 319, 321, 323, post.

Mr. Charles Sweet in a note to Challis, Real Prop. (3d ed.) 211, admits that the Rule against Perpetuities is not confined to interests arising under the Statutes of Uses and Wills, but says that executory devises of terms were void at common law. That depends upon what is meant by common-law interests; see § 296.1, post. See also §§ 297–298, 299–302, post.

# CHAPTER VI

## THE RULE AGAINST PERPETUITIES AND ITS COROLLARIES

**§ 201. Statement of the Rule.** In the first edition the Rule against Perpetuities was given in this form:

No INTEREST SUBJECT TO A CONDITION PRECEDENT IS GOOD, UNLESS THE CONDITION MUST BE FULFILLED, IF AT ALL, WITHIN[1] TWENTY-ONE YEARS AFTER SOME LIFE IN BEING AT THE CREATION OF THE INTEREST.

This appears to be correct if we assume that "condition" includes not only all uncertain future acts and events but also all certain future events with the exception of the termination of preceding estates.[2]

If we decline to make this assumption, and confine "condition" to uncertain future acts and events, then the Rule against Perpetuities will take this shape:

No INTEREST IS GOOD UNLESS IT MUST VEST, IF AT ALL, NOT LATER THAN TWENTY-ONE YEARS AFTER SOME LIFE IN BEING AT THE CREATION OF THE INTEREST.[3]

**§ 201.** [1] "At the expiration of" twenty-one years is within twenty-one years. English v. Cliff, [1914] 2 Ch. 376. Kolb v. Landes, 277 Ill. 440, 115 N. E. 539.

[2] "Die Bedingungen, unter denen ja auch er [Savigny] nur diejenigen versteht, welche das Dasein eines Rechtsverhältnisses von einem künftigen ungewissen Ereigniss abhängig machen, und die Befristungen sind in der That nur Unterarten eines Begriffs, und zwar . . . Unterarten des richtig gefassten Begriffs der Bedingung." Adickes, Die Bedingungen, p. 60. This may be para-

phrased thus: "Savigny uses the term 'condition' as including only those conditions which make a legal interest dependent on the happening of an uncertain future event. But the idea of a condition, properly conceived, includes not only conditions in the sense in which Savigny uses the term, but also all postponements." See also § 114, ante.

[3] Thus an estate devised to A. and his heirs, to begin from a day fifty years after the testator's death, is too remote, although the event upon which it

## 1. NATURE OF INTEREST

### § 202. Universal Application.
The Rule governs both legal and equitable interests, and interests in both realty and personalty.[1]

depends is certain to occur. Such an executory limitation is, to be sure, little if at all more objectionable on the ground of policy than a vested remainder after a long term of years. See 33 Harv. Law Rev. 526, 536. But in reality remainders after long terms are objectionable. See § 210, post. The reason such remainders do not infringe the Rule against Perpetuities is that the definition of the Rule excludes from its operation all completely vested interests. See Marsden, Perp. 65, 66; §§ 205, 970–974, post. This fact affords no reason for excepting from the operation of the Rule any executory limitations which logically fall within its scope. The circumstance that an executory limitation to an ascertained person is releasable is immaterial for the purposes of the Rule against Perpetuities. §§ 268, 269, post. See also Newhall, Fut. Int. in Mass., § 16. On the distinction between vested and contingent interests, see Chap. III., ante. And cf. Lawrence's Estate, 136 Pa. 354, 366, 367, 20 Atl. 521, 522, 523.

Professor Kales criticised the latter definition given in this section on account of the ambiguous meaning of the word "vest." 20 Harv. Law Rev. 198. 5 Ill. Law Rev. 387. The advantage of using the term "vest" is that the word, as employed in

connection with the Rule against Perpetuities, implies the assumption made with regard to the definition first above given and without which that definition is incomplete. It is true that the artificial character of the term "vested" as applied to a remainder to an increasable class asks for an explanation, but it seems better to give this explanation separately, as is done in §§ 205.2, 205.3, post, than to incumber the definition with it. See §§ 110.1, 118, ante, App. M, § 970, post. Indeed, the subject of class gifts presents such peculiar problems that probably no general definition could be framed that would carry the student very far in dealing with the topic. A separate and detailed treatment is required. See Chapter X., §§ 369 et seq., post.

The statement of the Rule above given seems also to assume that a vested interest may be defined as an interest which is subject to no condition precedent or postponement, except the expiration of preceding estates in accordance with their inherent limitations. See §§ 100, 101, ante, 205, note 2, post. This definition of a vested interest appears to be correct. As to the peculiar and unusual case of an executory limitation after a determinable fee, see § 114, note 3, ante.

§ 202. [1] Lewis, Perp. 169. The

§ **202.1.** The Rule applies not only to interests in particular pieces of property, but also to interests in changeable funds. Thus the interests of *cestuis que trust* may be too remote, although the trustees have full power to change investments.[1]

§ **203. A Practical Rule of Policy.** The Rule is not of feudal origin; it has its support in the practical needs of modern times. Therefore, although it is applied with great strictness, courts attend in applying it to the substance rather than to the form of future limitations. Thus a future interest, if destructible at the mere pleasure of the present owner of the property,[1] is not regarded as an interest at all, and the Rule does not concern itself with it. For instance, such limitations after an estate tail as must take effect, if at all, not later than the termination of the estate tail, are never too remote; the present tenant in tail can destroy them all at any moment by docking the entail.[2]

§ **204. Escheat.** In like manner, rights of escheat in realty and in the nature of escheat in personalty are not within

---

interests subject to the Rule are fully discussed in Chap. VIII., post. See Re Walkerly, 108 Cal. 627, 657, 41 Pac. 772, 779.

§ **202.1.** [1] See § 269, post.

§ **203.** [1] That is, the owner of the present interest.

[2] See Chap. XIV., post. In McMahon v. Swan, [1924] Vict. 397, a lease was given "for a period of 5 years, with option of purchase at £700," such tenancy not to cease "until notice in writing shall have been given by either party to the other." The learned judge held that the option was not too remote, because it could be destroyed at any time by notice to terminate the lease, and he referred to the cases on limitations after estates tail. But query if this conclusion is correct? The lessor can only destroy the option by terminating the lease, and the lease may be beneficial to him, as seems to have been the case here. If the owner of the present estate can destroy a future interest only by fulfilling an onerous condition, he is not free to destroy it at his mere pleasure, and the interest comes within the Rule against Perpetuities. Is not the termination of the lease here an onerous condition? See § 568, post. On options of purchase in leases, see § 230.3, post. See also Lewis Oyster Co. v. West, 93 Conn. 518, 107 Atl. 138.

the Rule.   The existence of these rights in no degree affects
the value of the interests which are subject to them.[1]

## 2. VESTED INTERESTS NOT SUBJECT TO THE RULE

**§ 205. Vested Interests not affected.**   A vested interest is
not subject to the Rule against Perpetuities.[1]   Thus, if land

§ 204. [1] See also § 205.1, post.

§ 205. [1] See §§ 101, ante, 970–974, post.

In Wood v. Drew, 33 Beav. 610, the testator bequeathed five leasehold houses, the leases of which had about fifty-four years to run, in trust for A. for life, remainder for her children; and on the expiration of the lease of any house he directed his trustees to convey to A. for life, remainder to her children in fee, one or more of his five freehold houses, so that the house thus conveyed should be of equal annual value, as near as could be, but not exceeding, the annual value of the leasehold house; and in case the annual value of the freehold house or houses should exceed the annual value of the leasehold house, then the difference should be paid by A. or her children to his trustees, upon the trusts of the will. The freehold houses were given to the trustees on trust to convey them, or such of them as might be necessary, to A. and her children, as provided, and until such conveyance to hold said houses, and all other the testator's property, in trust for B. and his heirs. Sir John Romilly, M. R., held that the interest of A. and her children in the freehold houses was not void for remoteness; that if it was bad for any cause it was bad for uncertainty; and he held that it was not bad for uncertainty. But the uncertainty seems to be this,—until remote periods it cannot be told which freehold house or houses will be conveyed in lieu of each leasehold house, or what the annual value of such houses will then be; that is, the uncertainty arises from the doubtfulness of a remote contingency. The objection is that of remoteness, and it is submitted that the gift was too remote. Apparently the annual value of the leasehold house for which a freehold house or houses of equal annual value was to be exchanged was the value at the expiration of the lease. Now, even assuming that the five freehold houses, less the amount by which their value should exceed the value of the leasehold houses at the expiration of the leases, could be considered as a distinct entity, and that this entity if ascertained could vest at once, yet such entity could not be ascertained until the leases fell in, and must consequently be contingent and therefore too remote. Cf. Re Wood, [1894] 2 Ch. 310, 316; Re Bewick, [1911] 1 Ch. 116.

**[G. R. P.]**

is devised to A., now a bachelor, for life, remainder to his children, as tenants in common, for life, remainder to B. in fee, B.'s remainder is vested, and is not too remote, although it may not come into possession until a period beyond the limits of the Rule against Perpetuities.[2] Reversions[3] and vested

[2] The idea of a particular estate, succeeded by a vested remainder or reversion, is peculiar to the common law. See §§ 8, 100, note 2, ante, 971, post. Under the common-law system, an estate for life, or a determinable fee, is an interest which comes to an end of itself by virtue of the intrinsic force of the terms by which it is created, and not because it is cut short by a condition subsequent, or by the substitution of another interest for it. Such estates expire as a consequence of the inherent limitation of their duration, whether that limitation results merely from the nature of the estate created, as in the case of an ordinary life estate, or from their being subject to an express special limitation. (As to special limitations, see § 32, ante.) Since the Rule against Perpetuities concerns only the validity of future interests, it cannot affect the duration of a present estate, except so far as the estate may be subject to be divested by a condition subsequent or executory interest. Therefore even if vested remainders, taking effect at a remote period, should be forbidden, there would still necessarily be a reversion after every estate that is subject to an inherent limitation. Cf. § 312, post. And see Chaplin, Suspension of Alienation (3d ed.), § 394. The possibly excessive duration of such a limited estate, and the consequent existence of an interest taking effect in the remote future, may be objectionable from the point of view of the general policy in favor of freedom from alienation (see §§ 210, 973, post); but that inconvenience can be remedied only by a law differing radically from the Rule against Perpetuities, and forbidding the creation of interests, less than absolute, which might last for longer than a prescribed period. Such a prohibition would apply to life estates to unborn persons. See § 974, post; and cf. the statutes mentioned in §§ 210, 735, 743, 747, 751–752.1, post. With respect to determinable fees, legislation has been proposed which would limit their duration to a fixed number of years. See 54 Harv. Law Rev. 248; Wis. Law Rev. (1940) 121; and the Uniform Estates Act, § 15, proposed by the State Commissioners for Uniform Laws (Handbook of Commissioners (1939) 275), and quoted in 54 Harv. Law Rev. 248, 253, note 22. It has even been suggested that the Courts, without the aid of legislation, acting on the analogy of Letteau v. Ellis, 122 Cal. Ap. 584, 10 Pac. 2d 496 (see § 282, note, at end, post), might declare that a special

remainders, and those equitable interests and interests in
personalty which, if they were legal interests in realty, would
be reversions and vested remainders, are vested interests.
Other future interests are not vested.

§ 205.1. Escheat. The right of escheat, if an interest at
all within the purview of the Rule against Perpetuities, is a
vested interest. At any rate, it has no effect on the tying up
of property.[1]

The right of escheat in real property is a future right; but
when the Crown or State takes personal property upon the
owner dying intestate and without kin, it is often said to take
as *ultimus heres,* that is, as continuing in succession the original owner's right.[2]

In the famous case of *Burgess* v. *Wheate,*[3] it was held that
when the owner of an equitable fee dies without heirs, the
trustee does not hold the land subject to a trust for the
Crown, and, in spite of Lord Mansfield's dissenting opinion,

limitation on a fee, originally good,
had become invalid on account of
changes in circumstances. See 54
Harv. Law Rev. 248, 268–276. In
any such case, the Court would
not merely declare the possibility
of reverter invalid. It would declare the special limitation of the
fee invalid, and, as a result of this,
the possibility of reverter would
disappear. See 2 Tiffany, Real
Prop. (3d ed.), § 404; 2 Simes,
Fut. Int., §§ 455, 602, 603, 611;
Amer. Law Inst. Restatement,
Property, § 44, Comment q.

[3] Including possibilities of reverter. See §§ 41, 113.3, ante.

§ 205.1. [1] §§ 115, 204, ante.

[2] In laico autem decedente ab
intestato, deficientibus consan-
guineis et uxore, succedet fiscus.
Lyndwood, Prov. 180. "Suppose
Lowe had been a bastard, or, being legitimate, had died without

any next of kin, The King, in
such case, would have taken, as
ultimus heres, but subject to the
debts of the intestate." Per
Lord Mansfield, Megit v. Johnson,
2 Doug. 542, 548. See also Johnston v. Spicer, 107 N. Y. 185, 13
N. E. 753; Matter of People
(Melrose Ave.), 234 N. Y. 48,
136 N. E. 235; People v. Richardson, 269 Ill. 275, 109 N. E. 1033.
Cf. Dyke v. Walford, 5 Moore P.
C. 434. But Re Barnett's Trusts,
[1902] 1 Ch. 847, seems to be a
decision contra; and see Delaney
v. State, 42 N. Dak. 630, 174 N.
W. 290; Re Estate of Miner, 143
Cal. 194, 76 Pac. 968; Re Estate
of O'Connor, 126 Neb. 182, 252
N. W. 826; 12 Neb. Law Bull.
378; 48 Harv. Law Rev. 129; 32
Mich. Law Rev. 226; 2 Univ.
Chic. Law Rev. 151.

[3] 1 Eden 177.

and of much criticism to which the decision has been subjected, this seems correct. When a man dies without natural heirs, the lord takes the land, not in succession as *ultimus heres*, but in the *post* by reason of tenure,[4] and there is no tenure of an equitable fee. The legal title is in the trustee subject to a trust in favor of the *cestui que trust*, and this trust has come to an end, and as it was not held of any lord, there is no person remaining having any claim against the trustee. But see remarks of Romer, L. J., in *Re Wells*.[5]

The contention may be made, that although the Crown cannot take as lord upon the death of the *cestui que trust* without heirs, there should be a resulting trust to the settlor or testator and his heirs. This question has not been presented in the cases, for in them the *cestui que trust* was the settlor or testator, so that not only the *cestui que trust*, but also the settlor or testator had died without heirs, and there was no one to whom a trust could result.[6]

If land is devised to trustees in trust for A. for life, and then in trust for A.'s children in fee, and A. never has any children, there is upon A.'s death a resulting trust to the testator's heirs; why then, it may be said, if land is devised to trustees in trust for A. and his heirs and A. dies without heirs, should there not be a resulting trust to the testator's heirs? It may be answered that in the former case the trust to A.'s children never arises, while, in the latter, though it has come to an end, it did once exist; but this does not seem a very solid

---

[4] See Attorney General v. Attorney General, [1928] A. C. 475.

[5] [1933] 1 Ch. (C. A.) 29, 57, 58.

[6] King's Attorney v. Sands, Freem. Ch. 129. Burgess v. Waite, 1 W. Bl. 123. Henchman v. Attorney General, 3 Myl. & K. 485. Taylor v. Haygarth, 14 Sim. 8. Davall v. New River Co., 3 De G. & Sm. 394. Beale v. Symonds, 16 Beav. 406. Cox v. Parker, 22 Beav. 168. Re Harrop's Estate, 3 Drew. 726. Sweeting v. Sweeting, 33 L. J. Ch. 211. Gallard v. Hawkins, 27 Ch. D. 298. See also Anon., Y. B. Mich. 5 Edw. IV. 7, pl. 18; Anon., 2 And. 197, 200; Henchman v. A. G., 3 Myl. & K. 485. The case of Keogh v. McGrath, 5 L. R. Ir. 478, seems to be the only exception. Cf. the St. 47 & 48 Vict., c. 71, § 4, giving the trust to the Crown; Re Wood, [1896] 2 Ch. 596; and an article on the Law of Escheat by Mr. Frederic W. Hardman, 4 Law Quart. Rev. 318.

distinction.  Again, as we shall see[7] when land is devised for a charitable purpose which comes to an end, and cannot be executed *cy pres,* there is a resulting trust; and this may be said to present the same case as a death without heirs.  Here again it may be answered there is a distinction between a charitable purpose and an individual *cestui que trust,* but this too seems a rather unsubstantial difference.  On the whole, in a jurisdiction where the common law still prevails, if A. devises real property in trust for B. and B. dies without heirs, it may be worth considering whether there should not be a resulting trust to A.'s heirs.  There seems to be nothing in the authorities to prevent it.[8]

If personal property is held in trust for A. and A. dies intestate and without widow or kin, the trust continues in favor of the Crown.  As with real estate, in all these cases the *cestui que trust* who has died without kin has been the same person as the settlor or devisor, and therefore there could be no question of resulting trust.[9]

Suppose, however, that A. bequeaths personal property to B. in trust for C. and C. dies intestate and without wife or kin, should the Crown or State take?  This seems to depend upon whether the Crown or State is really *ultimus heres* or not.  If the Crown or State is really *ultimus heres,* that is, if it takes in succession to the deceased owner, then it will succeed to the trust; if, on the other hand, *ultimus heres* is merely a piece of rhetoric, then either the trustee should take free from trust, or there should be a resulting trust to the next of kin of the testator as explained above with reference to real estate.

There is another possible view, however, which is suggested

7 § 603.9, post.

8 Except Keogh v. McGrath, note 6, supra.  For the cases in those of the United States where there is no tenure, and where, therefore, there can be no escheat, properly so called, vide infra.

9 Taylor v. Haygarth, 14 Sim.

8.  Powell v. Merrett, 1 Sm. & G. 381.  Cradock v. Owen, 2 Sm. & G. 241.  Read v. Stedman, 26 Beav. 495.  Re Hudson's Trusts, 52 L. J. Ch. 789.  Dillon v. Reilly, 9 L. R. Ir. 57.  See Re Harrop's Estate, 3 Drew. 726, and Re Jones, [1925] Ch. 340.

by the language of *Re Jones*.[10]  Even if the Crown or State
does not take the personalty of an intestate who dies without
wife or kin, as *ultimus heres* in a proper sense,[11] but merely
by virtue of its prerogative right to *bona vacantia*, it may
be said that nevertheless the equitable title of an intestate
*cestui que trust*, who has died without wife or kin, ought to
be treated as a property right of such a character as to come
within the description of *bona vacantia*, and ought therefore
to go to the Crown or State, notwithstanding that the trustee
has legal title to the property.[12]

Where there is no tenure, and therefore no escheat, the
passing of real estate on the death of the owner without heirs,
would, in the absence of statute, seem to rest upon the same
principles as underlie the passing of personal property.[13]

[10] [1925] Ch. 340.

[11] See Re Barnett's Trusts, [1902] 1 Ch. 847.

[12] Cf. Re Wells, [1933] 1 Ch. (C. A.) 29; and § 323, note 1, post.

[13] See Matthews v. Ward, 10 G. & J. 443; Matter of People (Melrose Ave.) 234 N. Y. 48, 136 N. E. 235; 3 Minn. Law Rev. 320, 327; 36 Mich. Law Rev. 226; and cf. Johnston v. Spicer, 107 N. Y. 185, 13 N. E. 753; Commonwealth v. Naile, 88 Pa. 429. With regard to the obsolescence of escheat to a mesne lord, see Re Holliday, [1922] 2 Ch. 695. In England, by the Administration of Estates Act (1925), §§ 45, 46, escheat on failure of heirs is abolished, and lands are disposed of together with the personal estate as bona vacantia, although tenure apparently continues to exist. See 75 Sol. J. 843. But cf. 69 L. J. 369, 385. In many of the United States legislation has apparently effected a similar result, and done away with escheat properly so called, whether or not tenure still exists. This situation as to the disposition of realty on the death of the owner without heirs exists, by reason either of the absence of tenure, or statutory provisions, in most if not all of the States. The American Law Institute, in its Restatement of the Law of Trusts, § 142, Comment e, states the American law, as to both realty and personalty, to be that the equitable interest of a cestui que trust, who has died intestate without heirs, goes to the State, although it does not clearly appear whether this conclusion is based on the notion that the State is ultimus heres, or on the theory as to bona vacantia mentioned in the next to the last paragraph of this section. See also § 411, Comment f, ibid.; 1 Scott, Trusts, § 142.2; 3 Scott, Trusts, § 411.4; 2 Univ. Chic. Law Rev. 151.

§ 205.2. **Remainders to a Class.** The preceding statement in § 205 must be subjected to one qualification. When a remainder is given to a class, and such remainder is vested in certain members of the class, subject to open and let in other members, born afterwards or afterwards fulfilling a condition,[1] the shares in such remainder or interest may be obnoxious to the Rule against Perpetuities, because their number and therefore their size may not be determinable until too remote a period.[2] For instance, suppose land is devised to A., a bachelor, for life, remainder to his eldest son for life, remainder to those children of B. who reach twenty-five. At the testator's death B. is living and one of his children, C., has reached twenty-five. The interest of C. is said to be vested, and yet the devise to B.'s children is invalid as too remote; for, although the minimum size of each child's share will be fixed at the death of B., the maximum may not be determined until twenty-five years after.[3] This qualification is rendered necessary by the artificial character of the rule which declares that a member of a class may have a vested interest in property given to the class although the number of the members in the class is uncertain. The fact is that, though it is certain that each member of the class will get something, the amount which he will get is dependent upon the contingency of the size of the class. Though the interest is called vested, it is in truth contingent.[4]

Where there is an escheat, or a succession in interest, or a taking by the Crown or State as bona vacantia, there is no room for the application of the Rule against Perpetuities; as to its application to cases of resulting trust, see § 327.1, post.

§ 205.2. [1] See §§ 110, 110.1, ante.

[2] See Chap. X., Limitations to Classes, post.

[3] See §§ 375, 381–385, post.

[4] Or at least it is treated as contingent for the purposes of the Rule against Perpetuities. §§ 110.1, ante, 375, post. McGill v. Trust Co., 94 N. J. Eq. 657, 665, 121 Atl. 760, 764. 1 Jarm. Wills (7th ed.) 303. 30 Cyc. Law & Proc. 1486. See Re Gage, [1898] 1 Ch. 498; and § 972, note 2, post. For a criticism of the correctness of this doctrine on principle, see 51 Harv. Law Rev. 1329; §§ 110.1, note, ante, 375, note 4, post.

As to the cases in which the right of possession of a vested interest is allowed to be post-

§ **205.3.** A *dictum* in the case of *Belfield* v. *Booth*[1] seems to have overlooked this qualification. The Court in that case held that the period at the end of which distribution was to take place would not extend beyond the limit fixed by the Rule against Perpetuities,[2] but they said: "Even if the period were one that might endure to a time beyond twenty-one years after the decease of the testator, the estate having vested at his decease in a definite class cannot be divested by any change in the membership of that class. It remains the same class, though composed from time to time of different individuals." It is respectfully submitted that this *dictum* is incorrect.[3]

§ **206. Vesting within Period.** An estate which, though now a contingent remainder or executory devise, must, if it is to take effect at all, become vested within twenty-one years after lives in being, is good. Thus upon a devise to A. in fee,

---

poned, and the application to them of the Rule against Perpetuities, see Chap. IV., ante.

§ **205.3.** [1] 63 Conn. 299, 306, 27 Atl. 585, 587.

[2] See § 214.2, post.

[3] In the following cases the Court likewise failed to discriminate between the vesting of a remainder in a class subject to be opened, and the complete vesting in each member of the class, which is held necessary for the purposes of the Rule against Perpetuities. See § 375, post. In each case, however, the remainders vested in the latter sense within lives in being, and therefore were properly held to be not too remote. Hoadley v. Beardsley, 89 Conn. 270, 93 Atl. 535. Holmes v. Connecticut Trust Co., 92 Conn. 507, 103 Atl. 640. Woodward v. Woodward, 184 Iowa 1178, 169 N. W. 464. See 10 Iowa Law Bull. 89, 100, note. Ed-

wards' Estate, 255 Pa. 358, 99 Atl. 1010. See 1 Tiffany, Real Prop. (3d ed.), § 401, note 43. But in Endsley v. Hagey, 301 Pa. 158, 151 Atl. 799, the Court, citing Edwards' Estate, erroneously held a gift to grandchildren when the youngest reached twenty-five not too remote, apparently on account of a failure to make this discrimination. In Lamkin v. Hines Lumber Co., 158 Ga. 785, 124 S. E. 694, reported only in the syllabus by Atkinson, J., the Court seems to have fallen into a similar error. There is also inaccurate language on this point in McKibben v. Pioneer Trust & Savings Bank, 365 Ill. 369, 6 N. E. 2d 619, as to which case see § 388, note 4, post. In First National Bank v. MacIntosh, 366 Ill. 436, 9 N. E. 2d 248, the time of vesting was immaterial, as the date of distribution was not too remote.

but if she dies unmarried then to B. and the heirs of her body,
and on failure of them to C. and the heirs of her body, C.'s
estate, though at the death of the testator an executory devise,
would be turned into a vested remainder by the death of A.
unmarried, and is therefore not too remote.[1] But the estate
must vest within the required limits; it is not enough that
it will vest during or at the end of a life interest which is itself good as beginning within them.[2] So there can be successive gifts for life to persons unborn, provided their estates
must vest within the required limits.[3]

§ 207. In *Ashley* v. *Ashley*,[1] an estate was given to A. for
life, remainder to A.'s children as tenants in common for life,
and for want of such issue remainder over. It was held that
cross-remainders for life to the children of A. should be implied. Malins, V. C., in *Stuart* v. *Cockerell*,[2] and Mr. Marsden[3] find fault with this decision on the ground that such
cross-remainders would be too remote. But the criticism

§ 206. [1] Craig v. Stacey, Ir.
Term R. 249. See Re Roberts, 19
Ch. D. 520. So in a devise to A.
for life, at A.'s death to any wife
of A. for life, and at her death to
A.'s children living at his death,
the devise to the children is contingent at first, but vests at A.'s
death. See Gray v. Whittemore,
192 Mass. 367, 78 N. E. 422; 51
Harv. Law Rev. 638, 647. If
property is held in trust, on the
termination of twenty-one years
after a life in being, to transfer
and pay over the same, the gift
over is not too remote, although
it may take some time for the
trustees to make the actual
transfer and payment. Bates v.
Spooner, 75 Conn. 501, 54 Atl.
305.

[2] Hodson v. Ball, 14 Sim. 558,
574. Lett v. Randall, 3 Sm. & G.
83. Buchanan v. Harrison, 1 J.
& H. 662, 665. D'Abbadie v.
Bizoin, Ir. R. 5 Eq. 205. See Re
Merrick's Trusts, L. R. 1 Eq. 551;
Goodier v. Johnson, 18 Ch. D.
441; Goodier v. Edmunds, [1893]
3 Ch. 455; §§ 509.2, 509.4, post.

[3] Brudenell v. Elwes, 1 East
442. Cadell v. Palmer, 1 Cl. & F.
372, 7 Bli., N. S. 202. The dictum
of Lord Tenterden, C. J., in Doe
d. Garrod v. Garrod, 2 B. & Ad.
87, 96, to the contrary, is not law.
See Marsden, Perp. 180. On the
question whether a remainder for
life to the child of an unborn
person, after a remainder for life
to such person, is good, if so limited that it must take effect
within lives in being and twenty-
one years, see §§ 284 et seq., post.

§ 207. [1] 6 Sim. 358.

[2] L. R. 7 Eq. 363, 370.

[3] Perp. 177 et seq.

seems not just. The cross-remainders all vested not later than the death of A.[4] The case is unlike a gift to the children of A. as tenants in common for life, remainder to the survivor in fee. There the remainder is contingent until all the tenants but one are dead.[5]

§ 207.1. In *Cooke* v. *Bowler*,[1] property was given in trust for the benefit of the testator's brother, A., and his sisters, B., C., and D., for life, then for their children for life, "with benefit of survivorship," and on the death of the survivor then to be distributed in accordance with the Statute of Distributions. Lord Langdale, M. R., is said to have held that the direction for distribution was void for remoteness, and that the property went, as on intestacy, to those who were the testator's next of kin at his death. The opinion is very brief. This case has been sometimes referred to as an authority that a vested interest is too remote if preceded by a life estate to an unborn person. But if the distribution to the next of kin was construed to mean a distribution to those who should be the next of kin at the termination of the children's life estates, the persons to take would remain uncertain until such termination, and the gift to them would be contingent, and of course too remote; while if the gift was vested, it vested in those who were next of kin at the testator's death, and they were the persons who did in fact take.[2]

§ 208. In *Donohue* v. *McNichol*,[1] after the devise of a life estate to an unborn person, there was a gift over to the testator's heirs. The Supreme Court of Pennsylvania said that even if the gift over was to those persons who were the testator's heirs at his decease, it would be too remote, and ques-

---

[4] See 1 Jarm. Wills (7th ed.) 324. Cf. 3 Jarm. Wills (7th ed.) 2048.

[5] On the case where the remainder is to joint tenants for life, see § 232.1, post.

§ 207.1. [1] 2 Keen 54.

[2] See 1 Jarm. Wills (7th ed.) 323; Lewis, Perp. 218 (a). Mr.

Marsden suggests, Perp. 179, 180, that perhaps Cooke v. Bowler is to be explained on the ground that the ultimate gift was bad as coming after cross-limitations for life to nephews and nieces which were themselves too remote. As to this, see §§ 251 et seq., post.

§ 208. [1] 61 Pa. 73.

tioned 1 Jarm. Wills 240.[2]  As the same persons took whether
the gift over so construed was valid or not, the remarks were
not called for.  They seem to have been clearly erroneous.[3]

§ 209. **Contingent Termination.**  If a remainder is vested,
that is, if it is ready to take effect whenever and however the
particular estate determines, it is immaterial that the particular estate is determinable by a contingency which may fall
beyond a life or lives in being.  For instance, if an estate is
given to the unborn child of A. until he dies or changes his
name, and then to B. and his heirs, B. has a vested remainder,
upon the birth of A.'s child, for B. will take the estate whether
the child dies or changes his name, although the contingent
determination of the estate before the child's death depends
upon an event which may not take place until beyond the limits prescribed by the Rule against Perpetuities.[1]  And it makes
no difference whether the provision for termination be expressed in the form of a condition or a limitation.[2]  So a remainder (so called) to a person ascertained and his heirs after
a term for years, however long the term, or whatever be the
conditions to which the term is subject, is not too remote.[3]

§ 209.1.  In *Morris* v. *Fisher*,[1] the Court of Common Pleas
of Philadelphia held that a vested remainder after a term
for ninety-nine years was too remote, and in ejectment by the
heir of the remainder-man judgment was given for the defendant.  The case was carried to the Supreme Court of Penn-

---

[2] 7th ed. 323.

[3] See Foulke, Treatise, § 348;
§ 353.1, post.

§ 209. [1] Wainwright v. Miller,
[1897] 2 Ch. 255.  See Boughton
v. James, 1 Coll. 26, 46; Re Gage,
[1898] 1 Ch. 498; Lawrence's Estate, 136 Pa. 354, 367, 20 Atl. 521,
523; Re Stevens, [1912] Vict.
194; § 232, post.

[2] See Re Roberts, 19 Ch. D.
520; Marsden, Perp. 71, 176, 177;
Lewis, Perp. 173.

[3] Gore v. Gore, 2 P. Wms. 28.
Wood v. Drew, 33 Beav. 610.

Switzer v. Rochford, [1906] 1 I.
R. 399.  Fearne, C. R. 431.  Marsden, Perp. 65.  Challis, Real Prop.
(3d ed.) 186.  See Redington v.
Browne, 32 L. R. Ir. 347, 356;
Todhunter v. D. M. I. & M. R. Co.,
58 Iowa 205, 12 N. W. 267; Toms
v. Williams, 41 Mich. 552, 572, 2
N. W. 814, 826; Rhodes's Estate,
147 Pa. 227, 23 Atl. 553; Sioux
City Terminal R. R. Co. v. Trust
Co. of N. America, 82 Fed. 124,
aff'd 173 U. S. 99, 19 S. Ct. 341,
43 L. E. 628.

§ 209.1. [1] 8 Pa. Dist. 161.

sylvania, and there the parties joined in an agreement request-
ing the Court to reverse the judgment below, which was done.[2]
This looks as if the learned counsel for the defendant had
little hopes of holding his judgment. It does not seem possible
that he could;[3] or that a like decision of the United States Circuit Court for the Western District of Arkansas can be sustained.[4]

§ 210. **Inconveniences of Exemption of Vested Interests.**
There can be no remainder after a fee simple; a remainder
after a fee tail is destructible; a remainder after life estates
must vest in possession not later than the end of life estates
which begin within the limits of the Rule against Perpetuities;[1] but an estate subject to a term for years may not come
into possession for centuries. Here there seems an oppor-
tunity for abuse. If an estate is devised to A. and his heirs,
but if he or they ever change their family name, then to B.
and his heirs, the gift to B. is an executory devise, and is too
remote. But suppose an estate is devised to A. for a thousand
years unless A. or his heirs sooner change their name, and,
subject to the term, the land is devised to B., here B. has an
interest theoretically vested, but practically contingent upon
A. or his heirs changing their name,—an event which may be
very remote. The trouble arises from terms being sometimes
of extravagant length. Some legislation, like that of Alabama,[2] which provides that "no leasehold estate can be created for a longer term than twenty years," seems judicious.[3]

[2] 46 Atl. 1102.

[3] See Foulke, Treatise, § 363.

[4] Hanley v. Kansas Coal Co., 110 Fed. 62.

§ 210. [1] But such a limitation
extends the period during which
freedom of alienation may be impaired from one to two generations. And where possibilities of
reverter after determinable fees
are allowed, they tie up property
for indefinite periods. See § 312,
post.

[2] Civil Code (1907), § 3418.

Now changed to ninety-nine
years. Ala. Civil Code (1923),
§ 6923. See § 742, post.

[3] See Roe v. Galliers, 2 T. R.
133, 140; 3 Prest. Abs. (2d ed.)
154, 155; 4 Property Lawyer 297,
298; Gray, Restraints on Alienation (2d ed.), § 103; App. M,
§§ 970 et seq., post. Statutes
limiting the duration of terms
for years have been passed in
other States; e. g. California,
Civil Code, §§ 717, 718; Nevada,
Comp. Laws (1929), § 1092, Gen.

### 3. Nature of Contingency

**§ 211. Failure of Issue.** The contingencies on which future interests may be conditioned are infinite in number. The one most in controversy has been the failure of issue. If a gift is made upon a failure of A.'s issue, the point to be determined is whether an indefinite failure of issue or a failure at A.'s death is intended. If the former, then it is meant that the gift over shall take effect whenever A.'s issue come to an end, even in the remotest generation. If the latter, then it is meant that the gift over shall take effect only in case A. has no descendants living at his death. For instance, suppose there is a gift to A. and his heirs with a gift over upon the death of A. without issue, and A. dies leaving a son B. surviving him, but B. dies unmarried, here, if an indefinite failure of issue is intended, the gift over is meant to take effect, for A.'s issue have become extinct; but if a definite failure of issue is intended, then the gift over is not meant to take effect, for A. left issue him surviving.

**§ 212.** In the case supposed, if the gift is of real estate the decision of the question whether a failure of issue is definite or indefinite is immaterial, so far as remoteness is concerned; for if an indefinite failure of issue is intended, then the first taker has an estate tail, to remainders on which the Rule against Perpetuities does not apply;[1] and if a definite failure is intended, then the gift over takes effect on the death of the first taker.[2] In the case of personal estate the question of indefiniteness or definiteness of failure of issue is vital on the question of remoteness; for if the failure of issue be indefinite, the gift over is too remote,[3] while if it is definite, the gift over is of course good.[4]

Sts. (ed. 1885), § 2647; North Dakota, Comp. Laws (1913), § 5289; South Dakota, Comp. Laws (1929), § 296; Montana, Rev. Codes (1935), §§ 6707, 6708. See also New York Const. (1894), Art. I., § 13; Mich. Const. (1908), Art. XVI., § 10.

§ 212. [1] See Chap. XIV., post.

[2] If there is no preceding gift to A., then a gift over of real estate on failure of A.'s issue will follow the analogy of limitations of personalty on the question of remoteness.

[3] Because there can be no estate tail in personalty.

[4] A definite failure of a man's

§ **213.** "Dying without issue" and equivalent expressions are presumed at the common law to mean an indefinite failure of issue, but this presumption can be overthrown by the context; and by statute in England[1] and in many of the United States the presumption is, in devises and bequests, reversed.[2] The number of cases is enormous. Mr. Lewis has devoted almost a third of his treatise to their consideration; but, with all respect for his authority, the discussion, however learned and valuable, seems out of place. There is no doubt how the Rule against Perpetuities applies either to gifts on indefinite or on definite failure of issue. Which is meant is a mere question of construction, and its discussion belongs to a treatise on the construction of wills, rather than to one on the Rule against Perpetuities.[3]

4. The Contingency must happen, if at all, within
the required Limits

§ **214. Probabilities Immaterial.** It is not enough that a contingent event may happen, or even that it will probably

issue is not necessarily a failure at his death; a failure in any particular generation or generations of his descendants is equally definite. Whether such gift would be too remote can easily be determined. Practically the question always arises between a definite failure at his own death, and an indefinite failure in any generation. Nor is it material how many generations of descendants may be born and die, before the period when the failure is to be determined. If that period is definitely fixed, the failure is not indefinite; and no failure which is to be determined within lives in being can be too remote a contingency. The opinion of the Chief Justice in Imbrie v. Hartrampf, 100 Ore. 589, 198 Pac. 521, shows a strange confusion on this point.

§ **213.** [1] 1 Vict., c. 26, § 29. See Re Thomas, [1921] 1 Ch. 306.

[2] See 14 Ind. L. J. 397, 416–424.

[3] The learned reader will find the cases collected and discussed in Lewis, Perp., c. 15, pp. 174–407, Suppl., pp. 68–96; Prior, Lim., §§ 97–171; 2 Jarm. Wills (6th ed.) 1958; 3 Jarm. Wills (7th ed.) 1914; Hawkins, Wills, (3d ed.), c. 17, 254–262; Theob. Wills (5th ed.), c. 42, pp. 619–625, (9th ed.), c. 48, pp. 542–548; Tud. L. C. in Real Prop. (4th ed.) 371; Marsden, Perp., c. 10, pp. 182–205; 2 Simes, Fut. Int., §§ 334–436; Amer. Law Inst. Restatement, Property, §§ 266–271. See § 632, note 1, post.

happen, within the limits of the Rule against Perpetuities;
if it can possibly happen beyond those limits, an interest
conditioned on it is too remote.[1]  A good illustration is fur-
nished by a mistake which has been often made.  Property is
devised to A. for life, remainder to his widow for life, remainder over on the death of the widow.  Here the remainder
over on the death of the widow, if contingent until that event,
is bad, because A. may marry a woman who was not born at
the testator's death; and the result is not affected by the fact
that A. is very old at the testator's death.[2]

§ 214. [1] See Re Wood, [1894]
2 Ch. 310, [1894] 3 Ch. 381; Re
Stratheden, [1894] 3 Ch. 265;
Thomas v. Thomas, 87 L. T. R.
58 (C. A.); Re Bewick, [1911]
1 Ch. 116; Ward v. Vander Loeff,
[1924] A. C. 653, 677; Spitzel's
Trusts, [1939] 2 All Eng. R. 266;
Irwin v. Whitehead, [1918] N. Z.
673. Cf. Gex v. Dill, 86 Miss. 10,
38 So. 193; Public Curator v.
Union Trustee Co., 31 Com. L. R.
666 (Aust.)

That subsequent events cause
an interest to vest in fact within
the limits of the Rule, is of
course immaterial.  If the opinion in Wentworth v. Wentworth,
77 N. H. 400, 92 Atl. 733, is to
be taken to mean that the limitation there, although it might not
have vested until too remote a
period, was sustained because it
in fact vested, as the events
turned out, in a person living at
the testator's death, that conclusion is contrary not merely to
the general doctrine in other jurisdictions, but to the law in New
Hampshire as stated in other
cases. See Downing v. Wherrin,
19 N. H. 9, 85; Asylum v.
Lefebre, 69 N. H. 238, 243, 45

Atl. 1087, 1089; McAllister v. Elliott, 83 N. H. 225, 229, 140 Atl.
708, 710. For criticisms of Wentworth v. Wentworth, see 1 Tiffany, Real Prop. (3d ed.), § 400,
note 37; 28 Harv. Law Rev. 639.
The decision can perhaps be sustained on the ground that the interest in question was vested at
the testator's death, but the will
seems rather to give contingent
interests, and the language of the
Court on this point is ambiguous.
On the general principle, see also
Re Roe, 281 N. Y. 541, 24 N. E.
2d 322.

[2] Hodson v. Ball, 14 Sim. 558,
574. Lett v. Randall, 3 Sm. & G.
83. Buchanan v. Harrison, 1 J.
& H. 662. Re Harvey, 39 Ch. D.
289. Sears v. Russell, 8 Gray 86.
Stone v. Nicholson, 27 Grat. 1.
Greenwich Trust Co. v. Shively,
110 Conn. 117, 147 Atl. 367.
Chenoweth v. Bullitt, 224 Ky.
698, 715, 6 S. W. 2d 1061, 1068.
Easton v. Hall, 323 Ill. 397, 154
N. E. 216. Camden Trust Co. v.
Guerin, 87 N. J. Eq. 72, 99 Atl.
105. Taylor's Trusts, [1912] 1
I. R. 1. American National Bank
v. Morgenweck, 114 N. J. Eq. 286,
168 Atl. 598. See Re Merrick's

## § 214.1. "After Settlement of My Estate."

§ 214.1. "After Settlement of My Estate." In *Brandenburgh* v. *Thorndike*,[1] a testator gave the residue of his property to trustees, in trust from the income to pay to his wife a certain sum annually, to add the balance to the capital, and after the death of the wife to add the whole income to the capital, and directed that "at the expiration of three years from the death of my wife, or at such time, whether earlier or later, as may, in the discretion of the trustees, be found expedient and practicable for the final settlement and distribution of my estate, the trustees shall pay, convey, and transfer said fund in equal shares, viz. one share to each of my following nieces and nephew, then surviving" (naming them) "and one share to the issue of each of said nieces and nephew then deceased leaving issue then surviving." The court held that the gift to the nieces and nephew and their issue was not too remote. They said: "Taking the view most favorable to the plaintiffs, the discretion of the trustees to delay the payment after the expiration of the three years is limited to such time

Trusts, L. R. 1 Eq. 551; Goodier v. Johnson, 18 Ch. D. 441; Re Allott, [1924] 2 Ch. (C. A.) 498; Stephens v. Evans, 30 Ind. 39; Klingman v. Gilbert, 90 Kan. 545, 135 Pac. 682; Marsden, Perp. 103. 175; 36 Yale L. J. 336. In Overby v. Scarborough, 145 Ga. 875, 90 S. E. 67, a life estate to a future wife of a living person was held too remote; and see language to the same effect in Shewmake v. Robinson, 148 Ga. 287, 96 S. E. 564, and semble in Hill v. Hill, 106 Neb. 17, 182 N. W. 578. The Court in these cases may have been influenced by an erroneous notion that a life estate to an unborn person is invalid. See §§ 232 et seq., post. And the Georgia cases may have been affected by the local statute. See § 735, post. It appears likely, however, that the Court simply overlooked the fact that, whenever the wife might be born, her interest vested not later than the death of the husband. The Georgia cases are discussed, apparently without disapproval, in Citizens Nat. Bk. v. Howell, 186 Ga. 47, 196 S. E. 741. In American Nat. Bank v. Morgenweck, 114 N. J. Eq. 286, 168 Atl. 598, a bequest to charity after the death of any wife of a son was held too remote, but the Court seems to have erred in not regarding the bequest as a remainder vested at the testator's death. In Lyman v. Sears, 283 Mass. 404, 186 N. E. 56, the Court avoided the difficulty by holding that only living spouses were referred to.

§ 214.1. [1] 139 Mass. 102, 28 N. E. 575.

as is reasonably necessary to settle the estate. They could not delay longer without violating their duty, and in case of unreasonable delay they would be compelled by a court of equity to make the payment and transfer. In no contingency could it be necessary or reasonable to delay the settlement and distribution of the estate for twenty-one years after the death of the widow."

§ 214.2. In *Belfield* v. *Booth*,[1] the will of a testator, who died in 1890, after making certain bequests and charges, continued thus: "After the above bequests have been complied with and the executor has settled with the judge of probate, my will is that the remainder of my estate be paid over to the trustee hereinafter named. I hereby appoint" P. "trustee of my estate for the following fourteen years from the time he receives said funds from the executor." The testator proceeded to direct that the trustee should make certain annual payments during the fourteen years, and at the expiration of that period should cause the remainder to be divided among a class to be then determined. P. was also named as executor. P. had been removed by the Court of Probate from his office as executor, but had appealed. He had not settled his administration account, and the date of the final settlement of the estate (which was mainly personalty) was uncertain on account of the pendency of the appeal. The Supreme Court of Errors of Connecticut held that the fourteen years began to run from the date of the settlement of the administration account, and they held that the period for final distribution was not too remote.[2] The Court said that the settlement of the estate of a deceased person in Connecticut was ordinarily completed within one or two years; that the executor was bound to offer the will for probate within thirty days from the testator's death; that "the form of probate bond, long prescribed by statute, obliged the executor to render his final account at a day set by the court, generally within a year

§ 214.2. [1] 63 Conn. 299, 27 Atl. 585.

[2] As to a dictum in the opinion, seemingly erroneous, on a vested gift to a class which can be increased and diminished, see § 205.2, ante.

from the grant of letters testamentary;"[3] that twelve months was the longest period that could be fixed by the Probate Court for the presentation of claims, and suits upon rejected claims must be brought promptly if at all; that if an executor neglected to settle an estate within a reasonable time, the Court of Probate could remove him on summary proceedings; that "the testator has a right to rely on the courts of his State to enforce the proper settlement of his estate, both as to the manner and the time of the proceeding;" that the executor "has been removed for cause, and within two months thereafter the construction of his [the testator's] will has been brought before the court of last resort for final determination;"[4] that the pendency of the executor's appeal from the decree of removal, although it rendered the time of the final settlement of the estate uncertain, could not render it remote, since such an appeal takes precedence of ordinary actions; that the Court was not to presume that the settlement of the estate will or can be delayed beyond a reasonable time; and that its opinion was that the trust would "commence at the time when the accounts of the executor or administrator of his estate are, or should be, settled in the due course of administration, and that this time cannot be delayed so long as seven years from his decease;" that it was "not necessary that such settlement should be the final accounting of the executor or administrator in the court of probate;" and that some of the persons to whom annual payments were to be made were over eighty.

§ **214.3.** The cases of *Brandenburgh* v. *Thorndike* and *Belfield* v. *Booth* call for serious consideration. The decision in the former case seems correct. A fair construction of the will was that the testator by the expression, "at the expiration of three years from the death of my wife, or at such time, whether earlier or later, as may, in the discretion of the trustees,

---

[3] The statute in force at the date of the will and subsequent proceedings did not, however, prescribe the form of the executor's bond. Conn. Gen. Sts. (1888),

§ 548.

[4] The case was argued before the Supreme Court of Errors in June, 1893, and decided in September, 1893.

be found expedient and practicable," meant "at such time, about three years, as the trustees may determine," and certainly a period exceeding twenty-one years is not "about three years." The decision in *Belfield* v. *Booth* is harder to support. That case rests upon the proposition that a period of fourteen years to begin after "the executor has settled with the judge of probate," must begin within seven years from the testator's death. Now, in the first place, the substitution of the time when the executor *should* have settled his accounts for the time when he has in fact settled them, seems a straining of the words of the will. But further to say that an executor ought necessarily, as matter of law under all circumstances, to settle his accounts within seven years after the testator's death seems to be to lay down doctrine which it is difficult to maintain. Suppose a man dies testate leaving a large property but much involved; suppose some of his relations are dissatisfied with his will; suppose plan after plan of compromise is tried in vain; suppose the will is offered for proof, an appeal taken to a jury from the decision in the Probate Court, an appeal to the Supreme Court on a question of the admissibility of evidence, and the appeal sustained; a new trial before a jury; a new appeal again sustained; the same process repeated a third time; suppose the will finally allowed, but that most of the assets are claimed by a third person, and the executor is obliged to prosecute or defend lawsuits in order to hold the assets and that these suits have the common incidents of appeals and new trials; suppose that the will is obscure, and a bill in equity has to be brought to construe it. None of these suppositions are impossible, few are improbable. Many other suppositions, neither impossible nor improbable, might be imagined. Between them it is certainly possible that the executor may not be bound in law to settle his accounts till more than seven years have elapsed since the death of the testator. Or if such delay is absolutely impossible in the *Saturnia regna* of Connecticut, the case can hardly be an authority in jurisdictions where justice is not so speedy.[1]

§ 214.3. [1] See Shoemaker v. Newman, 62 D. C. Ap. 120, 65 F. 2d 208; Miller v. Weston, 67 Colo. 534, 189 Pac. 610; Re Campbell's

§ **214.4.** The case of *Belfield* v. *Booth* is an interesting illustration how the introduction or rejection of a legal doctrine may bring about unexpected consequences. Connecticut repudiated the doctrine of *cy pres;* then came the case of *Coit* v. *Comstock*,[1] easily to be decided under the doctrine of *cy pres*, but for which the Court, to preserve the form of consistency, had to invent several novelties, among others this implication of "reasonable time," to avoid the objection of remoteness; and from *Coit* v. *Comstock*, this idea has travelled to *Belfield* v. *Booth*, and is there no longer confined to charities.[2]

Estate, 28 Cal. Ap. 2d 102, 82 Pac. 2d 22; 34 Harv. Law Rev. 644; 10 Rocky Mt. Law Rev. 249, 253; 27 Cal. Law Rev. 86; 37 Mich. Law Rev. 814. In Estate of Musgrove, [1927] P. 264, the will was not found for twenty years, at which time the estate was not yet completely settled by the administrator. In Re Stavely, 90 L. J. Ch. 111, mention is made of a will which was not found for thirty-one years. In Haddock v. Boston & Maine R. R., 146 Mass. 155, 15 N. E. 495, the will was not proved for sixty-three years.

§ **214.4.** [1] 51 Conn. 352. See §§ 621–624, post.

[2] See also §§ 617, 618, post. On limiting the exercise of powers to a reasonable period, see § 478, post. Cf. also Lennig's Estate, 31 W. N. C. (Pa.) 234.

In Johnson v. Preston, 226 Ill. 447, 80 N. E. 1001, a devise to an executor to hold "for the space of twenty-five years from and after the date of the probate" of the will was held void for remoteness. But in 41 Am. Law Rev. 613, and 42 Am. Law Rev. 112, the decision of this case is criticised, and with reason, on the ground that the words cited merely specify the date for the ending and not for the beginning of the term. In Ryan v. Beshk, 339 Ill. 45, 170 N. E. 699, property was bequeathed, at the termination of a life estate, to named persons, if they were then living, the share of any one who was deceased to go "to his executor or administrator to be applied by such as if the same had formed part of the estate of such person at his decease." This bequest was held too remote, as to the shares of persons dying before the life tenant, on the authority of Johnson v. Preston. This was an obvious slip, in an otherwise excellent opinion. All the shares vested at the termination of the life estate. The vesting of the interests of the legatees or next of kin of a deceased remainder-man did not depend on the existence of an executor or administrator. See Armstrong v. Barber, 239 Ill. 389, 88 N. E. 246; Mettler v. Warner,

**§ 214.5.** To avoid any doubt as to the points raised in these cases, the periods within which powers given by will to executors or others, e. g. to sell real estate, are to be confined, should be made to run, not from the date of probate, but from the time of the testator's death.

**§ 215. Possibility of Issue.** In one class of cases, from the difficulty and delicacy of determining the question involved, the occurrence of a contingent event beyond the required limits will be considered as possible although it is physically impossible. If a devise is made to those of a woman's children who reach twenty-five, the gift is too remote, although the woman be of such an age that it is certain she can have no more children, and therefore the event must occur, if at all, in the lives of persons in being, viz., of her children alive at the testator's death. In other words, for the purpose of determining questions of remoteness, men and women are deemed capable of having issue as long as they live. This was held by Sir Lloyd Kenyon in *Jee* v. *Audley,*[1] and his decision has never been questioned, at least in England.

**§ 215.1.** In *Sayer's Trusts,*[1] Malins, V. C., followed *Jee* v. *Audley;* but in *Cooper* v. *Laroche,*[2] apparently forgetting both *Jee* v. *Audley* and his own previous decision in *Sayer's Trusts,* he held that a future gift to the children of a woman sixty years old must be a gift to persons now *in esse.* The case might have been decided in the way it was on another ground,[3] and there can be little doubt that *Cooper* v. *Laroche* must be considered one of the not unfrequent blunders of that learned judge.[4] *Jee* v. *Audley* was followed, and the decision of Mal-

243 Ill. 600, 90 N. E. 1099; Ashmore v. Newman, 350 Ill. 64, 183 N. E. 1. Cf. McCutcheon v. Pullman Bank, 251 Ill. 550, 96 N. E. 510; Shoemaker v. Newman, 62 D. C. Ap. 120, 65 Fed. 2d 208 (see 48 Harv. Law Rev. 1251); Union Trust Co. v. Nelen, 283 Mass. 144, 186 N. E. 66 (see Newhall, Fut. Int. in Mass., § 32); Trautz v. Lemp, 329 Mo. 580, 46 S. W. 2d

135; Loehr v. Glaser, 133 S. W. 2d 394 (Mo.).

§ 215. [1] 1 Cox 324.

§ 215.1. [1] L. R. 6 Eq. 319.
[2] 17 Ch. D. 368.
[3] See Gray, Restraints on Alienation (2d ed.), § 272 f.
[4] See 71 L. T., 186; Challis, Real Prop. (3d ed.) 191. For other erroneous decisions or dicta of Vice-Chancellor Malins on

questions of remoteness, see § 207, ante, §§ 325, note 2, 382, 447, note 2, 631, note 2, post.

There is a class of decisions which must not be confounded with this. Sometimes A. has an absolute interest in personalty, subject to divestment by the contingency of there being children of herself or of some other person. In such cases the usual practice in Chancery is not to turn over the custody of the fund to A.; but when, from the age of A. or of the other person, there is no chance that there will ever be such children, the Court of Chancery will order the fund paid to A., on her giving security to turn it over to the children, if born. There is no question of title here, but only of custody and management. Leng v. Hodges, Jac. 585. Fraser v. Fraser, Id. 586, note. Hamilton v. Brickwood, 5 L. J., N. s. Ch. 144, Brown v. Pringle, 4 Hare 124. Davis v. Bush, 8 Jur. 1114, note. Miles v. Knight, 17 L. J. Ch. 458, 12 Jur. 666. Mackenzie v. King, 17 L. J. Ch. 448. Dodd v. Wake, 5 De G. & Sm. 226 (which perhaps goes further than any other case). Lyddon v. Ellison, 19 Beav. 565. Edwards v. Tuck, 23 Beav. 268. Ryan's Settlement, 9 W. R. 137. Price v. Boustead, 8 L. T. R. 565. Vidler v. Parrot, 12 W. R. 976. Haynes v. Haynes, 35 L. J. Ch. 303, 14 W. R. 361. Widdow's Trusts, L. R. 11 Eq. 408. Milner's Estate, L. R. 14 Eq. 245. Browne v. Taylor, [1872] W. N. 190. Summers's Trusts, 22 W. R. 639. Belt's Estates, 25 W. R. 901. Allason's Trusts, 36 L. T. R. 653. Archer v. Dowsing, [1879] W. N. 43. Taylor's Trust, 43 L. T. 795, 29 W. R. 350. Maden v. Taylor, 45 L. J. Ch. 569. Davidson v. Kimpton, 18 Ch. D. 213. Re Taylor's Settlement Trusts, [1881] W. N. 12. Re White, [1901] 1 Ch. 570. Estate of Mellon, 16 Phila. 323, s. c. sub nom. Gowen's Appeal, 106 Pa. 288. Frank v. Frank, 153 Tenn. 215, 280 S. W. 1012. Re Commissioners of Streets, 7 Ir. Eq. 484. Farrell v. Cameron, 29 Grant (Ont.), 313. See also Payne v. Long, cited 19 Ves. 571; Defflis v. Goldschmidt, 1 Mer. 417, 422, 19 Ves. 566, 572; Re Dawson, 39 Ch. D. 155, 164, 165; 2 Seton, Decrees (4th ed.) 976; Stirling v. Urquhart, 14 Rettie C. of Sess. 112; White v. Weed, 87 N. H. 153, 175 Atl. 814; 23 Columbia Law Rev. 50; 21 Cal. Law Rev. 126; 34 Mich. Law Rev. 453; 53 Harv. Law Rev. 490; 3 Scott, Trusts, § 340.1; Amer. Law Inst. Restatement, Property, § 273 and App.; Restatement, Trusts, § 340, Comment e. The cases of Re Riccards's Trusts, 97 Md. 608, 55 Atl. 384; Fletcher v. Los Angeles, 182 Cal. 177, 187 Pac. 425; and several other cases cited by the Solicitor General in U. S. v. Provident Trust Co., 291 U. S. 272, 273–276, 54 S. Ct. 389, 78 L. E. 793, are contra. And cf. Brandon v. Woodthorpe, 10 Beav. 463; Re Overhill's Trusts, 22 L. J. Ch. 485; 17 Jur. 342; Groves v. Groves, 12 W. R. 45; Conduitt v. Soane, 19 W. R. 817; Croxton v. May, 9 Ch. D. 388; Re Hocking, [1898] 2 Ch. (C. A.) 567; Re Deloitte,

ins, V. C., discussed, in *Re Dawson.*[5]

[1926] Ch. 56; Re Cazenove, 122 L. T. R. 181; Berry v. Geen, [1938] Ch. 575, 584; Oleson v. Somogy, 90 N. J. Eq. 342, 107 Atl. 798, 93 N. J. Eq. 506, 115 Atl. 526; Re Smith, 94 N. J. Eq. 1, 118 Atl. 271; Sterrett's Estate, 300 Pa. 116, 150 Atl. 159; Ansonia Bank v. Kunkel, 105 Conn. 744, 136 Atl. 588; Towle v. Delano, 144 Mass. 95, 10 N. E. 769; Bowlin v. R. I. Hosp. Trust Co., 31 R. I. 289, 76 Atl. 348; Flora v. Anderson, 67 Fed. 182; Re Stevens, [1923] Vict. 584, s. c. sub nom. Teague v. Trustees Co., 32 Com. L. R. 252 (Aust.); Commissioners of Inland Revenue v. Bone, [1927] S. C. 698 (Sc.).

In Browne v. Warnock, 7 L. R. Ir. 3, a title, good only on the presumption that a woman of sixty-three would not have a child, was forced on a purchaser, in accordance with Mr. Dart's opinion, 1 Dart, V. & P. (8th ed.) 344, but against that of Lord St. Leonards, Sugd. V. & P. (14th ed.) 418; and in accord with Browne v. Warnock are: Whitney v. Groo, 40 D. C. Ap. 496; Landers v. People's Building & Loan Asso., 190 Ark. 1072, 81 S. W. 2d 916; and Re Tinning and Weber, 8 Ont. L. R. 703. Contra, List v. Rodney, 83 Pa. 483; Aulick v. Summers, 186 Ky. 810, 217 S. W. 1024. See Miller v. Macomb, 26 Wend. 229, 234, affirming Macomb v. Miller, 9 Paige 265; Bacot v. Fessenden, 130 N. Y. A. D. 819, 115 N. Y. S. 698; Azarch v. Smith, 222 Ky. 566, 1 S. W. 2d 968; Jordan v. Jordan, 145 Tenn.

378, 413, 239 S. W. 423, 433; 23 Columbia Law Rev. 50. Evidence of impossibility of issue has been admitted in the United States Courts in questions of the assessment of inheritance taxes. U. S. v. Provident Trust Co., 291 U. S. 272, 54 S. Ct. 389, 78 L. E. 793. Farrington v. Commissioner, 30 Fed. 2d 915, 279 U. S. 873, 49 S. Ct. 513, 73 L. E. 1008. City Bank v. U. S., 74 Fed. 2d 692. Ninth Bank v. U. S., 15 Fed. Supp. 951.

[5] 39 Ch. D. 155. See also Re Hocking, [1898] 2 Ch. (C. A.) 567; Re Burnyeat, [1923] 2 Ch. (C. A.) 52; Ward v. Van der Loeff, [1924] A. C. 653; Re Cazenove, 122 L. T. R. 181; Stout v. Stout, 44 N. J. Eq. 479, 15 Atl. 843; Flora v. Anderson, 67 Fed. 182; Taylor v. Crosson, 11 Del. Ch. 145, 98 Atl. 375; Tyler v. Fidelity Trust Co., 158 Ky. 280, 194 S. E. 939; Gettings v. Grand Rapids Tr. Co., 249 Mich. 238, 228 N. W. 703; Loud v. St. Louis Tr. Co., 298 Mo. 148, 249 S. W. 629; Graves v. Graves, 94 N. J. Eq. 268, 120 Atl. 420; Austin's Estate, 315 Pa. 449, 173 Atl. 278; First National Bank v. Poynter, 174 Tenn. 472, 126 S. W. 2d 335; Blackhurst v. Johnson, 72 Fed. 2d 644; Will of Deane, [1913] Vict. 272, reversed on a question of construction in Brownfield v. Earle, 17 Com. L. R. 615 (Aust.). Cf. Wright's Estate, 284 Pa. 334, 131 Atl. 188. But in Exham v. Beamish, [1939] I. R. 336, 349–351, Gavan Duffy, J., uttered a strong dictum that he would re-

## 5. LIVES IN BEING

**§ 216. Any Number of Lives.** The contingency may be postponed for any number of lives, provided they are all in being when the contingent interest is created; and the persons whose lives are taken need have no interest in the estate.[1] In *Thellusson* v. *Woodford*,[2] the testator directed that the income of his property should be accumulated during the lives of all his sons and grandsons and grandsons' issue who were alive at his death, and that on their death the property with its accumulations should be divided into three lots, each lot to go to the eldest male lineal descendant of one of his sons respectively. It was earnestly urged by counsel that lives could not be taken in this way to prolong the period for the happening of the gift over.[3] But Lord Chancellor Loughborough, assisted by Lord Alvanley, M. R., and Lawrence and Buller, JJ., sustained the will; and his decree was affirmed in the House of Lords in accordance with the unanimous opinion of the judges.[4]

**§ 217.** The difficulties which might arise in case testators were allowed to select any number of lives for the purpose of prolonging the period within which a future estate might vest were strongly pressed by counsel in *Thellusson* v. *Woodford*. Suppose, for instance, they said, that "all the members of both Houses of Parliament, all the members of both Universities,"[1] "all the persons whose lives are comprised in the several existing tontines,"[2] were taken; or the executory devise was not to take effect "so long as any person can be found in Europe, or rather in any part of the known world, who was either living or in the womb at the death of the particular testator."[3]

ceive evidence of impossibility of issue. Observe the passages from Co. Lit. 40, a, b, cited 39 Ch. D. 163, 164, [1898] 2 Ch. (C. A.) 571.

**§ 216.** [1] Friday's Estate, 313 Pa. 328, 170 Atl. 123.

[2] 4 Ves. 227, 11 Ves. 112, 1 B. & P. N. R. 357.

[3] 4 Ves. 242–244, 277–279, 290–292, 300–303, 314, 11 Ves. 116–119, 2 Harg. Jurid. Arg. 128–142.

[4] See § 190, ante. For earlier cases to the same effect, see § 189, ante.

**§ 217.** [1] 4 Ves. 244.

[2] 4 Ves. 277.

[3] 4 Ves. 278, 2 Harg. Jurid. Arg. 131.

The only limitation suggested by the opposing counsel or by
the Court was that the number of persons taken must be so
limited that evidence of their death could be obtained. "When
it is asserted that the rule permits the vesting to be postponed
during as many lives as can be stated, it must be asserted
with this qualification; *provided,* they are not more than will
admit of making out, by reasonable evidence, at what time
the survivor ceases to exist."[4] Macdonald, C. B., in giving the
opinion of the judges in the House of Lords, cites the language of Twisden, J., in *Love* v. *Wyndham,*[5] and says: "By
this expression he must be understood to mean any number
of lives the extinction of which could be proved without difficulty."[6] And again: "But it is asked, shall lands be rendered unalienable during the lives of all the individuals who
comprise very large societies or bodies of men, or where other
very extensive descriptions are made use of? It may be answered that, when such cases occur, they will, according to
their respective circumstances, be put to the usual test, whether they will or will not tend to a perpetuity, by rendering
it almost, if not quite, impracticable to ascertain the extinction of the lives described; and will be supported or avoided
accordingly."[7] "The language of all the cases is, that property may be so limited as to make it unalienable during any
number of lives, not exceeding that to which testimony can
be applied, to determine when the survivor of them drops."[8]

§ **218.** In *Cadell* v. *Palmer,*[1] the executory devise was to
take effect on the death of twenty-eight persons.[2] The Real
Property Commissioners, in their Third Report (1832),[3]
treated the question fully, and rejected the suggestion of
limiting the number of lives, or of requiring the lives to be

[4] 4 Ves. 290.
[5] 1 Mod. 50, 54, 1 Sid. 450, 451.
See § 167, ante.
[6] 11 Ves. 134.
[7] 11 Ves. 136.
[8] Per Lord Eldon, C., 11 Ves.
146. See Harg. Thel. Act, § 18.
Cf. Re Lanyon, [1927] 2 Ch. 264.
§ **218.** [1] 1 Cl. & F. 372, 7 Bli.,

N. s. 202, 10 Bing. 140.
[2] See Bender v. Bender, 225
Pa. 434, where there were eleven
lives. The executory devise in
Cadell v. Palmer, took effect in
fact after ninety-nine years. See
Re Villar, [1928] Ch. 478, note.
[3] Pp. 37–39. Lewis, Perp. App.
xiv–xvii.

those of persons taking an interest in the property, but recommended that it should not be lawful to take lives arbitrarily, and that lives should not be made use of to limit a term or period within which to create interests too remote if created out of an estate of inheritance; e. g. an estate to A., for the lives of twenty persons, in trust to pay the income to B. for life, remainder to his unborn son for life, remainder to the son of such son, etc. These suggestions have not, however, been adopted in England.[4] It is quite possible that the whims of testators may some day compel the courts to lay down a rule limiting the number of lives which can be taken. At present there is no limit.

In *Re Villar*,[5] a testator gave property upon trusts such that the capital was not to vest until the expiration of twenty years from the death of the last survivor of all the descendants of Queen Victoria who should be living at the time of his death. It appeared that there were about one hundred and twenty descendants of Queen Victoria living at the testator's death, and it would be difficult to determine exactly who those persons were, and probably still more difficult in the future to determine the date of death of the survivor. It was held unanimously by the Judge of first instance and the Court of Appeals that the provisions of the will did not infringe the Rule against Perpetuities and were valid. Astbury, J., in the court below, and the Master of the Rolls in the Court of Appeals, showed much reluctance in reaching this conclusion; and their language may perhaps be construed as a warning that the courts may in the future draw the line against the use of periods measured by the lives of large numbers of persons who have no beneficial interest in the trust. The fact that the will adopted an old form which has been extensively used in England may have had an effect on the result.[6]

---

[4] On the legislative changes which have been made in some of the United States on this point see §§ 742, 747, 751, post.

[5] [1928] Ch. 471, [1929] 1 Ch.

243. See 75 L. J. 108, 196, 179 L. T. 331.

[6] It seems to have been assumed, or conceded, that if the period of vesting of the capital were

**§ 219. "For Longest Period Allowed."** In *Pownall* v. *Graham*,[1] a testator gave his estate in trust for his brothers for life, and on the death of the survivor to apply the income for the benefit of such of their children as should appear to the trustees to "stand most in need of the same, and that regularly, from year to year, as the law in such cases admits," and, "after the law, as mentioned aforesaid, admits of no further division among such of my brothers' children," then over. Lord Romilly, M. R., said: "The law would admit this trust for division amongst the children to go on as long as any person living at the moment of the testator's death was in existence, and during twenty-one years after the life of the longest liver of any person then in existence. But it would be impossible to ascertain when that period would cease; and, if it were, all the children of his brother would probably be then dead, and the gift over would fail of taking effect. I am of opinion, therefore, that it is impossible so to construe it, and that the period from which the twenty-one years must begin to be calculated is the death of the last surviving brother. In no other way can effect be given to this trust, for the testator might have directed it to endure as long as any of the children in a charity school should live and twenty-one years after; but unless he so expressed it, it could not be maintained, as it would be impossible for the trustees to ascertain when the trust ceased. The general scope and object of the will itself gives the explanation. No one contends that the trust is to go on until the death of too remote, the gift of income would be entirely void. If the gift of capital were valid, of course no question arose as to the income.

The suggestion has been made that the real objection to the limitation in this case was not remoteness but uncertainty. See the language of Lawrence, L. J., [1929] 1 Ch. (C. A.) 250, 251 (part of which is quoted in § 219.1, note 2, post), and also 166 L. T. 316. It is perhaps not important whether the requirement that it shall be reasonably practicable to ascertain the expiration of the period, is treated as a part of the Rule against Perpetuities, or as an independent requirement. The judges in Thellusson v. Woodford apparently took the former view. Cf. Amer. Law Inst. Restatement, Property, § 107.

§ 219. [1] 33 Beav. 242.

everybody in existence at the testator's death, and both parties have referred to the will as being the guide from which
the period from which the twenty-one years is to begin to run
is to be ascertained."

§ 219.1. **Re Moore.**[1] A testator bequeathed personal
property in trust to apply the income in keeping in repair
her brother's tomb in Africa, "for the longest period allowed
by law, that is to say, until the period of twenty-one years
from the death of the last survivor of all persons who shall
be living at my death." Joyce, J., held the legacy bad for
uncertainty.[2]

§ 219.1. [1] [1901] 1 Ch. 936.
[2] Mr. Sweet in 1 Jarm. Wills
(6th ed.) 297, 455, (7th ed.) 268,
430, says that the gift was not
void for uncertainty, but was
void within the Rule against
Perpetuities; but see below.

In Re Villar, [1929] 1 Ch. (C.
A.) 243, 250, Lawrence, L. J., referring to Re Moore, said: "Moreover I think that in cases of that
kind the question is not whether
the rule against perpetuities has
or has not been infringed, but
whether the gift is void for uncertainty. If it be impossible to
ascertain the lives upon the
death of the survivor of which
the vesting of the capital is to
take effect, such vesting is not
in fact postponed beyond the
permitted limit, but the gift is
void for uncertainty." It is submitted that the learned Lord
Justice overlooked the true
ground for the decision in Re
Moore. Whether or not a future
limitation to take effect on the
death of all persons living at the
testator's death would be void
for uncertainty or for remoteness, the immediate gift of in-

come during the indeterminate
period would be invalid on account of the uncertainty of the
period, apart from the lack of a
definite cestui que trust, or the
remoteness of the trustee's power of application, if the trust is
construed as a power. See §§ 894–
909, post. And cf. Pirbright v.
Salwey, [1896] W. N. 86; Re
Hooper, [1932] 1 Ch. 38.

In Re Vaux, [1939] Ch. (C. A.)
465, a testator left the residue
of his property to trustees with
power "to pay away and deal
with the same in all respects for
the benefit and provision of my
children or grandchildren as they
may think best or most expedient
and to act in all respects as I
could have done if living save
only that all such dealings with
the residuary trust fund and the
income and accumulations thereof shall be within the limitations
prescribed by law." It was held
by the Court of Appeal that this
clause provided in effect that appointments made by the trustees
under this power must be such
as to vest an interest in the
beneficiaries within the period of

§ 219.2. **Fitchie v. Brown.**[1] Here A., by will, directed that the residue of his estate should be "placed in trust for as long a period as is legally possible, the termination or ending of said trust to take place when the law requires it." He appointed a trustee, and directed the payment of annuities to some forty persons named, to them for life, and on their death to their heirs, except three who were to have only life interests. "On the final ending and distribution of the trust, the trust fund to be divided equally among those persons entitled at that time to the aforementioned annuities." By a codicil he gave an annuity to a charitable corporation "under the same conditions as the other annuitants." The Supreme Court of the United States, affirming the decree of the Supreme Court of Hawaii, followed *Pownall* v. *Graham,* and held that the trust continued for twenty-one years after the death of all the persons named as annuitants, and that the gift for distribution at the end of the trust was valid.[2]

the Rule against Perpetuities; and that the gift of the residue was therefore valid. The Court, at p. 476, commented on Re Moore.

§ 219.2. [1] 18 Hawaii 52, 211 U. S. 321, 29 S. Ct. 106, 53 L. E. 202.

[2] Acc. Gale v. Gale, 85 N. H. 358, 159 Atl. 122. See also Pirbright v. Salwey, [1896] W. N. 96, and Re Hooper, [1932] 1 Ch. 38.

The opinion in Fitchie v. Brown contains some inaccurate dicta. See 43 Yale L. J. 393, 399.

Note the difference between reference to lives of persons, in the description of the event on which the gift is to vest, and reference by a court, in passing on the validity of the gift, to lives of persons as a measure in the application of the Rule against Perpetuities. Where the first kind of reference is involved, the question is what was the testator's intent, and whether it is expressed with sufficient certainty. In Pownall v. Graham, Fitchie v. Brown, and Gale v. Gale, the question discussed by the Court is of this sort. And cf. Re Vaux, [1939] Ch. (C. A.) 465. But in every case, after the intent has been ascertained, the question remains whether the gift is valid under the Rule against Perpetuities. The testator's intention does not necessarily play any part here; often he did not have the Rule in mind. In deciding this question, reference must be made by the Court to lives by which to measure the period allowed by the Rule. For the purpose of sustaining a limitation, reference may be made by the Court to the lives of any per-

## 6. PERIOD OF GESTATION

**§ 220. Child Conceived.** Whatever may have formerly been the law, it is now generally agreed that a child *en*

sons living at the testator's death, whose lives have a necessary relation to the event on which the limitation vests, whether or not those persons take any interest in the property (see § 216, ante) or are mentioned in the will. A bequest to all the testator's grandchildren when they reach twenty-one is good, though none of the children are mentioned. Re Helme, 95 N. J. Eq. 197, 123 Atl. 43, contra, is a blunder; see § 370, post. That decision appears to be founded on an ill-considered dictum in Van Riper v. Hilton, 78 N. J. Eq. 371, 78 Atl. 1055. Likewise a bequest to all the testator's daughters-in-law, whether they become so before or after his death, would be good though the sons were not mentioned. In very few, if any, instances would the lives of any persons, other than parents, husbands or wives of persons mentioned, bear any necessary relation to the event; and perhaps it might be considered that the will referred by implication to such persons. But the testator need not expressly refer to any lives for the purpose of measuring the period allowed by the Rule. See 51 Harv. Law Rev. 638, 641. In Dwyer v. National Newark Banking Co., 103 N. J. Eq. 481, 143 Atl. 625, though Re Helme is not cited, there are dicta apparently indicating agreement with that case.

In Bonded Building & Loan Co. v. Konner, 118 N. J. Eq. 546, 180 Atl. 570, there is an erroneous dictum that a gift over on the marriage of the testator's son at any time would be contrary to the Rule against Perpetuities, the Court apparently overlooking the fact that the marriage must be during the life of the son, who was a life in being.

In Indiana, the statute against perpetuities requires that the lives be specified. § 743, post. Query whether this changes the law. Probably an implied reference to particular lives would be held sufficient. See 15 Ind. L. J. 261, 281.

In Brooker v. Brooker, 130 Tex. 27, 106 S. W. 2d 247, a testator created a trust to last "during the life of my last surviving legatee, and twenty-one years thereafter;" but later provided that his heirs should have a right to continue the trust by a majority vote, "if they legally can and do take such a vote." The Court held that the trust infringed the Rule against Perpetuities because it might last indefinitely. This decision seems clearly wrong. The provision for extension of the trust was not only separable in form, but the testator indicated that it was to be separated and disregarded if it was illegal. See 16 Tex. Law Rev. 121; §§ 331, 341, 353, post.

*ventre sa mere* is to be considered as born, when it will be for its benefit to be so considered.[1] Whether, as a general principle, such a child will be considered as born for the benefit of third persons is still *sub judice*.[2] But whether or not this is true as a general principle, it is true in questions of remoteness. Thus a devise to such of the grandchildren of the testator as reach twenty-one is valid; for although the testator may have a posthumous child, it will be considered as born at the testator's death. Yet here it will be so considered, not for its own sake, but for the sake of the grandchildren.

§ **221.** Often two periods of gestation are allowed. Thus, in the case suggested in the previous section, a grandchild may be a posthumous child of a posthumous child. And again, a very common form of testamentary gift is to the testator's children for life, and on their death to their children; but if these latter all die under twenty-one, then to B. and his heirs. Here the gift to B., a stranger, is good.[1]

§ 220. [1] Doe d. Clarke v. Clarke, 2 H. Bl. 399. Athey v. Pickerings, 96 L. J. K. B. 250. See Marsh v. Reed, 184 Ill. 263, 56 N. E. 306; Phillips v. Herron, 55 Ohio 478, 45 N. E. 720; Dexter v. A. G., 224 Mass. 215, 112 N. E. 946; Drobner v. Peters, 194 N. Y. A. D. 696, 186 N. Y. S. 278, 232 N. Y. 220, 133 N. E. 567; Re Brown, [1933] N. Z. 114; Reporter's note to Randolph v. Randolph, 40 N. J. Eq. 73; 51 Harv. Law Rev. 254, 272; Amer. Law Inst. Restatement, Property, § 266, Comment e, and App. Cf. 1 Scott, Trusts, § 112.1; Restatement, Trusts, § 112, Comment a.

[2] Blasson v. Blasson, 2 De G. & S. 665. Re Burrows, [1895] 2 Ch. 497. Villar v. Gilbey, [1907] A. C. 139. Re Salamon, [1907] 2 Ch. 46, [1908] 1 Ch. (C. A.) 4. Reid's Trustees v. Dashwood, [1929] S. C. 748 (Sc.). Elliot v. Joicey, [1935] A. C. 209. This last case has been much criticised. See 52 Law Quart. Rev. 1; 53 Law Quart. Rev. 19; 79 L. J. 127; 184 L. T. 196; 78 Sol. J. 185; 48 Harv. Law Rev. 1202, 1235; 33 Mich. Law Rev. 414; 42 W. Va. Law Quart. 344; 13 Can. Bar Rev. 594; 9 Aust. Law Rev. 294; Amer. Law Inst. Restatement, Property, § 266, Comment e, and App. Cf. Kembro v. Harper, 113 Okla. 48, 238 Pac. 840.

§ 221. [1] See Long v. Blackall, 7 T. R. 100; Thellusson v. Woodford, 11 Ves. 112, 143; 2 Harg. Jurid. Arg. 93–126; Lewis, Perp. 147–149.

§ **221.1.** In *Re Wilmer's Trusts*,[1] a testatrix devised land to trustees in trust to pay the income to M. during her life, and on her death to stand possessed of the land in trust for the sons of M. (with certain exceptions) born or to be born, successively for life, with remainder upon the death of each such son upon trust for his first and other sons successively in tail male. M. had a son S. (not within the exceptions) who was begotten, but not born, at the death of the testatrix. It was held by Buckley, J., and by the Court of Appeal that S. took a life estate, and that the remainder to his first and other sons was good, although it would have been for the advantage of S. if he had been considered as unborn at the testatrix's death, for, on that supposition, the remainder to his sons would have been too remote, and he would have taken an estate tail under a subsequent limitation in the will. Therefore, for the purposes of the Rule against Perpetuities, a child *en ventre sa mere* will be considered as born, even when it is actually prejudicial to it to be so considered.[2]

§ **222.** In some cases a third period of gestation would be allowed. Suppose, for instance, a devise to testator's children for life, on their death to be accumulated till the youngest grandchild reaches twenty-one, and then to be divided among all the grandchildren then living, and the issue then living of any deceased grandchild. The testator leaves a posthumous child, who dies leaving one child, A., born, and another, B., *en ventre sa mere*. B. is born and reaches twenty-one, but, before he does so, A. dies, leaving his wife *enceinte*, who gives birth to a child after B. reaches twenty-one. Here we have (1) the period until the testator's child is born; (2) the life of such child; (3) the period after the death of such child until B. is born; (4) the minority of B.; (5) the period from the time when B. reaches twenty-one until A.'s child is born. Here we have a life, a minority of twenty-one years, and three periods of gestation. This case was dis-

§ 221.1. [1] [1903]  1  Ch.  874, [1903] 2 Ch. 411.

[2] Acc. Equitable Trust Company v. McComb, 19 Del. Ch. 387,

168 Atl. 203. Cf. Matter of Backer, 148 Misc. (N. Y.) 318, 266 N. Y. S. 47.

cussed in *Smith* v. *Farr*,[1] but no decision was given on the
point.   Mr. Lewis[2] thought the gift to the issue of the deceased grandchild good, but afterwards[3] doubted it, on the
ground that, so far as the grandchildren were concerned, the
period of gestation of the great-grandchildren was a term
in gross, and that, so far as the great-grandchildren were concerned, the period of gestation of the grandchildren was a
term in gross.   This is true, but it would not seem to invalidate the gift.   It was determined in *Cadell* v. *Palmer*[4] that
the time of gestation could be allowed only when gestation
in fact existed;[5] but if gestation exists, a gift to take effect
on the reaching of majority by an infant now *en ventre sa
mere* is good, whether such gift be to a third person or not.
If Mr. Lewis's doubt was well founded, gifts over to third
persons on grandchildren dying under twenty-one, like that
given in section 220, *ante,* would be bad; for so far as the
children are concerned the period of gestation of the grandchildren is a term in gross, and so far as the grandchildren
are concerned the period of gestation of the children is a
term in gross; yet such limitations are exceedingly common,
and their validity is undoubted.   It is submitted that the true
doctrine is that in applying the Rule against Perpetuities a
child *en ventre sa mere* will be considered as born.

### 7. Term of Twenty-one Years

**§ 223. Term in Gross.**   The term of twenty-one years may
be taken in gross without reference to any infancy.   This
was settled in England by the case of *Cadell* v. *Palmer*,[1] and
seems to have never been questioned in America.   The curious

§ 222. [1] 3 Y. & C. 328.

[2] Perp., Addenda 726.

[3] Suppl. 22–26.

[4] 1 Cl. & F. 372, 7 Bli., N. s. 202,
10 Bing. 140.

[5] The rule is sometimes stated
as if an additional period of just
nine months was allowed for gestation.   But of course it is the

actual period of gestation which
is allowed and that may be considerably longer or shorter.   See
Gaskill v. Gaskill, [1921] P. 425;
Equitable Trust Co. v. McComb,
19 Del. Ch. 387, 168 Atl. 203.

§ 223. [1] 1 Cl. & F. 372, 7 Bli.,
N. s. 202, 10 Bing. 140.

[G. R. P.]

and illogical manner in which the Rule against Perpetuities was extended beyond lives in being has been stated in the preceding chapter.[2]

§ 224. As early as 1813, twenty-one years after lives in being was recognized in the United States by Judge Story as the limit of the Rule against Perpetuities,[1] and, as has been said, the doctrine has met with acceptance everywhere. In *Mayor of New York* v. *Stuyvesant,*[2] however, it appears to have been overlooked. There A., in 1825, conveyed a parcel of land to B. and C. for their own use, but in trust to permit A., his heirs and assigns, until the parcel was opened as a public square, to enjoy the rents, and after B. and C., their heirs and assigns, should have elected to lay open, and should actually lay open, the same as a public square, then in trust that the same be forever kept open and used as a public square; provided, that if the parcel should not within thirty years be so opened, then the land should revert to A., his heirs and assigns, for their own use. The parcel was actually laid open in 1850. It was held that A. had lost all claim to the land. It would seem that the dedication to the public was a shifting trust which was bad for remoteness, as it might not take effect for thirty years; but the point is not suggested in the opinion.

[2] See §§ 171–188. Here may be noted an odd point arising in England under the provision of the Administration of Estates Act (1925), sec. 47, that an interest in intestacy shall only vest absolutely on the person entitled attaining the age of twenty-one or marrying. Suppose A. gives property in trust for such of the children of B. as may attain twenty-one, then in default of such children, then to the persons who would have taken if A. had died at the date of the failure of the trust, possessed of the property and intestate. The trust may not fail till the expiration of lives in being and nearly twenty-one years, and the person then entitled may be an infant. The ultimate limitation, therefore, would be too remote. See 2 Conveyancer, N. s. 103; 185 L. T. 190.

§ 224. [1] Barnitz v. Casey, 7 Cranch 456, 469. See Pleasants v. Pleasants, 2 Call 319, 331.

[2] 17 N. Y. 34.

### 8. LIMITATIONS OF AN ESTATE FOR LIFE OR OF A TERM NOT EXCEEDING TWENTY-ONE YEARS

**§ 225. Life of Another.** No limitation of a present life estate, or of a present term of not more than twenty-one years, can be bad for remoteness. Thus if an estate for the life of A. (or a term for twenty years) is devised to such of the children of L. as reach twenty-five, but if none of them reach twenty-five then over to M. and his heirs, the devise to M. is good, because it must take effect, if at all, within the lifetime of A. (or within twenty years). This is so obvious that it is strange it should ever have been doubted. Yet it has been questioned, and there seems to be little authority directly deciding it.[1]

**§ 226.** In *Love* v. *Wyndham*[1] (1670), a term for ninety-nine years, if three lives so long lasted, was given by the testator to Dulcibella his wife, on her death to his son Nicholas for life, and if Nicholas should die without issue, then to his son Barnaby. It was held that the devise to Barnaby was void. No attention was paid on the bench or at the bar to the fact that the term was to last only during the lives of living persons; the term was treated like a simple term for ninety-nine years; and the gift to Barnaby was held bad because of the character of the contingency, not of its remoteness. The Rule against Perpetuities had not yet formulated itself.[2]

**§ 227.** In *King* v. *Cotton*,[1] the point was raised but not decided. The learned reporter says: "It seems rather to be a good limitation." In *Low* v. *Burron*,[2] an estate for three lives was devised to M. for life, remainder to her issue male, remainder to L. Lord Chancellor Talbot thought that the gift to L. was good, and that M. could not bar it.[3] He said:

§ 225. [1] See Marsden, Perp. 24, 25, 193.

§ 226. [1] 1 Mod. 50, 1 Sid. 450, 2 Keb. 637, 2 Ch. Rep. 14, 1 Vent. 79, 1 Lev. 290. See § 167, ante.
[2] See Lewis, Perp. 675.

§ 227. [1] 2 P. Wms. 674, 676.

[2] 3 P. Wms. 262.
[3] The last point has since been determined otherwise. See notes to Low v. Burron, Fearne, C. R. 496 et seq.; Tud. L. C. in Real Prop. (4th ed.) 101; Challis, Real Prop. (3d ed.) 362.

"Here can be no danger of a perpetuity; for all these estates will determine on the expiration of the three lives.  So if, instead of three, there had been twenty lives, all spending at the same time, all the candles lighted up at once, it would have been good; for, in effect, it is only for one life, viz. that which shall happen to be the survivor." This case seems authority for the proposition that limitations of an estate *pur auter vie* cannot be too remote.[4]

§ 228. In the United States the question presented itself in bequests of slaves.  If a female slave was bequeathed to A., but if he died without issue then to B., the gift was too remote; for the gift of a female slave included the gift of her issue.[1]  In *Matthews* v. *Daniel*,[2] a negro man and a horse were bequeathed to A. and her heirs, but if she died without issue then over.  The gift over was held too remote.  The case is very briefly reported.  The Court say: "The argument

---

[4] See Saltern v. Saltern, 2 Atk. 376; Campbell v. Harding, 2 Russ. & M. 390, 406; Harris v. Davis, 1 Coll. 416, 423; Mills v. Smith, 193 Mass. 11, 17, 78 N. E. 765, 768; Fearne, C. R. 496 et seq.; Id. 500, Butler's note; Lewis, Perp. 673–681; Prior, Lim., § 161; 8 Jur., pt. 2, 261.

In Wastneys v. Chappell, 3 B. P. C. (Toml. ed.) 50, a conveyance by a quasi tenant in tail of an estate pur auter vie was held not to bar the remainder over.  But the tenant in tail was himself a remainder-man, not in possession at the time of his conveyance, and a conveyance by such quasi tenant in tail in remainder does not bar subsequent remainders, without the concurrence of the holder of the particular estate (see Edwards v. Champion, 3 De G. M. & G. 202).  Therefore the decision was consistent with the power of a quasi tenant in tail in posses-

sion to bar remainders, and a future interest which can be barred is never too remote.  But this does not apply to Low v. Burron, for the remainder there was held not barrable by the tenant in possession.  That case, therefore, is authority for the proposition that no limitation of a life estate can be too remote.

If in an estate pur auter vie one or more of the cestuis que vie are not in esse, a limitation of such an estate might be too remote; but Mr. Charles Sweet, 49 Sol. J. 793, has shown reason to doubt whether, apart from the Rule against Perpetuities, cestui que vie can be a person not in esse. See further on this question 60 Sol. J. 57, 137, 187.  Cf. Amer. Law Inst. Restatement, Property, §§ 18, 107.

§ 228. [1] Johnson v. Lish, 4 H. & J. 411.

[2] 2 Hayw. 346.

that here the event must happen, if at all, in the lifetime of the negro, and that so the event is limited to a life in being, has at least the merit of novelty to recommend it, but will not bring the case within the legal limits." But it was easier to sneer at the argument than to refute it. It seems unanswerable. In *Biscoe* v. *Biscoe*,[3] there was a gift of a male slave to J., but if J. died without issue then over. It was held that the gift over was not too remote, and that this result was produced by the fact of the slave being male. But the case was not decided on the ground that no limitation of a male slave could be too remote, but because the subject matter of the gift showed that the testator intended a definite failure of issue; and consequently, in *Hatton* v. *Weems*,[4] a like gift over of both negro men and women was held void, on the ground that the same rule of construction must apply to both; that an indefinite failure of issue was meant; and that gifts of male and female slaves after an indefinite failure of issue were all bad.  *Sed qu.*[5]

**§ 228.1.** Must the lives in being be human lives? Suppose a limitation, in itself too remote, be made of a horse, or dog, or parrot, or of some animal of great longevity, real or supposed, such as an elephant, or crow, or tortoise, or carp, or of a female animal, such as a cow or hen, would it be void?[1]

**§ 229.** *Low* v. *Burron*,[1] seems to be the only direct adjudi-

---

3 6 Gill & J. 232.

4 12 Gill & J. 83.

5 See Johnson v. Lish, 4 H. & J. 441; Edelen v. Middleton, 9 Gill 161; Royal v. Eppes, 2 Munf. 479; M'Donald v. M'Mullen, 2 Mills, Const. 91; Hope v. Johnson, 2 Yerg. 123.

It was the law in Virginia that the Rule against Perpetuities did not apply to provisions for emancipation. Pleasants v. Pleasants, 2 Call 319. Wood v. Humphreys, 12 Grat. 333. See Peggy v. Legg, 6 Munf. 229; Crawford v. Moses,

10 Leigh 277, 284. But in Kentucky it has been held to apply to them. Ludwig v. Combs. 1 Met. (Ky.) 128. Compare Williams v. Ash, 1 How. 1, 13, 11 L. E. 25; Harris v. Clarissa, 6 Yerg. 227, 241; Smith v. Dunwoody, 19 Ga. 237, 260.

**§ 228.1.** 1 See Re Dean, 41 Ch. D. 552, and App. H, § 896.3, post; and cf. 18 Jurid. Rev. 36. See also Re Howells' Estate, 145 Misc. 557, 260 N. Y. S. 598; Re Kelly, [1932] I. R. 255.

**§ 229.** 1 3 P. Wms. 262.

cation that a limitation of a life estate cannot be too remote. But to hold such a limitation too remote would be so palpable a violation of the fundamental principle of the Rule against Perpetuities, that there can be little doubt that *Low* v. *Burron* is correct on this point.

### 9. COVENANTS TO RENEW LEASES

**§ 230. Perpetual Renewals.**  That a lease for lives or for years may be, as a matter of fact, renewed by the lessor does not make it bad, for the lessees have no right to a renewal.[1] Suppose, however, that the lease contains a covenant by the lessor for perpetual renewal? It is no objection to a lease that it contains such a covenant, if the entire control of the covenant is in the hands of those persons who have vested interests under the lease.[2]  Sir George Jessel, M. R., in *London & S. W. R. Co.* v. *Gomm*,[3] speaks of this as an exception to the Rule against Perpetuities;[4] but it seems hardly necessary to create any exception to meet the case,—the covenant to renew is part of the lessee's present interest.[5]  The right which the present possessor of land has to continue or to drop his possession is not a right subject to a condition precedent. The Rule against Perpetuities, as has been remarked before, although a strict rule, is yet a practical rule.  An estate for years with a perpetual covenant for renewal is, so far as questions of remoteness are concerned, substantially a fee,

§ **230.**  [1] 8 Jur., pt. 2, 273.

[2] Ross v. Worsop, 1 B. P. C. (Toml. ed.) 281.  Sweet v. Anderson, 2 B. P. C. 256.  Hare v. Burges, 4 K. & J. 45, 57.  Meller v. Stanley, 2 De G. J. & S. 183, 192.  Pollock v. Booth, Ir. R. 9 Eq. 229, 607.  Marsden, Perp. 15. See Banks v. Haskie, 45 Md. 207, 218.  Cf. Blackmore v. Boardman, 28 Mo. 420; Diffenderfer v. St. Louis Public Schools, 120 Mo. 447, 25 S. W. 542, in which cases the Supreme Court of Missouri, while declaring that the law does not favor a perpetual covenant for the renewal of a lease, recognizes that if the intention of the parties to create such a perpetual covenant, is unmistakable, the law will enforce it.

[3] 20 Ch. D. 562, 579.

[4] And see Challis, Real Prop. (3d ed.) 186.

[5] See Moore v. Clench, 1 Ch. D. 447, 452; Buckland v. Papillon, L. R. 1 Eq. 477, L. R. 2 Ch. 67; Muller v. Trafford, [1901] 1 Ch. 54, 61.

and as such it is regarded.[6]  If the right of renewal, however, is not within the control of those having vested interests
under the lease, and if the interest of the person within
whose absolute control the right will be may not vest within
the period required by the Rule against Perpetuities, the limitation to such person is bad.[7]  Thus, if an estate for lives
or years with a covenant for perpetual renewal is devised to
A. for life, and on his death to his (unborn) children and
their heirs, but if all his children die under twenty-five then
to C. and his heirs, the devise to C. is bad.[8]

§ 230.1.  The author's learned friend, Mr. T. Cyprian Williams, in an article in the Solicitor's Journal,[1] comments on

[6] See 2 Tiffany, Landl. and Ten.,
§ 221; 1 Tiffany, Real Prop. (3d
ed.), §§ 406, 410; 27 Yale L. J.
878; 35 Yale L. J. 214; Wis. Law
Rev. (1939) 147.  Late cases in
favor of the validity of covenants
for perpetual renewal are: Nak-
dimen v. Atkinson Co., 149 Ark.
448, 233 S. W. 694. Vokins v.
McGaughey, 206 Ky. 42, 266 S. W.
907.  Nichols v. Day, 128 Miss.
756, 91 So. 451.  Montana Consolidated Mines Co. v. O'Connell,
107 Mont. 273, 85 Pac. 2d 345.
Haeffner v. A. P. Green Fire
Brick Co., 76 S. W. 2d 122
(Mo.).  Rosson v. Bennett, 294
S. W. 660 (Tex. C. A.).  Todd v.
Light & Heat Co., 90 W. Va. 40,
110 S. E. 446.  Tipton v. North,
185 Okla. 365, 92 Pac. 2d 364.  Re
Jackson & Imperial Bank, 36
Dom. L. R. 589.  Such a covenant was held void as creating a
perpetuity in Morrison v. Rossignol, 5 Cal. 64; but in Becker v.
Submarine Oil Co., 55 Cal. Ap.
698, 204 Pac. 245, a similar covenant was sustained.  The law as
to perpetuities was changed in
California between these two cases

by the adoption of the Code (see
§ 752, post) and this change particularly affects the law as to
options.  See Blakeman v. Miller,
136 Cal. 138, 68 Pac. 587.  The
Court, however, in Becker v. Submarine Oil Co., does not mention
Morrison v. Rossignol, and the
language in the opinion in the
later case raises a doubt whether
the Court considered the law to be
as stated in the earlier case, even
in a common-law jurisdiction.
That a right to perpetual renewals
infringes the Rule, seems to have
been assumed in Syms v. Major,
18 Jones & Sp. 289 (N. Y. Super.),
Hudgins v. Bowes, 110 S. W. 178
(Tex. C. A.), and Gray v.
Stadler, 228 Wis. 596, 280 N. W.
675, but see dissenting opinion in
this last case.

[7] See Hope v. Gloucester, 7 De
G. M. & G. 647; A. G. v. Green-
hill, 9 Jur., N. S. 1307; Brush v.
Beecher, 110 Mich. 597, 68 N. W.
420; Hudgins v. Bowes, 110 S. W.
178 (Tex. C. A.); Redington v.
Browne, 32 L. R. Ir. 347, 357, 358.

[8] 8 Jur., pt. 2, 273.

§ 230.1. [1] 42 Sol. J. 628, 630,

the preceding section; and in reference to the language in the
text: "The covenant to renew is part of the lessee's present
interest. The right which the present possessor of land has
to continue or drop his possession is not a right subject to a
condition precedent," he says: "This explanation appears
sufficient in the case of an absolute covenant to renew a lease
for years, but is not equally satisfactory where the right of
renewal is limited to arise only on giving notice within a
particular time and paying a specified fine;" and that it does
"some violence to the language" of such a covenant to hold
that "in such a case the equitable interest created is not an
interest to arise in future on fulfilment of a condition precedent, but a present interest defeasible on the condition subsequent of not giving due notice to renew, or paying the
fine." The criticism has weight. The construction suggested
does do "some violence to the language." The choice seems
to lie between adopting such construction, or recognizing
that covenants to renew in the form suggested by Mr. Williams, are either void, or else are exceptions to the application
of the Rule against Perpetuities.

§ 230.2. That covenants for the renewal of leases are not
open to the objection of remoteness, and that this is an exception to the Rule against Perpetuities, seems now to be
recognized as law. In *Woodall* v. *Clifton*,[1] the opinion of Warrington, J., is valuable for a full discussion of these covenants.
He concludes[2] that he "must treat these covenants to renew
as exceptions to the general rule [against perpetuities]—exceptions for which it is very difficult to find a logical justification, but exceptions which have been probably recognized
because they were in existence long before the rule had been
developed." And in the same case Romer, L. J., in the Court
of Appeals,[3] said: "I have always understood that the exception of covenants to renew a lease from the Rule against
Perpetuities could not be justified on principle, but only by
a long series of decisions." And in *Re Tyrrell's Estate*,[4]

650; and see Guardian Realty Co.          [2] P. 265.
v. Stark, 70 Dom. L. R. 333, 342.         [3] P. 268.
    § 230.2. [1] [1905] 2 Ch. 257.        [4] [1907] 1 I. R. 194, 197.

Ross, J., said: "Contracts for the renewal of leases are an exception to the rule. Why they are an exception nobody can tell," and so *Re Garde Browne*[5] and *Rider* v. *Ford*.[6]

§ **230.3. Option to Tenant.** An option to a tenant for years to purchase the fee, exercisable at a remote time, is bad as violating the Rule against Perpetuities.[1] The matter is fully discussed by Mr. Williams in the article cited in § 230.1, *ante*. The only reason for considering the Rule against Perpetuities as inapplicable to such an option is the analogy to covenants for renewal treated in the three preceding sections. But the exemption from the Rule in the case of covenants for renewal is either an exception which there is no reason to extend, or is to be explained, as it is in § 230, *ante*, on the ground that the covenant to renew is part of the present interest, a ground which cannot well be taken when the present interest is a tenancy for years, and the interest to be purchased is a fee.[2]

---

[5] [1911] 1 I. R. 205. See Challis, Real Prop. (3d ed.) 186; 7 Holdsworth, Hist. Eng. Law, 260, 261; 11 Enc. Laws of Eng. (2d ed.) 70.

Under the Law of Property Act (1922), § 145, Sch. 15, perpetually renewable leaseholds are converted into terms of 2000 years. See Williams, Real Prop. (24th ed.) 627–631. See also Law of Prop. Act (1925), § 149.

[6] [1923] 1 Ch. 541.

§ **230.3.** [1] Woodall v. Clifton, [1905] 2 Ch. (C. A.) 257. Rider v. Ford, [1923] 1 Ch. 541. And see London & S. W. R. Co. v. Gomm, 20 Ch. D. (C. A.) 562; §§ 275, 330, post; 49 Sol. J. 64, 543, 547, 592, 740; 70 Sol. J. 55; Marsden, Perp. 14; 1 Dart, V. & P. (8th ed.) 252; 1 Wms. V. & P. (4th ed.) 423; Re Tyrrell's Estate, [1907] 1 I. R. 292, overruling s. c., [1907] 1 I. R. 194. Cf. Mann v. Land Registry, [1918] 1 Ch. 202; § 320.1,

post. In the United States there is little authority on this question, and much difference of opinion. See 2 Tiffany, Landl. and Ten., § 256; 1 Tiffany, Real Prop. (3d ed.), §§ 405, 410; 27 Yale L. J. 878; 29 Yale L. J. 87; 35 Yale L. J. 213; 17 Va. Law Rev. 461; 51 Harv. Law Rev. 638, 661; 15 Ind. L. J. 261, 293. Keogh v. Peck, 316 Ill. 318, 147 N. E. 266, is contra to the English cases. And by the local law of Maryland such options are valid. Hollander v. Central Metal Co., 109 Md. 131, 171 Atl. 442. See also Todd v. Citizens Gas Co., 46 Fed. 2d 855, 866. If an option to a stranger, unlimited in time, is valid, as is the law in some American jurisdictions (see § 330, note 2, post), of course an option to a tenant is good. As to McMahon v. Swan, [1924] Vict. 97, see § 203, note 2, ante.

[2] See Mr. Williams's article,

### 10. Time runs only from Testator's Death

**§ 231. Date of Will immaterial.** As the law should not take a wanton pleasure in thwarting the intention of a testator, it seems strange that it could ever have been supposed that the question of remoteness was to be determined by the state of things at the date of a testator's will, and not at the time of his death. The object of the Rule against Perpetuities is to confine the vesting of contingent estates to a short period after their creation; and if it is certain when the estate is created that the contingent event must happen within the required time, it seems a needless interference with the testamentary power to say that the estate is bad, because, at some time, before the estate was created and when its existence was entirely in the control of the testator, it was not certain that the contingent event would happen within the required time. For example, land is devised to those children of A. who reach twenty-five. If the testator die before A. the gift is too remote, because A. may have a child born after the testator; but if A. die before the testator, there can be no objection to the devise, because it must take effect, if at all, in the lives of A.'s children, and none of these can be born after the testator's death. Mr. Lewis in the Supplement to his treatise proves superabundantly that the time of the testator's death is the true period at which to judge of the remoteness of the provisions in his will.[1] The rule that the question of remoteness is to be determined from the time of the testator's death, and not of his will, is now settled.[2]

ubi supra; also Re Leeds & Batley Breweries, [1920] 2 Ch. 548; Sherwood v. Tucker, [1924] 2 Ch. (C. A.) 440, 444; Cornell-Andrews Co. v. Boston & Providence R. R., 209 Mass. 298, 307, 95 N. E. 887, 890. And cf. Batcheler v. Murphy, [1925] Ch. (C. A.) 220.

§ 231. [1] P. 27 et seq. But see A. G. v. Gill, 2 P. Wms. 369, 370;

Gower v. Grosvenor, 5 Mad. 337. 341.

[2] Vanderplank v. King, 3 Hare 1, 17. Faulkner v. Daniel, Id. 199, 216. Williams v. Teale, 6 Hare 239, 251. Cattlin v. Brown, 11 Hare 372, 382. Dungannon v. Smith, 12 Cl. & F. 546, et passim (see Lewis, Perp. Suppl. 53-57). Peard v. Kekewich, 15 Beav. 166.

Southern v. Wollaston, 16 Beav. 166, 276. Monypenny v. Dering, 2 De G. M. & G. 145, 170. Hale v. Hale, 3 Ch. D. 643, 645. O'Reilly v. Bellew, [1924] 1 I. R. 1. Hosea v. Jacobs, 98 Mass. 65, 67. 1 Jarm. Wills (7th ed.) 271. Tud. L. C. in Real Prop. (4th ed.) 595. 4 Kent, Com. (12th ed.) 283, note 1. See Rye's Settlement, 10 Hare 106, 112; Murphey v. Brown, 159 Ind. 106, 62 N. E. 275; Penfield v. Tower, 1 N. Dak. 216, 218, 219, 46 N. W. 413, 414. An inadvertent phrase in Pearce v. Pearce, 199 Ala. 491, 505, 74 So. 952, 958, is corrected in Crawford v. Carlisle, 206 Ala. 379, 389, 89 So. 565, 575.

So in New York, under the Revised Statutes. Lang v. Ropke, 5 Sandf. S. C. 363, 369, 370. Lang v. Wilbraham, 2 Duer 171, 175. Griffen v. Ford, 1 Bosw. 123, 137. In Odell v. Youngs, 64 How. Pr. 56, Beach, J., in the Court of Common Pleas, said that Schettler v. Smith, 41 N. Y. 328, Van Nostrand v. Moore, 52 N. Y. 12, and Colton v. Fox, 67 N. Y. 348, seemed to overrule Lang v. Ropke and Griffen v. Ford, and he held that the question of the remoteness of a devise must be determined as from the date of the will and not at the testator's death; but the three cases cited by him as overruling Lang v. Ropke and Griffen v. Ford have nothing whatever to do with the matter, and the decision in Odell v. Youngs is certainly wrong. See Tallman v. Tallman, 3 Misc. 465, 23 N. Y. S. 734; Adams v. McKee, 121 Misc. 215, 200 N. Y. S. 765. So also in Ohio, under St. of

1811, 2 Rev. Sts. (1880), § 4200, McArthur v. Scott, 113 U. S. 340, 382, 5 S. Ct. 652, 28 L. E. 1015; and in Michigan, under 2 How. Sts., § 5531, 3 Mich. Compiled Laws, § 8797, Mullreed v. Clark, 110 Mich. 229, 68 N. W. 138.

Suppose personal property is bequeathed to A. and the heirs of his body, and if A. dies without issue, then to B., and there is a lapse by reason of A.'s death without issue before the testator, does B. take? There has been a difference of opinion on this point. Sir Richard Pepper Arden, M. R., in Brown v. Higgs (1799), 4 Ves. 708, 717, thought that B. would take; so did Sir William Grant, M. R., in Donn v. Penny (1815), 1 Mer. 20, 22, 23; and so also did Lord Langdale, M. R., in Mackinnon v. Peach (1838), 2 Keen 555, 560. On the other hand, Vice-Chancellor Knight Bruce thought that B. would not take. Harris v. Davis (1844), 1 Coll. 416, 424–426; and see A. G. v. Gill, 2 P. Wms. 369. Cf. also Andrew v. Andrew, 1 Coll. 686, 690 et seq.; Hughes v. Ellis, 20 Beav. 193; Greated v. Greated, 26 Beav. 621; Stringer's Estate, 6 Ch. D. 1, 7, 15. The Court of Appeal has now held, in accordance with common sense, that B. will take. Re Lowman, [1895] 2 Ch. (C. A.) 348; and see Re Dunstan, [1918] 2 Ch. 304; Re Cobbett, 18 Tasmanian 47, aff'd 32 Com. L. R. 615 (Aust.); Murphey v. Brown, 159 Ind. 106, 62 N. E. 275. Cf. cases cited in Gray, Restraints on Alienation (2d ed.), § 64, note.

In Bullard v. Shirley, 153 Mass.

## 11. Enough if Interest begins within the Required Limits

**§ 232. Time of Commencement.**   An interest is not obnoxious to the Rule against Perpetuities if it begins[1] within lives in being and twenty-one years, although it may end beyond them.[2] If it were otherwise, all fee-simple estates would be bad. The law is the same with lesser estates. That an estate can be limited to an unborn person for life, whether there be a gift over or not, was repeatedly held or assumed down to 1820.[3] The only thing to the contrary was a *dictum* of

559, 27 N. E. 766, a testator gave $5,000 to A., and, on his death, for an illegal charitable purpose, "failing which it shall revert to my heirs." It was held that the gift to the heirs was not too remote.

**§ 232.** [1] I. e. vests at or before A.'s death. See § 206, ante.

[2] See Re Cassel, [1926] Ch. 358; Re Chardon, [1928] 1 Ch. 464; Pulitzer v. Livingston, 89 Me. 359, 365, 36 Atl. 635, 638; Brooks v. Belfast, 90 Me. 318, 323, 38 Atl. 222, 223; True R. E. Co. v. True, 115 Me. 533, 99 Atl. 627; Bancroft v. Maine Sanatorium, 119 Me. 56, 109 Atl. 585; Gray v. Whittemore, 192 Mass. 367, 372, 78 N. E. 422, 424; Minot v. Burroughs, 223 Mass. 595, 608, 112 N. E. 620, 625; Lennig's Estate, 31 W. N. C. (Pa.) 234; Owen's Pet'n, 34 W. N. C. (Pa.) 354, 3 Pa. Dist. 328; Johnston's Estate, 185 Pa. 179, 184, 185, 39 Atl. 879, 880, 881; Lyons v. Bradley, 168 Ala. 505, 512, 53 So. 244, 247; Madison v. Larmon, 170 Ill. 65, 73, 74, 48 N. E. 556, 558; Flanner v. Fellows, 206 Ill. 136, 68 N. E. 1057; Mettler v. Warner, 243 Ill. 600,

609, 90 N. E. 1099, 1102; Nicol v. Morton, 332 Ill. 533, 164 N. E. 5; Chenoweth v. Bullitt, 224 Ky. 698, 715, 6 S. W. 2d 1061, 1068; Eager v. McCoy, 143 Tenn. 693, 228 S. W. 709; Story v. First National Bank, 115 Fla. 436, 156 So. 101; Norman v. Jenkins, 73 S. W. 2d 1051 (Tex. C. A.); Holmes v. Walter, 118 Wis. 409, 95 N. W. 380; 1 Tiffany, Real Prop. (3d ed.), §§ 397, 408; §§ 205, note 2, 209, ante; App. M, §§ 972–974, post. This is equally true of equitable interests, as in most of the cases just cited. See 1 Bogert, Trusts, § 218; Amer. Law Inst. Restatement, Trusts, § 62, Comment k.

[3] Cotton v. Heath, 1 Roll. Ab. 612, pl. 3, Pollexf. 26 (1638). Marlborough v. Godolphin, 1 Eden 404, 415 (1759). Evans v. Astley, 1 W. Bl. 521, 523 (1764). Den v. Page, 3 T. R. 87, note (1783). Hay v. Coventry, Id. 83, 86 (1789). Routledge v. Dorril, 2 Ves. Jr. 357, 366, 367 (1794). Brudenell v. Elwes, 1 East 442, 452, 453 (1801). Foster v. Romney, 11 East 594 (1809). Beard v. Westcott, 5 Taunt. 393, 5 B. & Ald. 801 (1813). See Doe d. Liv-

Buller, J., in *Robinson* v. *Hardcastle*[4] (1788).  In 1820, however, Sir John Leach, in *Deerhurst* v. *St. Albans*,[5] when Vice-Chancellor, said that an estate for life to an unborn child was bad; and in *Hayes* v. *Hayes*[6] (1828), when Master of the Rolls, he expressly decided that such an estate was bad, unless followed by a vested interest.  This was undoubtedly, however, a slip of that learned judge.  He is said to have himself repented of it;[7] and it has been repeatedly overruled in England, sometimes *sub silentio*,[8] sometimes with pointed condemnation.[9]  And the textbooks join in this condemnation.[10]  The American authorities are to the same effect.[11]

ersage v. Vaughan, 5 B. & Ald. 464, 1 Dowl. & Ry. 52 (1822).

[4] 2 T. R. 241, 253.

[5] 5 Mad. 232, 278.

[6] 4 Russ. 311.

[7] Boughton v. James, 1 Coll. 26, 37.

[8] As in Bennett v. Lowe, 7 Bing. 535, 5 Moore & P. 485; Ashley v. Ashley, 6 Sim. 358; Burley v. Evelyn, 16 Sim. 290; Cattlin v. Brown, 11 Hare 372, 375; Boughton v. James, 1 Coll. 26, 36; Gooch v. Gooch, 14 Beav. 565, 3 De G. M. & G. 366, 383; Avern v. Lloyd, L. R. 5 Eq. 383; Stuart v. Cockerell, L. R. 7 Eq. 363, L. R. 5 Ch 713; Evans v. Walker, 3 Ch. D. 211; Re Roberts, 19 Ch. D. 520; Re Allott, [1924] 2 Ch. (C. A.) 498. So Hutchinson v. Tottenham, [1898] 1 I. R. 403; Re Crichton Estate, 23 Manitoba 594, 13 Dom. L. R. 169.

[9] Williams v. Teele, 6 Hare 239, 250, and especially Hampton v. Holman, 5 Ch. D. 183, 188, per Jessel, M. R.

[10] 1 Jarm. Wills (7th ed.) 322. Sugd. Pow. (8th ed.) 392, 393. Lewis, Perp. Suppl. 144. Leake, Law of Property in Land (2d ed.) 242. Gilb. Uses (Sugd. ed.) 268. Marsden, Perp. 174, 175.

[11] Otis v. McLellan, 13 Allen 339. Loring v. Blake, 98 Mass. 253. Lovering v. Worthington, 106 Mass. 86. Simonds v. Simonds, 112 Mass. 157, 163, 164. Minot v. Taylor, 129 Mass. 160. Seaver v. Fitzgerald, 141 Mass. 401, 6 N. E. 73. Peabody v. Tyszkiewicz, 191 Mass. 317, 77 N. E. 839. Dodge v. Bennett, 215 Mass. 545, 102 N. E. 916. Greenough v. Osgood, 235 Mass. 235, 126 N. E. 461. Loomer v. Loomer, 76 Conn. 522, 527, 57 Atl. 167, 169. Colonial Trust Co. v. Brown, 105 Conn. 261, 135 Atl. 555. Greenwich Trust Co. v. Shively, 110 Conn. 117, 147 Atl. 367. Stout v. Stout, 44 N. J. Eq. 479, 15 Atl. 843. Ogden v. McLane, 73 N. J. Eq. 159, 67 Atl. 695. Lawrence's Estate, 136 Pa. 354, 20 Atl. 521. Ronckendorff's Estate, 11 Pa. C. C. 447. Re Wickersham's Estate, 261 Pa. 121, 104 Atl. 509. Heald v. Heald, 56 Md. 300. See Wood v. Griffin, 46 N. H. 230; Hazen v. Amer. Security & Trust Co., 49 D. C. Ap. 297, 265 Fed. 447; Goldsborough v. Martin, 41 Md. 488.

As an estate for life is good if it begins within the required limits, even if it is to terminate upon a contingency,[12] so a term for years beginning within those limits is good likewise. Thus a devise of a term for twenty-five years to begin on the death of a person living at the testator's decease is good, although followed by a limitation bad for remoteness.[13] So easements and other rights in the land of other persons may be made terminable at remote periods.[14]

§ 232.1. If an estate is given to A. for life, remainder to his children as joint tenants for life, the remainder is valid.[1]

§ 233. One qualification must be made of the statement in § 232, *ante*. When there is a good absolute gift, and the settlor or testator goes on in a second clause to modify the gift

But cf. Bradford v. Griffin, 40 So. Car. 468, 471, 19 S. E. 76, 77, stated § 398.1, post; Brown v. Columbia Finance Co., 123 Ky. 775, 97 S. E. 421, see § 522, note 1, post.

If property is shared among a class for their lives, and some of the class may not come into existence within the required limits, of course the whole gift is bad. Barnum v. Barnum, 26 Md. 119. Deford v. Deford, 36 Md. 168. Goldsborough v. Martin, 41 Md. 488. § 246, post. See Chap. X., post.

[12] Wainwright v. Miller, [1897] 2 Ch. 255. Re Gage, [1898] 1 Ch. 498. See Boughton v. James, 1 Coll. 26, 46.

[13] Gooding v. Reed, 21 Beav. 478, 4 De G. M. & G. 510. Re Watson, [1892] W. N. 192. Re Wise, [1896] 1 Ch. 281. Cf. Rhodes's Estate, 147 Pa. 227, 23 Atl. 553. Hoadley v. Beardsley, 89 Conn. 270, 93 Atl. 535. Colonial Trust Co. v. Waldron, 112 Conn. 216, 152 Atl. 69. But see Johnston's Estate, 185 Pa. 179, 39

Atl. 879, § 249.2, post; O'Brien's Estate, 24 Vict. 360. In Re Blew, [1906] 1 Ch. 624, Warrington, J., said that when the trustees of a term exceeding twenty-one years had a discretion to apply the income, the trust of the term was void, and on that ground he disapproved Re Watson and Re Wise, supra. See 1 Jarm. Wills (7th ed.) 271, 279; 174 L. T. 4. On such discretionary trusts, see § 246, post.

[14] See §§ 17, ante, 279, post. In Hoover v. Ford's Coal Co., 145 Wash. 295, 259 Pac. 1079, it was said that the mining "lease" there in question must terminate "long before the rule against perpetuities would take effect." As the only matter in dispute was the duration of the rights granted, the Rule against Perpetuities could have no application.

§ 232.1. [1] Re Roberts, 19 Ch. D. 520. Re Price, 8 Tasmanian 95. Marsden, Perp. 178. See Re Stevens, [1912] Vict. 194; § 207, ante.

by directing that the donee shall have a particular estate, with a limitation over to his children, issue, etc., and this latter limitation is bad for remoteness, the whole modifying clause is disregarded, and the donee takes the absolute interest.[1]

§ 234. **Anomalous American Decisions.** Although the doctrine that an estate is not too remote if it begins within the limits prescribed by the Rule against Perpetuities is recognized on both sides of the Atlantic, and although an opposite view would conflict with the fundamental principles which govern questions of remoteness, yet there are some American cases which are not conformable to this doctrine, and which therefore should be examined. In some of them, absolute interests have been said to violate the Rule against Perpetuities, although beginning within lives in being; in others, life interests beginning in like manner have been said to be too remote. They will be taken up in succession.

§ 234.1. These decisions and *dicta* are generally sporadic, and are inconsistent with, or are overruled by, cases in the same jurisdictions in which they have occurred. In Maryland, however, a considerable series of cases seems to call for detailed consideration. There will here be taken up in succession: (I.) Cases generally in which absolute interests beginning within, or at the end of, lives in being have been said or held to violate the Rule against Perpetuities. (II.) Cases generally in which life interests beginning within, or at the end of, lives in being have been said or held to violate the Rule. (III.) The series of Maryland cases.

§ 235. **(I.) Absolute Interests beginning within Lives in Being.** *Slade* v. *Patten.*[1] In this case there was an immediate devise to trustees in trust for children and their heirs, and the devise was held to violate the Rule against Perpetuities. The Court said: "If the trustees are to hold the estate for the four daughters and the heirs of the daughters, then the trust is void as creating a perpetuity." The decision was that the daughters took a legal fee; undoubtedly it should

§ 233. [1] These cases are considered in Chap. XIII., post.     § 235. [1] 68 Me. 380.

have been that they took an equitable fee. But as they could have immediately demanded a conveyance from the trustees, the practical difference was small. However, the Court said that the trust could not be considered as for the daughters for life, remainder for their heirs in fee, and that even if this were the construction, it would "create a perpetuity, because it was possible that they might have heirs unborn at the testator's death, and in whom the estate would not vest within lives in being and twenty-one years and a fraction afterwards." But the daughters' heirs must take the fee on the daughters' death, and the daughters must be alive (or begotten) at the testator's death.[2]

§ 236. In this opinion very different things were confounded. There are two distinct rules of law, by the joint action of which the tying up of estates is prevented. 1. Estates cannot be made inalienable. 2. Future estates cannot be created beyond the limits fixed by the Rule against Perpetuities. If land is devised to A. in trust for B. and his heirs, the Rule against Perpetuities has no application. The trust is perfectly good.[1] B.'s equitable fee is no more objectionable because it may last forever than is a devise of a legal fee simple; that, too, may last forever. B. may at once demand from the trustee a conveyance of the legal fee.[2] An equitable fee cannot be made inalienable.[3]

§ 237. But *Slade* v. *Patten,* though cited as authority in *Hamlin* v. *Mansfield,*[1] was in *Pulitzer* v. *Livingston,*[2] after full and elaborate discussion, overruled.[3]

[2] The case was criticised in 14 Am. Law Rev. 237.

§ 236. [1] See Harlow v. Cowdrey, 109 Mass. 183; O'Rourke v. Beard, 151 Mass. 9, 11, 23 N. E. 576; Cooper's Estate, 150 Pa. 576, 585, 24 Atl. 1057, 1060; Hart v. Seymour, 147 Ill. 598, 613, 614, 25 N. E. 246, 250; Reimer v. Smith, 105 Fla. 617, 142 So. 603.

[2] On a contrary doctrine in Massachusetts, Illinois, and other States, and its connection with the Rule against Perpetuities, see §§ 121.3 et seq., ante.

[3] See § 119.1, ante; Gray, Restraints on Alienation (2d ed.), §§ 105 et seq.

§ 237. [1] 88 Me. 131, 138, 33 Atl. 788, 790.

[2] 89 Me. 359, 36 Atl. 635.

[3] See, however, Towle v. Doe, 97 Me. 427, 54 Atl. 1072; § 245.1, post.

**§ 237.1.** In *Pennsylvania Co.* v. *Price,*[1] property was conveyed to a trustee in trust for eight children, their heirs and assigns, with an option in the trustee, his heirs and assigns, to convey the principal to the *cestuis que trust*. It was held by the Court of Common Pleas of Philadelphia that the *cestuis que trust* had the right to a conveyance; that is, the Court held the attempt to restrain the alienation of the estate, or postpone its enjoyment, by giving the trustee, his heirs and assigns, an option to withhold it, to be void. This was certainly correct. The language of the Court is unfortunate, however, as lending countenance to the idea that an equitable fee is obnoxious to the Rule against Perpetuities.

**§ 237.2.** In *Williams* v. *Herrick,*[1] a testator gave all his estate to trustees in trust to erect a "brick block" on his land to be forever known as the "A. G. & A. W. Olney Block," and to pay the rents and income among such of his heirs as should present satisfactory proof of their claims to the trustees; vacancies among the trustees to be filled by the Court of Probate "ever thereafter." The heirs and next of kin of the testator brought a bill in equity to have the testator's estate conveyed to them, and the Court overruled a demurrer to the bill, rightly it would seem. But, as in *Pennsylvania Co.* v. *Price,* the Court uses language about "perpetuities," which had better have been avoided.

**§ 237.3.** In *Bigelow* v. *Cady,*[1] a testator directed that his land should be taken charge of by his executrix; that the income should be equally divided between his wife and his three children; that "in case of death of either of the four above-named heirs it shall go (their share) to the heirs of the deceased heir, if they have any; if not, it shall be equally divided between my remaining heirs above mentioned, and their heirs forever, share and share alike;" that if his wife "dies leaving no heir of mine, then her share (one-fourth) shall go to my heirs and their heirs forever, share and share

§ 237.1. [1] 7 Phila. 465.

§ 237.2. [1] 19 R. I. 197, 32 Atl. 913.

§ 237.3. [1] 171 Ill. 229, 48 N. E. 974.

alike;" and that in case of the death or inability of the executrix, the judge of the Probate Court "shall, from time to time and for all time to come, appoint" a successor. The testator's wife and children brought a bill for partition. As the Rule in *Shelley's Case* is in force in Illinois, it would seem that no one was interested in the land except the plaintiffs, and that therefore the Court was right in overruling a demurrer to the bill. The inaccurate language of the Court as to the Rule against Perpetuities is to be regretted.[2]

§ 237.4. A perpetual trust which is not charitable and which has no definite *cestuis que trust*,—for instance a trust to keep a grave in repair,—is invalid, either because there is no person who has a right to enforce it, or else because it is a discretionary power within the scope of the Rule against Perpetuities.[1]

§ 238. (II.) Life Interests beginning within Lives in Being. In *Smith* v. *Dunwoody*,[1] the question was whether a very illiterate and confused will should be admitted to probate. The Court, why is not very apparent, considered the legality of the provisions of the will. There was a gift of the income of the testator's estate to certain persons named and their heirs. It was held that this was a gift of the *corpus*. The executors were charged to pay annually to each of the testator's slaves $5, and $100 to some Baptist minister, and to keep the chapel on the estate in repair; and the testator also directed that every tenth slave born after his death should

[2] This language is the more matter of surprise, because of the then recent case of Hart v. Seymour, 147 Ill. 598, 613, 614, 35 N. E. 246, 250. See Davis v. Williams, 85 Tenn. 646, 4 S. W. 8; Johnson v. Preston, 226 Ill. 447, 80 N. E. 1001; Kales, Estates, § 659. In Kempson v. Hoskins, 88 N. J. Eq. 153, 102 Atl. 673, a remark that a provision in restraint of alienation violated the Rule against Perpetuities was evidently made without due consideration; and in Carter v. Boone County Trust Co., 338 Mo. 629, 92 S. W. 2d 647, the Court seems to have fallen into a similar confusion in saying that an equitable fee, subject to a restraint on alienation, would violate the Rule against Perpetuities.

§ 237.4. [1] See App. H, §§ 898–909, post. In Troutman v. De Boissiere, 66 Kan. 1, 71 Pac. 286 (stated in the third edition of this work, § 245 b), the trust was of such a character.

§ 238. [1] 19 Ga. 237.

be emancipated. All these provisions were held bad, on the ground, it is said, that they were too remote. So far as the gift of $5 a year was to slaves unborn at the testator's death it was, in part at least, bad, but so far as it was to slaves then living it seems good. The gift was not to a class, but to each slave separately; and the gift to one was not affected by the validity or invalidity of the gift to any other.[2] Very likely, however, no such bequest to a slave would have any legal validity.[3]

§ 239. In *Smith's Appeal*,[1] property was devised to trustees in trust to pay the income to B. for life, and on her death as B. might by will appoint. B. appointed to trustees in trust for her children for life without liability for their debts, and directed that on the death of each child its share should go over. All B.'s children were born before the testator's death. The Court held the appointment bad, because B. might have had children born after the testator's death. B. might certainly have had such children, but all B.'s children, whether born before or after the death of the testator, would have taken at B.'s death, and therefore the life estates to the children were good.[2] *Smith's Appeal*, on this point, has been overruled by *Lawrence's Estate*.[3]

[2] See § 389, post.

[3] The direction to emancipate was finally held void on the ground that it was repugnant to the gift of the property. See § 228, note 5, ante.

§ 239. [1] 88 Pa. St. 492.

[2] As all B.'s appointees were in fact born in the testator's lifetime, and as the share of each went over independently, not only were the life estates good, but the gifts over were good also. See §§ 395, 523 et seq., post.

If any of the appointees had been born after the testator's death, the restraint on the alienation of their shares was either good or ought to have been disregarded. See the following section.

It is to be observed that the effect of holding the gifts over to be void was to give the children of B., under a provision in default of appointment, the whole interest in the property in which, under the appointment of B., they took a life interest, and the question of the validity of the life interests may have therefore less attracted the attention of the Court. An error similar to that in Smith's Appeal was made in Johnston v. Cosby, 374 Ill. 407, 29 N. E. 2d 608. See § 370, note 1, post.

[3] 136 Pa. 354, 366, 20 Atl. 521, 522. See also Coggins' Appeal, 124

**§ 240.** In *Gardette's Estate,*[1] P. devised property to C. for life, and on her death to her children and issue in such shares and for such estates as she should by will apoint. C. appointed to trustees in trust for her daughter J. for life, without power of anticipation. J. was not born until after P.'s death. The Orphans' Court of Philadelphia held that the appointment was void. But as J.'s life estate began on the death of C., the appointment would seem to have been clearly good. The restraint on anticipation was either good, or if it was too remote, it should have been disregarded.[2]

**§ 241.** In *Thomson* v. *Livingston,*[1] property subject to a power was appointed to trustees to pay the income to A., who was not born at the time of the creation of the power, till he reached forty-five, and then to transfer the capital to him absolutely, but if he died before that age, to transfer the property to his next of kin. The Court held the whole appointment void. No opinion is reported, but the reporter says one was given orally, and went upon the ground stated in the headnote, which is "that the appointment was void because it suspended the absolute ownership of the personalty bequeathed beyond the period allowed by law before the Revised Statutes." The gift over was bad, but the appointment of the equitable interest to A. until he reached forty-five, if he lived so long, was an interest beginning within the required limits, and therefore good. The expression about "suspending the absolute ownership" is borrowed from the Revised Statutes, and is foreign to the conceptions of the common law.[2]

**§ 242.** In *Thorndike* v. *Loring,*[1] a fund was given by will

Pa. 10, 30, 16 Atl. 379, 581; Ronckendorff's Estate, 11 Pa. C. C. 447; Owen's Pet'n, 3 Pa Dist. C. 328; Glenn's Estate, 16 Pa. D. & C. 581.

**§ 240.** [1] 13 W. N. C. (Pa.) 315, s. c. 16 Phila. 264.

[2] See §§ 432–438, post.

**§ 241.** [1] 4 Sandf. S. C. 539.

[2] See § 748, post. The case is so imperfectly reported, that it is not clear what A. took, the appointment over on his reaching forty-five being invalid. If the fee came to him, then as he had the entire equitable interest he could compel an immediate transfer to himself.

**§ 242.** [1] 15 Gray 391.

# 246

to trustees to accumulate for fifty years, and then to pay over to those who would be entitled to the testator's estate if he had then died intestate. The short memorandum of the opinion says: "The gift to trustees was void for remoteness. . . . The gift being void in law, the gift by the residuary clause takes effect, and the residuary legatees are entitled to distribution." The residuary legatees were certainly entitled to distribution, but the mode by which that result was reached is perhaps not quite correctly stated. The term for fifty years was not too remote, although the gift over was.[2] The residuary legatees, therefore, took the property subject to the term, and having the whole interest they could stop the accumulation and demand a conveyance at once.[3] The same comment is applicable to *Fosdick* v. *Fosdick*,[4] which is discussed in the following sections on another point. It may also be fairly urged in support of the decision in *Thorndike* v. *Loring* that the trust was created solely for the purpose of making an invalid gift, and that its sole object being illegal the whole trust failed.[5]

§ 243. In *Fosdick* v. *Fosdick*,[1] a testatrix gave the residue of her estate to trustees in trust to accumulate the income until her youngest living grandchild should reach twenty-one, and then "to pay over annually to my grandchildren, in equal shares, all the annual interest and income of said trust fund or estate." She then directed to whom each grandchild's share of income should be paid in case of its death, and that the interest and income should continue to be paid during the life of the last survivor of the grandchildren, and on the death of such last survivor she gave the property over. It is clear that the equitable life interests of the grandchildren must vest within twenty-one years after lives in being at the

[2] Gooding v. Read, 4 De G. M. & G. 510. Re Watson, [1892] W. N. 192. Re Wise, [1896] 1 Ch. 281. Rhodes's Estate, 147 Pa. 227, 23 Atl. 553. Johnston's Estate, 185 Pa. 179, 39 Atl. 879. See Andrews v. Lincoln, 95 Me. 541, 50 Atl. 898; O'Brien's Estate, 24 Vict. 360. See also § 232, ante.

[3] See §§ 671, 672, post.

[4] 6 Allen 41.

[5] A like decision in a like case was made in Baker v. Stuart, 28 Ont. 439.

§ 243. [1] 6 Allen 41.

death of the testator, and they therefore seem to be good, although the gifts over on the death of the grandchildren are of course bad.  But the Court held the life estates of the grandchildren to be void, for a singular reason.  They say that no portion of the annual interest and income "will or can become payable to any one of the legatees until the end of one year after the fund itself is created and established; for no annual interest can before that time have accrued upon it.  And until that time it is impossible that any part of such income can become legally vested in any one to whom any portion of it is bequeathed, because until the arrival of that time it is and must remain uncertain who are the legatees who will then be entitled to receive it; for according to the provisions in the will the share or portion which each one of the grandchildren would, if living, be entitled to receive is, upon his or her death, bequeathed and to be paid either to the surviving brothers and sisters, or the surviving wife or husband, or the children, or the appointees under the will of the deceased, as certain particularly enumerated and pre- scribed events and contingencies shall or shall not occur. Thus it may happen that the earliest possible time when any portion of the interest or income of the accumulated fund can become vested in any one of the legatees may be twenty- two years after the birth of a child born after the death of the testatrix; and the end of this term of twenty-two years may be more than twenty-one years and ten months after the extinction of all said lives in being, that is, after the death of all of said grandchildren who were living at the time of the decease of the testatrix."[2]

§ **244.** In *Lovering* v. *Worthington*,[1] the Court say that in *Fosdick* v. *Fosdick* "property was bequeathed to trustees to be accumulated for a term which the Court held to be longer than the period prescribed by the Rule against Perpetuities." But this is not so; the period during which the property was to be accumulated was only a life in being and twenty-one years.  The fact that in *Fosdick* v. *Fosdick* the life interests of the grandchildren did not begin till twenty-one years after a

---

[2] 6 Allen 41, 46.                         § **244.** [1] 106 Mass. 86, 88.

life in being did not make them bad. As appears by the cases cited, § 232, *ante,* it has been repeatedly held in Massachusetts, as elsewhere, that a life interest beginning at the end of a life in being is good. Such life interest may extend beyond twenty-one years, and yet there has never been a suggestion that that part which fell beyond twenty-one years is bad, and *Gooch* v. *Gooch*² is a distinct authority to the effect that a life interest beginning at the expiration of lives in being and twenty-one years is good. Neither is it any objection that the life interest is merely an equitable one, entitling the *cestui que trust* only to the receipt of the income; for this has been so in the great majority of the cases where life interests to unborn persons have been supported.³

§ **245.** Nor does the decision in *Fosdick* v. *Fosdick* purport to rest upon any of these grounds, but because "the 'annual' interest and income of [the fund] is to be 'annually' paid over to and received by the respective legatees." The adjective "annual" adds absolutely nothing, in this connection, to the words "interest and income." Neither the amount to be received by the *cestuis que trust,* nor the time nor mode of receiving it, is in the least affected by the use of this word. Were it stricken out the sense would not be in any way changed. The effect attributed to this expression in rendering the gift too remote must lie in the words "annually paid over and received." The utmost force that can be attributed to the word "annually" is that the trustee need not pay over the income more than once a year. As soon as received by the trustee it belongs to the life tenant. Should the life tenant die in the course of the year, any dividends or interest received before his death belong to him. The fact that the life tenant may not be alive at the end of a year, to which the opinion refers, is nothing more than may happen in any life estate, and will not deprive the life tenant of income accrued before his death. The Court treat the gift as if it had been "to such of certain persons as are living at the end of one year after my youngest grandchild reaches twenty-one, and so on at the end of every year so long as any one of my

---

² 3 De G. M. & G. 366, 383.     ³ See cases cited, § 232, ante.

grandchildren is alive." Such a gift would have been too remote, for it would have been contingent on the condition precedent of a legatee being alive twenty-two years after lives in being; but that was not the gift in *Fosdick* v. *Fosdick*. The gift there was free from any condition precedent, and was vested in, and (if that be material) immediately alienable by, the grandchildren. If a life interest in any property is to be considered contingent except as to those instalments of income which have actually been received, then all that part of a life estate beginning at the determination of a life in being which falls beyond twenty-one years from its commencement is bad for remoteness; but in the numerous cases in which such life estates have been held good without qualification, no such suggestion has ever been heard.[1] It is confidently submitted that *Fosdick* v. *Fosdick* was wrongly decided.

§ **245.1.** In *Towle* v. *Doe*,[1] a testator gave the residue of his estate to his wife for life and on her death "to my children, viz.: Wm. M. Towle and his heirs, one-fourth part to be invested by my executor in United States bonds or State bonds, and the interest, deducting expenses, paid over to said Wm. M. Towle and his children so long as they live, and then the principal divided to his or their heirs." The Court held that Wm. M. Towle took a fee subject to a modifying clause, and that as the modifying clause created interests which were in part too remote, such clause, in accordance with the doctrine laid down, Chapter XIII., *post*, must be rejected. This, though rather an extreme application of that doctrine, may be accepted, but the Court seems to have thought that not only the final gift to the heir or heirs of Towle and his children was void, which was enough to support the decision, but also that the trust for Towle and his children during their lives was bad. This, it is respectfully submitted, was erroneous.[2]

§ 245. [1] See Re Allott, [1924] 2 Ch. (C. A.) 498, 514, and cf. remarks in § 246, post, criticizing Re Cassel, [1926] Ch. 358.

§ 245.1. [1] 97 Me. 427, 54 Atl. 1072.

[2] In the third edition, under the heading § 245 b, is a discussion

## § 245.2. (III.) Maryland Cases. *Barnum* v. *Barnum*,[1]

(1866). Here there was a devise to trustees in trust for children and their heirs, with a direction that the property devised should be permanently carried on as a hotel, and (as the Court interpreted the will), if the testator's views on this point were disappointed, judicially or otherwise, he devised the property over. The Court held that the trust for the children was void, and the "disappointment clause" took effect. Though the trust would seem to have been good, yet it was terminable at the will of the *cestuis que trust,* it might fairly be said that the testator's views were disappointed. There is therefore no occasion to quarrel with the decision, but the Court, disregarding or overlooking the fact that an equitable fee is alienable, and that the Rule against Perpetuities applies only to future estates, said (p. 171) : "In the case now under consideration, no question is presented as to the future vesting of an executory estate, in order to determine the validity of the preceding one; but simply whether the trusts of the will require in their execution a longer period than that prescribed by the Rule against Perpetuities, and, therefore, render the property devised to the trustees inalienable during that time. If so, the law denounces the devise in trust as a perpetuity, and declares it void."

In *Deford* v. *Deford,*[2] *Albert* v. *Albert,*[3] *Thomas* v. *Gregg,*[4] and *Reed* v. *McIlvain,*[5] equitable life estates to persons who might not be living at the death of the testator were held invalid, under the doctrine of *Barnum* v. *Barnum,* although they took effect within the period of the Rule against Perpetuities, apparently for the reason that the trusts might continue beyond that period.[6] On the other hand, in *Heald*

---

of Troutman v. De Boissiere, 66 Kan. 1, 71 Pac. 286. For this case, see § 237.4, ante, App. H, §§ 894–909, post.

**§ 245.2.** [1] 26 Md. 119.
[2] 36 Md. 168.
[3] 68 Md. 352, 12 Atl. 11.
[4] 76 Md. 169, 24 Atl. 418.
[5] 113 Md. 140, 77 Atl. 329.

[6] For a detailed discussion of these cases, see the third edition of this work, § 245 c and g. The language of Barnum v. Barnum was also cited with approval in Goldsborough v. Martin, 41 Md. 488, stated § 397, post. Cf. Allen v. White, 16 Ala. 181, and Johnston's Estate, 185 Pa. 179, 39 Atl.

**v. *Heald*[7] and *Graham* v. *Whitridge*[8]** the Court held, in accordance with the general and correct doctrine, that life estates to unborn grandchildren were valid.

Finally, however, the Court of Appeals has gone back to the Common Law. In *Gambrill* v. *Gambrill*,[9] a testator, who died in 1856, gave property in trust for his daughter E. for life, and on her death as she might by will appoint. E. married in 1869 and died in 1872, and by will appointed the property to her husband for life, and on his death to G., her only child, for life, with limitation over. The Court held that the limitation over was of course void, but that the life estate to G. was good. They said that the Rule against Perpetuities "is applicable to limitations of either legal or equitable estates in either real or personal property. It relates to the *commencement* of future interests, and not to their *duration*, and it is therefore immaterial whether the estate limited is in fee, for life, or for years." They rely on *Heald* v. *Heald* and *Graham* v. *Whitridge*. They disapprove of *Thomas* v. *Gregg* and *Reed* v. *McIlvain*. They say that in those cases "the principle of the *Barnum Case* was construed and applied as confining the *duration* of a trust within a life or lives in being and twenty-one years thereafter, and not as merely restricting the future vesting of an estate within that period. This theory of the rule is not in accord with its purpose and effect as defined in the earliest decisions of this court on the subject and in its statement in the recent cases of *Levenson* v. *Manly*,[10] *Starr* v. *Starr M. P. Church*,[11] and *Hollander* v. *Central Metal Co.*,[12] as well as in the cases of *Heald* v. *Heald* and *Graham* v. *Whitridge*, to which we have more particularly

879, § 249.2, post. See also a note on the Rule against Perpetuities in Md. in the 26th volume of Perkins's edition of Maryland Reports, p. 119.

[7] 56 Md. 300.

[8] 99 Md. 248, 290, 57 Atl. 609. For a further discussion of this case, see third edition, § 245 e, and 18 Harv. Law Rev. 232, 234.

Cf. Levenson v. Manly, 119 Md. 517, 87 Atl. 261; Lyon v. Safe Dep. Co., 120 Md. 514, 87 Atl. 1089.

[9] 122 Md. 563, 89 Atl. 1049.

[10] 119 Md. 517, 87 Atl. 261.

[11] 112 Md. 171, 182, 76 Atl. 595, 599.

[12] 109 Md. 131, 157, 71 Atl. 442, 447.

referred.  As we adhere to the principle of the rule as there expressed, and find it controlling in the present case, we must hold that this [limitation for the life of G.] is not in violation of the Rule against Perpetuities."  *Gambrill* v. *Gambrill* has been followed in *Bowerman* v. *Taylor*,[13] *Turner* v. *Safe Deposit and Trust Co.*,[14] *Hawkins* v. *Ghent*,[15] and *Safe Deposit and Trust Co.* v. *Sheehan*,[16] and was mentioned with approval in *Ortman* v. *Dugan*.[17]

Parallel with these cases with regard to equitable life estates has run another line of cases concerning equitable fees, in which the doctrine of *Barnum* v. *Barnum* has been referred to.

*Missionary Society* v. *Humphreys*.[18]  A devise was made to trustees and their successors to apply the rents from year to year to a number of incorporated bodies and boards for charitable purposes.  The Court held the trust void and declared that they felt "constrained to adhere to the law as announced in" *Barnum* v. *Barnum*.  Surely this is the *reductio ad absurdum* of the doctrine of *Barnum* v. *Barnum*. The Court expressly say that a devise directly to the charitable bodies would have been good.  That is:  A devise of a legal fee to a charity is good, but a devise of an equitable fee violates the Rule against Perpetuities.[19]

*Trinity Church* v. *Baker*.[20]  Here was a devise to trustees upon trust to convey land to a charitable organization, upon its complying with a condition precedent, which compliance might be at a remote period.  Remembering that the doc-

13 126 Md. 203, 94 Atl. 652.

14 148 Md. 371, 129 Atl. 294.

15 154 Md. 261, 140 Atl. 212.

16 167 Md. 138, 179 Atl. 536.

17 130 Md. 121, 100 Atl. 82, stated below.

18 91 Md. 131, 46 Atl. 320.

19 See also Bennett v. Humane Impartial Soc., 91 Md. 10, 45 Atl. 888; Woman's Foreign Missionary Soc. v. Mitchell, 93 Md. 199, 48 Atl. 737; Baltzell v. Church Home, 110 Md. 244, 73 Atl. 151; Gray v. Orphan's Home, 128 Md. 592, 98 Atl. 202; Conner v. Trinity Church, 129 Md. 360, 99 Atl. 547; Waters v. Order of the Holy Cross, 155 Md. 146, 142 Atl. 297; Home for Incurables v. Bruff, 160 Md. 156, 153 Atl. 403; Art Students' League v. Hinckley, 31 Fed. 2d 469.  Cf. Charles T. Brandt, Inc. v. Y. W. C. A., 169 Md. 607, 182 Atl. 452.

20 91 Md. 539, 46 Atl. 1020.

trine of *cy pres* does not prevail in Maryland, there seems
nothing to criticise in this decision, though it is not always
easy to follow the reasoning of the Court.

*Lee* v. *O'Donnell.*[21] Devise to trustees to hold in trust
for A. for life, and if he died without issue living at his
death (which happened) to hold for B., C., and D., and their
heirs as tenants in common. Of course B., C., and D. were
entitled to have the legal estate conveyed to them, but the
Court said: "If the trusts in this case are not to terminate
at this point of time [the death of A.], they must be held as
void, as tending to create a perpetuity."[22] This case brings
out into sharp relief the difference between what it is submitted is the true rule and the doctrine as laid down in the
Maryland cases, the former being that equitable fees are alienable, the latter being that they are void *ab initio.*

In *Brown* v. *Reeder,*[23] land was conveyed by A. to B. and
his heirs for their own use, but in trust for A. for life, and
on his death for C. and his heirs. After the death of A., C.'s
heir brought a bill in equity for a conveyance, and a conveyance was decreed. This appears to put the case on the correct
ground. The Court distinguish *Barnum* v. *Barnum* and the
following cases, because in them there were provisions imposing active duties on the trustee.[24]

In *Novak* v. *Orphans Home,*[25] and *American Colonization
Society* v. *Soulsby,*[26] gifts in trust for charitable purposes
were held void as infringing the Rule against Perpetuities,
following *Missionary Society* v. *Humphreys.*

In *Ortman* v. *Dugan,*[27] a devise was made in trust for the

[21] 95 Md. 538, 59 Atl. 979.

[22] See Hillen v. Iselin, 144 N.
Y. 365, 39 N. E. 368.

[23] 108 Md. 653, 71 Atl. 417.

[24] If the cestui que trust has
the equitable fee, query whether
such provisions are not voidable
at the suit of the cestui, without
any question of perpetuities, as
being against public policy. See
Gray, Restraints on Alienation
(2d ed.), §§ 105 et seq., and Chap.

IV., §§ 119–121.8, ante.

[25] 123 Md. 161, 90 Atl. 997.

[26] 129 Md. 605, 99 Atl. 944.
See also cases cited in the note
to Missionary Society v. Humphreys, in this section, ante, assuming the existence of this doctrine
as to charitable trusts; and on
charitable trusts generally in
Maryland, see 1 Md. Law Rev.
105.

[27] 130 Md. 121, 100 Atl. 82.

testatrix's son for life, and after his death to his issue and
their heirs, with a provision that if a child of the son should
die without exercising a power of disposition and without issue, its share should go to the testatrix's daughter for life, and
on the latter's death to her issue. The son died leaving no
issue, but survived by his sister. The question before the
Court was whether the daughter and her issue had a good
title in fee. It was held that the executory devise to the
daughter and her issue was too remote, because it took effect
on the death of grandchildren who might be unborn at the
testatrix's death. This decision was undoubtedly correct.[28] It
seems to have been assumed that the interests of the son's children, if any had survived him, would have been good. The
Court said: "In order that the estates limited upon this double contingency may be valid, according to the intent of the
rule against perpetuities, they must have been certain to vest
before the expiration of 21 years and 10 months after the
period of a life or lives in being when the will became oper-
ative. *Bowerman* v. *Taylor, Gambrill* v. *Gambrill, Graham*
v. *Whitridge, Heald* v. *Heald.* It is the time of vesting of
the estate, and not its duration after it has vested, that is to
be considered upon the question as to whether the limitation
upon which it depends is in conflict with the rule. But vested
trusts of unlimited duration, requiring the application of
funds to continuing uses, and involving the performance of
active fiduciary duties to that end, beyond the period prescribed by the rule, have likewise been held to be perpetuities
and consequently void. *Missionary Society* v. *Humphreys,
American Colonization Society* v. *Soulsby, Barnum* v.
*Barnum.*"

In *Turner* v. *Safe Deposit & Trust Co.*,[29] the Court, while
following *Gambrill* v. *Gambrill* in deciding that a life estate
to an unborn person is valid, made the following remarks:
"The most recent case cited in support of the opposite view

[28] See, however, for a possible
question as to the effect of the
power of disposition, § 524.1,
post.

[29] 148 Md. 371, 129 Atl. 298;
and see 24 Mich. Law Rev. 725.

is *American Colonization Society* v. *Soulsby*. In that case the rule against perpetuities was held to invalidate a trust of unlimited duration for the purpose of promoting emigration to Liberia. In *Missionary Society* v. *Humphreys,* the rule was declared to be violated by a devise in trust, without restriction as to time, for the benefit of certain religious and charitable institutions. There was no question in those cases as to the vesting of successive legal or equitable titles. The purposes which the trusts would serve were to be continuous and un-varying from their inception, and were sought to be projected into the remote future. The proposed duration of the trust being in evident excess of the time permitted by the rule against perpetuities, the principle of that rule was applied to prevent the property granted or devised in trust from be-ing rendered indefinitely or perpetually inalienable. The de-cisions to that end are entirely consistent with the view that an equitable estate, though held and administered under an active trust, is exempt from the operation of the rule, if lim-ited to vest within the period which it allows."

It may probably be taken as settled that both *Gambrill* v. *Gambrill* and *Missionary Society* v. *Humphreys* are good law in Maryland. The result seems to be that there exists in Maryland a doctrine as to perpetual trusts, which is consid-ered as an application of the Rule against Perpetuities, though in reality independent of the common-law rule known by that name. At the same time, the common-law Rule against Per-petuities exists in Maryland, and is applied in the same man-ner as in other common-law jurisdictions. The scope of the local doctrine as to perpetual trusts cannot be said to be clear-ly settled. The invalidity in Maryland of perpetual trusts for charitable purposes appears to be established by a long and uniform series of decisions. How far the principles an-nounced in *Barnum* v. *Barnum* and *Lee* v. *O'Donnell*, limited as those principles have been by the later cases, would be ap-plied to a trust for A. and his heirs, seems to be doubtful.

**§ 246. Indeterminate Interests.** Equitable interests begin-ning within the limits of the Rule against Perpetuities are

good ;[1] but not only must the persons taking be determined
within the required period,[2] but also the amount of the interest of each person must be determined within that period.
If the amount of the interest remains dependent upon future
events, the interest is not vested for the purposes of the Rule.[3]
Suppose, as, for instance, to save property from creditors, that
it is given to A. in trust to pay the income to B., a bachelor,
for life, and on B.'s death to distribute the income among
such of B.'s children during their lives as the trustee may in
his discretion think fit, or at his discretion to add the income
to the principal.   Here, in order to give any interest to any
child, or in order that any sum should be added to the principal, the trustee must exercise his discretion to that end ; the
exercise of such discretion is a condition precedent; and as
that discretion may not be exercised in that way till too remote a period, the whole gift upon B.'s death is void.[4]   And
likewise the gift is too remote even if there is no discretion
to add the income to the principal, but only a discretion to
distribute it; for though the whole class have a vested interest, yet the share of each member depends upon the prior exercise of discretion by the trustee.   Perhaps such a gift to unborn children may be held good as a gift to them in equal

§ 246. [1] See cases cited, § 232,
ante.

[2] A trust for a fluctuating class
which may include persons not
born till too remote a period is of
course bad.  See § 232, note 11,
second paragraph, ante; §§ 396–
398, and 896, post; and Peek v.
Peek, 17 W. R. 1059; Kennedy
v. Kennedy, [1914] A. C. 215; Dot-
ten v. Glennie, 93 Conn. 472, 106
Atl. 824; Sanford v. Sanford, 230
Ky. 429, 20 S. W. 2d 23; Rhode
Island Hospital Trust Co. v. Peck,
40 R. I. 519, 101 Atl. 430; St.
Paul's Church v. Attorney General, 164 Mass. 188, 195, 41 N. E.
231, 233; Amory v. Amherst College, 229 Mass. 374, 382, 118 N.
E. 933, 936; Talbot v. Riggs, 287
Mass. 144, 191 N. E. 360; Lockhart's Estate, 306 Pa. 394, 159
Atl. 874; First National Bank v.
Rice, 101 N. J. Eq. 520, 139 Atl.
396; City National Bank v. White,
337 Ill. 442, 169 N. E. 197; Re
Bullen, 17 W. Aust. 73; and Sied-
ler v. Syms, 56 N. J. Eq. 275, 38
Atl. 424, stated § 410.2, post.

[3] Re Whiteford, [1915] 1 Ch.
347, stated below.  Cf. §§ 205.2,
ante, 375, post.

[4] See Andrews v. Lincoln, 95
Me. 541, 50 Atl. 898.

shares, the discretion to modify the amount of the shares being rejected.[5] But this suggestion cannot be accepted in all
cases. To reject a modification, there must be an independent
gift,[6] and often there is none such. If the trustee can pay
over the income at such time as he sees fit, that time may be
too remote, and therefore the discretion is void.[7] But suppose, as may often be the case, that the trustee's discretion
cannot be exercised at any time he sees fit, but must be exercised every year. If the trust is to pay the income every year
to such children, now unborn, as the trustee sees fit, is such
trust wholly void, or is it good for twenty-one years, on the
ground that the annual payments are separable? On this see
§§ 410.1, 479, 480, *post*.[8]

It is immaterial whether the amount of the interest of an
unborn beneficiary is contingent on the exercise of discretion
by the trustee or on other future events which may occur at
too remote a period. In *Re Whiteford*,[9] A. by her will ap-

[5] See § 439, post; 1 Jarm. Wills
(7th ed.) 279.

[6] § 431, post.

[7] So if the discretion is to make
payment to, or for the benefit of,
a class, members of which may
come into existence at too remote
a date. Kennedy v. Kennedy,
[1914] A. C. 215. Re Canning's
Trusts, [1936] 1 Ch. 309. Cf. Re
Wright's Estate, 284 Pa. 334, 131
Atl. 188, in which the Court held
the discretionary trust good by
confining it to living persons. See
also § 232, note 13, ante; and the
case of Moore v. Moore, 6 Jones
Eq. 132, discussed § 396, post.
And so likewise any discretionary
trust for the lifelong maintenance
of a person unborn at the creation of the trust is invalid. Re
Bernard's Settlement, [1916] 1
Ch. 552. Re Benyon-Windsor,
143 L. T. 178. Re Coleman,

[1936] 1 Ch. 528. Bundy v. U.
S. Trust Co., 257 Mass. 72, 79,
153 N. E. 337, 339. See Re Blew,
[1906] 1 Ch. 624; Re Antrobus,
[1928] N. Z. 364; 1 Jarm. Wills
(7th ed.) 279; 174 L. T. 4. A
discretionary trust is in effect a
special power of appointment
given to the trustee; and if a
power can be exercised at a time
beyond the limits of the Rule
against Perpetuities, it is invalid,
§ 474.1, post. Cf. remarks of
Russell, J., in Re Cassel, [1926]
Ch. 358, 369, 370, discussed below
in this section.

[8] In Re Whiteford, Re Cassel,
and several of the other cases discussed in this section, a question
of this sort was, or might have
been, suggested. And see Re
Kelly, [1932] I. R. 255, § 410.3,
note, post.

[9] [1915] 1 Ch. 347.

pointed a fund under her marriage settlement, in trust to
apply the whole or so much of the income as should be required for making up the total income of her son W. to the
sum of two hundred pounds per annum, in such manner as
the trustees should in their discretion think proper, for the
maintenance of W. during his life, and to divide the residue,
if any, of such income equally between her four other sons.
The interests of W. and his brothers seem not to be dependent on the discretion of the trustees, and the judge therefore
properly omitted to refer to the words of discretion in the
will.  He held, however, the shares of each of the five brothers
in the income to be contingent each year on the facts in that
year.  "On the other side it is argued that it is a vested interest from the death of the appointor, although the amount
of income to be received by any one of the five could only be
ascertained from year to year and might have to be ascertained after the expiration of twenty-one years.  I think the
question really is whether you can have a vested interest depending in whole or in part upon the happening of a particular event.  It seems to me that to say you can is to state what
is a contradiction in terms, because the thing cannot be both
vested and contingent."  (P. 351.)  It is difficult to escape
from this reasoning.  The class as a whole may be said to have
a vested interest, but the amount which each person is to take
remains contingent on the facts existing from time to time.[10]

In *Re Cassel*,[11] A. bequeathed to trustees a house held on
a lease terminating in 1995, with covenants for repair and
maintenance, on trust for a series of persons.  The terms of
the trust were such that the property would necessarily vest
absolutely in some person at the expiration of lives in being.
The testator then directed that "the rent, outgoings, rates
and taxes for the time being payable in respect of the
said messuage and premises and keeping the same and the
contents thereof insured against fire and burglary and in a
proper state of preservation shall be always paid by my trustees out of the income of my residuary personal estate."  Rus-

10 Cf. §§ 375, 675, post.        11 [1926] Ch. 358.

[G. R. P.]

sell, J., held the trust to pay the rent, outgoings, etc., was to continue only during such time as the lease remained the property of a beneficiary deriving his title directly from the will, and that, so construed, the trust did not infringe the Rule against Perpetuities, because the right to the annual payments of rent, etc., must vest in some ascertained person not later than the termination of lives in being, although it might continue thereafter beyond the period allowed by the rule. The learned judge, after referring to the principle that an interest is not obnoxious to the rule if it begins within lives in being and twenty-one years, although it may end beyond them, continued as follows: "It was, however, further argued that the uncertainty of the quantum of the annual sum rendered the disposition void, because the exact quantum of the interest could not be ascertained within the limit of the rule. This contention, if sound, would produce far-reaching results. A bequest of an annuity of 100 pounds per annum for 1000 years to A. for life and after his death to any wife of his for her life and after her death to A.'s children for life would be good; but if given free of tax would be bad, for the actual amount payable to the children might not be ascertainable within the perpetuity period. The answer seems to me to be that the interest arises and is vested during the period, and that although the amount necessary to satisfy it is expressed in uncertain terms it is always capable of being rendered certain; and that the whole property (that is to say the interest in question and the property which is subject to that interest) is vested in some person or persons during the necessary period." He then referred to the cases of discretionary trusts, which he distinguished on the ground that the interest of the beneficiary in such cases remains contingent on the exercise of the discretion. In this case it seems that the trust for maintenance of the house might well have been treated as involving the exercise of discretion from year to year. But even if there was no discretion, it is difficult to support this decision on principle, or to distinguish it from *Re Whiteford*, which does not appear to have been mentioned by either court or counsel. No authority is cited for the proposition that an annuity free of income tax is a vested interest for the purposes of the Rule against Perpetuities, in a case where its enjoyment might continue during too remote a period. Moreover, the gift here was not of an annuity free from tax. The right to the use and income of certain property forever, or for life, or for a term of years, is regarded by the law as a single entire interest[12] in the property, which interest vests at the date of its commencement, and entitles its owner to the income of the property forever, or during the designated period, although the amount of income may vary. The right to a fixed sum annually is likewise regarded as a single entire interest, which vests at the date of its commencement; and possibly the right to a fixed sum annually, *plus* an amount equal to the tax on such sum, might be held to be a similarly vested interest. But it is hard to see how the right to a varying annual sum can be considered as vested, if its amount is dependent each year on the amount of taxes and other expenses payable with respect to other property and not with respect to such annual sum or the property from which it is derived. The answer given by the learned judge, to the objection of the continuing uncertainty of the amount payable, seems open to the reply above quoted from the opinion in *Re Whiteford*. The circumstance that a future interest is contingent, not on any person's volition, but on facts which can be definitely ascertained when a future date is reached, does not make it any the less contingent until that date arrives. The amount of the interest of each son in *Re Whiteford* was also capable of being rendered certain in each year as it arrived.[13]

## 12. EFFECT OF REMOTE INTERESTS ON PRIOR LIMITATIONS

**§ 247. Void Limitations omitted.** If future interests created by any instrument are avoided by the Rule against Perpetuities, the prior interests become what they would have been had the limitation of the future estates been omitted

---

[12] See Re Allott, [1924] 2 Ch. (C. A.) 498, 514. And see remarks in § 245, ante, criticising    Fosdick v. Fosdick, 6 Allen 41.
[13] Re Cassel is criticised in 174 L. T. 4.

from the instrument. Thus, if an estate is given to A. for life, remainder to his children and their heirs, but, if the children all die under twenty-five, then to B. and his heirs, the limitation to B. is too remote, and the children of A. take an indefeasible fee simple. The cases illustrating this are innumerable.[1] So when there is a devise on a remote condition, and no prior devise, the land descends to the heir who has an indefeasible fee.[2]

§ 248. If the devise of a future interest is void for remoteness, but the prior devise is for life only or other limited period,—for instance, if there be a devise to an unborn child for life, remainder to the unborn child of such unborn child, —the property after the termination of the prior interest goes to the person to whom property which has been invalidly devised or bequeathed goes. This person is generally the heir in case of realty, and the residuary legatee in case of personalty. There is no difference in this respect between a devise or bequest void for remoteness and a devise or bequest void for any other reason.[1]

§ 247. [1] See, for example, Brattle Sq. Church v. Grant, 3 Gray 142, 156 et seq. Cf. Amer. Law Inst. Restatement, Property, § 229, and App.; and § 788, note 2, post.

[2] See Ferguson v. Ferguson, 39 U. C. Q. B. 232, 1 Ont. Ap. 452, 2 Can. S. C. 497. Cf. Re Daveron, [1893] 3 Ch. 421; Goodier v. Edmunds, Id. 455.

§ 248. [1] Andrews v. Rice, 53 Conn. 566, 5 Atl 823. Tongue v. Nutwell, 13 Md. 415. Deford v. Deford, 36 Md. 168. Cf. Wainman v. Field, Kay 507; Blight v. Hartnoll, 23 Ch. D. 218; Loyd v. Loyd, 102 Va. 519, 46 S. E. 687. There is no question that personal property included in a void bequest goes to the residuary legatee. Shanley v. Baker, 4

Ves. 732. Cox v. Harris, 17 Md. 23. Deford v. Deford, ubi sup. 1 Jarm. Wills (6th ed.) 945. The better opinion seems to be that void devises, like lapsed devises, go to the heir. 1 Jarm. Wills (6th ed.) 946; 2 Jarm. Wills (7th ed.) 924. Van Kleeck v. Reformed Dutch Church, 6 Paige 600, 20 Wend. 457. Greene v. Dennis, 6 Conn. 292. Lingan v. Carroll, 3 H. & McH. 333. Tongue v. Nutwell, ubi sup. See Tregonwell v. Sydenham, 3 Dow 194. Contra, Ferguson v. Hedges, 1 Harring. 524. And see Hayden v. Stoughton, 5 Pick. 528, 536 et seq. Often, by modern legislation, lapsed and void devises go to the residuary devisee. 1 Vict. (1837), c. 26, § 25. Thayer v. Wellington, 9 Allen 283. See Massey's Ap-

§ **249.** In *Caldwell* v. *Willis*,[1] there was a bequest of personalty to A. for life, with what was held to be a too remote limitation over. The Court contrived to reach the extraordinary result that A. took an absolute interest. They quoted a remark by Smith, C. J., in *Harris* v. *McLaran*,[2] that the estate of the first taker was absolute "in those cases in which an intention to dispose of the whole interest is apparent, and where also conditional limitations are engrafted upon interests in the first takers, which, in the absence of the conditional limitations, would be held to be absolute interests." What Smith, C. J., meant was that when the first taker takes an absolute interest subject to a conditional limitation, if the conditional limitation is too remote, the first taker retains his absolute interest. The Court in *Caldwell* v. *Willis* must have understood the remark to mean that if the interest of the first taker *plus* the void limitation was meant to carry the whole interest, then the first taker takes the whole interest. That the remark of Smith, C. J., could have been so misunderstood, and that so misunderstood it could have been supposed to be law, seem equally inconceivable; but *Caldwell* v. *Willis* is not otherwise intelligible.[3]

§ **249.1. Missouri Cases.** Some recent cases in which the invalidity for remoteness of a subsequent limitation has been held to destroy prior limitations also, call for notice. The first of them is *Lockridge* v. *Mace*.[1] In this case there was a devise to the testator's wife for life, remainder to his children for life, remainder to his grandchildren for life, remainder to his great-grandchildren in fee. The Court of course held the last limitation void. It then asks the question whether all the life estates "share the fate of the clause which attempts to give to the great-grandchildren an estate in fee, or is the will void, only in so far as it exceeds the limitation prescribed

peal, 88 Pa. 470; Kirkpatrick v. Kirkpatrick, 112 Kans. 314, 211 Pac. 146.

§ **249.** [1] 57 Miss. 555.
[2] 30 Miss. 533, 570.
[3] As to an equally strange res-

olution on another point in this case, see § 398, post. And see 10 Va. Law Rev. 533, 542.

§ **249.1.** [1] 109 Mo. 162, 18 S. W. 1145.

by law?" It then proceeds to cite authorities and concludes thus: "Guided by these authorities, it must be held" that the devise "must fail *in toto.*" But in fact none of these authorities support the conclusion of the Court.[2] And if anything is now well settled in the law it is that a life estate, good in itself, is not destroyed by the remainder over being bad for remoteness or any other reason.[3] Even where the life estates are to unborn persons they are good. In Mr. Lewis's words "it occasions surprise to find the question treated as in any way doubtful or open to argument."[4] Sir John Leach, M. R., in *Hayes* v. *Hayes,*[5] held a life estate to an unborn person to be bad, but he lived to regret it.[6] In the second edition of this work it was said: "It is confidently to be hoped that the learned Court of Missouri will come into line." But this hope has been disappointed. *Lockbridge* v. *Mace* was followed in *Shepperd* v. *Fisher;*[7] and those two cases have been followed in *Loud* v. *St. Louis Tr. Co.,*[8] *Mockbee* v. *Grooms,*[9] and *Riley* v. *Jaeger.*[10] The last-named case went still farther and declared void a devise of a defeasible fee because the subsequent executory devise was too remote. In some of these cases, the

---

[2] They are Leake v. Robinson, 2 Mer. 363; Donahue v. McNichol, 61 Pa. 73, 78, 79; Hawley v. James, 16 Wend. 120, 121, 126; St. Armour v. Rivard, 2 Mich. 294, 2 Lead. Cas. in Amer. Law of Real Prop. 488. The first three have nothing to do with the subject. In St. Armour v. Rivard (see § 665, post), there seems to have been an estate tail (in Michigan by statute an estate in fee simple) with a proviso that each tenant should hold for life only; this proviso was declared invalid. The reference to 2 Lead. Cas. in Amer. Law of Real Prop. 488, is to an editorial note based on a mistaken view of St. Armour v. Rivard. See Rozell v. Rozell, 217 Mich. 324, 186 N. W. 489.

[3] Take, for instance, four cases from as many different jurisdictions. Stuart v. Cockerell, L. R. 5 Ch. 13. Wood v. Griffin, 46 N. H. 230. Lovering v. Worthington, 106 Mass. 86. Stout v. Stout, 44 N. J. Eq. 479, 15 Atl. 843. See Lewis, Perp. Suppl. 144; Marsden, Perp. 174, 175; Perry, Trusts (7th ed.), § 377.

[4] Perp. Suppl. 144.

[5] 4 Russ. 311.

[6] See § 232, ante.

[7] 206 Mo. 208, 245–247, 103 S. W. 989, 999, 1000.

[8] 298 Mo. 148, 185, 249 S. W. 629, 639.

[9] 300 Mo. 446, 467, 254 S. W. 170, 175.

[10] 189 S. W. 1168.

language of the Court suggested that the Missouri doctrine
was based upon a presumption of intent that all the provisions of the trust should stand or fall together. But in all
the cases the doctrine has been applied in such a sweeping
manner, without any apparant consideration of what the
testator would have wished in the particular case, that the
presumption, if so it is called, seems to amount to a positive
rule of law.[11]

§ 249.2. **Pennsylvania Cases.** *Johnston's Estate.*[1] A testator devised land to trustees for a term of seventy-five years,
to pay debts and legacies out of the income, and then on each
1st of May to divide the income "among all my children share
and share alike and the children of such of my children as
may during said period depart this life, the children of such
deceased children to have and take however only such portion
and share of said rents, issues, and profits as their deceased
parents would have taken if living; the said mode of distribution to obtain also in regard to said rents, issues, and profits,
among descendants of more remote degree than children's
children;" and at the expiration of the term of seventy-five
years, the land to be sold and the proceeds distributed among
all of his children then living, and the issue of those then
dead. One of the testator's heirs brought a bill to set aside
the trust, and obtain possession of a share in the land.

The case was heard in the Court of Common Pleas by Stewart, P. J., who delivered a very lucid opinion, granting the
prayer of the bill, and the decree was affirmed in the Supreme
Court, that Court adopting Stewart, P. J.'s opinion. The
learned judge held that the devise of the trust term for years
was good in itself and that the circumstance that it would
continue seventy-five years was immaterial. He then held
that the gift over at the end of the seventy-five years was
contingent, and therefore, of course, too remote. But he went

---

[11] See the discussion of the
Missouri Cases by Professor M.
O. Hudson in 3 Law Series, Univ.
of Mo. Bull. 3, 14, 22–28; 14 Law
Series 53. Cf. Chenoweth v. Bul-
litt, 224 Ky. 698, 716, 6 S. W. 2d
1061, 1067. See also 21 St. Louis
Law Rev. 209.

§ 249.2. [1] 185 Pa. 179, 39 Atl.
879.

on, and decided that although the term for years was good in itself it was bad *because* the contingent gift over at the expiration of the term was too remote. He admitted (p. 191) that "no cases are to be found in Pennsylvania supporting" this view, and he relied on three New York cases, and on *Thorndike* v. *Loring*.[2]

The New York cases were all decided, not at common law, but under the peculiar provisions of the New York Statutes.[3] The difference between *Thorndike* v. *Loring* and *Johnston's Estate* is this: In the former case the income was to be accumulated for fifty years in order that at the end of that time the accumulations might be given over, but the gift over was too remote, and could never take effect, therefore the object of the trust wholly failed; but in the latter case the object of the trust was not solely for the purpose of the remote gift over,—in fact, it had nothing to do with the gift over,—it was created solely to regulate the payment out of income during the seventy-five years. It would have effected its purpose had there been no gift over at all. There is a series of English cases opposed to *Johnston's Estate*,[4] and on the whole, with great submission, the decision seems difficult to maintain.[5] *Johnston's Estate* was followed in *Gerber's Estate*[6] and

[2] 15 Gray 391, § 242, ante.

[3] By N. Y. Rev. Sts., pt. 2, c. 1, Tit. 2, §§ 14, 15, 23, 63, and c. 4, Tit. 4, §§ 1, 2, as revised by c. 547 of the Laws of 1896, §§ 32, 39, 83, and c. 417 of the Laws of 1897, §§ 2, 3, all estates are void which suspend the power of alienation for more than two lives, and all trust estates are inalienable; therefore in New York such a term as existed in Johnston's Estate would be, of course, bad. The same is true in other States which have copied the N. Y. statute; see §§ 747–752.1, post.

[4] Gooding v. Read, 21 Beav. 478, 4 De G. M. & G. 510. Re Watson, [1892] W. N. 192. Re Wise, [1896] 1 Ch. 281.

[5] The passage in the text is quoted with approval in Lyons v. Bradley, 168 Ala. 505, 521, 53 So. 244, 249.

Although the reason given by Stewart, P. J., for invalidating the trust term seems insufficient, yet were not the trusts of the term, in part at least, bad? On each 1st of May for seventy-five years the income was to be divided among the children then living, and the issue per stirpes then living of children then deceased; the persons taking and the size of the shares at each period of distribution could not be determined until such period, which might be

*Kountz's Estate.*[7] The learned reader is referred to a severe but just criticism on the three cases by Mr. Foulke.[8]

In *Whitman's Estate,*[9] life estates were held valid, although followed by remote remainders. The Court said: "The Pennsylvania rule is . . . that a valid limitation which is associated with, but practically possible of separation from, one that transgresses the rule against perpetuities, will not be struck down, unless the will as a whole not only shows the void limitation, but that the general scheme and dominant purpose of the whole disposition in question were to tie up the testator's estate beyond the time allowed by law; when such is the case, however, the provision falls in its entirety. While the last part of this rule is freely criticised by some text-writers, yet the cases . . . show it to be implanted in our law; but we all agree that it has no application to the will at bar." *Whitman's Estate* was followed in *Lockhart's Estate,*[10] *Jones' Trusts,*[11] *Hecht's Estate,*[12] *Warren's Estate,*[13] *Quigley's Estate,*[14] and *Wanamaker's Estate.*[15] See also *Ewalt v. Davenhill,*[16] *Price's Estate,*[17] and *McCaskey's Estate.*[18] In *Kountz's Trusts,*[19] *Geissler v. Reading Tr. Co.,*[20] *Lilley's Estate,*[21] *Crolius v. Kramer,*[22] *Feeney's Estate,*[23] *Ledwith v. Hurst,*[24] and *Scott's Estate,*[25] the Court followed *Johnston's Estate.* In *Scott's Estate,* however, the Court admitted that: "It is not always easy to determine what was a testator's dominant purpose in so disposing of his estate as to violate the rule

long after the limits fixed by the Rule against Perpetuities. On the question whether such trusts could be sustained in part, see §§ 410.1 et seq., post.

6 196 Pa. 366, 46 Atl. 497.
7 213 Pa. 390, 62 Atl. 1103.
8 Treatise, §§ 472–476. And see a further criticism of the Pennsylvania cases in 77 Univ. Pa. Law Rev. 523.
9 248 Pa. 285, 93 Atl. 1062.
10 267 Pa. 390, 111 Atl. 234, 306 Pa. 394, 159 Atl. 874.
11 284 Pa. 90, 130 Atl. 314.

12 316 Pa. 12, 173 Atl. 324.
13 320 Pa. 112, 182 Atl. 396.
14 329 Pa. 281, 198 Atl. 85.
15 335 Pa. 241, 6 Atl. 2d 852.
16 257 Pa. 385, 101 Atl. 756.
17 260 Pa. 376, 103 Atl. 893.
18 293 Pa. 497, 143 Atl. 209.
19 251 Pa. 582, 96 Atl. 1097.
20 257 Pa. 329, 101 Atl. 797.
21 272 Pa. 143, 116 Atl. 392.
22 279 Pa. 275, 123 Atl. 808.
23 293 Pa. 273, 142 Atl. 284.
24 284 Pa. 94, 130 Atl. 315.
25 301 Pa. 509, 152 Atl. 560.

against perpetuities." Moreover, where there is a "dominant purpose" to create remote limitations, it does not follow that the testator would have wished the whole disposition to fail, because the "dominant purpose" could not be carried out. And now in *Quigley's Estate,* the Court appears inclined to abandon the notion of a "dominant purpose" and to adopt as its guide the presumed intention of the testator. Cf. *Friday's Estate,*[26] and *Wanamaker's Estate.* In *Feeney's Estate,* the Court seems to have been in error in deciding even that the remainder was too remote.[27]

§ **249.3. Illinois Cases.** *Eldred* v. *Meek.*[1] Here property was given to three of the testator's grandsons by name upon their becoming, respectively, twenty-five years of age; subsequent clauses provided that if any of the grandsons died without leaving children their shares should go to the survivor and survivors upon their reaching twenty-five, and then another clause provided that if any grandson should die before arriving at twenty-five leaving children, then such children becoming twenty-five years of age respectively should take their father's share. This gift to the children of the grandsons upon their attaining twenty-five was too remote, but the Court went on and held that the gifts to the grandsons were bad also. The Court rely on *Johnston's Estate* and *Lawrence* v. *Smith,*[2] and on New York decisions under statutes. *Eldred* v. *Meek* has been followed in *Pitzel* v. *Schneider.*[3] Cf. *Reid* v. *Voorhees.*[4]

§ **249.4.** The Supreme Court of Illinois has often distinct-

---

[26] 313 Pa. 328, 336, 170 Atl. 123, 126. But see Colladay's Estate, 32 D. & C. 644. And see also 37 Pa. B. A. Q. 37 (1938).

[27] See 51 Harv. Law Rev. 638, 647; § 206, ante.

§ **249.3.** [1] 183 Ill. 26, 55 N. E. 536.

[2] § 249.5, post.

[3] 216 Ill. 87, 74 N. E. 779; and also in Dime Savings Co. v. Watson, 254 Ill. 419, 427, 98 N. E. 777, 779; Barrett v. Barrett, 255 Ill. 332, 99 N. E. 625; Milliken National Bank v. Wilson, 343 Ill. 55, 174 N. E. 857; Keefer v. McCloy, 344 Ill. 454, 176 N. E. 743; Foley v. Nally, 351 Ill. 194, 184 N. E. 316; Northern Trust Co. v. Porter, 368 Ill. 256, 13 N. E. 2d 487; Johnston v. Cosby, 374 Ill. 407, 29 N. E. 2d 608.

[4] 216 Ill. 236, 74 N. E. 804.

ly recognized that a limitation is not void because it is followed by a remote limitation ;[1] but the Court distinguished the
cases mentioned in the preceding section on the ground that
where provisions in themselves valid are inextricably connected with invalid provisions the whole must fail. Undoubtedly this is a possibility,[2] but it is submitted that the application of such a doctrine in those cases went too far.[3]

§ 249.5. *Lawrence* v. *Smith*[1] is not a case of prior and subsequent limitations, but may conveniently be discussed here.
The testator gave all his estate to trustees in trust to pay
annuities to certain persons, including two sons and a daughter; to pay to each of three of his daughters, A., B., and C.,
$600 annually during her life; on her death to pay to each
of her children $300 annually until such child reached twen-
ty-five; and then to pay it $10,000. After the payment of all
these sums, he directed the principal of his estate to be paid
and conveyed to his grandchildren then living. The testator
died in 1892, leaving property, real and personal, worth about
$90,000. He left four daughters and three sons,—one of the
latter was in prison under a life sentence and was expressly
disinherited in the will. His three daughters aforesaid, A.,
B., and C., who at his death were respectively fifty-three, fifty-
two, and forty-nine years, had among them five children, the
oldest of whom was twenty-four and the youngest nine. His
other children, all of whom were "of mature age," had no
issue.

§ 249.6. The Court held that the final gift over was too
remote, and they also seem to have been of the opinion that

§ 249.4. [1] Howe v. Hodge, 152
Ill. 252, 38 N. E. 1083. Chapman
v. Cheney, 191 Ill. 574, 61 N. E.
363. Reid v. Voorhees, 216 Ill.
236, 74 N. E. 804. Johnson v.
Preston, 226 Ill. 447, 80 N. E.
1001. Quinlan v. Wickman, 233
Ill. 39, 84 N. E. 38. Moroney v.
Haas, 277 Ill. 467, 115 N. E. 648.
Beal v. Higgins, 299 Ill. 229, 132
N. E. 542. Aldendifer v. Wylie,
306 Ill. 426, 138 N. E. 143. Easton v. Hall, 323 Ill. 397, 154 N. E.
216.

[2] Cf. White v. Allen, 76 Conn.
185, 56 Atl. 519; Lepard v. Clapp,
80 Conn. 29, 66 Atl. 780; Russell
v. Hartley, 83 Conn. 654, 659, 78
Atl. 320, 322.

[3] See Kales, Estates, §§ 705–
710.

§ 249.5. [1] 163 Ill. 149, 45 N. E.
259, affirming Smith v. Lawrence,
27 Chic. L. News 155.

the provisions for payment to the grandchildren until each reached twenty-five, and then the payment to each of $10,000 were good so far as they concerned those living at the testator's death; but that if any children had been born, after the death of the testator, to A., B., or C., no one of such children could have taken the $10,000. These determinations seem of unimpeachable correctness. The gifts to the testator's grandchildren were clearly separable, and one born in fact in the testator's life could take, though one afterwards could not.[1] But the Court came to the conclusion that inasmuch as the testator's intentions towards all possible children of A., B., and C. could not be carried out, the trust should not be carried out for those who actually existed.

§ **249.7.** This decision is incomprehensible. The testator has by his will given $10,000 apiece to five of his grandchildren, and the Court takes it away. For what reason? Is it because the gift is against public policy as too remote? or is it because, under the circumstances, the testator would not have wished them to take it? It is not for the first reason: the Court assumes and admits that the gifts are in themselves perfectly good. It must be, then, for the second reason, —that the testator would not have wished these grandchildren to take. Let us see how it would have presented itself to the testator on his deathbed, under all the circumstances. Suppose some one had said to him: "You have five grandchildren, their ages running from twenty-four to nine. They are the children of three of your daughters, the youngest of whom is forty-nine. You have given to each of the children of your three daughters $10,000; the gift is good for all those grandchildren that you know; but if any grandchild is born after your death, it cannot take. The alternatives are these: If the will stands, these five grandchildren will get $10,000 apiece, and the rest of your property will go to all of your heirs,—that is, your children—and they, including the convict, will get about $6,000 apiece. If you destroy the will, none of the grandchildren will get a dollar, but your children, including the convict, will get over $12,000 apiece. These

§ 249.6. [1] See § 389, post.

(legally) possible grandchildren will get nothing either way.
There is no time to make a new will. Shall the present will
go into the fire or not?" Is it possible to doubt what the testator's answer would have been? Is it conceivable that he
would desire to deprive the grandchildren, whom he has
known and loved, of his bounty because he could not do the
same for some possibility whose chance of existence was a
thousand to one? Such pedantic fanaticism of uniformity in
a testator is incredible. The cases which establish the doctrine
of independent gifts are, of course, entirely opposed to the
doctrine of *Lawrence* v. *Smith*. The Court was probably influenced by the cases under the New York Revised Statutes.[1]
It is much to be regretted that a learned Court, walking in the
freedom of the Common Law, should put its neck under the
yoke of the New York Statutes, or adopt arbitrary and irra-
tional assumptions as to what testators would have intended
if they had known that their full intentions could not be carried out.[2]

§ 249.8. **New Jersey Cases.** In *Hewitt* v. *Green*,[1] a testator bequeathed $100,000 to his executors in trust to pay cer-
tain annuities out of the income; the rest of the income to be
accumulated for his grandchildren, but when each grandchild
should reach twenty-one the interest on his share to be paid
to him until the youngest grandchild should reach twenty-
five, when the principal should be distributed among the
grandchildren then living, the share which any grandchild
would have taken if then living to go to any issue he might
have left at his death. The gift of the principal was, of
course, too remote. Stevenson, V. C., said: "The limits of
this opinion already too wide will not permit the minute discussion of this provision for the distribution of accumulated
income and accruing income to adult grandchildren, or to
consider the various questions in regard to that provision
which might be raised. The whole matter may, I think, be
disposed of by the proposition that the gift of income to the
grandchildren is a mere incident to the tying up of the

§ 249.7. [1] See § 249.2, ante.    § 249.8. [1] 77 N. J. Eq. 345, 363,
[2] See Kales, Estates, § 707.    77 Atl. 25, 33.

$100,000 of the principal for their benefit when the youngest member of the class has reached the age of twenty-five years. When the main gift falls, the incidental gift falls with it." Disposing of the gift of income to the grandchildren when they reach twenty-one by calling it incidental, seems a rather rough and ready way of dealing with the question. *Hewitt* v. *Green* was followed in *Graves* v. *Graves*,[2] *Glock* v. *Glock*,[3] and *Central Hanover Bank* v. *Helme*.[4] But the application of the doctrine there stated is now greatly limited in New Jersey. See *McGill* v. *Trust Co.*,[5] in which the Court said: "It is true that there are more than a few authorities holding that where a trust is created with an ultimate gift of corpus thereunder and prior estates for years or lives, if the ultimate gift be too remote and hence invalid, the prior estates are invalid also, on the theory that it is to be conclusively presumed the ultimate gift was testator's main purpose or object and the prior estates merely incidental; and these authorities are reflected in some of the text books or the text of some of the digest writers. Such a holding is, however, utterly opposed to the rationale of the matter, and the weight of authority is overwhelmingly the other way."

§ 249.9. In most of the American cases, where particular limitations, not in themselves too remote, are held to be rendered invalid by the remoteness of subsequent provisions, this is done on the ground of the supposed intent of the testator that the partial disposition should not stand if the subsequent disposition of the principal failed. When it is said that the partial disposition should not stand, because the result would be unjust or would violate the testator's general scheme, or because the valid dispositions are inseparable from, or incidental to, the invalid disposition, the result seems to depend ultimately on what the Court supposes the testator would

2 94 N. J. Eq. 268, 120 Atl. 420.

3 110 N. J. Eq. 477, 160 Atl. 339.

4 121 N. J. Eq. 249, 190 Atl. 53.

5 94 N. J. Eq. 657, 672, 121 Atl. 760, 767, 96 N. J. Eq. 331, 125 Atl. 108. See also Penn Co. v. Robb, 118 N. J. Eq. 529, 180 Atl. 410, aff'd 123 N. J. Eq. 232, 196 Atl. 741; Camden Safe Dep. & Trust Co. v. Scott, 121 N. J. Eq. 366, 189 Atl. 653; Clark v. Union County Trust Co., 127 N. J. Eq. 221, 12 Atl. 2d 365.

have wished.[1] Under this heading fall the Illinois and New Jersey cases above cited, the Connecticut cases referred to in § 249.4, note 2, *ante,* and the Pennsylvania cases above cited, according to the doctrine adopted in *Quigley's Estate.*[2]

In the Missouri cases, however, the Courts seem to lay down a rule of law that the particular limitations are rendered void by the illegality of the subsequent limitations. The grounds and limits of this rule are not clear; but apparently it applies without consideration of what the testator would have wished in the particular case. It is submitted that any such rule of law is contrary to principle and to the weight of authority.

In some cases where limitations have been held void for remoteness, the Courts have treated as invalid other limitations, not prior to the void limitations, but concerning different property, or even have declared the whole will void, on the ground that the testator would have wished the whole to fail if a part could not stand. *Beatty* v. *Stanley.*[3] *Anderson* v. *Menefee.*[4] *Lawrence* v. *Smith*[5] seems to be such a case.[6]

§ 249.9. [1] See Estate of Whitney, 176 Cal. 12, 19, 167 Pac. 399, 402; Wanamaker's Estate, 335 Pa. 241, 6 Atl. 2d 852; Simes, Fut. Int., § 529.

[2] 329 Pa. 281, 198 Atl. 85, and confirmed in Wanamaker's Estate, ubi sup. See also Buck v. Tolar, 146 So. Car. 294, 144 S. E. 1; Woodruff Oil Co. v. Yarborough, 144 So. Car. 18, 142 S. E. 50; and § 397, note 3, post. In Reed v. McIlvain, 113 Md. 140, 77 Atl. 329, the invalidity of the particular limitations was conceded by the defendants.

[3] 298 Ill. 444, 131 N. E. 687.

[4] 174 S. W. 904 (Tex. C. A.).

[5] 163 Ill. 149, 45 N. E. 259, § 249.5, ante.

[6] It is impossible to do better than guess what a testator's wishes would have been in a situation which he did not anticipate. The American Courts which attempt to make such a guess, endeavor to aid themselves by the use of varying and uncertain rules, which in effect are rules of construction. The resulting situation is often very unsatisfactory, as, for instance, in Illinois (§§ 249.3–249.7, ante). It would seem better, except in very clear cases, to carry out the testator's expressed intentions as far as possible, and allow the remaining interests to go as the law provides. See Wilmington Trust Co. v. Wilmington Trust Co. 180 Atl. 597, 186 Atl. 903 (Del. Ch. Decree modified on other grounds in 15

**§ 250. Void Conditional Gift Over.** If a contingent event is too remote to serve as a condition precedent for a future estate, may it not yet serve as a condition subsequent to determine a present estate? Or, in other words, may not a contingent clause purporting to be a conditional limitation, though, on account of remoteness, inoperative to take effect as a conditional limitation creating a new estate, yet serve as a contingent termination of the prior estate? If the prior estate is for life or years, then it may be determinable by a contingent event, which yet is too remote to serve as the condition precedent of a subsequent estate. Such contingency may operate purely as a condition subsequent which in effect creates a special limitation of the preceding estate.[1] And if it is clear that the settlor or testator intended that on the occurrence of the event the prior estate should determine, whether the subsequent estate took effect or not, then on the happening of the event the prior estate will come to an end, although the subsequent estate is too remote.[2] But it will take clear language to show an intention to have the determining limitation taken separately from the remote gift. "When you find a forfeiture clause associated with a gift over, is it not reasonable to read them together?"[3] If the prior

---

Atl. 2d 153); Chenoweth v. Bullitt, 224 Ky 698, 716, 6 S. W. 2d 1061, 1068; Ligget v. Fidelity Trust Co., 274 Ky. 387, 118 S. W. 2d 720; Gump's Estate, 107 Pac. 2d 17 (Cal.); Amer. Law Inst. Restatement, Property, Chap. 16, Introductory Notes, and §§ 228, 229; Restatement, Trusts, § 65; 1 Bogert, Trusts, § 214, pp. 642–644; 38 Harv. Law Rev. 379; 77 Univ. Pa. Law Rev. 523; 14 Tex. Law Rev. 273. In England there are very few cases in which it has been contended that the invalidity of a subsequent limitation should affect the validity of a precedent limitation, and appar-

ently no cases in which such a contention has been successful. See Gooding v. Read, 21 Beav. 478, 4 De G. M. & G. 510; Re Wise, [1896] 1 Ch. 281. As to the effect of the remoteness of a power or an appointment, see §§ 531–537, post.

**§ 250.** [1] See Adams v. Adams, [1892] 1 Ch. (C. A.) 369, 376; and § 32, ante.

[2] See Lewis, Perp. 173.

[3] Hodgson v. Halford, 11 Ch. D. 959, 963. 2 Jarm. Wills (7th ed.) 1415, 1430. See Doe v. Eyre, 5 C. B. 713, and the discussion of that case in §§ 783–788, post;

estate be a fee simple the void conditional limitation cannot, it is submitted, thus operate as a contingent termination of the prior estate. The limitation purporting to be over to a third person cannot be a common-law condition, for that can be taken advantage of only by the grantor or his heirs by way of re-entry; and no right of re-entry in the heirs can be found in an express limitation over to a third person.[4] And except by a condition, the only way in which a fee can now be cut short is by the creation of a new estate through a conditional limitation. Since the Statute *Quia Emptores* there can be no fee with a contingent termination, apart from a condition or conditional limitation.[5] Therefore, if an estate is given to A. and his heirs until B.'s (unborn) children reach twenty-five, and then to such children, it cannot be contended that although the estate to B.'s children is too remote, yet A.'s estate has come to an end when B.'s children reach twenty-five.[6]

## 13. EFFECT OF REMOTE INTERESTS ON SUBSEQUENT LIMITATIONS

**§ 251. Vested Interests.** When an interest is vested it is

Boal v. Metropolitan Museum, 292 Fed. 299, 300, 303, 305, 298 Fed. 894, 906; 1 Tiffany, Real Prop. (3d ed.), § 386; Amer. Law Inst. Restatement, Property, § 229, and App. therein referred to.

[4] And such a right of re-entry would be too remote, in the case supposed. § 299, post. But it is otherwise in America. § 304, post.

[5] See §§ 31–41.1, ante. However, determinable estates in personalty, similar to determinable fees, seem to be possible. Re Chardon, [1928] Ch. 464, §§ 87.1, 90, note 1, ante. And in the United States determinable fees

generally are allowed, §§ 38–41, ante, and may be followed by conditional limitations. § 14, note 8, ante. Whether the estate preceding the void conditional limitation is a determinable fee, in a jurisdiction where such an estate is possible, is a question of construction. See Amer. Law Inst. Restatement, Property, § 229; and § 788, note 2, post.

[6] Where determinable fees are allowed, this reasoning does not apply; but as a matter of construction the fee would not be held to be terminated. § 778, note 2, post. On limitations after equitable fees, see §§ 327, 327.1, post.

[G. R. P.]

never too remote, although preceded by other interests which
are too remote. In the first and second editions it was said:
"Thus if an estate is given (1) to A. for life, (2) to A.'s unborn child for life, (3) to the child of such unborn child for
life, (4) to B. in fee, B.'s estate is good, although the remainder to the child of A.'s unborn child is too remote. So although the later interest is not vested at its creation, yet if it
must become vested within the limits fixed by the Rule
against Perpetuities, it will be good." But this is incorrect.
A vested estate is an estate which is subject to no condition
precedent except the termination of the precedent estates.[1]
In the case put the estate to B. is subject to the conditions
precedent of (1) the death of A., (2) the death of A.'s unborn child, (3) the death of the child of A.'s unborn child.
A. and A.'s unborn child have estates for life, but the gift
to the child of A.'s unborn child being remote, said child has
no estate; and therefore as B.'s estate is subject not only to
the termination of the life estates of A. and of A.'s unborn
child, but also to the contingency of the death of an unborn
person who has no estate, the estate given to B. is not a remainder but an executory devise, which takes effect at too
remote a period; and so it was held in *Re Mortimer*.[2]

§ 251. [1] See §§ 8, 101, ante.
[2] [1905] 2 Ch. (C. A.) 502. A note by the author, 23 Law Quart. Rev. 127, is wrong. See Re Backhouse, [1905] 2 Ch. 51; Re Ramadge's Settlement, [1919] 1 I. R. 205; § 258.1, post; Re Benyon-Windsor, 143 L. T. 178; 1 Jarm. Wills (7th ed.) 324–328. In Re Canning's Trusts, [1936] Ch. 309, and Re Coleman, [1936] Ch. 528, these cases and those cited in the next section are discussed, and it is said that a limitation is invalidated by the remoteness of a preceding limitation only where it is dependent on the preceding limitation. The opinions, however, cast little light on the reasons for holding a subsequent limitation to be dependent on the preceding limitation in any particular case. The question does not seem to be treated as one of intent. (See also Macpherson v. Maund, 58 Com. L. R. 341 (Aust.).) In the Canning and Coleman cases, the limitations which were invalid for remoteness were discretionary trusts. These discretionary trusts, however, were in effect powers of appointment or disposition (see § 246, note 2, ante). Whether such powers are exercisable by the trustees or by a beneficiary, the invalidity of the power does not affect the validity of the lim-

§ 252. **Life Interests to Living Persons.** As all life interests to persons now in being must take effect, if at all, within lives in being, all such interests would seem to be good,[1] although preceded by interests that are too remote. Thus suppose personalty is bequeathed to A., and if A. dies without issue then to B., and if B. dies without issue then to C. for life, and on C.'s death to D., B.'s interest is too remote; but although C. cannot take until both A. and B.'s issue are extinct, yet inasmuch as C.'s interest must come into possession in his lifetime, if it comes at all, it would seem as if it were not too remote; while D.'s interest, not being limited to his life, is again too remote. So if property is devised to A. for life (or for ninety-nine years if he live so long) and then to his first son (then unborn) for a like estate, followed by remote limitations, and then to C., a living person, for a like estate, the gift to C. seems not too remote. There are decisions, however, that in such a case C.'s estate would be bad. It was probably so held in *Somerville* v. *Lethbridge*,[2] though the case is too imperfectly reported for any certain conclusion.[3] And such a limitation in the case of *Beard* v. *Westcott*,

itation in default of exercise of the power or the validity of subsequent limitations. §§ 258, 535, post. See also 53 Law Quart. Rev. 13; 25 Harv. Law Rev. 1.

§ 252. [1] See Re Norton, [1911] 2 Ch. 27. But see discussion of that case in Re Hewett's Settlement, [1915] 1 Ch. 810. A gift to those of certain named persons now living who shall survive at the end of thirty years is good. Lachlan v. Reynolds, 9 Hare 796. 1 Jarm. Wills (7th ed.) 270, 300. The decision in Kirkpatrick v. Kirkpatrick, 112 Kan. 314, 211 Pac. 146, contra, seems to be due to an oversight. See § 378, post. So if a trust is created to last for twenty-five years, but it nevertheless is to come to an end at the death of survivor of living persons, the distribution at the termination of the trust cannot be too remote. Cunningham v. Fidelity Nat. Bank, 186 Okla. 429, 98 Pac. 2d 57.

[2] 6 T. R. 213.

[3] In 6 T. R. 213, the devise by the testator is said to have been in trust for the use of A. "for the term of ninety-nine years if he should so long live, and after that term to the use of the first, second, third, and fourth sons of" A. "and the issue male of their bodies lawfully begotten for the like term of ninety-nine years, as they should be in seniority of birth, and in default of such issue male in him or them, then to the use of his kinsman" B. "and

after having been held good by the Court of Common Pleas,[4] was adjudged bad by the Court of King's Bench;[5] and the decision of the Court of King's Bench was approved by Lord St. Leonards, C., in *Monypenny* v. *Dering,*[6] and by Lord Romilly, M. R., in *Thatcher's Trusts.*[7] *Burley* v. *Evelyn,*[8] before Vice-Chancellor Shadwell, is to the same effect; and so appears to be *Palmer* v. *Holford.*[9] *Re Hewett's Settlement*[10]

the issue male of his body lawfully begotten for the like term of ninety-nine years," and then over. The devise is stated in the same terms in Southey v. Somerville, 13 Ves. 486, 487; but the certificate of the judges says that the first son of A. would take an estate for ninety-nine years, ·determinable with his life. Sugden, in a note to his edition of Gilbert on Uses, 269, says that successive terms of ninety-nine years, determinable on their lives, were given to A. and to his first, second, third, and fourth sons, and the issue male of their bodies; and in Beard v. Westcott, 5 Taunt. 393, 403, 404, where the interest of each successive taker was limited to an estate for ninety-nine years, determinable on his life, it was said by Serjeant Manley, in argument, that the devise "appears to have been penned by the same hand" as that in Somerville v. Lethbridge. It would seem, therefore, probable that all the issue were to take as purchasers, and that perhaps B. also was to have only an estate for ninety-nine years, determinable by his death. The Court of King's Bench certified to the Court of Chancery that A. took an estate for ninety-nine years determinable by his death, and

then his first son an estate for ninety-nine years determinable by his death, and that the other limitations were void. If the devise to B. (a living person) was determinable by his death, it was good in itself, and was only rendered bad by its following limitations bad for remoteness.

[4] 5 Taunt. 393. Quære were there not here separable limitations?

[5] 5 B. & Ald. 801.

[6] 2 De G. M. & G. 145.

[7] 26 Beav. 365.

[8] 16 Sim. 290.

[9] 4 Russ. 403. In this case personal property was bequeathed in trust to accumulate the income for twenty-eight years, and then to pay the fund to the children of A. who were then living, and if no children of A. were then living, then to the children of B. who were then living, and if no children of B. were then living, then to B. if he was living; and in case of B.'s not being then alive, there were other gifts over. The Master of the Rolls, Sir John Leach, said that the gift to the children of A. was too remote, "and the gifts over, not being to take effect until after the same period, which is too remote, are necessarily void also." It does not appear whether it was nec-

adopts the same doctrine on the authority of *Thatcher's Trusts*
and the earlier cases above mentioned in this section.

§ **253.** *Somerville* v. *Lethbridge* and *Beard* v. *Westcott*
were cases from Chancery, and we have merely the certificates
of the judges, without any reasons for their decision. All
that is said in *Palmer* v. *Holford* on the point in question is
given in the note to the preceding section. *Thatcher's Trusts*
goes entirely upon *Beard* v. *Westcott;* and in *Burley* v.
*Evelyn* the counsel conceded that a limitation subsequent to
a remote limitation was invalid. The reasons and authorities,
therefore, for the doctrine that a life interest given to a living person is bad if it follows an interest too remote are to be
found in the argument of Sir Edward Sugden in *Beard* v.
*Westcott*,[1] and his judgment, when Chancellor, in *Monypenny*
v. *Dering*.[2] And with all respect for so distinguished a name,
it must be said that his reasons are not satisfactory, and the
authorities cited by him are not in point.

§ **254.** In *Beard* v. *Westcott*,[1] Sir Edward Sugden said, as
counsel, that life interests to living persons were void "because it was the intention of the testator that those limitations should take effect only in case the previous limitations
were capable of taking effect, and had failed;" and in *Monypenny* v. *Dering*[2] he said that in *Beard* v. *Westcott* the Court
of King's Bench "held that the gift over was void, not because it was not within the line of perpetuity, but expressly
on the ground I have adverted to, namely, that that limitation over was never intended by the testator to take effect,
unless the persons whom he intended to take under the previous limitation would, if they had been alive, been capable
of enjoying the estate, and that he did not intend that the

essary to pass upon this latter
point or not.

10 [1915] 1 Ch. 810. See Re
Abbott, [1893] 1 Ch. 54, 57; Re
Davey, [1915] 1 Ch. (C. A.) 837.
See also remarks in Re Canning's
Trusts, [1936] Ch. 309, and Re
Coleman, [1936] Ch. 528, com-
mented on in § 251, note 2, ante.

§ **253.** 1 5 B. & Ald. 801, 808.
2 De G. M. & G. 145, 180 et seq.
See Gilb. Uses (Sugd. ed.) 270,
note, et seq.; 1 Jarm. Willis (5th
ed.) 254, 255; Marsden, Perp. 291,
292.

§ **254.** 1 5 B. & Ald. 808.
2 2 De G. M. & G. 182.

estate should wait for persons to take in a given event, where
the person to take was actually in existence but could not
take."[3]  But the imputation of such an intent to a testator
seems unwarranted.  Take the case suggested at the beginning of § 252, *ante,*—personalty bequeathed to A., and if A.
dies without issue to B., and if B. dies without issue then to
C. for life.  Suppose the testator had been told: "Your bequest to B. is bad; but if, in fact, A. and B. both die before
C. without issue, would you like C. to take?  There is no legal
objection to his doing so, should you wish it."  What reason
is there to suppose that the testator would have answered
in the negative?  If the precise contingency has happened on
which he directed C. to take, why should it be supposed that
he does not wish C. to take simply because another bequest
cannot take effect?  It is not as if C. would step into B.'s
place, and take what the testator meant B. to have, for C. is
to have nothing until B. has died without issue.  The testator
did not mean that the bequest to C. should take effect until
the families of A. and B. had run out, and it is not suggested
that it shall take effect until they have run out.  But when
they have run out, why should it not take effect?  This supposed intention is not merely an arbitrary assumption, but
one directly the opposite of the probable intention.

§ **255.**  The cases cited by Sir Edward Sugden in *Beard* v.
*Westcott*[1] as authorities in support of his position are *Alexander* v. *Alexander,*[2] *Robinson* v. *Hardcastle,*[3] *Routledge* v.
*Dorril,*[4] *Brudenell* v. *Elwes.*[5]  They are cases where there had
been an excess in the execution of powers.  In *Alexander* v.
*Alexander,* under a power to appoint to children, the fund
was appointed to A., a daughter, for life, remainder to her
children living at her death, but on default of such children

[3] And see further his language
on pp. 181, 182, to the effect that
the testator in Beard v. Westcott had an actual intent that
the gift in question should not
take effect after a gap in the enjoyment caused by the invalidity
of the preceding limitation.

§ **255.** [1] 5 B. & Ald. 808.
[2] 2 Ves. Sr. 640, 643.
[3] 2 Bro. C. C. 22, 344, 2 T. R.
241, 380, 781.
[4] 2 Ves. Jr. 357.
[5] 1 East 442.

of A. then to B., another daughter. A. died leaving children.
It was held that although A.'s children were not objects of
the power, yet that B. could not take; for the appointment
was to her only on the contingency of A.'s dying without
children, which had not occurred. In the other cases there
were appointments to persons who were not objects of the
power, and then contingent appointments over to persons who
were within the power. The contingencies occurred, in fact,
within the limits required by the Rule against Perpetuities;
but as they might not have so occurred, the appointments
made dependent on them (not being life interests) were of
course too remote.[6] These cases are no authority for *Beard*
v. *Westcott* and the decisions which have followed it. In
these cases of powers, the reason why a future interest could
not take effect was either that the contingency upon which
it depended had never occurred, or that the interest might
come into possession at too remote a time. But in *Beard* v.
*Westcott* the contingency upon which the gift over depended
would have occurred, and the gift could not possibly have
taken effect at too remote a time.

§ 256. If in these cases of powers there had been an appointment to persons not objects of the power, with an appointment over to persons who were objects of the power,
and the event on which the gift over was to take effect had
been one which must have occurred, if at all, within the limits
of the Rule against Perpetuities, and which in fact had
occurred, then those cases would have been in point in *Beard*
v. *Westcott*. Such a case has occurred, and was decided by
Sir Edward Sugden himself in favor of the validity of the
limitation over. In *Crozier* v. *Crozier*,[1] a donee of a power to
appoint among his children appointed to his wife for life,
remainder to his eldest son. The Lord Chancellor of Ireland
held that during the life of the wife the property went as in
default of appointment, but that the appointment to the eldest
son in fee was good. In commenting on *Beard* v. *Westcott,* he
said he thought the decision of the Court of Common Pleas

---

6 See Reid v. Reid, 25 Beav.    511; Marsden, Perp. 258, 289.
469; Sugd. Pow. (8th ed.) 508–    § 256. 1 3 Dr. & W. 353.

was wrong, "for the consequence was that there might be a person *in esse* entitled to take according to the words of the first limitation in the will, but incapable in law, and a remainder-man *in esse* capable of taking by law, but incapable of taking under the will because the contingency has not happened, which was to determine the preceding estate."[2] It is true these were the consequences in *Beard* v. *Westcott*, but they were also the precise consequences of the decision in *Crozier* v. *Crozier*. There was the wife, "a person *in esse* entitled to take according to the words of the first limitation but incapable in law;" and there was also the eldest son, "a remainder-man *in esse* capable of taking by law but incapable of taking under the will, because the contingency had not happened which was to determine the preceding estate," i. e. the death of the wife. These consequences were not deemed objectionable in *Crozier* v. *Crozier*: why should they have been in *Beard* v. *Westcott?*[3]

§ **257.** The doctrine that a vested limitation or a limitation for life to a living person is void if it follows an interest which is too remote, cannot be traced clearly beyond *Beard* v. *Westcott*, in which the Courts of Common Pleas and of King's Bench came to opposite conclusions. As it introduces an arbitrary element into the Rule against Perpetuities, and defeats the intentions of testators without any pretext of public policy, under the false pretence supporting them, it is submitted that it ought not to be followed in America.[1]

---

[2] P. 369.

[3] In Armstrong v. West, 8 Ir. Jur., N. S. 144, the limitation over might have taken effect at too remote a period. The same was true of all the limitations that were declared invalid in Re Manning's Trusts, 49 Ir. L. T. R. 143; Re Benjamin, [1926] Vict. 378, 397; and Re Zahel, [1931] Queensl. 1. As to Willson v. Cobley, [1870] W. N. 46, see 48 L. T. 388.

§ **257.** [1] Mr. Lewis, Perp. 421,

661, states distinctly the doctrine here maintained as law. Singularly enough, however, he notices in this connection the decision of Beard v. Westcott, only in the Court of Common Pleas, 5 Taunt. 393, and not in the Court of King's Bench, 5 B. & Ald. 801. See 1 Tiffany, Real Prop. (3d ed.), § 414; 1 Jarm. Wills (7th ed.) 324–328; 51 Harv. Law Rev. 638, 657.

**§ 258. Interests subject to a Power.** As the existence of a power does not affect the vesting of a limitation in default of appointment,[1] a power under which only appointments that may be too remote can be made, will not invalidate limitations in default of appointment.[2] And if under a good power no appointment or a good appointment is made, the fact that a bad appointment might have been made will not render the gift in default of appointment bad.[3]

**§ 258.1.** In *Re Ramadge's Settlement*,[1] the limitations under the marriage settlement of A. were in effect to A. for life, then to his younger sons for their lives, and after their deaths to such of his daughters as should then be living, for their lives, and after the death of the survivor of the younger children to his eldest son. The Court held the gifts to the daughters bad as taking effect on too remote a contingency, and remarked that the fact that the gift to them was for their lives was immaterial, referring to *Thatcher's Trusts.* But that case was not in point, for none of the children in *Re Ramadge* were in being at the date of the settlement, so that the life estates to the daughters were clearly too remote, and moreover all the preceding limitations were held good. The Court then held the gift to the eldest son void because expectant and dependent on remote prior limitations. That gift, which was not for life only, took effect on too remote a contingency. If the provisions for the daughters had not been invalid, it seems that the limitation to the eldest son would have been valid as a remainder vesting at A.'s death, subject only to the life interests of the younger children. On the supposition that the limitation to the eldest son would have been vested, if the preceding limitations had been valid, the case is similar to *Re Mortimer.*[2]

---

§ 258. [1] See §§ 112, 112.1, ante.

[2] Wollaston v. King, L. R. 8 Eq. 165. Re Abbott, [1893] 1 Ch. 54. Re Canning's Trusts, [1936] 1 Ch. 309. Re Coleman, [1936] 1 Ch. 528. Re Hay, [1932] N. Ir. 215. See Re Hobson's Will, [1907] Vict. 724, 736, 737; §§ 251, note 2, ante, 535, post.

[3] Re Bowles, [1905] 1 Ch. 371. Re Davies & Kent's Contract, [1910] 2 Ch. (C. A.) 35.

**§ 258.1.** [1] [1919] 1 I. R. 205.

[2] [1905] 2 Ch. (C. A.) 502, § 251, ante.

## 14. CONFLICT OF LAWS

**§ 259. Differences in Law.** When from statutory changes or otherwise,[1] there is a different law on the subject of remoteness in one jurisdiction from that which prevails in another, questions may arise under the Conflict of Laws.

**§ 259.1. Real Estate.** When the title to land situated in a certain jurisdiction is transferred, either *inter vivos* or by will, whether the transfer be direct or in trust, and whatever be the domicil of the grantor, testator, grantee, devisee, trustee, or *cestui que trust*, the transfer cannot be on limitations or trusts which the law of that jurisdiction considers too remote, but can be on limitations or trusts which such law does not consider too remote, whatever be the law of any other jurisdiction.[1] And as the true rule is that immovables are governed by the *lex rei sitæ*, whether they are technically real estate or not, the remoteness of a conveyance or devise of a term for years is to be determined by the law of the place where the land lies.[2]

§ 259. [1] As to which, see Appendices B, C, and D, §§ 686–773, post.

§ 259.1. [1] White v. Howard, 52 Barb. 294, 46 N. Y. 144. Knox v. Jones, 47 N. Y. 389. Brewer v. Brewer, 11 Hun 147, sub nom. Brewer v. Penniman, 72 N. Y. 603. Draper v. Harvard College, 57 How. Pr. 269. Hobson v. Hale, 95 N. Y. 588. Lee v. Tower, 124 N. Y. 370, 26 N. E. 943. Butler v. Green, 65 Hun 99, 19 N. Y. S. 890. Trowbridge v. Metcalf, 5 N. Y. A. D. 318, 39 N. Y. S. 241, sub nom. Trowbridge v. Trowbridge, 158 N. Y. 682, 52 N. E. 1126. Bishop v. Bishop, 257 N. Y. 40, 177 N. E. 302, 258 N. Y. 216, 179 N. E. 391. Woolley v. Hutchins, 114 Misc. 11, 186 N. Y. S. 769. Fischer v. Steuart, 104 N. J. L. 78. Ford v. Ford, 70 Wis. 19, 33 N. W. 188; 72 Wis. 621, 40 N. W. 502. Miller v. Douglass, 192 Wis. 486, 213 N. W. 320. Penfield v. Tower, 1 N. Dak. 216, 46 N. W. 413. See Fellows v. Miner, 119 Mass. 541; Wheeler v. Fellowes, 52 Conn. 238; Clarke's Appeal, 70 Conn. 195, 39 Atl. 155, 178 U. S. 186, 20 S. Ct. 873, 44 L. E. 1028; Chaplin, Suspension of Alienation (1st ed.), §§ 517–522; Amer. Law Inst. Restatement, Confl. of L., §§ 218, 241, 249. Cf. Mount v. Tuttle, 183 N. Y. 358, 364, 76 N. E. 873, 874.

[2] So held by Lord Selborne, C., in Freke v. Carbery, L. R. 16 Eq. 461. And in Re Moses, [1908] 2 Ch. 235. See Duncan v. Lawson, 41 Ch. D. 394; Goods of Gentili, Ir. R. 9 Eq. 541; De Fogassieras v. Duport, 11 L. R. Ir. 123; Dicey, Confl. of L. (5th ed.) 58; Amer.

**§ 259.2.** In *Ellis* v. *Maxwell*,[1] an English testator directed the rents of his Irish estates to be accumulated and "become a part of his personal estate." The direction for accumulation was in violation of the Thellusson Act.[2] It was held that the rents of the estates could be accumulated as directed, the Act not applying to Ireland, but that the income of the accumulated rents could not.

**§ 260. Personal Property.** Direct future limitations of personalty by deed are not allowed in England or in North Carolina,[1] but future limitations of personalty can be everywhere created by deed through the means of a trust.

**§ 260.1. Transfer Inter Vivos.** Questions arising under the Conflict of Laws concerning conveyances of personalty *inter vivos* present great theoretical difficulties. For whereas, in bequests, the law of the testator's domicil is undoubtedly that to which reference must in the first place be made,[1] it is very doubtful what is the proper law to apply in cases of transfers *inter vivos*.[2] There are but few cases of a transfer *inter vivos* where a question as to the Conflict of Laws on remoteness has actually arisen.

**§ 261. Heywood v. Heywood.**[1] Here upon the marriage in Ireland of a domiciled Englishman to the daughter of a

Law Inst. Restatement, Confl. of L., § 249, Comment d; 2 Beale, Confl. of L., §§ 208, 249, 303.5. The contrary was decided in Despard v. Churchill, 53 N. Y. 192, and in Craig v. Craig, 140 Md. 322, 117 Atl. 256, but the English and Irish decisions seem preferable. Cf. Chatfield v. Berchtoldt, L. R. 7 Ch. 192; Macpherson v. Stewart, 28 L. J. Ch. 177; 32 L. T. R. 143.

**§ 259.2.** [1] 12 Beav. 104.

[2] 39 & 40 Geo. III., c. 98.

**§ 260.** [1] §§ 78, 92, ante.

**§ 260.1.** [1] Cf. Hewitt v. Green, 77 N. J. Eq. 345, 362, 366, 77 Atl.

25, 32, 34. See §§ 263–263.3, post.

[2] Dicey, Confl. of L. (5th ed.), Rules 152–154, pp. 608–627. 2 Beale, Confl. of L., §§ 255–262, 294–299. Goodrich, Confl. of L. (2d ed.), §§ 149, 150, 155. 32 Columbia Law Rev. 680. 44 Harv. Law Rev. 161. 45 Harv. Law Rev. 969. See Robb v. Washington and Jefferson College, 103 N. Y. A. D. 327, 93 N. Y. S. 92, 185 N. Y. 485, 78 N. E. 359; Hutchison v. Ross, 262 N. Y. 381, 187 N. E. 65. Cf. Am. Law Inst. Restatement, Confl. of L., §§ 257, 258, 261, 262, 294, 297, 348–352.

**§ 261.** [1] 29 Beav. 9.

domiciled Irishman, in accordance with the terms of the marriage settlement, which was drawn and executed in Ireland,
£3,000, Irish currency, were paid to the trustees of the settlement by the bride's father, to accumulate during the lives of
the husband and wife. The Thellusson Act[2] provides that
accumulation under a settlement shall not continue longer
than the life of the settlor. The Act does not extend to Ireland. The Master of the Rolls held that the accumulation
was good at least during the life of the husband. He said
that if the husband was to be regarded as the settlor, accumulation during his life was lawful under the Thellusson Act,
and that if the settlement was by the bride's father, it "must
be considered as an Irish settlement by a domiciled Irishman," in which case it was not subject to the Thellusson Act.
Regarding the bride's father as settlor, the settlor was an Irishman, the marriage took place in Ireland, the settlement was
drawn and executed in Ireland, and the money was paid to
the trustees in Ireland. It does not seem clear to which of
these circumstances it is due that the case was considered as
governed by Irish law. According to the English cases, a
marriage settlement is generally governed by the law of the
matrimonial domicil.[3]

§ 262. Fowler's Appeal.[1] Here a resident of Chicago by
deed executed in Chicago gave certain Western railroad bonds
to a Philadelphia trust company in trust for a resident of
Colorado and her issue. The actual *situs* of the bonds does
not appear. The trust deed contained provisions for accumulation which were invalid by the laws of Pennsylvania, but
not (it was assumed) by the law of Illinois or of Colorado.

---

[2] 39 & 40 Geo. III., c. 98.

[3] Quære, does this rule apply
to the determination of the validity of a settlement? See Dicey,
Confl. of L. (5th ed.), Rule 184,
pp. 758–762, and cf. Rule 150, pp.
583–598. The matrimonial domicil means the husband's domicil
at the time of marriage, Id. p.

598. See also Hutchison v. Ross,
262 N. Y. 381, 187 N. E. 65; 2
Beale, Confl. of L., § 294; 44
Harv. Law Rev. 161, 178, 182–
186, 191–198; 13 Boston Univ.
Law Rev. 219; Amer. Law Inst.
Restatement, Confl. of L., § 294.

§ 262. [1] 125 Pa. 388, 17 Atl.
431.

It was held by the Supreme Court of Pennsylvania that the provisions for accumulation were valid.[2]

**§ 262.1. Curtis v. Curtis.**[1] Two settlors, domiciled one in New Jersey, the other in New York, executed in New Jersey an instrument creating a trust of securities. The trust property was kept in New York, but its *situs* at the date of the creation of the trust did not appear. The original trustees were the settlors. The New Jersey trustee died, and was succeeded by a New York trust company. A question arose as to the validity of provisions for accumulation, which were good in New Jersey under the common law, but bad under the New York statutes. The Court said that if both settlors had been domiciled in New Jersey, the law of that State would have governed, but that under the circumstances the law of New York governed, and the accumulations were prohibited.

**§ 262.2. Liberty National Bank v. New England Investors Shares.**[1] A Massachusetts corporation executed a deed conveying shares of stock of various corporations to a New York trust company, as trustee. It did not appear where the instrument was executed or what was the *situs* of the certificates of stock at the time of execution. The deed provided that the trust should be exclusively governed by the law of Massachusetts. It was contended that the trust was void under the New York statutes against suspension of alienation. The Court held that the validity of the trust was governed by the law of the settlor's domicil, and that under Massachusetts law its provisions were good.[2]

[2] Sed quære. See De Renne's Estate, 12 W. N. C. (Pa.) 94; § 725, post.

§ 262.1. [1] 185 N. Y. A. D. 391, 173 N. Y. S. 103. See 33 Harv. Law Rev. 17, 44 Harv. Law Rev. 161, 176.

§ 262.2. [1] 25 Fed. 2d 493 (Dist. of Mass.). See 27 Mich. Law Rev. 464; 44 Harv. Law Rev. 161, 181.

[2] See § 263.3, post. And see also Greenough v. Osgood, 235 Mass. 235, 126 N. E. 461; Bundy v. U. S. Trust Co., 257 Mass. 72, 153 N. E. 337; Swetland v. Swetland, 105 N. J. Eq. 608, 149 Atl. 50; Second National Bank v. Curie, 116 N. J. Eq. 101, 172 Atl. 560; Hutchison v. Ross, 262 N. Y. 381, 187 N. E. 65; Equitable Trust Co. v. Pratt, 117 Misc. 708, 193 N. Y. S. 152; City Bank v. Whiteing, 136 Misc. 416, 241 N. Y. S. 398; Shannon v. Irving Trust Co., 246 N. Y. A. D. 280,

**§ 263. Wills.** Coming, then, to wills: If a bequest in the will of A. who has died domiciled in State X., is given to B. who is resident in State Y., the limitations or trusts upon which the legacy is given may be too remote either by the law of X. or by the law of Y.; if they are too remote by the laws of both States, or of neither, *cadit quæstio.*

**§ 263.1.** Suppose then, *first,* that a legacy is made on limitations or trusts which are valid by the law of the testator's domicil, but are too remote by the law of the residence of the legatee or *cestui que trust.* If the legacy is direct, it will be valid; the residence of the legatee is immaterial. So if the legacy is in trust it will be good; the residence of either the trustee or the *cestui que trust* is immaterial.[1] A change of residence by the trustee or *cestui que trust* cannot affect the validity of the trust.[2]

**§ 263.2.** Suppose, *secondly,* that a legacy is given on limitations or trusts which are too remote by the law of the testator's domicil, but not by the law of the residence of the legatee. Here, according to the general rule that the law of

285 N. Y. S. 478, aff'd 275 N. Y. 95, 9 N. E. 2d 792; Miller v. Douglass, 192 Wis. 486, 506, 213 N. W. 320, 327; Wilmington Trust Co. v. Wilmington Trust Co., 186 Atl. 903, 15 Atl. 2d 153 (Del. Ch.); Land, Trusts in Confl. of L., §§ 21–23; 19 Corn. L. J. 282; 23 Corn. L. J. 624; 37 Columbia Law Rev. 125; 25 Georgetown L. J. 464; 45 Yale L. J. 438; 47 Harv. Law Rev. 350; 50 Harv. Law Rev. 1119, 1156.

**§ 263.1.** [1] Cross v. U. S. Trust Co., 131 N. Y. 330, 30 N. E. 125. Dammert v. Osborn, 140 N. Y. 30, 40, 35 N. E. 407, 410, 141 N. Y. 564, 35 N. E. 1088. Guaranty Trust Co. v. Leach, 168 Misc. 526, 5 N. Y. S. 2d 628. National City Bank v. Smith, 87 N. Y. L. J.

3373 (June 15th, 1932). See Bishop v. Bishop, 257 N. Y. 40, 177 N. E. 302, 258 N. Y. 216, 179 N. E. 391; De Renne's Estate, 12 W. N. C. (Pa.) 94; Land, Trusts in Confl. of L., §§ 18, 19.

Nor is the actual situs of the personal property material. Cross v. U. S. Trust Co., ubi sup. But as to a possible distinction in the case of tangible chattels, see Land, Trusts in Confl. of L., § 13.

[2] Whitney v. Dodge, 105 Cal. 192, 38 Pac. 636. Hussey v. Sargent, 116 Ky. 53, 75 S. W. 211. Cf. Swetland v. Swetland, 105 N. J. Eq. 608, 149 Atl. 50; Wilmington Trust Co. v. Wilmington Trust Co. 186 Atl. 903 (Del. Ch.), but now see 15 Atl. 2d 153, and § 540.2, note 9, post.

the testator's domicil must govern, the limitations or trusts would seem to be invalid.[1]

§ 263.3. **Influence of Law of Place of Administration.** If a legacy is given on a charitable trust which is to be carried out in another jurisdiction where it would be valid, sometimes the law of the domicil forbids such a legacy absolutely, and in that case the legacy is void; but sometimes the law only forbids such trusts within the state of the domicil, and then the legacy is good. And in this latter case it seems that the trust will be subject to the law of the other jurisdiction in matters of administration.[1] If the law of the place of administration prevents such a trust from being carried out,

§ 263.2. [1] But query as to the effect in New York of the Decedent Estate Law, § 47 (last sentence), providing that where a testator has declared that the provisions of his will shall be regulated by the laws of New York, the validity and effect of such provisions shall be governed by such laws. See Re Tabbagh, 167 Misc. 156, 3 N. Y. S. 2d 542; Re Slade, 154 Misc. 275, 277, 276 N. Y. S. 956, 958; Re New York Life Ins. and Trust Co., 139 N. Y. S. 695, 712, 209 N. Y. 585, 103 N. E. 315. See also Personal Property Law, § 12-a, and Hutchison v. Ross, 262 N. Y. 381, 187 N. E. 65. For questions of the Conflict of Laws arising on the execution of powers of appointment, see § 540.2, post.

§ 263.3. [1] Manice v. Manice, 43 N. Y. 303, 387. Matter of Huss, 126 N. Y. 537, 27 N. E. 784. Hope v. Brewer, 136 N. Y. 126, 32 N. E. 558. St. John v. Andrews Inst., 117 N. Y. A. D. 698, 191 N. Y. S. 254. Kennedy v. Palmer, 1 T. & C. 581. Mapes v. Home Miss. Soc., 32 Hun 360. Draper v. Harvard College, 57 How. Pr. 269. Matter of Feehan, 135 Misc. 903, 241 N. Y. S. 669. Mena v. Virnard, 124 Misc. 637, 207 N. Y. S. 504. See Matter of Rathbone, 170 Misc. 1030, 1044, 11 N. Y. S. 2d 506, 520; Lamborn's Estate, 171 Misc. 734, 13 N. Y. S. 2d 732; Matter of Idem, 256 N. Y. A. D. 124, 8 N. Y. S. 2d 900, aff'd 280 N. Y. 756, 21 N. E. 2d 522; Re Chappell's Estate, 124 Wash. 128, 213 Pac. 684, 221 Pac. 336; Re Risher's Will, 227 Wis. 104, 277 N. W. 160; Vansant v. Roberts, 3 Md. 119; Johns Hopkins Univ. v. Uhrig, 145 Md. 114, 125 Atl. 606; State v. Lodge, 16 Atl. 2d 250 (Del.); 2 Beale, Confl. of L., § 294.7; Land, Trusts in Confl. of L., § 18, p. 66. Cf. McAuliffe's Estate, 167 Misc. 783, 4 N. Y. S. 2d 605. If the laws of both the domicil and the place of administration forbid such charitable trusts, the legacy is void. Catt v. Catt, 118 N. Y. A. D. 742, 103 N. Y. S. 740.

the courts of the domicil will strive to give effect to it by *cy pres* or otherwise.[2] The language of several of the New York cases cited in note 1 to this section indicates that the chief reason why the charitable trust would have been invalid, if it had to be carried out in New York, was that the trust would have violated the New York statutory rules which have been substituted for the common-law Rule against Perpetuities.[3] There do not seem to be any cases in any jurisdiction, in which trusts invalid by the law of the testator's domicil, under the Rule against Perpetuities or corresponding statutory rules, other than charitable trusts, have been sustained because valid by the law of the place of administration. Probably in New York such trusts would be sustained on that ground.[4] But when a trust is valid under the Rule against Perpetuities at the testator's domicil, the circumstance that it would be invalid under the law of New York, where it is to be administered, is disregarded.[5] It may well be that the courts of other jurisdictions will follow New York in sustaining trusts which are valid under the Rule against Perpetuities in force in the place where the trust is to be administered although invalid by the law of the testator's domicil.[6] It may

[2] See Fellows v. Miner, 119 Mass. 541, 546. Cf. 33 Harv. Law Rev. 358, 360–364.

[3] See, for instance, Hope v. Brewer, Kennedy v. Palmer, Draper v. Harvard College. See also Chamberlain v. Chamberlain, 43 N. Y. 424; Dammert v. Osborn, 140 N. Y. 30, 35 N. E. 407, 141 N. Y. 564, 35 N. E. 1088; Chaplin, Suspension of Alienation (3d ed.), § 509.

[4] See Chamberlain v. Chamberlain, 43 N. Y. 424, 434; Robb v. Washington and Jefferson College, 103 N. Y. A. D. 327, 356, 93 N. Y. S. 92, 109; Second National Bank v. Curie, 116 N. J. Eq. 101, 104, 172 Atl. 560; 39 Yale L. J.

100, 103; 13 Columbia Law Rev. 243.

[5] Cross v. U. S. Tr. Co., 131 N. Y. 330, 30 N. E. 125. National City Bank v. Smith, 87 N. Y. L. J. 3373 (June 15th, 1932). Cf. Rosenbaum v. Garrett, 57 N. J. Eq. 186, 41 Atl. 252; Klumpert v. Vrieland, 142 Iowa 434, 121 N. W. 34. In Bishop v. Bishop, 257 N. Y. 40, 177 N. E. 302, 258 N. Y. 216, 179 N. E. 391, the place of administration does not appear, but seems to be regarded as unimportant when the law of the domicil supports the trust. See 13 Columbia Law Rev. 243.

[6] See the remarks of the Lord Chancellor in Fordyce v. Bridges,

be contended, on the other hand, inasmuch as the policy of a State on the subject of remoteness is concerned only with property to be administered within that State, that trusts invalid under the law of the place of administration should not be sustained, though valid under the rule of the testator's domicil. But there is little or no authority on this last point except the New York decisions to the contrary.[7] A change in the residence of trustee is immaterial.[8]

§ 263.4. Re Luck's Settlement Trusts.[1] Under a settlement made in contemplation of the marriage of A. and B., both domiciled in England, and a special power therein reserved, property was appointed in trust for all the children of the marriage, the income of each child's share to be paid to it for its life; and after its death its share divided among

2 Phil. 497, 515, § 266.1, post; Vansant v. Roberts, 3 Md. 119; Second National Bank v. Curie, 116 N. J. Eq. 101, 172 Atl. 560; Wilmington Trust Co. v. Wilmington Trust Co., 186 Atl. 903, 15 Atl. 2d 153 (Del. Ch.), § 540.2, note 9, post; 44 Harv. Law Rev. 161. But cf. Re De Noailles, 114 L. T. R. 1089.

7 See 44 Harv. Law Rev. 161; 32 Columbia Law Rev. 680. The Am. Law Inst. Restatement, Confl. of L., § 295, reads: "The validity of a trust of moveables created by a will is determined by the law of the testator's domicil at the time of his death." The Rule against Perpetuities, however, is not mentioned, and the question appears to be left open, whether the application of the Rule against Perpetuities may not be governed to some extent by the law of the place of administration. See Restatement, §§ 297–299; 39 Yale L. J. 100,

106–110; 23 Minn. Law Rev. 527; 23 Corn. L. J. 624; and the remarks of the Court in Re Risher's Will, 227 Wis. 104, 277 N. W. 160. The same question might be raised in trusts inter vivos. In Curtis v. Curtis, 185 N. Y. A. D. 391, 173 N. Y. S. 103, stated in § 262.1, ante, and many of the cases cited in §§ 262–262.2, the law actually applied was that of the place of administration. See also Wilmington Trust Co. v. Wilmington Trust Co., 186 Atl. 903, 15 Atl. 2d 153 (Del. Ch.), § 540.2, note 9, post; and Second National Bank v. Curie, 116 N. J. Eq. 101, 172 Atl. 560.

8 Swetland v. Swetland, 105 N. J. Eq. 608, 149 Atl. 50. 2 Beale, Confl. of L., § 1024. But see Wilmington Trust Co. v. Wilmington Trust Co., 186 Atl. 903, 15 Atl. 2d 153 (Del. Ch.), § 540.2, note 9, post.

§ 263.4. 1 [1940] 1 Ch. 323, 864.

[G. R. P.]

its children who should have been born within twenty-one years after the decease of the survivor of A. and B. The survivor of A. and B. died in 1898. In 1908, C., a son of A. and B., (who was married, and had children), had an illegitimate son D. born in California. Later C. became domiciled in California; and in 1925 he acknowledged D. as his son in a form which, according to a California statute, made him legitimate. C. died in 1938; and D. thereupon claimed a share in the fund with C.'s other children. Farwell, J., sustained D.'s claim, on the ground that in 1938, at the time of distribution, he was entitled, by force of his father's acknowledgment and the California statute, to be treated as legitimate from his birth, notwithstanding the fact that the act of legitimation took place after the expiration, in 1919, of the period of twenty-one years from the death of his grandparents. This conclusion appears to be highly doubtful. Assuming that D. came within the description of the settlement, and that the Court was right in recognizing the act of legitimation in California, it seems that his interest in the fund did not become vested until 1925, after the expiration of the period of twenty-one years from the death of his grandparents, and was therefore too remote.[2] The implied requirement that a grandchild should be of legitimate birth, was as much a condition precedent to D.'s interest vesting as if it had been expressed. Not until 1925, when the act of legitimation took place, was it ascertained, or ascertainable, that D. fell within the description. This was not a question of evidence. In 1919, it was clearly a fact that D.'s interest was subject to an unfulfilled condition precedent. No statute or decree could alter the fact that if D. was allowed to take a share, the property remained tied up by the existence of a contingent interest until 1925, the date of the act of

---

[2] The question of remoteness was raised, but it does not appear what argument was made upon it, and it received only slight consideration in the opinion. Most of the discussion was on the question whether the Court ought to recognize the legitimation in California of a child born when the father was not domiciled in California.

legitimation.  If the California statute would oblige a California court, in a similar situation arising with regard to California property, to treat D. as if he had been born legitimate,
the Californa Court in thus giving a retroactive effect to the
statute, would be creating in substance a statutory exception
to the Rule against Perpetuities.[3]  But an English court,
dealing with property in England, ought not, merely on account of a California statute, to allow the tying up of such
property for a period longer than that sanctioned by the
English Rule against Perpetuities.  The question is not merely one of the status of D.; it is a question as to how long a
fund shall be tied up in England.[4]  The Court of Appeal, by
two judges to one, reversed the decree below, on the question
of C.'s status only, holding that the English courts could not
recognize for any purpose a legitimation of D. by a declaration of his father, if the father was not domiciled in California at the time of the birth.  The appellants appear to
have conceded, in the Court of Appeals at least, that if the
father had been then domiciled in California the legitimation
would have been good.  Whether this concession was correct,
with reference to the question of the son's right to take under
the settlement, may be doubted.  But the Court of Appeals
expressly declined to consider the question whether the son
might be debarred from taking under the settlement if
his legitimation were valid and operated retrospectively.

§ 264. Conversion.  When a testator directs land to be
sold, or personalty to be invested in land, the laws of his
domicil and of the *situs* of the land may differ.  Suppose land

[3] Whether a California court
would have given such an effect
to the statute on legitimation
may be doubtful, especially in
view of that court's view as to
the effect of the mention of the
Rule against Perpetuities in the
California Constitution. See § 752,
post.

[4] The fund here is subject to
English law, whether the domicil

of the settlors, the place of administration, or the actual situs
of the property at any particular
time, is regarded as the important circumstance.

This case was discussed in 53
Harv. Law Rev. 1201, and 18 Can.
Bar Rev. 491, but without considering the point as to the Rule
against Perpetuities.

is settled or devised on limitations or trusts which are too remote according to the *lex rei sitæ*, but the conveyance or devise is accompanied with a direction that the land shall be
sold and the proceeds held as personalty, or invested in land,
in a State where such limitations or trusts are allowed, is
such settlement or devise valid? In the case of *Freke* v. *Carbery*,[1] Lord Selborne, C., held that it was not.[2]

§ **265.** The view now generally adopted in America is that
the decision of the foregoing question must depend upon
whether there is an immediate absolute equitable conversion.
If the deed or will directs such immediate absolute conver-

---

§ **264.** [1] L. R. 16 Eq. 461.

[2] And the same seems to have
been held in Parkhurst v. Roy, 27
Grant 361, 7 Ont. Ap. 614. Cf.
Anderson v. Kilborn, 13 Grant
219. In Macpherson v. Stewart,
28 L. J. Ch. 177, 32 L. T. R. 143,
an English testator gave his property to trustees, directing them
to place it in such funds, stocks,
or securities, either in Europe or
India, as they might deem advisa-
ble, in trust to make certain payments to certain persons, and on
their death to apply the fund,
with all accumulations, in the
purchase of land in Scotland, to
be strictly entailed on A. The
Thellusson Act (39 & 40 Geo. III.,
c. 98), § 3, provided that nothing
in the Act contained should extend "to any disposition respecting heritable property within that
part of Great Britain called Scotland." Vice-Chancellor Kinders-
ley held (1) that during the lives
named the Thellusson Act applied
to the accumulations of income;
and (2) that during this period
the income of so much of the fund
as was invested in Scotch heritable bonds formed no exception.

The first holding was certainly
correct. The second holding
would seem correct also; for,
First. The provisions for investment during the life interests
hardly amounted to a direction
to convert. Second. If Freke v.
Carbery is correct, a trust as to
converted property is not good,
unless it would be good as to the
property unconverted. Third. If
Freke v. Carbery is not correct,
heritable bonds, though considered heritable property in Scotland, Bell's Principles, § 1485, are
yet in their nature movables, and
it should seem, out of Scotland,
ought to be considered, for the
purpose of applying the Rule
against Perpetuities, as movables;
just as leaseholds, though personal property, are considered for
such purpose as immovables. See
§ 259.1, ante. But it seems to be
settled in England that such
bonds are immovables. See Re
Fitzgerald, [1904] 1 Ch. (C. A.)
573, 588; Re Berchtold, [1923] 1
Ch. 192, 201; Foote, Priv. Internat. L. (5th ed.) 246–249; Dicey,
Confl. of L. (5th ed.) 579–582;
Cheshire, Priv. Internat. L. 319.

sion, then the validity of the settlement or devise is governed
by the law of the testator's or settlor's domicil, but if there
is no such direction for immediate absolute conversion, the
devise or settlement is governed by the law of the *situs* of
the land.[1]

§ **266.** The American doctrine seems preferable to that of
Lord Selborne, C. In *Freke* v. *Carbery,* as reported, almost
the whole attention of court and counsel was directed to
the question whether leaseholds were governed by the *lex rei
sitæ*. The only authority cited by counsel to support the
ruling as to conversion was *Curtis* v. *Hutton*.[1] In this case
land in England was devised to be sold, and the proceeds were
directed to be applied for the maintenance of a charity in
Scotland. Sir William Grant, M. R., held the devise bad.
He said: "The disinheriting of the lawful heirs by languish-
ing or dying persons, which is treated by the Statute as a
mischief, cannot be less so, where the effect is to carry the
property out of England." But the holding of real or personal estate in foreign jurisdictions on remote limitations is
not within the mischief of the Rule of Perpetuities of a State,
which is only concerned with property within that State.[2]

§ **265.** [1] Clarke's   Appeal.   70
Conn. 195, 39 Atl. 155, sub nom.
Clarke v. Clarke, 178 U. S. 186,
20 S. Ct. 873, 44 L. E. 1028.
Draper   v.   Harvard   College,
57   How.   Pr.   269.   Hobson
v. Hale, 95 N. Y. 588. Butler v. Green, 65 Hun 99, 19 N. Y.
S. 890. Trowbridge v. Metcalf.
5 N. Y. A. D. 318, sub nom.
Trowbridge v. Trowbridge, 158
N. Y. 682, 52 N. E. 1126. Hope
v. Brewer, 136 N. Y. 126, 32 N. E.
558. Ford v. Ford, 80 Mich. 42.
44 N. W. 1057. Ford v. Ford, 70
Wis. 19, 33 N. W. 188, 72 Wis.
621, 40 N. W. 502. Penfield v.
Tower, 1 N. Dak. 216, 46 N. W.
413. The case of Wood v. Wood,
5 Paige 596, is probably not law.

See Chamberlain v. Chamberlain,
43 N. Y. 424, 435; Peabody v.
Kent, 153 N. Y. A. D. 286, 138
N. Y. S. 32. Cf. Mena v. Virnard,
124 Misc. 637, 207 N. Y. S. 504.
See also App. I, § 916, post.

According to the Amer. Law
Inst. Restatement, Confl. of L.,
§ 249, Comment c, "A will of an
interest in land is governed by
the law of the state where the
land is in spite of a direction in
the will to convert the land into
personalty." See 2 Beale, Confl.
of L., § 251. But query whether
this statement applies to questions arising under the Rule
against Perpetuities.

§ **266.** [1] 14 Ves. 537.

[2] Cf. § 263.3, ante. At the time

§ **266.1.** In *Fordyce* v. *Bridges*[1] personal property was bequeathed to trustees to invest in either English or Scotch estates, the Scotch estates to be settled in strict Scotch entail. Lord Cottenham, C., held that investments could be made in Scotch estates. It was objected that the bequest of a fund to be invested in a regular Scotch entail was void as a perpetuity, but the Chancellor said: "The rules acted upon by the courts in this country with respect to testamentary dispositions tending to perpetuities relate to this country only."[2]

§ **267.** When a testator domiciled in one State directs land situated in another State to be sold and the proceeds invested in land in the State of his domicil, on trusts which are illegal by the law of the latter State, though allowed by the *lex situs*, such trusts are void.[1]

of the first edition, the author was inclined to the contrary opinion. Freke v. Carbery is doubted in 1 Jarm. Wills (7th ed.) 3, 4.

§ **266.1.** [1] 2 Phil. 497, 515.

[2] It should be observed that "perpetuity" is here used in the sense of an unbarrable entail. See §§ 141.1–141.6, ante. Fordyce v. Bridges was followed in Re Mitchner, [1922] Queensl. 252.

§ **267.** [1] Hawley v. James, 7 Paige 213. See Ellis v. Maxwell, 12 Beav. 104; § 259.2, ante; Bible Soc. v. Pendleton, 7 W. Va. 79. In White v. Howard, 52 Barb. 294, 46 N. Y. 144, a Connecticut testator ordered his land in that State to be sold, and the proceeds invested in certain specified personal securities, or in real estate in New York, or any of the New England States, and to be held on trusts which were good in Connecticut but invalid by the law of New York. The trustees invested some of the property in New York lands. It was held that the trusts failed as to these lands so purchased. Certainly land in New York could not be held on trusts illegal by the law of that State. But it would seem to have been improper for the trustees to have invested the trust fund in property which could not be held on the trust. See 46 N. Y. 166, 167; Bishop v. Bishop, 257 N. Y. 40, 177 N. E. 302, 258 N. Y. 216, 179 N. E. 391.

In Jenkins v. Guarantee Trust Co., 53 N. J. Eq. 194, 32 Atl. 208, a Pennsylvania testatrix gave the residue of her estate, real and personal, to a Pennsylvania trust company, in trust, among other things, to pay a legacy to a Pennsylvania charity. The legacy was in violation of the provisions of the Pennsylvania Mortmain Act. The testatrix left property in Pennsylvania, and also land in New Jersey. The Pennsylvania property was insufficient to pay the debts. The New Jersey Court of Errors and Appeals held that the legacy was void. Cf. Decker v. Vreeland, 220 N. Y. 326, 115 N. E. 989; Hailey v. McLaurin's Estate, 112 Miss. 705, 73 So. 727.

Suppose all the persons interested in such a provision as is given in the text should elect to take the realty unconverted, could they hold against the heirs? See Norris v. Loyd, 183 Iowa 1056, 168 N. W. 557.

On the doctrine of election as applicable to the questions discussed in the preceding sections, see Staples v. Hawes, 39 N. Y. A. D. 548, 57 N. Y. S. 452.

## CHAPTER VII

## INTERESTS, THOUGH ALIENABLE, MAY BE TOO REMOTE

**§ 268. Inalienability and Remoteness.** As has been said,[1] the tying up of property was attempted in two ways, first, by making vested estates inalienable, and when the judges stopped this, then by the creation of indestructible future contingent estates; and, to restrain these last, the Rule against Perpetuities was devised. The tying up of property is therefore restrained, as to present estates, by making them alienable, and, as to future estates, by subjecting them to the Rule against Perpetuities. Since the original purpose of the Rule against Perpetuities was to restrain one mode of tying up estates, it would not have been inconsistent with that purpose to have held that contingent interests, if alienable, did not come within the Rule, but, as will appear in this chapter, the Rule has been extended so as to cover all future interests whether alienable or not, and this extension, though not a logically necessary consequence of the establishment of the rule, is now well settled, and it is a reasonable extension. If there is a gift over of an estate on a remote contingency, the market value of the interest of the present owner will be greatly reduced, while the executory gift will sell for very little, or, in other words, the value of the present interest *plus* the value of the executory gift will fall far short of what would be the value of the property if there were no executory interest. Further, if the owner of the present interest wishes to convey an absolute fee, the holder of the executory gift can extort from him a price which greatly exceeds what it ought to be, if based on the chance of his succeeding to the property.[2] And again, just as it has been for centuries the policy of our law to allow a man full power of disposition of

§ **268.** [1] §§ 140 et seq., ante.     ed.), §§ 392, 398; 2 Wis. Law Rev.
[2] See 2 Tiffany, Real Prop. (3d     449, 451–453.

his property, under the belief that thereby the activity of
the owner will be increased and the public benefited, so it is
against public policy to allow such activity to be diminished
by the fear of losing the property on a future contingency;
and while near future interests may be desirable modifications
of ownership, remotely contingent interests are likely to
diminish the activity in ownership to an extent greater than
any advantages which will follow from allowing them. To
put it in other words, it is desirable that a man's motives to
make the most of his property should not be diminished by
the danger of losing it on a future contingency; on the other
hand each generation should have the power of providing for
those who come immediately after it in the way it thinks best
by limiting the interests given them; and the Rule against
Perpetuities, as extended, is the line which the law has laid
down so as to give both these desirable objects a reasonable
field without encroaching on the other.

§ 269. **Remote Alienable Interests.** It has been sometimes, and indeed often, said that if future interests can be
alienated or released, they cannot be too remote, and that the
Rule against Perpetuities is aimed only at such limitations as
tie up property, and take it absolutely out of commerce.
Every executory devise was said, by Powell, J., in *Scatterwood* v. *Edge*,[1] to be "a perpetuity as far as it goes, that is to
say, an estate unalienable, though all mankind join in the
conveyance;" and this definition of a perpetuity has been
frequently cited in the cases, and has been laid hold of in
support of the view that conditions are free from the restraints
of the Rule.[2] But without going here into disputed questions,
it is clear that the Rule applies to cases where there is no
tying up of property. For instance, suppose real and per-

§ **269.** [1] 1 Salk. 229.

[2] See also Keppell v. Bailey, 2
Myl. & K. 517, 527, 528 (cf. Challis, Real Prop. (3d ed.) 184);
Gooch v. Gooch, 3 De G. M. & G.
366, 384 (see Re Legh's Settlement Trusts, [1938] Ch. (C. A.)
39, 43, 46, 51); Brattle Square

Church v. Grant, 3 Gray 142, 148,
"in which a single ambiguous or
inaccurate expression has sometimes led to a misunderstanding
of the law intended to be stated;"
Winsor v. Mills, 157 Mass. 362,
365, 32 N. E. 352, 353; 8 Jur., pt.
2, 284, note.

sonal property are given to trustees and their heirs, with full
power of changing investments, but upon trusts which may
arise more than twenty-one years after lives in being, such
trusts are void, yet no property is tied up.[3] But, further,
conditional limitations may be bad for remoteness, though
they are releasable or alienable.[4] It is true that a conditional
limitation to an uncertain person cannot be released because
there is no one to release it; but when a conditional limitation
is to a known person and his heirs, and the contingency is
only in the happening of the event on which the conditional
limitation is to take effect, it may be released (or, if equitable,
either released or assigned); yet if such event may occur more
than twenty-one years after lives in being, the conditional
limitation is too remote. Thus a bequest of personalty is too
remote if to take effect after the failure of issue of A., either
to a living person[5] or to a corporation.[6] So a conditional
limitation of real estate may be too remote, although made to
a living person in fee.[7] In like manner, if the persons to whom
a gift is made may not be ascertained within the required
limits, the gift is too remote, although the class to which they
belong must be determined within those limits, and a conveyance by the whole class would pass the entire interest.[8]
It may be said that although an executory devise can be released, it cannot be assigned to a stranger. But it can be

3 4 Kent, Com. (14th ed.) 283.
Wheeler v. Fellowes, 52 Conn. 238,
244. See § 202.1, ante.

4 "The possibility or impossibility of obtaining releases is not
the test by which to determine
the validity or invalidity of a
limitation." Winsor v. Mills, 157
Mass. 362, 366, 32 N. E. 352, 353.

5 Grey v. Montagu, 2 Eden
205, 3 B. P. C. (Toml. ed.) 314.

6 Johnson's Trusts, L. R. 2 Eq.
716.

7 Re Brown & Sibly's Contract, 3
Ch. D. 156. Re Norton, [1911] 2
Ch. 27, 37, 40. Brattle Square

Church v. Grant, 3 Gray 142.
Society for Theological Educa-
tion v. A. G., 135 Mass. 285.
Winsor v. Mills, 157 Mass. 362,
32 N. E. 352. Bundy v. U. S.
Trust Co., 257 Mass. 72, 80, 153
N. E. 337, 340.

8 See cases cited in § 277, post.
See also Marsden, Perp., c. 3;
Sanders on Uses (5th ed.) 203,
204; London & S. W. R. Co. v.
Gomm, 20 Ch. D. (C. A.) 562,
573–575 (explaining Washborn v.
Downs, 1 Ch. Cas. 213); Curtis
v. Lukin, 5 Beav. 147; § 675, post.

released to the owner of the present estate, and he can convey a fee,—that is, the two, by joining, can convey an absolute
estate,—and therefore the case does not come within Powell's
definition.    Besides, an equitable executory interest can be
assigned to a stranger, yet the Rule applies equally to such
interests as to legal estates.[9] Again, modern statutes have very
generally made legal executory interests alienable as well as
releasable;[10] but this has made no change in the Rule against
Perpetuities.[11]

§ 270. Cases to the Contrary.    There were, however, three
decisions which seemed opposed to this:    *Gilbertson* v.
*Richards*,[1] *Birmingham Canal Co.* v. *Cartwright*,[2] and *Avern*
v. *Lloyd*.[3]

§ 271. In *Gilbertson* v. *Richards*,[1] there was a mortgage to
H. to secure the payment of £5,000, the equity of redeeming
which was in B.  The mortgage deed, made in 1838, declared
that if there was any default in payment of the £5,000, H.
might sell and dispose of the land, and contained a proviso
that if the mortgagee or any persons claiming by, through, or
under him should, by virtue of any power therein contained,
enter upon or otherwise become possessed of the land, the land
should immediately become charged with a rent of £40 in
favor of B.  There was a default, and in 1847, H. sold the
land.  B. contended that thereupon the rent arose; the purchaser contended that the provision for its creation was void
for remoteness.  The Court of Exchequer held that the rent
was duly created.  They said:  "It seems to be an error to call
this rent a perpetuity, in an illegal sense.  It is vested in
Thomas Billings and his heirs.  He or his heirs may sell it,
or release it, at their pleasure.  A rent in fee simple may be
granted to a man and heirs to continue forever.  Why, therefore, may not one be granted to commence at any time

9 See Grey v. Montagu and Johnson's Trusts, ubi supra, and the cases cited in § 277, post.

10 For instance, 8 & 9 Vict., c. 106, § 6.

11 Lewis, Suppl. 13–20. Marsden, Perp. 66.

§ 270. 1 4 H. & N. 277, 5 H. & N. 453.

2 11 Ch. D. 421.

3 L. R. 5 Eq. 383.

§ 271. 1 4 H. & N. 277.

however remote? It is only a part of the estate in fee simple of the rent. A perpetuity arises when a rent is granted to a person who may not be *in esse* until after the line of perpetuity be passed; but when the estate in the rent is vested in an existing person and his heirs in fee simple, who may deal with it at his or their pleasure, and as he or they think fit, we think it is not subject to the objection of remoteness, notwithstanding that its actual enjoyment may depend upon a contingency which may never happen, or may happen at any time however distant."[2]

§ 272. But the Court of Exchequer Chamber, to which the case was carried,[1] rested the decision, not on the fact that the mortgagors could release their right to the rent charge, but on the ground that the case was analogous to that of a power of sale in a mortgage. They said: "The real effect of the limitations in the deed before us is, that the mortgagees are to take possession or sell, subject to the payment of this rent to Billings. It is a restriction on the amount of the estate of the mortgagees, and seems within the cases as to the power of sale in a mortgagee, which, as incidental to his estate, is held not to be within the Rule as to Perpetuities."[2] So Lord St. Leonards,[3] after saying that the distinction taken by the Court of Exchequer was not necessary for the decision of the case, adds: "No perpetuity was created by the power of sale in the mortgagees, or by the right of them or their heirs to take possession of the land, but in exercising that right they took, subject to a perpetual rent of £40 a year, in favor of the mortgagor. It was a charge on the estate and had no tendency to a perpetuity."[4]

§ 273. The Court of Exchequer Chamber, however, did not distinctly repudiate the doctrine of the Exchequer. They said: "There may be considerable doubt also on the point raised by counsel, whether the Rule as to Perpetuities applies to a case like the present, where the party who or whose heirs

[2] 4 H. & N. 297, 298.

§ 272. [1] 5 H. & N. 453.

[2] 5 H. & N. 459.

[3] Sugd. Pow. (8th ed.) 16.

[4] And see Williams on Settlements 31, 32; Marsden, Perp. 248; Chap. XVI., post, on Mortgages.

are to take is ascertained, and who can dispose of, release, or alienate the estate, either at common law or at all events since the passing of 8 & 9 Vict. c. 106, § 6."[1]

§ **273.1.** Perhaps *Gilbertson* v. *Richards* may be supported on the ground that the future right to the £40 annually was not a right of property, but simply a contract obligation. A contract right, as such, is certainly not subject to the Rule against Perpetuities.[1] A rent charge is a right to a sum of money which can be enforced by distraint on certain land. The right to distrain is simply a remedy, and perhaps fairly enough to be considered not a right in property, and therefore not within the purview of the Rule against Perpetuities. In *Morgan* v. *Davey*,[2] a lessee covenanted for himself, his heirs and assigns, to pay certain sums "by way of rent charge or royalty or reservation" if he should mine coal. Mathew, J., at *nisi prius*, ruled, on the authority of *Gilbertson* v. *Richards,* that this covenant was not within the Rule against Perpetuities. Except so far as it created a rent charge, it certainly was not subject to the Rule. Even viewed as creating a rent charge, it may be sustained on the ground, above suggested, that it gave merely a remedy and not a right of property.[3]

§ **274.** The case of *Birmingham Canal Co.* v. *Cartwright*[1] was a clear decision that an executory interest which could be released was not within the Rule against Perpetuities. The vendor of lands, reserving the mines, covenanted with the vendee that should he ever sell the mines under adjoining land, he would sell the reserved mines to the vendee at the

§ 273. [1] 5 H. & N. 459. The section of the statute referred to provides that executory and contingent interests in realty may be disposed of by deed.

§ 273.1. [1] § 329, post.

[2] 1 Cab. & El. 114.

[3] Rents charge have generally been dealt with in the common law together with property, and not simply as obligations. But the Rule against Perpetuities deals with the substance of things. Does the right to distrain on land in order to enforce a right in personam make that right a right in rem? A question not easy to answer. The distinction between substantive rights and remedies is sometimes hard to draw. See §§ 303, 316, post.

§ 274. [1] 11 Ch. D. 421.

same rate as that at which he should have sold the adjoining mines. Fry, J., held that the covenant was not obnoxious to the Rule against Perpetuities, and that specific performance could be enforced by the assigns of the vendee against the devisees of the vendor. The learned judge said: "I think that wherever a right or interest is presently vested in A. and his heirs, although the right may not arise until the happening of some contingency which may not take effect within the period defined by the Rule against Perpetuities, such right or interest is not obnoxious to that Rule, and for this reason. The Rule is aimed at preventing the suspension of the power of dealing with property,—the alienation of land or other property. But when there is a present right of that sort, although its exercise may be dependent upon a future contingency, and the right is vested in an ascertained person or persons, that person or persons, concurring with the person who is subject to the right, can make a perfectly good title to the property. The total interest in the land, so to speak, is divided between the covenantor and the covenantee, and they can together at any time alienate the land absolutely. I think that *Gilbertson* v. *Richards* is a distinct authority in favor of that conclusion."[2]

§ **275.** But *Birmingham Canal Co.* v. *Cartwright* has been overruled, and the true doctrine clearly stated by the Court of Appeal in *London & S. W. R. Co.* v. *Gomm.*[1] In that case the plaintiff company in 1865 conveyed land to Powell in fee, and Powell covenanted with the company that he, his heirs or assigns, would, at any time, on receipt of £100, reconvey the land to the company. In 1879 Gomm purchased the land from Powell with notice of the covenant, and in 1880 the

[2] 11 Ch. D. 432, 433. In Collison v. Lettsom, 6 Taunt. 224, there came in question a covenant in a lease for a term of twenty-eight years, by which the lessor covenanted that if he, his heirs or assigns, should, during the term, have an advantageous offer to dispose of certain adjoining land, the lessee, his executors, administrators, or assigns, should have a right of preemption. The Court held that there had, in fact, been no breach of the covenant. Whether or not the covenant was too remote was not mooted.

§ **275.** [1] 20 Ch. D. (C. A.) 562.

company demanded a conveyance, and, upon Gomm's refusal, brought a bill for specific performance. Kay, J., discussed the cases very fully, and declared that he was unable to agree with what had been said in *Gilbertson* v. *Richards* and *Birmingham Canal Co.* v. *Cartwright.* "In my opinion," he said, "a present right to an interest in property which may arise at a period beyond the legal limit is void, notwithstanding that the person entitled to it may release it."[2] The learned judge, however, thought that the Rule against Perpetuities was "a branch not of the law of contract but of property." "A contract not creating any estate or interest properly so called in property, at law or equity, is not, in my opinion obnoxious to the Rule;"[3] and as the covenant in this case did not run with the land at law, and a purchaser without notice would not be bound by it, he thought it was not within the Rule against Perpetuities at all, and made a decree for specific performance. Gomm appealed. The Court of Appeal (Jessel, M. R., Sir James Hannen, and Lindley, L. J. J.) reversed the decree. The Court held that the option to purchase gave an equitable interest which was within the Rule against Perpetuities, and that judged by that Rule it was void.[4] The Master of the Rolls said[5] he considered that Mr. Justice Kay was "quite right in the view he takes of the doctrine of remoteness and of the authorities cited before him, not forgetting the case of the *Birmingham Canal Co.* v. *Cartwright,* which must be treated as overruled," and that he had "most correctly and accurately defined the law," but that he was in error in thinking that the covenant did not create any interest in land.

§ **275.1.** *Winsor* v. *Mills,*[1] following the case of *London & S. W. R. Co.* v. *Gomm,* held that an option in M., his heirs and assigns to purchase land was too remote; and previous inaccurate *dicta* were corrected.[2] To the same effect are

[2] 20 Ch. D. (C. A.) 573.
[3] 20 Ch. D. (C. A.) 575.
[4] See § 330, post.
[5] 20 Ch. D. (C. A.) 582.

§ **275.1.** [1] 157 Mass. 362, 32 N. E. 352.

[2] It is to be regretted that this case, while clearing the law con-

*Starcher* v. *Duty*[3] and *Barton* v. *Thaw*.[4]

§ **276.** The third case which favored the idea that an alienable interest cannot be too remote was *Avern* v. *Lloyd*.[1] In that case there was a bequest of personal property to A. for life, and after A.'s death to his issue for life, and to the executors, administrators, and assigns of the survivor. Stuart, V. C., held, rightly it would seem, that it was intended to give the absolute interest to the survivor; but he went on to say: "Each of the tenants for life in this case had as much right to alien his contingent right to the absolute interest as to alien his life estate; and the person claiming under an assignment of the whole estate and interest of the tenant for life would, as soon as his assignor became the survivor of the other tenants for life, be entitled to the possession and enjoyment as absolute owner. It seems obvious that such a case is not within the principle on which the law against perpetuity rests, and that the limitation in question of the absolute interest does not fail as being too remote."

§ **277.** But[1] in *Edmondson's Estate*,[2] the report of which, before Wood, V. C., immediately follows that of *Avern* v. *Lloyd,* it was conceded that limitations over to the survivors of a class who must all have been born within a life in being were too remote, although if the whole class had joined in a conveyance they could have made a good title. The Vice-

cerning remoteness from prevalent misconceptions, contained dicta on the invalidity of provisions restraining a trustee from selling without the consent of the cestuis que trust which were of very questionable soundness. But this has now been set straight in Howe v. Morse, 174 Mass. 491, 55 N. E. 213. See §§ 509.13–509.15, post.

3 61 W. Va. 373, 56 S. E. 524.

4 246 Pa. 348, 92 Atl. 312. For further authorities and discussion, see § 330, post. That the

[G. R. P.]—20

alienability of an interest does not prevent its being obnoxious to the Rule against Perpetuities was expressly declared in Starcher v. Duty, 61 W. Va. 373, 379, 56 S. E. 524, 526; Woodall v. Bruen, 76 W. Va. 193, 195, 85 S. E. 170, 171; and Redington v. Browne, 32 L. R. Ir. 347, 358. See also Lewis Oyster Co. v. West, 93 Conn. 518, 107 Atl. 138.

§ **276.** 1 L. R. 5 Eq. 383.

§ **277.** 1 As pointed out in Wms. Settlements 33.

2 L. R. 5 Eq. 389.

Chancellor said that "of course" the gift over was void for remoteness. In *Hobbs* v. *Parsons,*[3] Stuart, V. C., himself had held that after a bequest to the testator's grandchildren a gift over, if any one of them died under twenty-two, to the survivors or survivor was void. Yet all the grandchildren could have made a good title. And also in *Courtier* v. *Oram*[4] and *Garland* v. *Brown,*[5] limitations to survivors were held too remote, although the class to which the survivors belonged could have made a good conveyance, and must have been determined within a life in being. But further than this, there are very many cases in which a gift to such of the children of a living person as reach some age greater than twenty-one have been held too remote.[6] It is true that in such cases all the children could not convey a good title, because none of them might reach the prescribed age; but all the children, together with the heirs, next of kin, or residuary legatees of the testator, who would take should none of the children reach that age, could make a good title. All the modern English text-writers have condemned *Avern* v. *Lloyd,*[7] and it has now been expressly overruled by the Court of Appeal in *Re Hargreaves.*[8]

§ **278. Alienability and the Rule.** A remark seems here in place. There are two propositions which are often confounded, but which are, in truth, distinct.

*First.* Future contingent interests, if alienable, are not subject to the Rule against Perpetuities.

*Second.* The Rule against Perpetuities is directed at preventing a suspension of alienation of present interests.

3 2 Sm. & G. 212.
4 21 Beav. 91.
5 10 L. T. R. 292.
6 See §§ 372–374, post.
7 See Wms. Settlements 32, 33; 1 Jarm. Wills (7th ed.) 275, 324; Theob. Wills (9th ed.) 491; Marsden, Perp. 178; 45 L. T. R. 339. See also Curtis v. Lukin, 5 Beav. 147. Cf. Stuart v. Cockerell, L. R. 7 Eq. 363, 368, 369.

8 43 Ch. D. (C. A.) 401; followed in Re Ashforth, [1905] 1 Ch. 535, 541, where Farwell, J., says: "Three void contingent remainders will not make one good vested remainder." In Stevens v. Annex Realty Co., 173 Mo. 511, 73 S. W. 505, there was no future estate. The opinion shows the confusion of ideas referred to in the following section.

[G. R. P.]

Both propositions are erroneous,—but in a very different degree.

To subject future contingent interests presently alienable to the Rule against Perpetuities is an extension of the Rule beyond the needs which gave it birth. The extension is well settled and reasonable, as is shown in this Chapter, but it is not necessary.

But to suppose that the Rule against Perpetuities is needed to restrain a suspension of alienation, or that present interests in property might be made inalienable were it not for the Rule, is to throw the fundamentals of the law into confusion.

§ 278.1. The fullest and ablest presentation of the view that future contingent interests, if alienable, ought not to be subject to the Rule against Perpetuities, is to be found in Professor Reeves's Treatise on Special Subjects of the Law of Real Property, Boston, 1904.[1] Professor Reeves argues that there is no sufficient justification for the extension of the Rule to cover alienable contingent future interests; and that, as an original question, such interests should not be subject to the Rule. He contends that the provisions of the New York Revised Statutes touching these matters which are based on the conception of "suspension of alienation," are more consonant with what was the original object and with what should be the true extent of the Rule.

§ 278.2. The difficulty lies here. If by "suspension of alienation" is meant suspension of alienation through future interests,—and this is the meaning, it would seem, which Professor Reeves attaches to it,—then, according to his view, as well as according to the common view, the Rule against Perpetuities is aimed at the control of future estates, and should appropriately be called the Rule against Remoteness. The only difference between the two views is that by one, future interests alienable *in præsenti* are considered too remote; and by the other, they are not.

§ 278.3. An interest void for remoteness is an interest whose invalidity arises from its being a future and not a pres-

§ 278.1. [1] And now cf. an article by Mr. Charles Sweet, 18 Jurid. Rev. 132, 138, 139.

ent interest. Not all future interests are remote. Thus everyone agrees that an interest presently vested is not remote; that an interest vesting within twenty-one years after lives in being is not remote; that an interest destructible by the owner of the present interest is not remote. If Professor Reeves's view were correct, it would only mean that we should have to add that an interest alienable or releasable presently or within twenty-one years after lives in being is not remote. The conception of the Rule against Perpetuities as applying solely to future and never to present interests would not be changed.

§ 278.4. But the phrase "suspension of alienation" and still more "restraint of alienation" includes the suspension or restraint of alienation of present interests by direct provisions, and, therefore, when it is said that the Rule against Perpetuities is aimed at the suspension or restraint of alienation, it is natural to suppose that the Rule has something to do with provisions directly suspending or restraining the alienation of present interests, an idea which, as has been said, has thrown the fundamentals of the law into confusion. To see how great that confusion may be one has only to read the Maryland decisions stated § 245.2 *et seq., ante,* or the decisions made under statutes based on restraining "suspension of alienation."[1]

§ 278.4. [1] See further in the application of the Rule against Perpetuities to alienable future interests, 2 Wis. Law Rev. 449, 451–453; 10 Iowa Law Bull. 275, 289–292; 9 Corn. L. J. 422, 426; 6 Minn. Law Rev. 560. For the statutes of New York and other States restraining suspension of alienation, see §§ 747–752.1, post.

# CHAPTER VIII

## INTERESTS SUBJECT TO THE RULE AGAINST PERPETUITIES[1]

**§ 279. Rights in Lands of Others.** Easements, profits *a prendre*, and other rights over the lands of others are not future but present interests, and the Rule against Perpetuities has no application to them.[1] This statement would seem superfluous, were it not for the remark of Sir George Jessel, M. R.,[2] that exceptions to the rules against remoteness had "been thoroughly established in many cases at law as regards easements."[3] There is no need to create any exception; easements are present interests, and the Rule applies to future interests only.[4] And further, as the Rule against Perpetuities

---

Chap. VIII.   [1] The question whether the Rule against Perpetuities is good against the Crown is stated without discussion in Cooper v. Stuart, 14 Ap. Cas. 286, 293. But the point was not decided. See s. c. below, 7 N. S. W. L. R. Eq. 1.

§ 279.   [1] Lewis, Perp. 599.

[2] London & S. W. R. Co. v. Gomm, 20 Ch. D. (C. A.) 562, 583.

[3] See Marsden, Perp. 20; Challis, Real Prop. (3d ed.) 186, 187; 10 Iowa Law Bull. 275, 286, note 73.

[4] Cawthon v. Stearns Culver Lumber Co., 60 Fla. 313, 53 So. 738. Council v. Sanderlin, 183 No. Car. 253, 111 S. E. 365. Post v. Bailey, 110 W. Va. 504, 159 S. E. 529. Cameron v. Dalgety, [1920] N. Z. 155, 164. See South Eastern R. Co. v. Associated Portland Cement Manuf., [1910] 1 Ch. 12, §§ 330.2, 330.3, post. Easements, etc., created in *futuro* are subject to the Rule.

These will be considered, §§ 314–316, post.

The Law of Property Act (1925), § 162, provides as follows. "For removing doubts, it is hereby declared that the rule of law relating to perpetuities does not apply and shall be deemed never to have applied." . . . (d) "To any grant, exception, or reservation of any right of entry on, or user of, the surface of land or of any easements, rights, or privileges over or under land for the purpose of"—(1) working mines; (2) felling timber; (3) executing repairs or alterations on adjoining land; (4) constructing and maintaining sewers, water-courses, pipes, electric wires, or other like works. This section seems to be intended to validate certain sorts of profits or easements as to which doubts might be raised whether they vested presently. See opinion of Swinfen Eady, J., in South East-

affects the beginning only of future interests, and does not
concern itself with conditions subsequent, except so far as

ern R. Co. v. Associated Portland
Cement Manuf., [1910] 1 Ch. 12;
1 Wolst. & Ch. Conv. (11th ed.)
414, 415; and cf. 25 W. Va. Law
Quart. 30. A grant may create
a presently vested easement or
profit, although the enjoyment of
the granted right may be postponed by circumstances, or by the
character of the estate to which
it is appurtenant. See Threlkeld
v. Inglett, 289 Ill. 90, 96, 124 N.
E. 368, 370; Cameron v. Dalgety,
[1920] N. Z. 156, 164; 55 Law
Quart. Rev. 434. Nor does the
circumstance that a payment is
to be made when the easement or
profit is used, prevent it from being a present right, not contingent upon the payment. Post v.
Bailey, 110 W. Va. 504, 159 S. E.
529. Cf. Barton v. Thaw, 246 Pa.
348, 92 Atl. 312. Although an
easement may undoubtedly be a
future interest, yet the tendency
of the courts has been to construe them as present rights,
when the question has actually
become material. See § 316, note
6, post. The rights in question
in Francis v. Superior Oil Co.,
102 Fed. 2d 732 (C. C. A. Okla.),
and many other cases of grants
or leases of rights in minerals or
timber, seem to be present rights
of that character, although in
that case it was said that the
grant was unobjectionable under
the Rule against Perpetuities for
the reason that the parties contemplated that it should take effect in enjoyment within a reasonable time.

In Beloit Building Co. v. Quinn,

145 Kan. 507, 60 Pac. 2d 549 (see
also 141 Kan. 408, 41 Pac. 2d
762), two adjoining landowners
made an agreement with regard
to a party-wall erected by one of
them partly on the land of each,
by which the builder agreed to
sell to the other, whenever the
latter should wish to build, "one
half of their said wall" for a sum
to be determined by arbitration.
The Court held that the right of
the landowner subsequently
building was not within the scope
of the Rule against Perpetuities,
for the reason that it was vested.
If this right of the adjoining
landowner could properly be
treated as an easement, it seems
that the decision can be supported on the doctrine stated in
the preceding paragraph of the
note. And it seems also that such
a view can properly be taken, although at first sight the language of the agreement seems
rather to contemplate a right of
ownership which might be acquired at a future date. Such a
construction of the agreement, as
creating only easements, would
carry out all the practical purposes of the arrangement. And
although the language of the
Court is not clear, it apparently
did take this view. The interest in question was said to be an
"option appurtenant." Now although the term option ordinarily imports contingency, the only
interests in property which can
be appurtenant are easements
and profits, and these are usually
treated as present interests even

they are also conditions precedent, a provision that an easement or other *jus in alieno solo* shall terminate on a certain
contingency is not invalidated by the remoteness of the contingency.[5] A remote conditional limitation is invalid, not be-

when in form they appear to be
contingent.    Cf.  a  case  in  the
same court, Long v. Smyre, 87
Kan. 182, 123 Pac. 765, in which
it was held that a party-wall,
built by one of two adjoining
landowners, was owned one half
by each, with mutual easements.
For a case showing that this result may be reached, although the
language of the agreement appears inconsistent with it, see
Shiverick v. Gunning Co., 58 Neb.
29, 33, 78 N. W. 480. And cf. the
draft of American Law Institute,
Restatement of the Law of Property (Group No. 2), Tentative
Draft No. 8, § 23. "Creation of
Easement or Profit by Conveyance Contrasted With Creation of
Estate."  Comment b.  "Whether
a  conveyance  creates  an  easement or a profit, or an estate, depends upon the intent of the parties as determined by construction of the conveyance. Classification of an interest in land as an
easement or a profit or as an estate is a legal classification rest-
ing ultimately upon the nature
of the legal relations which the
parties intended to create.   If
these legal relations bring the interest within the definition of an
easement or a profit, or of an estate, the interest will be classified
accordingly even though the parties would have given it a different classification."  Cf. Barton
v. Thaw, ubi supra, where the
Court held that a future right of
ownership, and not a mere ease-

ment, was intended to be given.
    The law as to party-walls dif-
fers considerably in England and
the United States; and in the
United States at least is not well
settled.  There appear to be no
decisions on the application of the
Rule against Perpetuities to agreements concerning such walls, except
the Kansas case, and the questions
of that nature which might arise
have been the subject of much discussion in the United States.   It
would be desirable, in order to
avoid raising such questions, that
the form of party-wall agreement
ordinarily employed in the United
States should be treated as giving no rights (other than con-
tractual obligations) except rights
of the nature of easements.   See
Clark, Real Covenants and Other
Interests Which Run With Land
118–139 (the substance of these
pages appeared previously in 37
Harv. Law Rev. 301) ; 3 Tiffany,
Real Prop. (3d ed.), §§ 770, 777;
but cf. 8 Tenn. Law Rev. 239.
    [5] In Switzer v. Rochford, [1906]
1 I. R. 399, a legal rent charge
for 500 years was granted on
leasehold land with a proviso that
it might be redeemed by payment
of £300, and that it should then
become void.  It was held that
the proviso was not void for remoteness.   Switzer v. Rochford
appears to have been doubted by
the Irish Court of Appeal in Re
Tyrrell's Estate, [1907] 1 I. R.
292, 297, 303, but it seems to be

cause the old estate ends at a remote period, but because the
new estate begins at a remote period. The ceasing of one interest in possession of a corporeal hereditament is the beginning of another interest in possession,—it is a transfer of possession; but the termination of an easement is not the beginning of another easement,—the easement is not transferred;
it is extinguished altogether.[6]

§ 280. **Equitable Easements.** Covenants as to the use of
land are often regarded in equity, according to the familiar
doctrine of *Tulk* v. *Moxhay*,[1] and the numerous cases following it, as imposing a trust or burden on the land for the benefit of other land belonging to the grantor or to third persons.
The rights thus created are sometimes called equitable easements; they are present interests, and are no more subject
to the Rule against Perpetuities than are common-law easements. "There seems some difficulty in understanding the
objection to such a modified enjoyment of property on the
ground of its supposed tendency to a perpetuity."[2]

correct (and see § 209, ante).
The duty to give up the rent
charge on payment of the £300
did not call for any transfer of a
property right, but only for the
extinction of the rent charge. See
§ 329, post. And cf. Re Lyster
Smythe's Estate, [1938] I. R. 231,
243. In Re Tyrrell's Estate a
perpetual equitable charge on
land was redeemable by the exercise of an option to pay the
interest on a certain kind of
bonds. The Court held that the
equitable charge "could not be
thus redeemed." This seems
wrong. The Court rely on London & S. W. R. Co. v. Gomm, but
there the option called for the
transfer of a property right,
while in Re Tyrrell's Estate there
was only an extinction of an
equitable charge. But in Re

Donoughmore's Estate, [1911] 1
I. R. 211, and Re Ramadge's Settlement, [1919] 1 I. R. 205, 223,
Switzer v. Rochford was not followed. Cf. Law of Prop. Act
(1925), § 4(3).

[6] Ardley v. Guardians of the
Poor, 39 L. J. Ch. 871 (fully
stated, § 316, note 6, post). Cleve-
land, etc. R. Co. v. Coburn, 91
Ind. 557. Hall v. Turner, 110 No.
Car. 292, 14 S. E. 791. Wiggins
Ferry Co. v. Ohio & Miss. R. Co.,
94 Ill. 83. See Battelle v. Worcester, 236 Mass. 395, 400, 128 N. E.
631, 633; Brownlee v. Douslin, N.
Z. L. R. 2 S. C. 363, N. Z. L. R.
3 C. A. 57, 63; § 17, ante.

§ 280. [1] 2 Phil. 774.

[2] Per Sir J. L. Knight Bruce,
Ex parte Ralph, De Gex 219, 225.
Mackenzie v. Childers, 43 Ch. D.
265, 279. Hall v. Turner, 110 No.
Car. 292, 14 S. E. 791. **Lewis,**

§ **281.** A right given to the grantee of a legal or equitable easement to enter upon the servient tenement and abate any structure put up to the injury of such easement does not bring the easement within the scope of the Rule against Perpetuities. It does not affect the title to the land, but merely gives the grantee the right to do for himself what the law would do for him.[1]

§ **282. Easement or Condition.** It is immaterial how such equitable easement is created. According to the modern cases, when to a conveyance of land a condition restraining the mode of its use is attached, and such a condition is for the benefit of the land of other persons (and sometimes when it is for the benefit of land of the grantor himself), this condition is not regarded as a true condition, on breach of which the grantor or his heirs may enter and be in of their old estate, but as simply an inapt way of declaring a trust or equitable charge. To determine when words of condition constitute a true condition and when they create a trust is a question of construction outside the scope of this treatise.[1]  It is

Perp. ͵12. Sugd. V. & P. (14th ed.) 596. 2 Dav. Prec. Conv. (4th ed.) 511, note. Marsden, Perp. 12, 13, 16. Challis, Real Prop. (3d ed.) 186, 187. 11 Enc. Laws of Eng. (2d ed.) 69. See London & S. W. R. Co. v. Gomm, 20 Ch. D. (C. A.) 562, 583; Heald v. Ross, 47 Atl. 575 (N. J.); Wakefield v. Van Tassell, 202 Ill. 41, 66 N. E. 830; Stevens v. Annex Realty Co., 173 Mo. 511, 73 S. W. 505; Noel v. Hill, 158 Mo. Ap. 426, 138 S. W. 364; Pierce v. St. Louis Union Tr. Co., 311 Mo. 262, 294, 278 S. W. 398, 408; Clem v. Valentine, 155 Md. 19, 141 Atl. 710. Cf. Aspden v. Seddon, 1 Ex. D. 496.

§ 281. [1] Tobey v. Moore, 130 Mass. 448. In Ex parte Ralph, De Gex 219, 228, 229, there was a contract to convey land subject to

equitable easements, with proper provisions for their observance. The Court ordered a clause, giving a right to enter and abate any obstruction to the easements, to be inserted in the conveyance. The deed actually drawn limited this right to lives in being and twenty-one years, but this seems to have been unnecessary. 2 Dav. Prec. Conv. (4th ed.) 511, note. Marsden, Perp. 62. But see Smith v. Colbourne, [1914] 2 Ch. (C. A.) 533.

§ 282. [1] In the time of Lord Coke, words of condition restraining the use of land, although manifestly imposed for the benefit of other land in the neighborhood, would undoubtedly have been deemed to create a condition enforceable by entry. In Eng-

enough to say here that when they create a present equitable
easement by way of trust, such equitable easement is not with-

land, however, for nearly, if not
quite, two centuries, the remedy
by entry for breach of condition
attached to a conveyance in fee
simple has been practically obsolete. In mortgages all remedies have been had in equity, and
if in devises clauses in the form
of a condition have been inserted
to secure the payment of legacies
to the heir or third persons, the
right to such legacies has not
been enforced by entry. The last
instance in which an heir is reported to have entered for breach
of a condition to pay a legacy to
him is Grimston v. Bruce, 1 Salk.
156 (1707), as was said by counsel
in Wright v. Wilkin, 2 B. & S. 232,
262; and in that case the heir was
enjoined by the Court of Chancery. The only case found in either
the eighteenth or the nineteenth
century in England where the heir
has entered for breach of a condition attached to a fee simple
is Doe d. Gill v. Pearson, 6 East
173 (1805), and there no trust
could be raised, and the decision
has been doubted. Attwater v.
Attwater, 18 Beav. 330. Billing
v. Welch, Ir. R. 6 C. L. 88. See
Gray, Restraints on Alienation
(2d ed.), §§ 31 et seq. The practice
of entry undoubtedly fell into disuse, because when the condition
was for the payment of money,
which it generally was, equity
would restrain a forfeiture, and
would in many cases enforce the
payment as a trust. Yet it was
a bold statement for Sugden to
make in his treatise on Powers

(1st ed.) 96 (1808), "That what
by the old law was deemed a
devise *upon condition* would now,
perhaps, in almost every case, be
construed a devise in fee upon
trust, and by this construction,
instead of the heir taking advantage of the condition broken, the
cestui que trust can compel an
observance of the trust by a suit
in equity." But this statement,
which is repeated by the learned
author in all the subsequent editions (see 8th ed. (1861) 106),
though bold, was prophetic. In
1860 the Court of Queen's Bench,
and on appeal the Exchequer
Chamber, held, in the case of
Wright v. Wilkin, 2 B. & S. 232,
259, that upon a devise on condition that the devisee should pay
certain legacies, the heir could not
enter for breach of condition, but
that the devisee took the land on
trust; and this view was adopted
by the House of Lords in A. G. v.
Wax Chandlers' Co., L. R. 6 H. L.
1 (1873), overruling Lord Romilly, M. R., L. R. 8 Eq. 452; and
Lord Hatherley, C., L. R. 5 Ch.
503. See also A. G. v. Southmol-
ton, 14 Beav. 357; Merchant Tay-
lors' Co. v. A. G., L. R. 11 Eq. 35;
Re Richardson, 56 L. J. Ch. 784.
The same doctrine has been
adopted in the Supreme Court of
the United States, after elaborate argument, in Stanley v. Colt,
5 Wall. 119, 18 L. E. 502. See also Columbia Ry. Co. v. South Carolina, 261 U. S. 236, 43 S. Ct. 306,
67 L. E. 629. So in Massachusetts. Sohier v. Trinity Church,

in the Rule against Perpetuities; and that when they constitute a true condition, the effect of the Rule will be considered,
§§ 299 et seq., post.

109 Mass. 1, 19. Episcopal City
Mission v. Appleton, 117 Mass.
326. Ayling v. Kramer, 133
Mass. 12. Skinner v. Shepard,
130 Mass. 180. Stone v. Houghton, 139 Mass. 175, 31 N. E.
719. Cassidy v. Mason, 171 Mass.
507, 50 N. E. 1027. These later
decisions must be taken to have
overruled anything to the contrary in the earlier Massachusetts cases of A. G. v. Merrimack
Manuf. Co., 14 Gray 586, and
Guild v. Richards, 16 Gray 309.
See also Jeffries v. Jeffries, 117
Mass. 184. In Clapp v. Wilder,
176 Mass. 332, 57 N. E. 692, it
was held by four judges to three
that a certain condition was not
imposed for the benefit of land,
but for the benefit of the grantor
personally. Whether this decision was consistent with the law
as previously held in Massachusetts this is not the place to consider. But see also Wilson v.
Middlesex Co., 244 Mass. 224, 138
N. E. 699; Boston Consolidated
Gas Co. v. Oakes, 279 Mass. 230,
235, 181 N. E. 225, 227. In accord with the statement in this
note (as to both gifts and devises) are also Neely v. Hoskins,
84 Me. 386, 24 Atl. 882; Ashuelot
Nat. Bank v. Keene, 74 N. H. 148,
65 Atl. 826; Fuller v. Arms, 45
Vt. 400; Brice v. All Saints Mem.
Chapel, 31 R. I. 183, 76 Atl. 774;
Avery v. N. Y. Central R. R. Co.,
106 N. Y. 142, 154, 155, 12 N. E.
619, 624, 625; Post v. Weil, 115

N. Y. 361, 22 N. E. 145; Cunning-
ham v. Parker, 146 N. Y. 29, 40
N. E. 635; Countryman v. Deck,
13 Abb. N. C. 110; Freer v. Glen
Springs Sanatorium, 131 N. Y.
A. D. 352, 115 N. Y. S. 734; Mills
v. Davison, 54 N. J. Eq. 659, 35
Atl. 1072; Clark v. Martin, 49
Pa. 289; St. Peter's Church v.
Bragaw, 144 No. Car. 126, 56 S.
E. 688; Hinton v. Vinson, 180 No.
Car. 393, 104 S. E. 897; Watrous
v. Allen, 57 Mich. 362, 24 N. W.
104; Lake Erie & W. R. R. Co. v.
Priest, 131 Ind. 413, 31 N. E. 77;
Wier v. Simmons, 55 Wis. 637,
13 N. W. 873; Carroll County
Academy v. Gallatin Academy
Co., 104 Ky. 621, 47 S. W. 617;
Thornton v. Natchez, 129 Fed.
84; Federal Land Bank v. Luck-
enbill, 213 Ind. 616, 13 N. E. 2d
531; Delaware Land Co. v. First
Church, 16 Del. Ch. 410, 147 Atl.
165; Self v. Billings, 139 Ga. 400,
77 S. E. 562; Kent v. Stevenson,
127 Miss. 529, 90 So. 241; Victoria Hospital v. All Persons, 109
Cal. 455, 147 Pac. 124; Queen
City Park Asso. v. Gale, 110 Vt.
110, 3 Atl. 2d 529. And in Connecticut it is said that all conditions which are not for the benefit of some individual or the public are void. Mitchell v. Leavitt,
30 Conn. 587. And see Barrie v.
Smith, 47 Mich. 130, 10 N. W.
168. But cf. Adams v. Valentine,
33 Fed. 1. (The decision of the
Maryland cases, Bennett v. Humane Impartial Soc., 91 Md. 10,

316THE RULE AGAINST PERPETUITIES[§ 283

## I. LEGAL INTERESTS

### A. REAL ESTATE

**§ 283. Reversions and Vested Remainders.** These are vested interests, *i. e.* not subject to a condition precedent, and therefore are not within the scope of the Rule against Perpetuities.[1]

**§ 284. Contingent Remainders.** Whether contingent remainders are subject to the Rule against Perpetuities has been much discussed. As the Rule governs all shifting and springing uses and executory devises, and all contingent limitations of personal property, whether in the form of remainders or not, it seems very desirable that contingent remainders should be subjected to the Rule also. Some reasons have, however, been suggested for exempting legal contingent remainders from the operation of the Rule against Perpetuities.

**§ 285. I. Contingent Remainders Destructible.** It is said that a contingent remainder can be destroyed by the tenant of

45 Atl. 888, and Woman's Foreign Missionary Soc. v. Mitchell, 93 Md. 199, 48 Atl. 737, was affected by the doctrine, peculiar to that State, that property cannot be given upon an express charitable trust. See § 245.2, ante.) Cf. May v. Boston, 158 Mass. 21, 31, 32 N. E. 902, 904; Everett Factories v. Oldtyme Corp., 300 Mass. 499, 15 N. E. 2d 829; Upington v. Corrigan, 151 N. Y. 143, 45 N. E. 359; Blanchard v. Detroit, etc., R. R. Co., 31 Mich. 43; Underhill v. Saratoga R. R. Co., 20 Barb. 455; Aikin v. Albany, etc., R. R. Co., 26 Barb. 289; Douglas v. Hawes, Ritchie Eq. Dec. 146, 152; Rooks Creek Church v. First Church, 290 Ill. 133, 124 N. E. 793; New Edgewood Lake Corp. v. Kingston Trust Co. 246 N. Y. A. D. 163,

283 N. Y. S. 130; and see 1 Tiffany, Real Prop. (3d ed.), § 192; 1 Simes, Fut. Int., § 143; 54 Harv. Law Rev. 248; 14 Univ. Cinn. Law Rev. 524; 27 Am. B. A. J. 737; 11 Law Rep. Ann., N. S. 509 et seq.; §§ 308, note 1, 309, note 1, post. In Letteau v. Ellis, 122 Cal. Ap. 584, 588, 10 Pac. 2d 496, and Forman v. Hancock, 3 Cal. Ap. 2d 291, 39 Pac. 2d 249, the California Court of Appeals held that a condition, imposed for the purpose of enforcing a restriction on the use of land, while valid in its inception, had become invalid on account of changed circumstances. See 54 Harv. Law Rev. 248, 266–271.

**§ 283.** [1] See §§ 205–210, ante, and especially the qualification as to remainders to classes in § 205.2.

the particular estate, inasmuch as a contingent remainder must be supported by an estate tail or an estate for life, and a tenant in tail can bar all remainders by a fine or recovery, while a tenant for life by a feoffment, fine, or surrender can destroy all contingent remainders dependent upon his estate. This view is advocated in two articles in the Jurist for 1844.[1] It is true that the indestructibility of executory devises led to the establishment of the Rule against Perpetuities, while the ease with which contingent remainders might be destroyed prevented or postponed the starting of any question as to their remoteness.[2] But while it is true that no remainder after an estate tail can be too remote, since it can be destroyed by docking the entail, the case is different with a contingent remainder after an estate for life. The docking of an estate tail is a lawful act, which no condition can restrain, while on the other hand a tortious conveyance by a tenant for life exposes him to a forfeiture of his estate; and if a trustee to support contingent remainders joins in a conveyance to destroy them, he commits a breach of trust.[3] If a remainder cannot be too remote, the whole doctrine of *cy pres* with regard to estates tail[4] falls to the ground; on a remainder to an unborn person for life, with remainder to his issue, there is no occasion to give such a person an estate tail, if the remainder to his issue is good.

§ 286. But it is needless to discuss this theory, the unsoundness of which Mr. Lewis has exposed,[1] for both in England and very generally in America contingent remainders have by statute ceased to be destructible.[2] If they were exempt from the operation of the Rule against Perpetuities, because

§ 285. [1] 8 Jur., pt. 2, 20, 283.

[2] § 192, ante.

[3] Mansell v. Mansell, 2 P. Wms. 678, 680.

[4] See §§ 643 et seq., post. Query, if remainder is invalid under doctrine of Whitby v. Mitchell, § 298.1, post.

§ 286. [1] Lewis, Perp. Suppl. 130–136, 140–142.

[2] See Wood v. Chase, 327 Ill. 91, 158 N. E. 470; 1 Simes, Fut. Int., §§ 111–113; 4 Ill. Law Rev. 355; 11 Corn. Law Quart. 408; Amer. Law Inst. Restatement, Property, § 240, and explanatory notes thereto.

they could be destroyed, now that they have become indestructible they must fall within it.

§ **287. II. Successive Life Estates.**  It has been supposed that the old notion that you cannot have a possibility on a possibility has survived in the form of a prohibition of life estates to successive generations, and that this, and not the Rule against Perpetuities, governs the creation of remainders. The suggestion had been made before,[1] but it was brought into prominence by Sir Edward Sugden.  In *Cole* v. *Sewell*,[2] as Lord Chancellor of Ireland, he held that a contingent remainder dependent on an estate tail was barrable.  There can be no doubt of the correctness of the decision, which was affirmed in the House of Lords.  But the Lord Chancellor of Ireland not only held that contingent remainders after an estate tail were good, but he said that in all remainders remoteness was out of the question.  His language is far from clear.  It is given in the note.[3]  Mr. Lewis having commented on *Cole* v. *Sewell*,[4]

§ 287. [1] See §§ 195–199, ante.

[2] 4 Dr. & W. 1, 2 Conn. & L. 344.  See 5 Ir. L. 190, 595.

[3] "As to the question of remoteness, at this time of day, I was very much surprised to hear it pressed upon the Court, because it is now perfectly settled, that where a limitation is to take effect as a remainder, remoteness is out of the question: for the given limitation is either a vested remainder, and then it matters not whether it ever vest in possession, because the previous estate may subsist for centuries, or for all time; or it is a contingent remainder, and then, by the rule of law, unless the event, upon which the contingency depends, happen, so that the remainder may vest eo instanti the preceding limitation determines, it can never take effect at all.  There was a great difficulty in the old law, because the Rule as to Perpetuity, which is a comparatively modern rule (I mean of recent introduction, when speaking of the laws of this country), was not known, so that, while contingent remainders were the only species of executory estate then known, and uses, and springing and shifting limitations were not invented, the law did speak of remoteness and mere possibilities as an objection to a remainder, and endeavored to avoid remote possibilities; but since the establishment of the Rule as to Perpetuities, this has long ceased, and no question now ever arises with reference to remoteness; for if a limitation is to take effect as a springing, shifting, or secondary use, not depending on an estate tail, and if it is so limited, that it may go beyond a life or lives in being, and twenty-one years,

Lord St. Leonards, in *Monypenny* v. *Dering*,[5] remarked: "In *Cole* v. *Sewell*, I said that the rule against a limitation to an unborn son of an unborn son was unaffected by what I there laid down;" and again: "The rule of law forbids the raising of successive estates by purchase to unborn children, that is to an unborn child of an unborn child. With this rule I have never meant to interfere, for it is too well settled to be broken in upon." And in his Law of Property he said that in *Cole* v. *Sewell* "the rule was admitted to be a continuing one, which forbids the creation of successive life estates to successive unborn classes of issue. So far the old law was admitted to operate. . . The limitation was not within the old rule

and a few months, equal to gestation, then it is absolutely void; but if, on the other hand, it is a remainder, it must take effect, if at all, upon the determination of the preceding estate. In the latter case, the event may or may not happen, before, or at, the instant the preceding estate is determined, and the limitation will fail, or not, according to that event. It may thus be prevented from taking effect, but it can never lead to remoteness. That objection, therefore, cannot be sustained against the validity of a contingent remainder. . . . The first instance of Mr. Fearne is taken from Coke, Littleton, 378 a, and the passage shows there was then a difficulty about remote possibilities which does not exist at this moment. Lord Coke, speaking of this, says: 'So it is if a man make a lease for life to A., B., and C., and if B. survive C., then the remainder to B. and his heirs: here is another exception out of the said rule, for albeit the person be certain, yet inasmuch as it depends upon the

dying of B. before C., the remainder cannot vest in C. presently: and the reason of both these cases in effect is, because the remainder is to commence upon limitation of time, viz. upon the possibilitie of the death of one man before another, which is a common possibilitie.' The concluding words show that in those early times they were looking to the period when the contingency might arise. The effect, however, of the modern Rule against Perpetuities has been to render this doctrine obsolete, although it has rendered void successive life estates to successive unborn classes of issue. In Nicholls v. Sheffield, 2 Bro. C. C. 215, the Court held that a proviso for shifting an estate after an estate tail was valid; and Lord Kenyon, who was then at the Rolls, would not listen to an argument founded on remoteness, because the limitation over might at any time be barred by the previous tenant in tail." 4 Dr. & W. 28–32.

4 Perp. Suppl. 103–111.

5 De G. M. & G. 145, 168, 171.

forbidding the providing for a possibility upon a possibility." [6]

§ 288. The notion that there could not be "a possibility
upon a possibility" was no part of the common law. It was
a conceit introduced by Chief Justice Popham in 1598,[1] due,
as Mr. Williams himself says, to "the mischievous scholastic
logic which was then rife in our courts of law;"[2] and it was
a passing conceit. Within twenty years Lord Coke, C. J.,
said: "If Popham's opinion should be law, it would shake
the common assurances of the land;"[3] and in *The Duke of
Norfolk's Case*,[4] in 1681, Lord Nottingham, C., said: "That
there may be a possibility upon a possibility, and that there
may be a contingency upon a contingency, is neither unnatural nor absurd in itself; but the contrary rule given as a reason by my Lord Popham in the *Rector of Chedington's Case*
looks like a reason of art; but in truth has no kind of reason
in it, and I have known that rule often denied in Westminster
Hall." [5]    Not until 1765, in the case of *Chapman* v. *Brown*,[6]

[6] P. 120. See Sugden, Real
Prop. Statutes (2d ed.) 274, note
(a).

Mr. Justice Kay, in Re Frost,
43 Ch. D. 246, 253, says that
"Lord St. Leonards in Cole v. Sewell used language which has been
read as meaning that the doctrine
of remoteness never could apply
to a contingent remainder," but
that "the language refers simply
to the case of an estate for life
or an estate tail limited to a person in esse, when the limitation
takes effect." "But none of that
language contemplates the case of
there being interposed a possible
estate for life to a person not in
existence, and a contingent remainder over on the death of that
person." This is a just comment
on Cole v. Sewell, but in the extract from his treatise on Real
Property it must be conceded

that Lord St. Leonards recognizes
the continued existence of the doctrine of a possibility upon a possibility. Cf. Gilbert, Uses (Sugd.
ed.) 119, note (2); Sugd. Pow.
(8th ed.) 677; 1 Jarm. Wills (7th
ed.) 328, note (m).

§ 288. [1] Rector of Chedington's
Case, 1 Co. 153 a, 156 b; §§ 125–
133, ante, where the matter is
more fully treated.

[2] Wms. Real Prop. (24th ed.)
435.

[3] Blamford v. Blamford, 3 Bulst.
98, 1 Roll. R. 318, 321.

[4] 3 Ch. Cas. 1, 29.

[5] § 133, note, ante. Wms. Real
Prop. (22d ed.) 370. "I do not
think that much reliance can be
placed on the existence of an independent rule of law forbidding
a possibility on a possibility."
Per Farwell, J., in Re Ashforth,
[1905] 1 Ch. 535, 543. See also

is any suggestion to be found that such a theory is at the basis of the prohibition of a gift to the issue of an unborn child; and except as furnishing a ground for such prohibition, it is now universally admitted to be entirely exploded.[7]

§ 289. So much for the alleged ground of the supposed rule that, apart from the question of remoteness, you cannot limit successive life estates in remainder. But no trace of the rule itself is found until *Marlborough* v. *Godolphin*[1] (1759), and then it is not based on the "possibility upon a possibility" theory; and *Manning* v. *Andrews*[2] shows that before the establishment of the Rule against Perpetuities such limitations were deemed unobjectionable.[3]

§ 290. In short, the substitute offered to take the place of the Rule against Perpetuities as to remainders is a non-existent rule based on an exploded theory.[1]

§ 291. Let us consider, however, this supposed rule a little more closely. It is sometimes said to be that you cannot give

Re Nash, [1910] 1 Ch. (C. A.) 1, 9, 10. And Mr. Charles Sweet, while contending that the rule against contingent remainders being limited to successive generations still continues, condemns, in the strongest terms, the notion of double possibilities. Challis, Real Prop. (3d ed.) 118, 206; 12 Columbia Law Rev. 200, 216, 219; 30 Law Quart. Rev. 353; 27 Yale L. J. 977. In Re Bullock's Will, [1915] 1 Ch. 493, 500, Sargant, J., remarks: "the theory of double possibilities as a ground for avoiding limitations has received its quietus in the case of *In re Nash*." See further § 933, post.

6 3 Burr. 1626. § 197, ante.

7 § 133, note, ante. But now see § 298.8, post.

§ 289. 1 Eden 404. §§ 195, 196, ante.

[G. R. P.]—21

2 1 Leon. 256 (1576), stated §§ 132, 132.1, ante.

3 §§ 191–199, ante.

§ 290. 1 This and the six preceding sections appeared in substantially the same form as above in the first edition of this work, published in 1886. In England, a rule of the sort above said to be non-existent was established by the case of Whitby v. Mitchell, 42 Ch. D. 494, 44 Ch. D. (C. A.) 85 (see § 298.1, post); only to be abolished by the Law of Prop. Act (1925), § 161; see § 298.8, post. It had also been decided, previous to that statute, that the rule of Whitby v. Mitchell was not a substitute for the Rule against Perpetuities, and that the latter rule applies to contingent remainders. See § 298.9, post.

a remainder to the issue of a person unborn.[1]   But on a devise to A., a bachelor, for life, remainder to A.'s grandchildren in fee, the remainder is to the issue of unborn persons, yet it is unquestionably good,[2] and the creation of such a remainder by the exercise of a power is of constant occurrence in practice.[3]

§ 292. The form in which the alleged rule is stated by Mr. Joshua Williams, its chief defender, is: "An estate cannot be given to an unborn person for life, followed by any estate to any child of such unborn person."[1]   But suppose an estate is given to A., a bachelor, for life, remainder to A.'s eldest son for life, remainder to the eldest son of the eldest son of B., another bachelor, in fee.   This does not come within Mr. Williams's rule.   The eldest son of the eldest son of B. is the child of an unborn person, but the remainder to him does not follow an estate to that unborn person, but an estate to another unborn person; yet undoubtedly such remainder would be bad.

§ 293. Suppose, therefore, the rule is put in this form: "A remainder to the issue of an unborn person is bad if preceded by a life estate to an unborn person."   But if an estate is given to A., a bachelor, for life, remainder to his eldest son for life, remainder to such of the other children of A. as survive his eldest son, the remainder to the younger children of A. is not to the issue of an unborn person but of a living person; but as it will not vest till the death of an unborn person, can any one doubt that it would be held bad?

§ 294. Suppose the rule takes this shape.   A contingent remainder is not good unless it must vest within lives in

§ 291. [1] Leake, Law of Property in Land (1st ed.) 334.

[2] See Brown v. Brown, 86 Tenn. 277, 291–297, 6 S. W. 869, 873–875.

[3] See Routledge v. Dorril, 2 Ves. Jr. 357, 366; Robert v. West, 15 Ga. 122, 142.   These were cases of personalty, it is true, but it has never been doubted that the same rule holds in legal remainders.   See Hockley v. Mawbey, 1 Ves. Jr. 143, 150; Sugd. Pow. (8th ed.) 397, 677.

§ 292. [1] See Challis, Real Prop. (3d ed.) 115; Wms. Real Prop. (24th ed.) 435, 494.

being at the time of its creation; or, as Wood, V. C., puts it in *Cattlin* v. *Brown*,[1] "a contingent remainder cannot be limited as depending on the termination of a particular estate, whose determination will not necessarily take place within the period allowed by law."[2]  Now this is the Rule against Perpetuities, less the allowance of twenty-one years.  But the allowance of the period of twenty-one years beyond lives in being formed no part of the original Rule.  As has been shown,[3] it was established by erroneous reasoning, though it has now become a settled part of the Rule.  There is no ground why it should not be added to the Rule in the case of contingent remainders if it is to be added in the case of other future limitations, and there is decided inconvenience in introducing arbitrary distinctions.  If the period of twenty-one years has been adopted in the latter class it should be in the former.  "The rule is stated in the able argument of Mr. Preston in *Mogg* v. *Mogg*.[4]  He says: 'A gift to an unborn child for life is good, if it stops there; but if a remainder is added to his children or issue as purchasers, it is not good, unless there be a limitation of the time within which it is to take effect.'[5]  That is, I think, a perfectly accurate statement of the law which I am to apply to this case." [6]

§ **294.1.** The rule then must take this form: a contingent remainder is good, if it must vest within twenty-one years after lives in being, but to this there is an exception, viz. such remainder is bad if it is preceded by a contingent remainder to such remainder-man's parent now unborn.[1]  What is the reason for this exception?  It must be, either because

§ **294.** [1] 11 Hare 372, 374.

[2] This is not quite exact.  If the contingent event must happen within the required limits the remainder is good, although it follows an estate which may not terminate within those limits; e. g. to A., a bachelor, for life, remainder to his eldest son for life, remainder to A.'s other children in fee.  Here the remainder to A.'s younger children is contingent at

its creation, but it must become vested, if ever, during the life of A., and is, therefore, unquestionably good.  But see § 298.8, post.

[3] §§ 186-188, ante.

[4] 1 Mer. 654.

[5] 1 Mer. 664.

[6] Per Wood, V. C., Cattlin v. Brown, 11 Hare 372, 375.

§ **294.1.** [1] But now see § 298.8, post.

it is required by the general policy of the law as to remoteness, or because it is required by a doctrine of the Common Law settled before the policy of the law as to remoteness had been established. It is not required for the former reason, for the general policy of the law as to remoteness calls for no such exception. It is not required by the second reason, because there is no evidence that such doctrine had been adopted into the Common Law, and it is no answer to say that if the policy of the law as to remoteness had not been established, the courts would, not improbably, have done something to meet this particular case.

§ 295. Mr. Williams's chief argument[1] for the doctrine that the Rule against Perpetuities does not apply to remainders was that no conveyancer had ever drawn a settlement giving remainders to those children of unborn children who should be born within twenty-one years after the settlor's death; but the answer is that no such settlements had in fact been drawn of personalty, and yet such limitations Mr. Williams himself would have agreed were good; and they have now been decided to be good. *Re Bowles.*[2]

§ 296. **Statutes of Uses and Wills.** The notion which has led to the belief that contingent remainders are exempt from the operation of the Rule against Perpetuities seems to be that contingent remainders are common-law interests, and that the Rule was called into existence by the enactment of the Statutes of Uses and Wills, and for the purpose of restraining the creation of the interests first allowed by those Statutes, viz. shifting and springing uses and executory devises, and that it is confined to those interests. This is historically incorrect. It is true that contingent remainders came into the law without the aid of any statute, but they were not allowed till the fifteenth century, and they did not come into actual use in settlements until after the passage of

§ 295. [1] Real Prop. (18th ed.) App. E.

[2] [1902] 2 Ch. 650. So the rule against "double possibilities" does not apply where there is a duty on a trustee to convert realty into personalty. Fonseca v. Jones, 21 Manitoba 168, 184. See §§ 910–917, post. Cf. Re Clarke's Settlement Trust, [1916] 1 Ch. 467.

the Statutes of Uses and Wills;[1] and even when they were
introduced into practice, as they were easily destructible, any
inconvenience on the score of remoteness was little felt.  Instead of the Rule against Perpetuities coming in upon the
enactment of the Statutes of Uses and Wills, it was not distinctly announced from the Bench until *The Duke of Norfolk's Case*,[2] in 1681, one hundred and forty odd years after
the passage of those Statutes.  And how novel a doctrine
it then was appears from the fact that the decree of Lord
Chancellor Nottingham, though finally approved by the House
of Lords, was opposed to the opinions of the heads of the three
superior courts of common law, and was reversed by his successor, Lord Keeper North.  And so far is it from being true
that the Rule against Perpetuities was introduced only
against interests created by the Statutes of Uses and Wills,
that, in fact, it was to a common-law limitation that the Rule
owed its development.  Executory devises of chattels real
were common-law interests.  There could be no use of a chattel, and chattels were always devisable at common law.  But
it was in the long line of cases touching these common-law
interests, culminating in *The Duke of Norfolk's Case* itself,
that the Rule against Perpetuities grew and took its shape.[3]

§ **296.1.** Mr. Sweet in a note to Challis, Real Prop. (3d
ed.) 210, while not denying that executory devises of chattels
were allowed at the time when the Rule against Perpetuities
was established, and that it was in the consideration of them
that the Rule was formulated, says that they were not allowed
until *Manning's Case*,[1] and that therefore they were not common-law interests.  If no doctrine is to be considered as part
of the common law unless it was in force at the time of the
Heptarchy, or the Norman Conquest, or some other selected
date in the Middle Ages, then few doctrines are parts of the
common law; for instance, contingent remainders themselves
are not common-law interests.  It is submitted that it is both
usual and accurate to describe a doctrine which has become
settled in the law without the aid of a statute as a common-

§ **296.** [1] § 134, ante.    [3] §§ 148–158, 160–169, ante.
[2] 3 Ch. Cas. 1. § 169, ante.    § **296.1.** [1] 8 Co. 94 b.

law doctrine. The real point in issue is whether, before the
Rule against Perpetuities was developed, such a doctrine
had become established without the aid of statutes. Mr.
Sweet, surely, cannot be suspected of holding to the vulgar
error that judges cannot make law.[2]

§ 297. If it were true that contingent remainders are not
subject to the Rule against Perpetuities, because they are
common-law interests, then bequests of chattels, real or personal, would not be subject to the Rule, for they owe nothing
to any statute; and easements, rents, and terms for years (to
say nothing of rights of entry for breach of condition) could
be created to begin on the most distant contingencies.[1] So,
again, if it was necessary in order that an interest should be
subjected to the Rule against Perpetuities, that it should owe
its existence to the Statute of Uses or of Wills, all equitable
interests of every description would be free from any restraint
of the Rule, for equitable interests existed long before those
Statutes. Yet no one questions that to-day they are within the
scope of the Rule.[2]

§ 298. **Rule is Product of Common Law.** The Rule
against Perpetuities is, comparatively speaking, a modern
rule. No need of restraining future interests was felt in the
early times. The need was first felt in connection with executory devises of chattels, which were common-law interests.
As to springing and shifting uses and executory devises of
freeholds, the courts hesitated at first whether they should
be held indestructible; finally they were held indestructible,
and a need then arose for the application of the Rule against
Perpetuities to these statutory interests also. Contingent remainders long remained destructible, and no practical necessity therefore was felt of considering the Rule in connection
with them. The Rule was created and was gradually shaped
by the courts to restrain future interests within twenty-one
years after a life in being. When formed, it was applied to
common-law and statutory interests, to executory devises of

[2] See Gray, Nature and Sources
of the Law (2d ed.) 218–240.

§ 297. [1] See §§ 300–302, 312,
315, 316, 319, 321, post.
[2] § 323, post.

leaseholds and of freeholds alike; it was created to effect a
general end of public policy, and there is no reason in history
or policy why all future interests should not fall within it.
Such is the spirit, if not the actual decision, in *London &
S. W. R. Co. v. Gomm*.[1] The advocates of the view that the
Rule against Perpetuities should not apply to common-law
interests treat the Rule as if it was a statute directing only
how springing and shifting uses and executory devises should
be dealt with. They admit that the judges have applied the
Rule to common-law interests, but they think the judges have
been wrong in so doing.[2] But the Rule is not a statute, it
is judge-made law, and there seems no reason why, as cases
arise, the judges should not define the scope of the law that
they have made. The phenomenon is common enough, as,
for instance, in mercantile law.

§ **298.1. Whitby v. Mitchell.** After the first edition of
this book the case of *Whitby* v. *Mitchell*[1] was decided. Kay,
J., there held that the rule that successive life estates could
not be limited is "not only an application of the law against
perpetuities; it is something more than that." "For that
proposition I do not want any higher authority than that of
the late Mr. Joshua Williams. . . . He says . . . that

§ **298.** [1] 20 Ch. D. 562. See
Chap. V., ante. Mr. Lewis is the
ablest advocate of the view that
remainders are subject to the Rule
against Perpetuities. Lewis, Perp.,
c. 16, and especially Suppl. 97–
153. See, to the same effect, 1
Jarm. Wills (4th ed.) 255–258,
260–263, (5th ed.) 218–221, 223–
226; 2 Jarm. Wills (4th ed.) 845;
60 L. T. 247; 69 L. T. 360; Theob.
Wills (2d ed.) 424–429, (5th ed.)
520, (9th ed.) 485; Tud. L.
C. in Real Prop. (3d ed.) 470–475;
1 Hayes, Conv. (5th ed.) 494, 495;
7 Holdsworth, Hist. Eng. Law (3d
ed.) 235, 236; 55 Law Quart. Rev.
422, 426; Wood v. Griffin, 46 N.

H. 230, 235. Contra, Wms. Real
Prop. (13th ed.) 274–277, (24th
ed.) 435–437, 492–500; 8 Jur., pt.
2, 20, 283; 69 L. T. 336; Challis,
Real Prop. (3d ed.) 115, 187 et
seq., 197 et seq. See generally
Sugd. Pow. (8th ed.) 393, 394;
Fearne, C. R. 501; 3 Dav. Prec.
Conv. (3d ed.) 270, 336–338;
Third Rep. Real Prop. Comm. 29–
31; Marsden, Perp., c. 8; 2 Vaizey,
Settlements 1154. But now see
§ 298.9, post.

[2] See Mr. Challis and Mr. Sweet,
in Challis, Real Prop. (3d ed.)
passim.

§ **298.1.** [1] 42 Ch. D. 494, 44 Ch.
D. (C. A.) 85.

it is an absolute rule independent of the rule against perpetuities. With that I entirely agree." The learned judge
made no examination of the authorities. In this case legal
remainders to unborn children of unborn children after life
estates to their parents were declared to be bad, although
they were so limited as not to infringe the Rule against Perpetuities. This decision was affirmed by the Court of Appeal.[2]
Cotton, L. J., said: "You cannot have a limitation for the
life of an unborn person, with a limitation after his death to
his unborn children to take as purchasers. That is the same
thing as what has been called 'a possibility upon a possibility.'
But it is said that, although there is such a rule in existence,
that is superseded by the more modern rule against perpetuities. In my opinion the old rule with regard to a possibility
on a possibility has not been done away with by this modern
rule." Lindley, L. J., said: "I entertain no doubt myself
that Mr. Joshua Williams' observations on this subject are
correct from beginning to end, and I do not know that I
could express my views better than he did. I do not know,
any more than he seems to have done, the exact meaning of
the old rule as to a possibility upon a possibility; and if any
one turns to the passage in Coke upon Littleton where it is
discussed, I hope he will understand it better than I do. I
confess I do not understand it now and never did. But, at
all events, it gave rise to the rule which everybody can understand . . . 'that, if land is limited to an unborn person
during his life, a remainder cannot be limited, so as to confer
an estate by purchase on that person's issue.' . . . The
rule against perpetuities was invented much later, on account
of the law of shifting uses and executory devises. . . . The
old rule against double possibilities is a rule that has not been
abrogated." Lopes, L. J., said: "That there was an old rule
that an estate could not be limited to an unborn child of an
unborn person has been admitted, and, in fact, cannot be denied. It was an old rule originating out of the feudal system.
But it is said that, although this old rule did once exist, it
has been superseded by the rule against perpetuities. . . .

[2] 44 Ch. D. (C. A.) 85.

I have no doubt . . . that these are two independent and co-existing rules."

§ 298.2. The most striking thing about the opinions both of Kay, J., and of the judges of the Court of Appeal in *Whitby* v. *Mitchell* is the way in which they rest on the opinion of Mr. Joshua Williams. A writer in the Solicitors' Journal[1] says that this "shows the advantage of having text-books of such authority that judges of the Court of Appeal and the youngest students can alike take their law from them."

§ 298.3. The decision in *Whitby* v. *Mitchell* was criticised by Mr. J. Savill Vaizey in the Law Quarterly Review,[1] by an anonymous writer in the Law Times,[2] and by Mr. T. Cyprian Williams in the Law Quarterly Review.[3] Mr. Vaizey and Mr. Williams discussed elaborately the authorities given in the preceding sections, and their conclusion coincided with the result reached in the first edition of this book.

§ 298.4. Mr. Ernest C. C. Frith and Mr. Charles Sweet have published articles[1] defending *Whitby* v. *Mitchell*. The matter has now been so thoroughly threshed out, that the only important addition to be hoped for in aid of the discussion would seem to be the discovery of authorities previously unknown or unnoticed. Mr. Sweet has recognized this, and believes that he has found two authorities previously unnoticed, which bear upon the question. The first of these is a *dictum* of Popham, C. J., in *Chudleigh's Case:*[2] "He said, if a feoffment be made to the use of A. for life, and after to the use of every person who should be his heir, one after another, for the term of the life of every such heir only; in this case, if this limitation should be good, the inheritance would be in nobody; but this limitation is merely void, for the limitation of a use to have a perpetual freehold is not agreeable with the rule of law in estates in possession." To this may be added a later *dictum* of his in the same case:[3] "If the said case

§ 298.2. [1] 34 Sol. J. 343, 344.

§ 298.3. [1] 6 Law Quart. Rev. 410.

[2] 88 Law Times 95.

[3] 14 Law Quart. Rev. 234.

§ 298.4. [1] 14 Law Quart. Rev. 133, and 15 Law Quart. Rev. 71.

[2] 1 Co. 120 a, 138 a.

[3] 1 Co. 139 b.

before put of a perpetual freehold should be maintained, that
no heir shall have but an estate for life, and that the inheritance shall be in nobody, what escheat, or ward, or heriot, or
other profit will accrue to the King or other lords ?"

§ **298.5.** On these *dicta* it may be remarked that they do
not appear in Popham's own report of his opinion.[1]  And
again no one doubts that Chief Justice Popham had a private
conceit that there could not be "a possibility upon a possibility;" a conceit which was condemned as bad law by Lord
Coke and Lord Nottingham.[2]  But, it is submitted, Chief
Justice Popham had not here in mind any rule that there
could not be a possibility upon a possibility, either in the
form given to it in modern times that after a life estate to
an unborn person you cannot give an estate to that person's
child, or in any other form.  If he had, he would have said
that A. would have had an estate for life and his heir, a
remainder for life, and that the other limitations would be
void.  What he meant was that if you give an estate in fee
you cannot add a provision that each successive tenant shall
hold only for life, a proposition which is undoubtedly good
law,[3] but which has nothing to do with a possibility upon a
possibility.  To make Popham's *dictum* any authority for the
proposition that you cannot have an estate in remainder after
a life estate to an unborn person, we have to suppose that he
meant to say that the life estate to A. was good; that the life
estate to A.'s heir was good; and that the other estates were
void; it is submitted that it is impossible to extract such a
meaning from the passage.

§ **298.6.** Mr. Sweet's second authority is a passage in the
Touchstone: "Uses that are against the rules of the common
law, shall not be executed by this statute: and therefore, if a
feoffment be made to the use of A. for life, and after to the
use of every person that shall be his heir one after another for
term of his life . . . these uses shall not be executed, because these limitations are wholly void."[1]  This is evidently

§ **298.5.** [1] Pop. 70, 76, 84.          [3] §§ 656, 934, 937, post.
[2] See §§ 125, 133, ante.          § **298.6.** [1] Shep. Touch. 506.

taken from Popham's *dictum,* and the same remark is applicable to it as to that *dictum.*

§ **298.7.** It is likely enough that if the case of a remainder to an unborn person for life, with remainder to such unborn person's son, had been presented to the courts, they would have invented some rule to declare the latter remainder void, but that any such rule had in fact been invented before the Rule against Perpetuities is, so far as the evidence goes, a pure fiction. Some rule restraining the creation of remote interests was certain some time or other to be formulated. The rise and development of the Rule against Perpetuities through a series of years is plainly to be read in the reports. No reference to any prior rule is to be found until a hundred years after the Rule against Perpetuities was established. It requires a pretty robust faith in the infallibility of Mr. Joshua Williams to believe in the real existence of such prior rule. The matter is in this singular condition. On the one hand there are assertions by some of the most distinguished judges and writers that before the Rule against Perpetuities was adopted there was in existence a rule that after a life estate to an unborn person there cannot be a remainder to his issue; and on the other hand there is absolutely no evidence whatever that those assertions are correct.[1]

§ **298.8.** Mr. Sweet was finally of opinion, "after some hesitation," that there was a rule against "two successive contingent remainders" or "a contingent remainder on a contingent remainder," which was not identical with the rule in *Whitby* v. *Mitchell* against a contingent remainder to the issue of an unborn person preceded by a contingent remainder to such unborn person.[1] There have been some judicial ex-

§ **298.7.** [1] For a further discussion of Mr. Sweet's view see App. K, § 931, post; and cf. the opinions of the learned judges in Will of Malin, [1912] Vict. 259. See also 7 Holdsworth, Hist. Eng. Law (3d ed.) 209, 210, 236, 237; Powell, Cases on Fut. Int. 786, note.

§ **298.8.** [1] 12 Columbia Law Rev. 199, 216. 29 Law Quart. Rev. 304. 30 Law Quart. Rev. 304. 27 Yale L. J. 977. He also advanced the opinion, in which he seems to stand alone, that a similar rule applies to executory limitations of land.

pressions supporting this view: *Re Frost;*[2] *Whitting* v. *Whitting;*[3] *Will of Malin;*[4] and a single decision, *Re Park's Settlement.*[5] It is impossible to say what would be the limits of such a doctrine. It seems almost as objectionable as the notion of a possibility on a possibility. Mr. Sweet himself says, with regard to *Re Park's Settlement,* the only case ever decided squarely on such a doctrine: "Having regard to these authorities [*Re Frost* and *Whitting* v. *Whitting*] it is difficult to see how the learned judge could have decided differently, but the result is unsatisfactory, not to say absurd." [6]

In the cases of *Re Bullock's Will*[7] and *Re Garnham,*[8] the Court, while assuming the correctness of *Whitby* v. *Mitchell,* overrule *Re Park's Settlement,* and disapprove much of the language in *Re Frost* and *Whitting* v. *Whitting.* In the case of *Re Clarke's Settlement Trust,*[9] the Court, while applying *Whitby* v. *Mitchell,* says: "Some lawyers, and probably most publicists, do regret that the American view has not prevailed in this country and that a rule so artificial, and now without defenders or necessity, has not been abrogated by the more modern rule against perpetuities." The Law of Property Act (1925), § 161, provides: "The rule of law prohibiting the limitation, after a life interest to an unborn person, of an interest in land to the unborn child or other issue of an unborn person is hereby abolished, but without prejudice to any other rule relating to perpetuities."[10]

2 43 Ch. D. 246.

3 53 Sol. J. 100.

4 [1912] Vict. 259, 269.

5 [1914] 1 Ch. 595.

6 30 Law Quart. Rev. 135, 357. And see § 947, note, post.

7 [1915] 1 Ch. 493.

8 [1916] 2 Ch. 413. See also Wms. Real Property (23d ed.) 396, note, 449, note (c), (24th ed.) 436, note r, 499; 7 Holdsworth, Hist. Eng. Law (3d ed.) 213; 26 Yale L. J. 257.

9 [1916] 1 Ch. 467, 476.

10 This provision does away entirely in England with the rule of Whitby v. Mitchell, and all similar doctrines, except as to instruments which took effect previous to January 1, 1926. Even as to limitations previous to that date, it is probable, in view of Re Bullock's Will and Re Garnham, that English courts will not extend the rule of Whitby v. Mitchell beyond the decision in that case. Nevertheless the doctrine of Whitby v. Mitchell continues to be a subject of controversy (see 26 Yale L. J. 257; 27 Yale L. J. 977) and a

**§ 298.9.** The case of *Whitby* v. *Mitchell* decides that there is a doctrine other than the Rule against Perpetuities which applies to contingent remainders, but it does not decide that the Rule does not apply to them; on the contrary, it rather implies that it does; and it has now been determined that the Rule does apply to them. *Re Frost.*[1] *Re Ashforth.*[2] *Whitby* v. *Von Luedecke.*[3]

cause of confusion in legal thought. In Re Watson, [1930] 2 Ch. 344, 348, Eve, J., says that a certain supposed limitation "would involve a breach of what has been called the rule against double possibilities, otherwise the rule which prohibits the limitation of an estate to the unborn child of an unborn person." The limitation in question seems to be not a contingent remainder, but an executory devise, and would infringe the Rule against Perpetuities. For further historical discussion of the Rule in Whitby v. Mitchell, see 25 Iowa Law Rev. 1.

In America the so-called Rule of Whitby v. Mitchell has never been passed upon by the courts. But see 22 Wash. Univ. L. Q. 31. Dahlgren v. Pierce, 270 Fed. 507, 516 (C. C. A. Ohio), contains dicta unfavorable to such a doctrine. The weight of opinion among recent American text-writers is that no such rule ought to be, or is likely to be, applied here. 2 Simes, Fut. Int., § 487. Powell, Cases on Future Interests 786, note. 3 Law Series, Univ. of Mo. Bull. 3, 29. 37 Yale L. J. 179, 195. But cf. 25 Iowa Law Rev. 1. Mass. Acts (1916), c. 108, Gen. Laws (ed. 1932), c. 184, § 3, provides that contingent remainders "shall like executory devises, be subject to the rule respecting remoteness known as the rule against perpetuities, exclusively of any other supposed rule respecting limitations to successive generations or double possibilities." Iowa has a similar statute, Iowa Code (1935), § 10046. The statutory abolition in England of the rule of Whitby v. Mitchell may properly influence the courts of the English colonies and the United States not to follow that case. See McGibbon v. Abbott, 10 Ap. Cas. 653; Amory v. Meredith, 7 Allen 397, 400; 35 Columbia Law Rev. 787; and Professor Landis in Harvard Legal Essays 213, 230–233.

**§ 298.9.** [1] 43 Ch. D. 246.

[2] [1905] 1 Ch. 535.

[3] [1906] 1 Ch. 783, and so Will of Malin, [1912] Vict. 259. See 7 Holdsworth, Hist. Eng. Law (3d ed.) 235, 236; and 55 Law Quart. Rev. 422.

Mr. Charles Sweet (1 Jarm. Wills (7th ed.) 343, 344) did not regard these decisions as satisfactory; as is natural, for they are inconsistent with his view that the Rule against Perpetuities does not apply to common-law interests, as to which see §§ 299 et seq., post.

The rule of Whitby v. Mitchell applied to equitable interests in

**§ 299. Rights of Entry for Condition Broken.** When a feoffment was made on condition at common law, a right of entry for condition broken remained in the feoffor.[1] Such a right was not affected by the Statute *Quia Emptores.*[2] In the older books there are instances of feoffments and grants on condition, but the objection of remoteness was no more taken to them than it was to other future interests.[3] Afterwards the practice of entering for condition broken became obsolete. Provisions conditional in form were construed as creating a present trust, and not as true conditions, and consequently there came to be little occasion for applying the Rule against Perpetuities.[4] It is true that in some English cases words of condition could not have been held to create a trust, but as giving only a right of entry to determine an estate. But no instance has been discovered of such a condition, for longer than a lifetime, attached to a fee simple,[5] except *Flower* v. *Hartopp,*[6] where the condition was held to be destroyed, and no question of remoteness was raised. The Real Property Commissioners, indeed, in their Third Report, say: "The following case frequently occurs in practice, and, as far as we know, has never been determined; an estate is devised to A. B., 'his heirs and assigns,' on condition that he and they should take, and continue to use, the name and arms of C. D."[7] One hesitates to doubt a statement of this kind made by so distinguished a body, but considerable research has disclosed, neither in the reports, nor in the textbooks, nor in the books of precedents, any suggestion of adding such a condition extending beyond a lifetime to a conveyance in fee simple. Nor does it seem a likely occurrence. A person with so strong a desire to preserve an estate in his family

land. Re Nash, [1909] 2 Ch. 450, [1910] 1 Ch. 1, § 325.1, post; and to copyholds, Re Clarke's Settlement Trust, [1910] 1 Ch. 467. But not to any interests in personalty. Re Bowles, [1902] 2 Ch. 650.

§ 299. [1] § 12, ante.
[2] § 30, ante.
[3] § 123, ante.

[4] § 282, note, ante.
[5] Such conditions, for instance, names and arms clauses, are often attached to estates tail; but as they can be destroyed by fine or recovery, no question of remoteness arises with regard to them.
[6] 6 Beav. 476.
[7] P. 36.

name as to insert such a clause would be almost certain to put the estate into strict settlement.  Besides if the estate were given in fee simple, it would either be to the heir, in which case the condition would be inoperative, or it would be given with the desire to exclude the heir, and in that case it would be unlikely that a condition should be inserted which would carry the estate to the heir.

§ 300.  The Real Property Commissioners, in their Third Report,[1] also say of such rights of entry that they seem not to be confined within the Rule, but that "they are clearly within the policy, which the law has adopted with respect to perpetuities."

§ 300.1.  The two reasons which have been suggested for excluding rights of entry for breach of condition from the operation of the Rule against Perpetuities are:  (1) That they are common-law interests.  But the Rule applies to common-law interests.[1]  (2) That they can be released.  But interests which can be aliened or released are within the Rule.[2]

§ 301.  The theory of the Real Property Commissioners that rights of entry for breach of condition are not within the Rule is denied by Mr. Lewis[1] and by Mr. Sanders.[2]  In *Re Macleay*,[3] there was a devise to the testator's brother, "on the condition that he never sells out of the family."  Jessel, M. R., held that the condition was good.  He remarked: "First of all, it is to be observed that the condition, good or bad, is confined within legal limits; it is applicable merely to the devisee himself, and therefore is not void on any ground of remoteness."[4]  And again: "It is not, strictly speaking, limited as to time, except in this way, that it is limited to the

§ 300. [1] P. 36.

§ 300.1. [1] See the remarks on this objection in connection with contingent remainders, §§ 296-298, ante.  See also §§ 312, 315, 316, 319, 321, 323, post.
[2] See Chap. VII., ante.

§ 301. [1] Perp. 616, 617.  Whether the condition attached at common law to an exchange is without the Rule against Perpetuities, as Mr. Lewis thinks (Perp. 615) is idle to inquire, since exchanges became obsolete before the Rule was established.
[2] 1 Sand. Uses (5th ed.) 207.
[3] L. R. 20 Eq. 186.
[4] L. R. 20 Eq. 187, 188.

life of the first tenant in tail;[5] of course, if unlimited as to time, it would be void for remoteness under another rule."[6]

§ 302. Afterwards, in *Dunn* v. *Flood*,[1] there was a bill by a vendor for specific performance. The land was subject to a condition that if it was used for certain trades, the grantor might enter and take the rents until the trades were discontinued, and for three months longer. North, J., held that the condition was void for remoteness and no objection to a decree for specific performance, although he refused the decree on other grounds.[2] And now in *Re Hollis's Hospital*,[3] Byrne, J., in an elaborate opinion, has held that common-law conditions are subject to the Rule against Perpetuities, although he refused to force a title dependent on the invalidity of such a condition upon a purchaser. And in *Re Da Costa*,[4] Eve, J., held that a common-law condition was obnoxious to the Rule against Perpetuities. In face of these opinions and cases, the statement of the Real Property Commissioners, unsupported by any case or *dictum*, must be deemed erroneous.[5]

[5] It should be "tenant in fee simple."

[6] L. R. 20 Eq. 190.

§ 302. [1] 25 Ch. D. 629.

[2] In the Court of Appeal judgment was affirmed. Baggallay, L. J., said: "We have not heard the counsel for the defendant, but as at present advised I concur with Mr. Justice North that this right could not be enforced, being void under the Rule against Perpetuities." Dunn v. Flood, 28 Ch. D. 586, 592.

[3] [1899] 2 Ch. 540. This case was followed in Re St. Patrick's Market, 1 Ont. W. N. 92; Matheson v. Town of Mitchell, 51 Dom. L. R. 477; and approved in Williams v. Perpetual Trustee Co., 17 Com. L. R. 469 (Aust.).

[4] [1912] 1 Ch. 337.

[5] See Marsden, Perp. 4, 5; Gray, Restraints on Alienation, (2d ed.), §§ 42, 51; 7 Holdsworth, Hist. Eng. Law (3d ed.) 233. Mr. Challis, in his treatise on Real Prop. (3d ed.) 187–190, is of a contrary opinion; and agreeing with him are Mr. Charles Sweet in his editions of Challis and Jarman (Challis, Real Prop. (3d ed.) 210 et seq.; 1 Jarm. Wills (7th ed.) 349), and Mr. Cyprian Williams, 1 V. & P. (4th ed.) 691, 692. See also 51 Law Quart. Rev. 668. And that a common-law condition was not within the Rule against Perpetuities was said, after full discussion, in Ireland in 1895. A. G. v. Cummins, [1906] 1 I. R. 406. This was followed in Walsh v. Wightman, [1927] No. Ir. 1.

The Law of Property Act (1925), § 4 (3), provides: "All rights of entry affecting a

## § 303. Entry for Arrears of Rent.

Mr. Lewis, although holding that rights to enter for condition broken are in general obnoxious to the Rule against Perpetuities, yet believes that rights of entry for non-payment of rent are not within it.[1] This is true as to conditions attached to leases for years; the interest of the reversioner is a vested interest, and to that the Rule does not apply.[2] So the right to enter and hold until the arrears of rent are discharged is, perhaps, like the right to distrain, merely a matter of remedy and not within the Rule.[3] But a right contained in a conveyance in fee for the grantor, on failure of payment of rent, to enter and be in of his old estate seems like any other condition, to be within both the letter and the spirit of the Rule.[4] Such rights, indeed, existed in early years, when no objection to the remoteness of any future interests had been made;[5] but in later

legal estate which are exercisable on condition broken or for any other reason may, after the commencement of this Act, be made exercisable by any person and the persons deriving title under him, but, in regard to an estate in fee simple (not being a rent-charge held for a legal estate) only within the period authorized by the rule relating to perpetuities." See Cheshire, Real Prop. (4th ed.) 515; 37 Yale L. J. 197.

§ 303. [1] Perp. 618, 619.

[2] § 209, ante. See Knightsbridge Estates Trust v. Byrne. [1938] Ch. 741, 759, 760. But cf. Wms. Contract for the Sale of Land 63, note x, and authorities cited.

[3] See §§ 273.1, ante, 316, post; 1 Wms. V. & P. (4th ed.) 476. 477; 17 Law Quart. Rev. 32. So though the right is to enter on lands not included in the grant or demise. Lewis, Perp. 619. See

Daniel v. Stepney, L. R. 7 Ex. 327, L. R. 9 Ex. 185, in which the Court of Exchequer Chamber, overruling the Court of Exchequer, held that a right under a lease for forty years to distrain for rent on other land of the lessee was good, without the objection of remoteness being raised. Marsden, Perp. 248, 249. It was perhaps good as a matter of remedy. Such rights are expressly declared by the Law of Prop. Act (1925), §§ 121 (6), 162 (a), 190 (8), not to be subject to the Rule against Perpetuities.

[4] See 99 L. T. 596; Elphinstone, Introd. to Conv. (7th ed.) 140; Copinger & Munro, Rents, 64–68; 1 Wms. V. & P. (4th ed.) 476. But in 17 Law Quart. Rev. 32, Mr. Arthur J. Mackey in a learned article contends that such a right to enter is not obnoxious to the Rule. Cf. Foulke, Treatise, § 367.

[5] Lit., §§ 325–327.

times they have been disused, and rights to enter and hold until rent is paid have been employed instead; and, even when absolute in form, they are treated in equity as only entitling the grantor to hold until rent is paid.[6]

§ 304. **American Cases.** Though rights of entry for condition broken are within both the letter and the spirit of the Rule against Perpetuities; though there is nothing in the history of the Rule to exempt them from its operation; though they are held to be subject to it in England; though the practical inconvenience of excluding them is very great; and though this inconvenience is especially great in America, where the heirs from whom a release must be sought may, and often do, multiply enormously with every succeeding generation,—yet in America conditions violating the Rule against Perpetuities have been repeatedly upheld, and forfeitures for their breach enforced.[1]

§ 305. It is true that in almost none of these instances has the objection of remoteness occurred to either court or counsel. Those cases in which it is reported to have been mentioned, either at the bar or from the bench down to 1886, the date of the first edition of this book, are as follows:—

§ 305.1. **Canal Bridge v. Methodist Religious Society.**[1] (1847). Mr. Fletcher, as counsel for the tenant, objected to a condition that land granted should be forever appropriated to the maintenance of public worship, on the ground that it at-

6 Co. Lit. 203 a, Butler's note, (3). 3 Cruise, Dig. 286. 2 White & Tud. L. C. in Eq. (5th ed.) 1117–1120. Tud. L. C. in Real Prop. (4th ed.) 61. See Gilbert, Rents 135–137. Cf. Dunn v. Flood, in the preceding section, where a right to enter and hold not only till the default ceased, but for three months more, was considered to be bad. Such rights are not expressly mentioned in the Law of Property Act (1925) probably because they are prac- tically obsolete in England; and the effect of Section 4 of that Act on the question whether they are subject to the Rule against Perpetuities is not clear. See Cheshire, Real Prop. (4th ed.) 514; 37 Yale L. J. 197.

§ 304. 1 See Kales, Estates, § 662; Foulke, Treatise, § 367; 2 Simes, Fut. Int., § 506; Walsh, Real Prop. (2d ed.), § 270, note 15; 3 Minn Law Rev. 320, 337

§ 305.1. 1 13 Met. 335, 348.

**[G. R. P.]**

tempted to create a perpetuity, citing Lewis on Perpetuities. This is the first reported instance of the question of remoteness being discussed by counsel in connection with conditions. The Court decided in favor of the tenants on another ground, and took no notice of the objection.

§ 305.2. **Brattle Square Church v. Grant**[1] (1855). Here is a *dictum* of Bigelow, J., that the Rule against Perpetuities does not govern rights of entry for condition broken, because such rights can be at all times released. The unsoundness of this reason has been shown.[2] The most singular thing about the remark is that in this very case an executory devise which could at any time have been released, precisely like a right to enter for breach of condition, was held void for remoteness.

§ 305.3. **Indian Orchard Canal Co. v. Sikes**[1] (1857). Land was conveyed to A. on condition that no building thereon should be occupied or used for the sale of spirituous liquors. On a writ of entry by the grantor, based on a breach of condition, the judge ruled that a sale with the knowledge of A. was a breach, but that a sale without A.'s knowledge was not a breach. The jury found for the tenant, and the demandant alleged exceptions. At the argument on the exceptions the counsel for the tenant contended, *inter alia*, that the condition was void as an attempt to create a perpetuity. The full Court gave judgment on the verdict without delivering any opinion, presumably on the grounds stated at the trial.

§ 305.4. **Sharon Iron Co. v. Erie**[1] (1861). Counsel argued that a condition violated the Rule against Perpetuities; but as the Court held that there had been a waiver of the breach, if any, it had no occasion to consider, and did not consider, the objection on the score of perpetuity.

§ 305.5. **Hunt v. Wright**[1] (1867). An undivided part of land was conveyed to H. and his heirs, on condition that the premises should be held by H. and his heirs and assigns in common with the tenants of the other undivided parts, without partition or division, subject to certain articles of associ-

§ 305.2. [1] 3 Gray 142, 148.  
[2] Chap. VII., ante.  
§ 305.3. [1] 8 Gray 562.  
§ 305.4. [1] 41 Pa. 341.  
§ 305.5. [1] 47 N. H. 396.

ation.  Held, on a petition by H. for partition, that he was
estopped to have it.  The Court were of opinion that this
condition was not "invalid as creating a perpetuity;" that the
condition was not repugnant; that tenancies in common were
not compulsorily partible at common law; that there was no
restraint on alienations; and that the articles could be dissolved at any time.  Assuming that the condition was not
repugnant, and would have been good if confined within limits, there would seem to be no difference between it and any
other remote contingent interest.  Though the Court speak
of the condition as creating a perpetuity, they do not seem
to have contemplated the question of remoteness, but to have
used this term as meaning "an inalienable interest."[2]

§ 305.6.  **French v. Old South Society**[1] (1871).  This is the first
case in the books in which the question of a condition being
bad for remoteness was presented by counsel and passed upon
by the Court.  A pew was there sold by the defendants, on
condition that the grantee and his legal representatives should
pay to the defendants the tax assessed on the pew, and also
on the condition that he or they should offer the pew to the
defendants upon leaving the meeting-house.  Chapman, C. J.,
said: "The doctrine that conditions against alienation in a
conveyance are void has never been held to be applicable to
conveyances of pews, for the reasons stated by Chief Justice
Shaw, and cited above.  The tenure by which pews are held
in this Commonwealth is peculiar.  It is objected that the
Rule against Perpetuities makes the conditions of the plaintiff's deed void.  If a perpetuity may be defined as 'an estate
unalienable though all mankind join in the conveyance' (see
*Scatterwood* v. *Edge*, 1 Salk. 229), or 'where, if all that have
interest join, yet they cannot bar or pass the estate' (see
*Washborn* v. *Downs*, 1 Ch. Cas. 213), here is no violation of
the Rule; for the plaintiff and defendants could at any time
join in a conveyance of the property.  The grantee took an
estate on condition subsequent, and the possibility of reverter
remaining in the grantor on breach of the condition is not

[2] See § 141.5, ante; Gray, Re-    § 30.
straints on Alienation (2d ed.),    § 305.6.  [1] 106 Mass. 479.

subject to the Rule against Perpetuities, even if the pew is held as real estate, *Brattle Square Church* v. *Grant*, 3 Gray, 142." But the suggested definition of a perpetuity is incorrect;[2] and the case of *Washborn* v. *Downs,* and the remark cited from it, had reference to the barring of an estate tail. The opinion of the learned Chief Justice goes upon the assumption that the alienation of pews can be indefinitely restrained. This takes them out of the class of ordinary interests to which the Rule against Perpetuities applies, and classes them with charities, which are not obnoxious to the objection of remoteness. How far this assumption is correct, and how far a pew in a church can be considered as devoted to charity, particularly if it is in the church of a religious body which is not itself a charity,[3] this is not the place to consider. It is obvious that the case is of slight authority on the objection of remoteness to conditions generally.[4]

§ 305.7. **Tobey v. Moore**[1] (1881). Here it was held that restrictions on the use of land, not involving any risk of forfeiture, were free from any objection on the ground of remoteness. The Court said: "The rule against perpetuities, which governs limitations over to third persons to take effect in the future, has never been held applicable to conditions, a right of entry for the breach of which is reserved to the grantor or devisor and his heirs, and may be released by him or them at any time. Sugd. Vend. (14th ed.), 596. *Gray* v. *Blanchard*, 8 Pick. 284. *Austin* v. *Cambridgeport Parish*, 21 Pick. 215. *Brattle Square Church* v. *Grant*, 3 Gray 142, 148, 161. *French* v. *Old South Society*, 106 Mass. 479. *Cowell* v. *Springs Co.*, 100 U. S. 55. But this case does not require us to consider whether there are any conditions strictly so called to which the rule should be applied." The above, with *Giles*

---

[2] See Chap. VII., ante.

[3] Old South Soc. v. Crocker, 119 Mass. 1. But now cf. Sears v. A. G., 193 Mass. 551, 79 N. E. 772; McNeilly v. First Pres. Church, 243 Mass. 331, 338, 137 N. E. 691, 694.

[4] In Lowe v. Hyde, 39 Wis. 345, counsel contended that a condition for the maintenance of a college was bad as a perpetuity. The Court held that there had been no breach.

§ 305.7. [1] 130 Mass. 448.

v. *Boston Society*,[2] *Piper* v. *Moulton*,[3] and *Coit* v. *Comstock*,[4] considered later,[5] were the only reported cases in which the objection of remoteness with reference to conditions had, at the date of the first edition of this book (1886), been passed upon or suggested by court or counsel in America.[6]

§ **306.** But although *French* v. *Old South Society* was the only case, down to 1886, in which any court in America had passed upon the objection of remoteness in a condition, and the facts of that case make it of little value as a precedent, yet there have been numerous decisions in America by which conditions violating the Rule against Perpetuities have been sustained. They are given in a note.[1]

[2] 10 Allen 355.
[3] 72 Me. 155.
[4] 51 Conn. 352.
[5] § 311, post.
[6] See 1 Am. Law Rev. 265.

§ **306.** [1] In the following cases, no objection of remoteness appears to have occurred to any one. Cowell v. Springs Co., 100 U. S. 55, 25 L. E. 547. Carter v. Doe, 21 Ala. 72. Barnesville v. Stafford, 161 Ga. 588, 131 S. E. 487. Dunne v. Minsor, 312 Ill. 333, 143 N. E. 842. Stock v. Stipe, 12 Ind. 74. Indianapolis R. R. Co. v. Hood, 66 Ind. 580. Taylor v. Cedar Rapids, etc., R. R. Co., 25 Iowa 371. O'Brien v. Wetherell, 14 Kans. 616. Gray v. Blanchard, 8 Pick. 284. Austin v. Cambridgeport Parish, 21 Pick. 215. Guild v. Richards, 16 Gray 309. Langley v. Chapin, 134 Mass. 82. Smith v. Barrie, 56 Mich. 314, 22 N. W. 816. Estes v. Agricultural Asso., 181 Mich. 71, 147 N. W. 553. Sioux City St. P. R. Co. v. Singer, 49 Minn. 301, 51 N. W. 905. Cornelius v. Ivins, 2 Dutch. 376. Jackson v. Topping, 1 Wend. 388. Plumb v. Tubbs, 41 N. Y. 442. Howell v.

Long Island R. R. Co., 37 Hun 381. Upington v. Corrigan, 151 N. Y. 143, 45 N. E. 359. Sperry v. Pond, 5 Ohio 387. Pickle v. M'Kissick, 21 Pa. 232. Courtney v. Keller, 4 Pennyp. 38. Lehigh Coal Co. v. Gluck, 5 Pa. C. C. 662. Fly v. Guinn, 2 Tex. Unrep. Cas. 300. Martin v. Ohio River R. R. Co., 37 W. Va. 349, 16 S. E. 589. Horner v. Chicago, etc., R. R. Co., 38 Wis 165. Pepin County v. Prindle, 61 Wis. 301, 21 N. W. 254. Goyeau v. Gt. West R. Co., 25 Grant (Ont.) 62. Re Melville, 11 Ont. 626. Cf. Hardy v. Galloway, 111 No. Car. 519, 15 S. E. 890.

In the following cases the topic of remoteness has been expressly referred to. Theological Education Society v. A. G., 135 Mass. 285. Tappan's Appeal, 3 Gray 142, 148. First Universalist Society v. Boland, 155 Mass. 171, 29 N. E. 524. Palmer v. Union Bank, 17 R. I. 627, 24 Atl. 109. Hopkins v. Grimshaw, 165 U. S. 342, 356, 17 S. Ct. 401, 406, 41 L. E. 739. Wakefield v. Van Tassell, 202 Ill. 41, 49, 66 N. E. 830, 833. (These

§ 307. In very many cases also in which the effect of conditions extending beyond the limits of the Rule against Perpetuities has been involved, but in which the courts have held that there has been no forfeiture, either because there has been no breach or no entry, or because the right to enter has been waived, released, or destroyed, the validity of the conditions has been declared or assumed as unquestioned without any objection on the ground of remoteness.[1]

§ 308. And further, in those cases in which the condition must be broken, if at all, within lives in being and twenty-one years, no suggestion has ever been made in America that

cases are discussed in detail in the third edition of this work, § 310 a.) More recent cases are: Libby v. Winston, 207 Ala. 681, 93 So. 631. Hinton v. Gilbert, 221 Ala. 309, 128 So. 604. Erie v. Pennsylvania R. R., 246 Pa. 238, 92 Atl. 192. Koehler v. Rowland, 275 Mo. 573, 586, 205 S. W. 217, 220. See also Strong v. Shatto, 45 Cal. Ap. 29, 187 Pac. 139.

§ 307. [1] Among such cases are Henry v. Etowah County, 77 Ala. 538; Collins Manufacturing Co. v. Marcy, 25 Conn. 242; Warner v. Bennett, 31 Conn. 468; Price v. School Directors, 58 Ill. 452; Carter v. Branson, 79 Ind. 14; Gray v. Chicago, M. & St. P. Ry. Co., 189 Ill. 400, 59 N. E. 950; Lyman v. Suburban R. R. Co., 190 Ill. 320, 60 N. E. 515; Trego County v. Hays, 93 Kans. 829, 145 Pac. 847; Kenner v. Amer. Contract Co., 9 Bush 202; Hooper v. Cummings, 45 Me. 359; Osgood v. Abbott, 58 Me. 73; Crane v. Hyde Park, 135 Mass. 147; Michigan State Bank v. Hastings, 1 Doug. (Mich.) 225; Memphis & Charleston R. R. Co. v. Neighbors, 51 Miss. 412; Gillis v. Bailey, 17 N. H. 18, 21 N. H. 149; Gage v. School District in Boscawen, 64 N. H. 232, 9 Atl. 387; Den d. Southard v. Central R. R. Co., 2 Dutch. 13; McKelway v. Seymour, 5 Dutch. 321; De Peyster v. Michael, 6 N. Y. 467, 506; Ludlow v. N. Y. & H. R. R. Co., 12 Barb. 440; Underhill v. Saratoga R. R. Co., 20 Barb. 455; Tinkham v. Erie R. Co., 53 Barb. 393; Woodworth v. Payne, 5 Hun 551, 74 N. Y. 196; Towle v. Remsen, 70 N. Y. 303; McKissick v. Pickle, 16 Pa. 140; Sharon Iron Co. v. Erie, 41 Pa. 341; Hammond v. Railroad Co., 15 So. Car. 10; Bolling v. Petersburg, 8 Leigh 224; Congregational Soc. v. Stark, 34 Vt. 243; Mills v. Evansville Seminary, 58 Wis. 135, 15 N. W. 133; Douglas v. Hawes, Ritchie Eq. (Nov. Sc.) 146, 152. See Conn. Spiritualist Camp-Meeting Assoc. v. E. Lyme, 54 Conn. 152, 5 Atl. 849; Barrie v. Smith, 47 Mich. 130, 10 N. W. 168; Watrous v. Allen, 57 Mich. 362, 24 N. W. 104; Bad River Lumbering Co. v. Kaiser, 82 Wis. 166, 51 N. W. 1100.

this circumstance is what saves the condition from being too remote.[1]

§ 309. So conditions on conveyances in fee, reserving rent, and giving the grantor the right on default of payment to enter, and be in as of his old estate, have been held good without any suggestion that they were too remote.[1]

§ 308. [1] See, for instance, Taylor v. Sutton, 15 Ga. 103; Voris v. Renshaw, 49 Ill. 425; Plummer v. Worthington, 321 Ill. 450, 152 N. E. 133; Wilson v. Wilson, 86 Ind. 472; Rowell v. Jewett, 69 Me. 293, 71 Me. 408; Hayden v. Stoughton, 5 Pick. 528; Clapp v. Stoughton, 10 Pick. 463 (cf. Brattle Square Church v. Grant, 3 Gray 142, 161); Blake v. Blake, 56 Wis. 392, 14 N. W. 173; Delong v. Delong, 56 Wis. 514, 14 N. W. 591; Gilchrist v. Foxen, 95 Wis. 428, 70 N. W. 585.

In the cases in the two preceding sections a forfeiture was enforced, or there was an attempt to enforce it. There are also cases in which a condition extending beyond the limits of the Rule against Perpetuities has been held good where the question presented was whether land was subject to a valid incumbrance. Such are Keening v. Ayling, 126 Mass. 404; Gibert v. Peteler, 38 Barb. 488, 38 N. Y. 165; Anon., 2 Abb. N. C. 56; Post v. Weil, 8 Hun 418; Post v. Bernheimer, 31 Hun 247. These cases, however, may generally be sustained on the ground that equitable easements and not true conditions were created. § 282, note, ante.

§ 309. [1] Wartenby v. Moran, 3 Call 491. Jackson v. Demarest, 2 Caines 382. Van Rensselaer v. Snyder, 13 N. Y. 299. Van Rensselaer v. Smith, 27 Barb. 104. Van Rensselaer v. Ball, 19 N. Y. 100. Van Rensselaer v. Slingerland, 26 N. Y. 580. Van Rensselaer v. Dennison, 35 N. Y. 393. Van Rensselaer v. Barringer, 39 N. Y. 1. Hosford v. Ballard, 39 How. Pr. 162, 39 N. Y. 147. Cruger v. McLaury, 41 N. Y. 219. See Garrett v. Scouten, 3 Denio 334; McCormick v. Connell, 6 S. & R. 151; Kenege v. Elliott, 9 Watts 258; Robert v. Ristine, 2 Phila. 62; Stephenson v. Haines, 16 Ohio St. 478; Cadwalader, Ground Rents, c. 8, §§ 359–372. See § 303, ante.

The bad results of allowing conditions to operate at remote periods of time have been alleviated, though not removed, by the strictness with which courts have construed conditions, often holding them as personal to the grantors and not passing to their heirs. Emerson v. Simpson, 43 N. H. 475. Page v. Palmer, 48 N. H. 385. Skinner v. Shepard, 130 Mass. 180. See also Merrifield v. Cobleigh, 4 Cush. 178; Den d. Southard v. Central R. R. Co., 2 Dutch. 13; Voris v. Renshaw, 49 Ill. 425; Hunt v. Beeson, 18 Ind. 380; Jeffersonville, etc., R. Co. v. Barbour, 89 Ind. 375; Lawe v. Hyde, 39 Wis. 345. So in Mitchell v. Leavitt, 30 Conn. 587, it is said

§ **310.** This great consensus of authority, although without any consideration of the question involved, must be held to settle the law for the United States, and to create in this country an exception, arbitrary though it be, to the Rule against Perpetuities.

§ **311. Conditions to maintain a Tomb.** In *Giles* v. *Boston Society*,[1] property was given to the defendant on condition that it should keep the testator's tomb in repair. The Court held that on the facts there had been no breach of the condition, but they say: "It may well be doubted whether this condition to maintain a private tomb or burial-place was not void as tending to create a perpetuity." If these words of condition are to be held as imposing a trust,[2] then the authorities cited by the Court are strong to show that such a trust is void;[3] but if the words are not held to impose a trust, but simply to impose a common-law condition, such condition seems no more obnoxious to the Rule against Perpetuities than any other would be; and if conditions generally are exempt from the operation of the Rule, this ought to be also. The same remarks apply to *Piper* v. *Moulton*[4] and *Coit* v. *Comstock*.[5]

§ **311.1.** The case of *Re Tyler*[1] confirms the correctness of

that a "restriction on the use of real estate, where it does not appear that either some individual or the public would be benefited by it, would be contrary to public policy and void." That is, a condition which does not create an easement or trust is void, — a very sensible conclusion. See Barrie v. Smith, 47 Mich. 130, 10 N. W. 168; § 282, note, ante; 54 Harv. Law Rev 248, in which is given a summary of legislation in several States on this subject, and 27 Am. B. A. J. 727.

§ 311. [1] 10 Allen 355.
[2] See § 282, ante.
[3] And see Re Waldron, 109 N. Y. S. 681; 2 Perry, Trusts (7th

ed.), § 706. But see Jones v. Habersham, 107 U. S. 174, 183, 184, 336, 344, 345, 2 S. Ct. 336, 27 L. E. 401; Smart v. Durham, 77 N. H. 56, 86 Atl. 821; §§ 894–909, post.
[4] 72 Me. 155.
[5] 51 Conn. 352. That a condition like that in Giles v. Boston Society is valid, seems to be assumed in Dunne v. Minsor, 312 Ill. 333, 143 N. E. 842, and in Giblin v. Giblin, 173 Wis. 632, 182 N. W. 357. See also Williams v. Williams, 215 No. Car. 739, 3 S. E. 2d 334; Hunt v. Wright, 47 N. H. 396; § 305.5, ante.

§ 311.1. [1] [1891] 3 Ch. (C. A.) 252. See §§ 603.3, 603.4, post.

the view which was taken in the preceding section. There a fund was bequeathed to a charity on condition that it kept the testator's vault in repair; upon breach of the condition the fund to go to another charity. In England it has been held that a gift from one charity to another on a remote contingency is not within the Rule against Perpetuities,[2] and consequently the Court of Appeals (affirming the decision of Stirling, J.) held that the condition in this case was good. As Lindley, L. J., said, "There is nothing illegal in keeping up a tomb."[3] So in those jurisdictions in America in which conditions are held to be not within the Rule against Perpetuities, there is no reason why a condition to keep a tomb in repair should not be held valid. "There is nothing illegal in keeping up a tomb."[4]

§ 312. **Possibilities of Reverter.** Possibilities of reverter after determinable fees were probably put an end to by the Statute *Quia Emptores*.[1] Where the Statute *Quia Emptores* is not in force, and tenure exists, *i. e.* in South Carolina and, perhaps, Pennsylvania,[2] such interests can be created;

[2] Likewise in many of the United States. See §§ 597–603.8, post.

[3] And see Roche v. M'Dermott, [1901] 1 I. R. 394; § 603.3, post.

[4] See §§ 894–909.2, post. In such a case not only is no trust imposed, but the condition is not that the tomb be maintained out of the income of the devise, but simply that it be maintained out of any resources which the devisee may have. If the condition were of the former sort, it might perhaps be held invalid as constituting an inducement for the devisee to so apply the income of the property devised, which would tend, in effect, to tie up the property to nearly the same extent as if it were subject to a trust. The condition actually imposed, however, constitutes only an inducement to meet in some manner the costs of maintenance, and can be considered as imposing, at the most, a virtual obligation so to do. But such an obligation, if expressly undertaken, would seem to be valid, and certainly would not be affected by the Rule against Perpetuities. See § 329, post. The only tying up here is that resulting directly from the condition itself, which is not obnoxious to the Rule against Perpetuities, according to the American doctrine. See §§ 603.3, 603.4, post, and 28 Ky. L. J. 424.

§ 312. [1] See §§ 31 et seq., ante.
[2] §§ 26, 27, ante.

so also they have been allowed in many other States.[3] It would seem they are not too remote.[4] It is true that such rights are not like rights of escheat, which in no degree affect the value of the estates which are subject to them, and in no way hamper the transfer of such estates,[5] and that they are of a most objectionable character as restraining the free commerce in land; but this arises from the fundamental error of allowing determinable fees at all. When these are once allowed to exist, possibilities of reverter taking effect at a remote period become a necessity.[6]

[3] See §§ 40–41.1, 113.3, ante, 603.9, post.

[4] So held in Re Chardon, [1928] Ch. 464; Lougheed v. Dykeman Baptist Church, 40 N. Y. S. 586; and Yarbrough v. Yarbrough, 151 Tenn. 221, 269 S. W. 36. See also Atkins v. Gillespie, 156 Tenn. 137, 299 S. W. 776; Shee v. Boone, 295 Mo. 212, 243 S. W. 882; Kasey v. Fidelity Trusts, 131 Ky. 609, 115 S. W. 739; A. G. v. Cummins, [1906] I. R. 406, 407, 410; and note 6, infra. In practically all of the many American cases where a possibility of reverter is said to exist, it would have been invalid for remoteness if subject to the Rule. See 2 Simes, Fut. Int., § 507. Cf. Amer. Law Inst. Restatement, Property, §§ 23, 44, where almost all the illustrations of estates in fee simple determinable are of estates which obviously might last till remote periods. In Comment o to § 44, it is assumed that such an estate may last beyond the period of the Rule. See also illustration 20 under that Comment, and Comment b to § 47. If a possibility of reverter is a vested interest, as appears to be the case (see § 113.3, ante), then it is nec-

essarily not subject to the Rule. But further, whether it is called vested or contingent, it cannot be eliminated by the application of the Rule. The Rule against Perpetuities, being directed only to invalidating future estates, cannot operate to enlarge an estate which is in its origin self-limited by a special limitation. See 2 Tiffany, Real Prop. (3d ed.), § 404; § 205, note 2, ante. In Copenhaver v. Pendleton, 155 Va. 463, 155 S. E. 802, though the opinion contains language which may be taken to mean that possibilities of reverter are contingent interests, they are assumed to be valid, however remote the period at which they may take effect.

[5] See §§ 204, 205.1, ante.

[6] See § 205, note 2, ante, and 54 Law Quart. Rev. 258. The Supreme Judicial Court of Massachusetts in First Universalist Society v. Boland, 155 Mass. 171, 29 N. E. 524, has said that rights of entry for breach of condition and possibilities of reverter "should be governed by the same rule. If one is not held void for remoteness, the other should not be;" and that, therefore, as rights

**§ 313.** At any rate the possibility of reverter as it exists after that form of a determinable fee known as a conditional fee,—that is, an estate to a man and the heirs of his body, as it existed at common law before the Statute *De Donis*, and as it still exists in South Carolina,[1]—can never be too remote;

of entry are not in America deemed subject to the Rule against Perpetuities, possibilities of reverter ought not to be. But it is respectfully submitted that the cases rest on totally different grounds. An entry for condition broken cuts short an existing estate which, but for the entry, would continue. It has precisely the same effect as a conditional limitation, and the error in the American doctrine is to make a difference in the matter of remoteness, according as the divesting condition is in favor of a third person, or is in favor of the grantor, when in truth there is no rational distinction in the cases. But the possibility of reverter does not cut short the preceding interest. If there be an error in the Massachusetts decision of First Universalist Society v. Boland, as it is submitted there is, it is not in failing to apply the Rule to possibilities of reverter, but in recognizing determinable fees, which render such possibilities necessary. See Institution for Savings v. Roxbury Home, 244 Mass 583, 139 N. E. 301; Yarbrough v. Yarbrough, 151 Tenn. 221, 269 S. W. 36. Cf. Brattle Square Church v. Grant, 3 Gray 142, 148. The difficulty, however, in distinguishing possibilities of reverter from rights of re-entry, and the confusion between them which frequently occurs in the American cases, is a practical reason for not making a difference between them as to validity. The objections in practice to possibilities of reverter are the same as those to rights of entry.

A different, and, it is thought, a more correct view, of the application of the Rule against Perpetuities to possibilities of reverter is taken in the second and subsequent editions than in the first one.

The possibility of reverter which is held to exist in Illinois, and perhaps in some other States, upon a statutory dedication (see § 42, ante), has never been objected to as too remote. Probably if the question were raised, the statutory character of the interest would be considered as taking it out of the Rule. Under a common-law dedication the fee continues in the dedicator (see Town v. Leonard, 177 Iowa 337, 158 N. W. 655; Badeaux v. Ryerson, 213 Mich. 642, 182 N. W. 22), and the abandonment of the public use no more raises a question of remoteness, than does the extinguishment of an easement. The Rule of Perpetuities is concerned with the beginning only and not with the termination of estates and interests. See § 279, ante. Cf. §§ 973, 974, post.

**§ 313.** [1] § 14, ante.

for if the grantee has no issue, the estate terminates with his life; and if he has issue born to whom the estate descends, the estate can be at any time alienated, and the possibility of reverter destroyed.[2]

**§ 313.1. Curtesy and Dower.** These share the fate, as to remoteness, of the estates to which they are incident.

**§ 314. Rights less than Ownership.** Rights of this sort, in land of others, such as profits, easements, rents, could be granted at common law *de novo* to begin *in futuro*.[1] These rights were probably seldom granted to begin at any distant date, and no objection on account of remoteness seems to have been taken to them in early times, any more than to contingent remainders or to conditions. It is not improbable that a common-law grant to a person not *in esse* is void, and that therefore no such grant could be made except to a living person;[2] but a grant to A. and his heirs of a profit to begin fifty years or a thousand years from the date of the deed is good, unless it violates the Rule against Perpetuities.

**§ 315.** The only reasons given for exempting such a right so granted from the operation of the Rule against Perpetuities are that a grant is a common-law conveyance, and that the right is releasable. Neither of these is a valid reason.[1] So remote a right is greatly against public policy. If created by will it would be an executory devise void for remoteness; and such a distinction between a common-law grant and a devise is, to say the least, undesirable.

**§ 316.** In *Gilbertson* v. *Richards*,[1] it was held that a rent to begin at a possibly distant day was good; but no question was raised as to the effect of a common-law grant, for the rent in that case was created by way of use, and the case cannot now be considered as law.[2] The Real Property Commission-

[2] See Jones v. Postell, Harp. 92, 99, 100, note. On executory devises after fees simple conditional, see § 14, note 8, ante, and § 455, post.

**§ 314.** [1] § 16, ante.
[2] Perk. Grant 52.

**§ 315.** [1] See §§ 296–298, 302, 312, ante; §§ 319, 321.2, 323, post.

**§ 316.** [1] 4 H. & N. 277.
[2] As to Gilbertson v. Richards, see §§ 271–273.1, ante, and London & S. W. R. Co. v. Gomm, 20 Ch. D. (C. A.) 562; § 275, ante.

ers in their Third Report [3] seem to have considered that grants
of incorporeal hereditaments were not within the Rule against
Perpetuities, although they ought to be. But the leading
text-writers all agree that they are within the Rule.[4] Rents
indeed, although incorporeal hereditaments in the contemplation of the common law, may be perhaps fairly considered
as obligations, and therefore their creation as not within the
scope of the Rule against Perpetuities; the only right in any
property given by a rent is a right to distrain, and this
is matter of remedy to which the Rule does not apply.[5] But
grants of profits or easements *in futuro* seem to give true
rights in property, and should therefore be subjected to the
Rule.[6]

[3] P. 36.

[4] Lewis, Perp., c. 29. Gilbert,
Rents 59, 60. Fearne, C. R. 529,
Butler's note. Gilbert, Uses
(Sugd. ed.) 195, note. 1 Sand.
Uses (5th ed.) 203–305. Sanders
indeed, loc. cit., refers to Hartopp
v. Carbery, in the King's Bench in
Ireland, as deciding the point; but
in that case, which is not reported. the rent seems from his statement to have been created by executory devise. In Hope v.
Gloucester, 7 De G. M. & G. 647,
a covenant to grant leases at remote periods was held invalid as
creating a perpetuity. And see, as
to leaseholds in futuro, § 319,
post.

[5] See §§ 273.1, 303, ante; § 329,
post, and Law of Prop. Act
(1925), §§ 121, 162.

[6] South Eastern R. Co. v. Associated Portland Cement Manuf.,
[1910] 1 Ch. (C. A.) 12, 27;
and § 330.2 post. Per Farwell, L. J., "I see no reason to
doubt the accuracy of that passage [in Lewis on Perpetuities,

pp. 619, 620, that the Rule
against Perpetuities applies to
easements] in the case of a right
against real estate." So Sharpe
v. Durrant, 55 Sol. J. 423, § 330.3,
note 2, post. See Smith v. Colbourne, [1914] 2 Ch. (C. A.) 533;
Westropp v. Congested Districts
Board, [1918] 1 I. R. 265, aff'd
[1919] 1 I. R. 224; 11 Enc. Laws
of Eng. (2d ed.) 72, 73; 54 Sol.
J. 471, 501, 502. In all these cases,
however, the easements or profits
in question were either held to be
present rights, or were practically
enforced by indirect means.

In Ardley v. Guardians of the
Poor, 39 L. J. Ch. 871, T. demised
land for ninety-five years to R.,
reserving to T. and his heirs a
right of way over the east side of
the demised premises during the
time they should hold the adjoining land, with liberty to erect
scaffolding thereon for repairing
and building, and after he or they
should dispose of the adjoining
land, then reserving to T., his
heirs and assigns, a right of in-

**§ 316.1. Escheat.** This has no effect on the tying up of property and is not subject to the Rule against Perpetuities.[1]

**§ 317. Shifting and Springing Uses and Executory Devises.** These are all, without question, subject to the Rule against Perpetuities.[1]

**§ 318. Copyholds.** There appear to be no cases concerning remoteness in limitations of copyholds. But so far as future limitations of copyholds are allowed,[1] they would seem to be subject to the same rules as the corresponding limitations of freehold.[2]

### B. PERSONAL PROPERTY

**§ 319. Chattels in General.** Chattels real may be created, and chattels real and personal transferred, *in futuro*.[1] Unless the Rule against Perpetuities applies to them, they may be created or transferred fifty or a thousand years from the

gress and egress unto and upon the said eastern part of the demised premises for the purpose of rebuilding or repairing any buildings on said adjoining land. T. disposed of the adjoining land. Lord Romilly, M. R., held that when T. alienated the adjoining land, the first easement came to an end, and the second came into existence. No objection to the second easement on the ground of remoteness was made, but it seems to have been invalid on that score, unless it can be said that the new easement was merely a retention of part of the old easement. Perhaps in view of the fact that the first easement was reserved to T. and his heirs, and the latter to T., his heirs and assigns, this position might be difficult to maintain.

The tendency of the courts is to construe easements as present interests. And the Law of Property Act (1925), § 162, provides

that certain sorts of easements and profits which might be considered as commencing in the future shall not be subject to the Rule. See § 279, note 4, ante.

**§ 316.1.** [1] See §§ 204, 205.1, ante.

**§ 317.** [1] See § 114, ante.

**§ 318.** [1] See § 70, ante.

[2] Surrenders to future uses, if allowed, which is doubtful, give common-law interests; but it is highly improbable that they would be exempted from the operation of the Rule against Perpetuities on this ground. §§ 296–298, 300–302, 312, 315, 316, ante; §§ 319, 321, 323, post. Cf. Re Clarke's Settlement Trust, [1916] 1 Ch. 467, 478, in which it was held, citing this section, that the rule of Whitby v. Mitchell, 42 Ch. D. 494, 44 Ch. D. 85, § 298.1, ante, applied to copyholds.

**§ 319.** [1] §§ 71–85, ante.

date of the instrument creating or transferring them. The same considerations show that the Rule should govern them as show that it should govern incorporeal hereditaments.[2]

§ 320. Whether future interests in a chattel remaining in the grantor, or limited over to a third person, after a present gift, are within the Rule against Perpetuities or not depends upon whether they are to be deemed vested or contingent.[1] All such interests, if contingent, are within the Rule.[2]

§ 320.1. **Future Terms for Years.** (1) If a term for 100 years is created, and then at the same time, or later, another term is granted to begin on the termination of the first term, the latter is vested, though the reversion is not granted by it. It is ready to come into possession whenever the first term determines. The *interesse termini* is treated like an estate.[1] (2) If the second term is granted on a contingency which is too remote, then the second term is not good. (3) If there is no preceding term, and the period at which the term is to begin, though certain, is too remote, it is not good. In *Redington* v. *Brown*,[2] (1) is said to be clearly law, and (2) is decided. *Smith* v. *Day*[3] and *Knight* v. *City of London Brewery Co.*[4] come within (1) even if the question of remoteness, which was not suggested in either case by court or counsel, was material, which it would seem not to have been. (3) Seems correct. In *Mann* v. *Land Registry*,[5] a landlord gave to a tenant in possession, under a lease terminating in 1946, a "reversionary lease" of a term "to commence from the date

2 §§ 315, 316, ante. See also §§ 296, 298, 300–302, 312, ante; §§ 321, 323, post.

§ 320. 1 This matter is discussed in Chap. III., Vested and Contingent Interests, §§ 117 et seq., ante; App. F, §§ 789 et seq., post.

2 On covenants to renew leases, see §§ 230 et seq., ante.

§ 320.1. 1 See Bowen, J., in Gillard v. Cheshire Lines Committee, 32 W. R. 943. "When that demise

was made to the plaintiff he had vested in him an interest known to the law as an interesse termini. That is more than a right of entry; it is an interest which the law recognizes in a future term coupled with a right to complete that interest by possession."

2 32 L. R. Ir. 347.

3 2 M. & W. 684, Murphy & Hurlstone 185, 6 L. J., N. S. Exch. 219.

4 [1912] 1 K. B. 10.

5 [1918] 1 Ch. 202.

of the expiration of the existing lease, namely, Midsummer, 1946." This lease appears to be in a usual form for a reversionary lease, properly so called, in which the term granted is to begin on the termination of the existing term.[6] And Neville, J., seems so to construe the lease. The result of his decision sustaining it is therefore in accord with (1) *supra.* He seems, however, not to consider the presence of an existing term as significant for the question of the validity of the future term; and his opinion indicates that he considers that the future term would be outside the scope of the Rule against Perpetuities, for the reason that it was presently vested, even if there were no term preceding it. This view, it is submitted, is incorrect. The future term, without any subsisting intermediate term, would not be a vested interest for the purposes of the Rule against Perpetuities. Such a term may be spoken of as a "vested interest" in some connections,[7] but it is not vested in a strict sense for the purposes of the Rule.[8]

[6] See Smith v. Day, ubi sup.; Woodfall, Landl. & Ten. (24th ed.) 217; 1 Wms. V. & P. (4th ed.) 425, note t; 1 Key & Elphinstone, Precedents in Conv. (10th ed.) 1073.

[7] See § 118, ante.

[8] See 1 Tiffany, Real Prop. (2d ed.), § 183, p. 604, 2 Tiffany, Real Prop. (3d ed.), § 406; 11 Aust. L. J. 219. But cf. 1 Jarm. Wills (6th ed.) 307, (7th ed.) 351; 1 Wms. V. & P. (4th ed.) 424, 425; 11 Enc. Laws of Eng. 72, 73; 22 Halsbury, "Laws of England," § 658; 1 Simes, Fut. Int., §§ 197, 198, 227; 30 Law Quart. Rev. 66; 50 Sol. J. 760; 62 Sol. J. 50; 27 Yale L. J. 878, 886. See also §§ 117, 201, 210, ante.

The Law of Property Act (1925), § 149, reads as follows:

(1) "The doctrine of interesse termini is hereby abolished.

(2) "As from the commencement of this Act all terms of years absolute shall, whether the interest is created before or after such commencement, be capable of taking effect at law or in equity, according to the estate interest or powers of the grantor, from the date fixed for commencement of the term, without actual entry."

(3) "A term, at a rent or granted in consideration of a fine, limited after the commencement of this Act to take effect more than twenty-one years from the date of the instrument purporting to create it, shall be void, and any contract made after such commencement to create such a term shall likewise be void; but this subsection does not apply to any term taking effect in equity under a settlement, or created out of an equitable interest under a

**§ 321. Remainders.** As there are no true contingent remainders of personalty, no such question as has been discussed with regard to contingent remainders [1] can arise on limitations of personalty.[2]

**§ 321.1. Conditions.**[1] The arbitrary exemption in America from the Rule against Perpetuities of conditions attached to conveyances of real estate seems to be extended to conditions in conveyances of personalty. In *Palmer* v. *Union Bank*,[2] there is a *dictum* so extending it. The same doctrine appears to be applied in *Curtis* v. *Central University* [3] and it is expressly so decided in *Green* v. *Old People's Home*.[4]

**§ 321.2.** Nothing, as has been remarked, shows more conclusively the falsity of the idea that the Rule against Perpetuities governs only interests arising under the Statutes of Uses and Wills, and does not touch common-law interests, than its application to executory limitations of chattels. Such limitations can be made in England by will, and in America they can be made by either deed or will. They do not owe their existence to the Statute of Uses, for that Statute concerns only freeholds; nor to the Statute of Wills, for chattels could be disposed of by will before that Statute. They are purely common-law interests. Yet no one questions that they are subject to the Rule. Indeed, the Rule had its origin and development in cases concerning executory devises of leaseholds.[1]

## II. EQUITABLE INTERESTS

**§ 322. Vested Equitable Interests.** Such interests, either

settlement, or under an equitable power for mortgage, indemnity or other like purposes."

There seem to be no decisions on these provisions, and their effect is not clear. See 1 Wolst. & Ch. Conv. (11th ed.) 392; 11 Aust. L. J. 219.

**§ 321.** [1] §§ 284–298, ante.
[2] Re Bowles, [1902] 2 Ch. 650. And see § 325, post.

**§ 321.1.** [1] §§ 304–310, ante.
[2] 17 R. I. 627, 24 Atl. 109.
[3] 188 Iowa 300, 176 N. W. 330.
[4] 269 Ill. 134, 109 N. E. 701.

**§ 321.2.** [1] §§ 148–158, 160–169, 296–298, 300–302, 312, 315, 316, 319, ante, § 323, post.

On the doctrine of conversion as affecting questions of remoteness, see the case of Rous v. Jackson, App. I, §§ 910 et seq., post.

[G. R. P.]

of realty or personalty, are not subject to the Rule against Perpetuities.[1]

§ 323. **Contingent Interests.** All future equitable interests, not vested, are subject to the Rule against Perpetuities.[1]

§ 322. [1] Rhodes's Estate, 147 Pa. 227, 23 Atl. 553.

§ 323. [1] A theory has been advanced that when an equitable interest terminates, leaving the legal title free of trust either in the trustee or in a transferee from the trustee, the resulting change of beneficial interest is not within the scope of the Rule against Perpetuities. The only effect of the equitable limitations of the trust instrument, it is said, is to terminate the existing equitable estate. And it is insisted that such termination does not infringe the Rule against Perpetuities, because that Rule is concerned only with the commencement of estates. This line of reasoning has been applied to interests arising under certain powers exercisable by trustees, particularly powers of sale. See 3 Tiffany, Real Prop. (3d ed.), § 712; 16 Columbia Law Rev. 537, 545–553; and see also 2 Simes, Fut. Int., § 555. So far as the results attained by this reasoning are valid, they can be reached by other lines of argument. See §§ 509.18, post. To what classes of cases the proposed theory is to apply, does not clearly appear. It seems that, according to its terms, it would be applicable to several cases of powers exercisable by trustees, in which it would lead to results contrary to established law. Powers to give maintenance, for instance, or to pay over principal before the period fixed for termination of the trust, are undoubtedly subject to the Rule against Perpetuities; although the equitable interests of the persons taking in default of appointment are terminated, not by the creation of any new equitable interest, as distinct from a legal interest, but by the extinguishment of all equitable interests in the property and the creation of a new legal estate derived from the legal title of the trustee. Re Coleman, [1936] Ch. 528; §§ 474–476, post. The doctrine in question would apparently also cover the following case: A gift to A. (a bachelor) for life, then to A.'s eldest son in fee, in trust for certain purposes, but on a particular contingency, then to hold for his own use free of trust. There is little doubt that the last limitation would be held invalid under the Rule against Perpetuities. Yet the only event occurring at too remote a period is the change of the trustee's interest from a bare legal title to a legal title free of trust. The suggested course of reasoning assumes that no new equitable interest arises when the equitable and legal interest merge in the same person. Such an assumption, however, does not hold good for the purposes of the Rule against Perpetuities. A change of beneficial title, whether by the creation of a new

This is not questioned, and it furnishes another proof that the Rule is not confined in its scope to interests arising under the Statutes of Uses and Wills, for equitable interests created both *inter vivos* and by will existed before those Statutes.[2]

**§ 324. Quasi Remainders.** As no equitable future interest requires a previous estate to support it, there is no such distinction as exists at common law between contingent remainders and executory limitations. There are strictly no equitable remainders, and there can be no question in equity, such as there may be at law, whether contingent remainders are within the Rule against Perpetuities or not.[1]

**§ 325.** A curious result of the fact that there are no remainders in equity is that a limitation may be too remote in equity which would be good at law. Thus, suppose an estate is devised to A. for life, and on his death to such of his children as reach twenty-five. The limitation to A.'s children is a contingent remainder, and is not too remote. It is true that A.'s children may not reach twenty-five until more than twenty-one years after his death; but unless they have reached twenty-five at A.'s death they will never take at all, apart from any question of remoteness. The remainder, if it ever vests, must vest at A.'s death, and can therefore never be too remote.[1] Suppose, on the other hand, that land is given to trustees in trust to pay the rents to A. during his life, and on his death to convey the land to such of A.'s children as reach twenty-five. This limitation to the children, being equitable,

equitable interest or the extinction of an existing one, has the same effect, with respect to the Rule against Perpetuities, as if the same change had taken place in the legal title. This is in accordance with the principle that equitable limitations should follow legal limitations. See §§ 116, ante, 325.1, post; and cf. Re Jones, [1925] Ch. 340, discussed in § 205.1, ante. The exception as to contingent remainders, dis-

cussed in § 325, post, rests on grounds peculiar to real estate under the old common law, and not on any difference between legal and equitable estates in general.

[2] Cf. §§ 296–298, 300–302, 312, 315, 316, 319, 321, ante, and Chap. XII, § 411 et seq., post.

**§ 324.** [1] See §§ 116, 284–298, ante. Cf. 20 Law Quart. Rev. 285; 21 Law Quart. Rev. 126, 265.

**§ 325.** [1] § 377, post.

is not a remainder, and is too remote. For A.'s children may
not reach twenty-five until more than twenty-one years after
his death; and, apart from the question of remoteness, they
can take whenever they reach that age, although A. may have
died more than twenty-one years before.[2]

[2] Abbiss v. Burney, 17 Ch. D.
211, by the Court of Appeal, overruling Malins, V. C. (whose decision had been much criticised,
69 L. T. 335; 70 L. T. 146; 24
Sol. J. 816; 25 Sol. J. 717). See
Blagrove v. Hancock, 16 Sim. 371;
Bull v. Pritchard, 5 Hare 567;
Lewis, Perp. 424, 425; 3 Dav.
Prec. Conv. (3d ed.) 338–340. In
Abbiss v. Burney, two of the
judges of the Court of Appeal, it
is true, thought there was no particular equitable estate preceding
the estate over, which was held
too remote; but they all agreed
that had there been, the (so-
called) equitable remainder would
have been too remote. See Marsden, Perp. 167 et seq.

Vice-Chancellor Malins rested
his decision largely upon Lord
Hardwicke's opinion in Hopkins v.
Hopkins, West (Temp. Hardwicke)
606. Lord Hardwicke, indeed, in
that case discussed the question
whether a future equitable interest
was a contingent remainder or an
executory device, and held it to be
a contingent remainder; but he
then went on to say that an equitable contingent remainder want-
ed the essential characteristic of
a legal contingent remainder, viz.
the need of a freehold to support
it. Now it is this very characteristic which requires a legal remainder to vest, if at all, at the
termination of a life estate. Lord

Hardwicke's judgment therefore
amounts to this: that the limitation in question, if legal, would be
a contingent remainder, but that
in equitable estates there is no
difference between contingent remainders and executory devises.
But see Marsden, Perp. 169, note.

By the Law of Property Act
(1925), § 1, all remainders are
turned into equitable interests.
Consequently the point above discussed cannot arise with respect
to instruments subject to this
Act. See Williams, Real Prop.
(24th ed.) 434; Wolst. & Ch.
Conv. (11th ed.) 413; 18 Iowa
Law Rev. 289. The same result
is effected by statutes giving to
the personal representative of a
testator legal title to devised
realty. Re Robson, [1916] 1 Ch.
116. Barrett v. Barrett, [1918] N.
S. W. 637. See 64 Sol. J. 171; 6
Conveyancer 44. Likewise by
Mass. Acts (1916), c. 108, Gen.
Laws (ed. 1932), c. 184, § 3, providing that a contingent remainder shall take effect as if it had
been an executory devise. See 30
Harv. Law Rev. 226; 61 Sol. J.
572. Also by the New South
Wales Conveyancing Act (1919),
section 16, providing that contingent remainders shall take effect
as equitable interests. See 64
Sol. J. 421. And apparently by
other statutes rendering contingent remainders indestructible.

**§ 325.1.** The doctrine laid down in *Whitby* v. *Mitchell*,[1] that a remainder to the children of an unborn person, after a life estate to such person, is void apart from the Rule against Perpetuities, has been extended to an equitable limitation, which if it were legal, would be a contingent remainder. *Re Nash*.[2] This seems the logical result of *Whitby* v. *Mitchell*. Equitable limitations should follow legal limitations, unless, as in the instance in the preceding section, the doctrine of seisin is concerned in the result.[3]

**§ 326.** Future equitable interests in chattels which, if legal limitations of realty, would be contingent remainders are, of course, executory interests, require no preceding interest to support them, and are subject to the Rule against Perpetuities.[1] Even Vice-Chancellor Malins, in attempting to lay down a different doctrine as to (so-called) equitable contingent remainders in realty, does not pretend that any limitations of personalty can have the peculiar characteristics of legal contingent remainders.[2]

**§ 327. Resulting Trusts.** As possibilities of reverter are purely legal interests, the question above discussed [1] as to the exemption of such rights from the Rule against Perpetuities cannot arise in considering equitable interests. But equitable interests analogous to possibilities of reverter may exist in connection with certain charitable trusts.

**§ 327.1.** Trusts may result either: (1) Because the express trusts created do not exhaust the equitable fee, as when only equitable life estates or equitable estates tail are created. Here the resulting trust is a vested interest, like a reversion.

See § 286, ante; and Amer. Law Inst. Restatement, Property, § 240, where it is proposed that contingent remainders should be treated as indestructible, even in the absence of any statute bearing on the point.

**§ 325.1.** [1] 44 Ch. D. 85. See §§ 298.1 et seq., ante. [2] [1909] 2 Ch. 450, [1910] 1 Ch. (C. A.) 1. And see Re

Clarke's Settlement Trust, [1916] 1 Ch. 467. [3] See 1 Jarm. Wills (6th ed.) 286. Cf. Eve, J., in Re Nash, [1909] 2 Ch. 450, at 456, 458.

**§ 326.** [1] Bull v. Pritchard, 1 Russ. 213. Wms. Pers. Prop. (18th ed.) 453, 454. [2] Abbiss v. Burney, 17 Ch. D. (C. A.) 211, 221, 223.

**§ 327.** [1] §§ 312, 313, ante.

It is ready to take effect whenever and however the preceding estates determine. (2) Because the *cestui que trust* dies without heirs. If there is a resulting trust in such a case,[1] such resulting trust is an interest in the nature of an escheat and not within the Rule. (3) Because property has been given for a charitable purpose and that purpose has been accomplished. Equitable determinable fees ought not to have been allowed any more than legal determinable fees. We shall see,[2] however, that determinable charitable trusts have been allowed. Wherever such a trust is allowed, there must be *ex necessitate rei,* a valid resulting trust, and therefore a trust which is not avoided by the Rule against Perpetuities.[3]

§ 328. **Charitable Trusts.** In the case of a charitable trust there is generally no defined *cestui que trust,* but this unde-

---

§ 327.1. [1] As to whether there is a resulting trust in such a case, see § 205.1, ante.

[2] See § 603.9, post.

[3] See §§ 205, note 2, 312 ante. There is some authority in England for resulting trusts, analogous to possibilities of reverter, in cases other than those of determinable charitable trusts. See §§ 34, note 1, ante, 784, post. In many of the United States, legal possibilities of reverter are allowed. See §§ 38–41, ante. In jurisdictions where legal possibilities of reverter are allowed, there seems to be no objection to resulting trusts of an analogous nature, though no charitable trust is involved. But there is little or no American authority on the point. It is sometimes difficult to ascertain, in the American cases on terminable interests, whether there is a legal right of reverter or a resulting trust.

Rights to enter for condition broken are, like possibilities of reverter, interests existing only at law. But there may be analogous interests in equity. On principle they are even more clearly subject to the Rule against Perpetuities than legal rights of entry. See § 323, ante. In the American cases it is often doubtful whether the rights arising on breach of condition are treated as legal or equitable. But it seems to be generally assumed that the distinction is immaterial for the purpose of the application of the Rule against Perpetuities, and that such rights are equally exempt from the application of the Rule, whether legal or equitable. See Hopkins v. Grimshaw, 165 U. S. 342, 356, 17 S. Ct. 401, 406, 41 L. E. 739; Palmer v. Union Bank, 17 R. I. 627, 24 Atl. 109; Green v. Old People's Home, 269 Ill. 134, 109 N. E. 701; Curtis v. Central University, 188 Iowa 300, 176 N. W. 330.

fined interest is subject to the Rule against Perpetuities, and
cannot begin at too remote a period.[1] But although a charitable trust is to begin at a remote period, yet if it is preceded
by another charitable trust, it has been held not to be void,
even if there be a change of the trustee. This is considered
in the chapter on Charitable Trusts.[2]

## III. CONTRACTS

§ **329. Not within Rule.** The Rule against Perpetuities
concerns rights of property only, and does not affect the making of contracts which do not create rights of property. Thus
a promise to A. to pay him or his executors or administrators
a sum of money on a future event is good, although such event
may not happen within twenty-one years after lives in being;[1]

§ **328.** [1] §§ 595, 596, post.
[2] §§ 597–603.8, post.

§ **329.** [1] See Walsh v. Secretary
of State for India, 10 H. L. C.
367; Witham v. Vane, in Dom.
Proc. (printed in Challis, Real
Prop. (3d ed.) 440, at 451, 452);
Green v. Green, 255 Pa. 224, 99
Atl. 801; Kennedy v. McMullen,
39 S. W. 2d 168 (Tex.); Marsden,
Perp. 25, 26; Challis, Real Prop.
(3d ed.) 184. See also § 693, post.
Although the Rule does not affect the creation of such a contract, it does apply to a transfer
of the contract when created.
Thus if the promisee in such a
contract should bequeath it to A.
on a remote contingency, the bequest would be void. The creation of an obligation is no part of
the law of property; but the
transfer of such obligation when
created is as much part of the
law of property as the transfer
of a house or of a table. The attempt of North, J., to support his
decision in Re Randell, 38 Ch. D.
213, on Walsh v. Secretary of
State for India, is not happy. In
the last-mentioned case there was
no trust fund. In the former
there was. In Borland's Trustee
v. Steel Brothers & Co., [1901] 1
Ch. 279, a company's articles of
association provided that a shareholder should, upon demand,
transfer his shares upon certain
terms and to certain persons.
Farwell, J., held that this proviso was not too remote because
it was a personal contract. Sed
quaere. Assuming that the right
of the shareholder against the
company had its origin in a
personal contract, yet when once
created the transfer of that contract right (i. e. the share) would
seem to be subject to the Rule
against Perpetuities. If, as is
often the case with such articles,
the shares have to be surrendered
on the death of the shareholder,
he has only a life interest, and
such proviso will not be too remote. Probably such articles of

and this is not altered by the fact that the covenant runs with
the land (as, for instance, a covenant of warranty), or can,
in any way, be enforced by or against other persons than the
original parties and their representatives,[2] nor that the obli-

association in many cases could
be supported on the ground that
they did not create an executory
limitation, but were in reality a
restraint on the alienation of
property, and though the alienation of property cannot generally
be restrained for the benefit of
its owner, it can be restrained for
the benefit of persons other than
the owner, such as fellow members of a partnership, club or corporation. See New England
Trust Co. v. Abbott, 162 Mass.
148, 152, 38 N. E. 432, 433;
Longyear v. Hardman, 219 Mass.
405, 408, 106 N. E. 1012, 1013;
Brown v. Little, Brown & Co., 269
Mass. 102, 110, 168 N. E. 521,
525; Sixty-eight Beacon Street
v. Sohier, 289 Mass. 354, 194 N.
E. 303; Blue Mt. Forest Assoc. v.
Borrowe, 71 N. H. 69, 51 Atl. 670;
Fitzsimmons v. Lindsay, 205 Pa.
79, 54 Atl. 488; Lawson v. Household Finance Co., 17 Del. Ch. 1,
147 Atl. 312, 17 Del. Ch. 343, 152
Atl. 723, and cases there cited;
Gray, Restraints on Alienation
(2d ed.), §§ 29 d, 279, p. 280; 42
Harv. Law Rev. 555; 26 Va. Law
Rev. 354. Whether the Borland
case could be supported on such a
principle is not clear on the facts
as reported. Cf. A. G. v. Jame-
son, [1904] 2 I. R. 644, [1905]
2 I. R. 218.

In Loring v. Lamson Co., 249
Mass. 272, 143 N. E. 916, an option to purchase stock not yet
issued was held to give no interest in any property. In Kingston v. Home Life Ins. Co., 11
Del. Ch. 258, 101 Atl. 898, aff'd
11 Del. Ch. 428, 104 Atl. 25, it
seems that a similar option might
likewise have been treated as not
creating a right in property; but
the Court held the option not
subject to the Rule against Perpetuities on the ground that the
Rule does not apply to options to
buy shares in corporations. If a
contract relates to specific existing personal property, and the
property is of such a nature that
the courts will entertain a suit
for specific performance of the
contract by delivery, it seems
that the Rule against Perpetuities should apply to such a contract. It seems also that shares
of stock and corporate bonds
might under some circumstances
properly be considered as of such
nature. See 51 Harv. Law Rev.
638, 662; 2 Dodd & Baker, Cases
on Business Organizations 494–
496, note.

[2] See Aspden v. Seddon, 1 Ex.
D. 496; Morgan v. Davey, 1 Cab.
& El. 114; Cameron v. Dalgetty,
[1920] N. Z. 155, 164; § 273.1,
ante. But the fact that a covenant runs with the land does not
necessarily prevent it from con-
flicting with the Rule against
Perpetuities, if it creates a right
of property. § 330, post. See remarks of Warrington, J., in

gation has a right of distraint attached to it, for that is only matter of remedy, and not a future limitation of any particular property.[3]

**§ 330. Options.** Where, however, a contract raises an equitable right in property which the obligee can enforce in chancery by a decree for specific performance, such equitable right is subject to the Rule against Perpetuities. This was decided by the Court of Appeal in *London & South Western R. Co.* v. *Gomm*,[1] where an option to purchase land, unlimited as to time, was held void; overruling *Birmingham Canal Co.* v. *Cartwright*.[2]

Woodall v. Clifton, [1905] 2 Ch. 257, 264; and 49 Sol. J. 740. Cf. 3 Holdsworth, Hist. Eng. Law (3d ed.) 164, and 55 Law Quart. Rev. 434.

[3] See §§ 273.1, 316, ante.

§ 330. [1] 20 Ch. D. 562.

[2] 11 Ch. D. 421. So Trevelyan v. Trevelyan, 53 L. T. R. 853; Woodall v. Clifton, [1905] 2 Ch. (C. A.) 257; Worthing Corporation v. Heather, [1906] 2 Ch. 532; Lewis Oyster Co. v. West, 93 Conn. 518, 107 Atl. 138; Turner v. Peacock, 153 Ga. 870, 113 S. E. 585; Henderson v. Bell, 103 Kan. 422, 173 Pac. 1124; Winsor v. Mills, 157 Mass. 362, 32 N. E. 352; Eastman Marble Co. v. Vermont Marble Co., 236 Mass. 138, 128 N. E. 177; Barton v. Thaw, 246 Pa. 348, 92 Atl. 312; Starcher v. Duty, 61 W. Va. 373, 56 S. E. 524; Woodall v. Bruen, 76 W. Va. 193, 85 S. E. 170; Skeen v. Clinchfield Coal Co., 137 Va. 397, 119 S. E. 89; Kauri Timber Co. v. District Land Registrar, 21 N. Z. 84. See Mackenzie v. Childers, 43 Ch. D. 265, 279; Savill Brothers v. Bethell, [1902] 2 Ch. (C. A.) 523; Edwards v. Edwards,

[1909] A. C. 275; Hardy v. Galloway, 111 No. Car. 519, 15 S. E. 890; Rice v. Lincoln and N. W. Ry., 88 Neb. 307, 129 N. W. 425; Re Lilley's Estate, 272 Pa. 143, 116 Atl. 392; Shirley v. Van Every, 159 Va. 762, 167 S. E. 345; Redington v. Browne, 32 L. R. Ir. 347, 358, 359; Switzer v. Rochford, [1906] 1 I. R. 399; Re Tyrrell's Estate, [1907] 1 I. R. 194, 292; Re Doyle's Estate, [1907] 1 I. R. 204; Kenrick v. Dempsey, 5 Grant (Ont.) 584, § 485, post; Bennett v. Stodgell, 28 Dom. L. R. 639, 642; United Fuel Supply Co. v. Volcanic Oil Co., 3 Ont. W. N. 93; Carter v. Hyde, 33 Com. L. R. 115, 132 (Aust.); Hasker v. Summers, 10 Vict. L. R. Eq. 204, 210; McMahon v. Swan, [1924] Vict. 397; Marsden, Perp. 14; Challis, Real Prop. (3d ed.) 183 et seq., Kales, Estates, §§ 664, 665; 2 Simes, Fut. Int., § 512; 25 W. Va. Law Quart. 30, 36, 236; 25 Columbia Law Rev. 77; 22 Mich. Law Rev. 279; 48 Harv. Law Rev. 1253; 38 Can. L. T. 242, 322; and § 275, ante. But see also Tod v. Citizens' Gas Co., 46 Fed. 2d 855, 866 (C. C. A.

**§ 330.1.** But though an equitable right in property under such a contract is subject to the Rule against Perpetuities,

Ind.); Keogh v. Peck, 316 Ill. 318, 147 N. E. 266; Kingston v. Home Life Ins. Co., 11 Del. Ch. 258, 101 Atl. 898, § 329, note 1, ante; Coley v. Hord, 250 Ky. 250, 62 S. W. 2d 792; 23 Case & Comment, 835; 17 Va. Law Rev. 461. The decision in Weber v. Texas Co., 83 Fed. 2d 807 (C. C. A. Tex., cert. refused, 299 U. S. 561, 57 S. Ct. 23, 81 L. E. 413) that an option to purchase at the best price offered by any third party did not give such an interest as was within the purview of the Rule against Perpetuities, seems questionable. Such an option might render the property, to which it related, less saleable. It was immaterial that no state of facts had arisen in which the option actually had that effect.

Under statutes limiting the suspension of alienation, options unlimited in time have been held valid. Matter of City of New York, 246 N. Y. 1, 29, 157 N. E. 911, 920. Blakeman v. Miller, 136 Cal. 138, 68 Pac. 587. Mineral Land Investment Co. v. Bishop Iron Co., 134 Minn. 412, 159 N. W. 966. Windiate v. Lorman, 236 Mich. 531, 211 N. W. 62. The circumstance that an option is releasable is of importance under such statutes. See Chaplin, Suspension of the Power of Alienation, §§ 179, 397; 1 Wis. Law Rev. 180; 22 Mich. Law Rev. 279; 21 Cal. Law Rev. 1, 30; 15 Ind. L. J. 261, 292. Cf. §§ 274, 275, ante. Also under such statutes no suspension of alienation is generally allowed for a term of years in gross, so that options even for short terms would be invalid if the statutory prohibition were held to apply to them.

An agreement for sale is not void because it does not expressly limit the time within which the agreement is to be carried out. The vendee has an equitable interest, subject only to the condition that the price shall be paid, which must be done within a reasonable time, and that would be less than twenty-one years. Re Doyle's Estate, [1907] 1 I. R. 204. But an agreement which gives the vendee the right to call for a conveyance only on the fulfillment of a condition which may be too remote, is unenforceable in equity. Horticultural Development Co. v. Lark, 224 Ala. 193, 139 So. 229; discussed in 48 Harv. Law Rev. 1253. And it seems that if the right to a conveyance were postponed to a remote certain date, the agreement would likewise be invalid, even though the price had been paid and there was no unfulfilled condition except the lapse of time. See § 201, ante.

On the application of the Rule against Perpetuities to trusts for the payment of debts, see §§ 415 et seq., post; to mortgages and sinking funds, see Chap. XVI., post; to covenants to renew leases, and to options to lessees to purchase the fee, see §§ 230–230.2, ante. On the question whether a direction to pay premiums on a policy of life insur-

that Rule is no bar to an action at law on the contract for damages.[1]

In *Eastman Marble Co.* v. *Vermont Marble Co.*,[2] the Court held that a covenant giving an option to buy land, at any time within twenty-five years, was void at law as well as in equity. Rugg, C. J., said: "There seems to us to be an irreconcilable inconsistency in refusing to enforce specifically covenants concerning an interest in property which violate the rule against perpetuities and yet at the same time enforcing an action for damages for refusal to perform such a covenant. Since it is settled that such covenants cannot be enforced specifically, it must follow that damages cannot be recovered for such refusal. Any other conclusion would afford simple and direct means, at least for corporations which ordinarily have unlimited existence, through the form of options to buy covering long periods and binding heirs and assigns, to circumvent the rule against perpetuities and restraints upon alienation. Since such contracts are held to create 'no interest in the property' (*Thacher* v. *Weston*, 197 Mass. 143, 147, 83 N. E. 360, 361, and cases collected 39 Cyc. 1238, note 19), there would be no difficulty in enforcing such agreements either by specific performance or by action for their breach no matter how long might be their term. The mischiefs would easily arise against which those rules were established." [3]

It is not clear what sort of contract is referred to by the Court in this passage and elsewhere in the opinion as creating "no interest in the property," or as a "mere option." Contracts giving options to purchase do not give the holder of

ance violates the Thellusson Act, see § 693, post.

§ 330.1.   [1] Worthing Corporation v. Heather, [1906] 2 Ch. 532. See South Eastern R. Co. v. Associated Portland Cement Manuf., [1910] 1 Ch. 12; Bennett v. Stodgell, 28 Dom. L. R. 639, 642. Mr. T. Cyprian Williams in two articles, 51 Sol. J. 648, 669, contends that, though the contract in Worthing Corporation v. Heather did not come within the Rule against Perpetuities, it should have been held void as an illegal restraint on alienation. See 54 Sol. J. 502; 33 Law Quart. Rev. 236, 247; and note 7, infra.

[2] 236 Mass. 138, 128 N. E. 177.
[3] P. 155.

the option a present interest, nor make him in any sense the equitable owner until he exercises his right to buy. But the usual form of option contract will be specifically enforced against a purchaser of the property with notice.[4] And the specific enforcement of the contract, at least when it is enforced against a purchaser of the property, involves a finding that the contract creates some sort of equitable interest in the property.[5] The Court, however, seems to consider that options do not generally create any interest in the land, and further, that an option which did not give any such interest could nevertheless be enforced specifically against the promisor if he still held the land.[6] They seem, therefore, to have found it necessary, in order to prevent the enforcement of options extending over too long a period, to declare such options void at law. Whether this line of reasoning is correct, may be doubted; although the conclusion that such options are wholly void, at law as well as in equity, may well be supported on the ground that they would constitute illegal re-

[4] See Parkhurst v. Maynard, 285 Mass. 59, 188 N. E. 510; Crowley v. Byrne, 71 Wash. 444, 129 Pac. 113; 1 Williston, Contracts (Rev. Ed.), § 61, note 9.

[5] London S. W. Ry. Co. v. Gomm, 20 Ch. D. (C. A.) 562, 580, 582, 586. Worthing Corporation v. Heather, [1906] 2 Ch. 532, 539. Barton v. Thaw, 246 Pa. 348, 92 Atl. 312. Ball v. Milliken, 31 R. I. 36, 43, 76 Atl. 789, 792. Carey v. Roots, 5 Alberta L. R. 125, 141. Carter v. Hyde, 33 Com. L. R. 115, 132 (Aust.). Cf. 52 Harv. Law Rev. 77, 92, 95. In Thacher v. Weston, ubi supra, for instance, the holder of the option attempted to do acts upon the land which could only be justified if he were the present owner thereof, and the Court held that he had no right so to act. If the owner, however, had conveyed the property to a purchaser with notice of the option, there can be little doubt that the Court would have enforced the option against that purchaser. See Parkhurst v. Maynard, cited in the preceding note. The language of the able judge who wrote the opinion in Thacher v. Weston must be taken to mean that the contract gave no present interest in the property such as was necessary to sustain the claim of the option-holder in that case. Cf. Cornell-Andrews Co. v. Boston & Providence R. R., 209 Mass. 298, 306, 95 N. E. 887.

[6] Pp. 152, 155. Both these propositions are extremely doubtful. As to the latter, see South Eastern R. Co. v. Assoc. Portland Cement Manuf., [1910] 1 Ch. 12, discussed below.

straints on alienation if damages were allowed for their breach.[7]

§ **330.2.** In *South Eastern R. Co.* v. *Associated Portland Cement Manuf.*,[1] a railroad company, being about to purchase a strip through C.'s land, agreed with C., in a writing not under seal, that C., his heirs and assigns, might at any time make a tunnel under the strip. Subsequently C., by a deed poll, conveyed the strip to the railroad company, reserving to himself, his heirs and assigns, the right to make the tunnel. The assignee of C. started to make the tunnel, and the railroad company applied for an injunction. The deed from C., being a deed poll, created no legal easement in his favor,[2] but the agreement gave him an equitable right to an easement. The question was whether this was a present right or a future right. Swinfen Eady, J., held that it was a present right, and therefore was not obnoxious to the Rule against Perpetuities,[3] and so he refused the injunction. This, it is submitted, was correct.[4]

§ **330.3.** The case was carried to the Court of Appeals (Cozens-Hardy, M. R., Fletcher, Moulton, and Farwell, L.JJ.).[1] The Court affirmed the decree below refusing the

[7] See further on this point 25 Columbia Law Rev. 77; 1 Wis. Law Rev. 180, 182.

§ 330.2. [1] [1910] 1 Ch. 12.

[2] By an anomalous but widely spread doctrine in the United States, such a provision is held to create a legal easement.

[3] See § 279, ante. And see Threlkeld v. Inglett, 289 Ill. 90, 96, 124 N. E. 368, 370; Post v. Bailey, 110 W. Va. 504, 159 S. E. 524. Cf. Barton v. Thaw, 246 Pa. 348, 92 Atl. 312.

[4] But see 54 Sol. J. 471; 32 Law Quart. Rev. 71, 241, 427.

§ 330.3. [1] The learned judges seem to have decided the case quasi in furore. "I have listened with some amazement to the contention that the rule of perpetuities applies where the action is brought, not against an assignee of the covenantor, but against the covenantor himself, and I have listened with still more amazement when I heard the case of London & South Western R. Co. v. Gomm, 20 Ch. D. (C. A.) 562, cited as an authority for that purpose." [1910] 1 Ch. 28. "I do not think that in my whole experience I have ever had to decide upon a more utterly unmeritorious claim." (Ib. 31.) "If they were right in law, the fact that I am thoroughly disgusted with the railway company for putting forward such a claim

injunction, but apparently not on the ground taken by Swinfen Eady, J.  They said that the agreement between C. and the railroad company was a contract which could be enforced against the railroad company, and that specific performance of this contract could be compelled.  Apparently the contract created an obligation on the part of the company which could be enforced by a suit at law, because, *qua* contract, it was not subject to the Rule against Perpetuities, but it does not follow that it could be enforced by a decree for specific performance; for to have a right to specific performance of a contract to convey an interest in land is to have a right of property in the land which is subject to the Rule against Perpetuities.  With the greatest respect for the eminent judges, it does seem that, in their disgust for the conduct of the railroad company, they overlooked this distinction.[2]  *South*

would not affect me in the slightest . . . but the law on which the claim is founded seems to be as bad as the morals." (Ib. 32.) "There is certainly no honesty in the company's case." (Ib. 34.)

[2] See criticisms on this case in 54 Sol. J. 471, 501; 27 Law Quart. Rev. 150. In 42 Sol. J. 650, 54 Sol. J. 471, 501, and 27 Law Quart. Rev. 150, it is suggested that in the case of an option given by an individual the obligation of the promisor is severable from that of his heirs and assigns, and may be enforced against him during his life.  But does not the contract, considered apart from the Rule against Perpetuities, create a single continuous equitable interest in the property enforceable against the promisor and his heirs and assigns?  It seems that it would be so considered in a case where the option was limited to twenty-one years.  And the fact that the Rule against Perpetu-

ities is applicable ought not to alter the construction.  The cases of Starcher v. Duty, 61 W. Va. 373, 56 S. E. 524, and Henderson v. Bell, 103 Kan. 422, 173 Pac. 1124, are inconsistent with the theory suggested, as well as with the opinion in South Eastern R. Co. v. Assoc. Portland Cement Manuf.; for in those two cases the Courts refused to enforce the contract specifically against the original promisors, who were individuals, on the ground that the contract attempted to create an interest which was obnoxious to the Rule against Perpetuities.

It has often been remarked that the period of lives and twenty-one years is not very appropriate as a limit for the duration of options and other commercial contracts creating future interests in property.  Yet it has generally been conceded that some limit is desirable; and no other limit has ever been sug-

*Eastern R. Co.* v. *Associated Portland Cement Manuf.* was followed by Warrington, J., in *Sharpe* v. *Durrant.*[3]

gested. The real source of the dissatisfaction with the state of the law respecting options and similar contracts, is the fact that the parties so frequently omit to name any limit for the duration of the contract, although they would usually be willing to do so if the matter were called to their attention. It would perhaps be proper for the Court in such a case to indulge in a presumption that the intention was that the contract should be good only for a reasonable period, not exceeding twenty-one years. In London & South Western R. Co. v. Gomm, and all the cases following it, cited under § 330, ante, the Court construed the contract as perpetual, so that the decision would have been the same, whatever period was adopted for the permissible duration of such a contract.

3 55 Sol. J. 423 (1911). In this case the learned judge, on grounds which do not clearly ap-

pear in the imperfect report, went so far as to enforce by injunction against a purchaser from the original covenantor a negative covenant not to interfere with the enjoyment of a right of way granted to begin in futuro, although he held that the legal easement was too remote. See 32 Law Quart. Rev. 71, 73; 55 Law Quart. Rev. 434, and cf. § 316, note 6, ante. South Eastern R. Co. v. Associated Portland Cement Manuf. was also followed in New Federal Oils Co. v. Rowland, [1929] 1 Dom. L. R. 472, apparently on the supposition that the provision in question in the latter case constituted an agreement to reconvey land. The decision in the Canadian case can be supported, however, on other grounds. The property concerned was oil rights, which were in substance profits a prendre, and the provision for their ceasing was not within the Rule against Perpetuities. See § 279, ante.